Women in
Landscape Architecture

Women in Landscape Architecture

Essays on History and Practice

Edited by LOUISE A. MOZINGO
and LINDA JEWELL

McFarland & Company, Inc., Publishers
Jefferson, North Carolina, and London

LIBRARY OF CONGRESS CATALOGUING-IN-PUBLICATION DATA

Women in landscape architecture : essays on history and practice /
edited by Louise A. Mozingo and Linda Jewell.
p.   cm.
Includes bibliographical references and index.

ISBN 978-0-7864-6164-6
softcover : acid free paper ∞

1. Women landscape architects.   2. Landscape architecture —
History.   I. Mozingo, Louise A.   II. Jewell, Linda L.
SB469.375.W66 2012   712.082 — dc23   2011039648

BRITISH LIBRARY CATALOGUING DATA ARE AVAILABLE

On the cover: Italian Garden at the Cummer Museum of Art and
Gardens, Jacksonville, Florida (photograph by Judith B Tankard)

Manufactured in the United States of America

*McFarland & Company, Inc., Publishers
Box 611, Jefferson, North Carolina 28640
www.mcfarlandpub.com*

Contents

Introduction

Louise A. Mozingo

In 1899, Beatrix Jones was one of the eleven founding members of the American Society of Landscape Architects, at the same table with the sons of Frederick Law Olmsted, John Charles and Frederick Jr. In examining landscape architecture through the lens of gender, Beatrix Jones's practice as a landscape architect defies simplistic feminist formulations. While she was roundly excluded from the public work commanded by Olmsted and his many followers, she had been educated and encouragingly mentored by Charles Sprague Sargent, the Arnold Arboretum's formidable director and close ally of the Olmsted firm. She maintained an office with a lively practice, employing women in unprecedented numbers as her staff. Yet in a 1916 address to students at Bryn Mawr, warned that to sustain herself a woman landscape architect had better have an independent income "as the money return is not large."[1] Beatrix Jones Farrand (as she was known after her marriage in 1913) operated under the burden that the feminine creative enterprise, however committed and redolent of talent, could not hope to approach the livelihood enjoyed by male counterparts. Nonetheless her presence at the foundation of the ASLA was an important public testament to that talent. It was perhaps as well recognition of the social prominence of her clients, and even of her own family. In addition to gender, access to education, the formulations of capitalist exchange, the privileging of technological over aesthetic invention, and the trump card of class all inflected the level of power and autonomy that Beatrix Jones Farrand was able to exercise as a landscape architect.

Papers presented at the symposium "A Century of Women: Evaluating Gender in Landscape Architecture," held at the Department of Landscape Architecture of the University of California, Berkeley, provide the basis for this book. The "century" that the title refers to is the century since the formation of the American Society of Landscape Architects. The editors' presumption in convening a conference is that gender is central but not all-encompassing in examining landscape architecture. Admittedly, the editors did not begin with this presumption. In preparing for the conference we assumed that gender was a determinant factor in landscape architecture — indeed gender had fundamentally shaped our own experience as women in the profession and academia. Consulting with women in contemporary practice in preparation for the symposium, specifically women who had entered the profession in the previous decade, dissuaded us from this absolutism. In soliciting papers for the symposium, the editors stated: "On the one hand, feminism avers that femaleness is a defining factor in experience, landscape architectural or otherwise. On the other hand, as women take on the roles that feminism opened, to many this essentialist position

1

is belied by experience." In keeping with the intent of the symposium, the book addresses the diverse ways that gender has influenced the creation, design, and experience of land-scapes.

The essays coalesce around the central idea that women both make and experience the landscape in distinct ways framed by gender, but not determined entirely by it. The book chapters are organized into four groups. First, we present an overview of women and land-scape architecture both as an interpretive history (the only essay solicited for the book that did not begin as a paper presented at the symposium) and as a summary timeline highlighting key events that mark the chronicle of women's relation to landscape architecture present and past. A second set of essays explores the early training of women as mentorship and educational institutions variously afforded women entrée into the field. The third section presents the professional efforts of early to mid-century women with numerous plans of ground-breaking projects. These may be hard to read in every detail in book-scale repro-ductions but are nonetheless illuminating as evidence of accomplishment and influence in the field of landscape architecture. The chapters that follow explore both the perception and experience of landscapes by women, a more elusive yet equally powerful form of gender construction as access to education and employment. The book concludes with essays that speculate on ways to re-imagine and reconsider gender and the landscape.

The essays on pioneering practitioners elucidate that the landscape was a realm of endeavor that did provide an alternative to domesticity — qualified, constricted, and unher-alded at times — but nonetheless more receptive than architecture, much less engineering or science. Given the contention of Sally Schauman's essay that both nature and women are diminished in actuality while proclaimed as precious in rhetoric, this line of opportunity arguably might have something to do with the landscape's besieged position, yet women were in the field while they were not in so many others. The leap from home and garden to playgrounds, community gardens, and estate design while straining at social strictures did not snap them.

Unlike other fields that have to mine small veins to include feminine contributions, women's work proves fundamental to the history of American landscape architecture. As the present work demonstrates, women are largely responsible for inventing landscape types now taken for granted in American cities — community gardens, playgrounds, streetscapes, ecological planting, and the shared open spaces of clustered housing. Significantly, women's work was central and not exceptional to estate design. As writers and speakers about the landscape they were eloquent, introducing forefront subjects — plant communities as base-lines for design, the nature of children's play, the importance of humane housing for the working class — to myriad audiences.

What characterized this work was a fine-grained, additive quality and the eschewing of a grand vision approach. Community gardens reclaimed from abandoned parcels, play-grounds formed on small city lots, and collective yards for housing were small gestures with telling consequences that transformed the vocabulary of city space. Close observation of the vegetation groupings of wildlands suggested alternative regionally appropriate designs for the garden, composed plant by plant. Even the estate designers, Farrand in particular, worked one piece of the garden at a time, adjusting, refining, and trying out as the projects evolved. Given smaller canvases on which to project their creativity, they made an avant-garde of the increments of the landscape at their disposal.

Their social visions too reflected this virtue of the small scale. One child at a time in playground and garden, one citizen at a time walking down an orderly street, one family at a time in decent housing surrounded by green all reflected a humbler ambition than the transformative societal reordering promoted by Frederick Law Olmsted and his followers. While Central Park was and is magnificent, no one any longer imagines that it will induce widespread temperance. Yet we continue to understand with even more precision that a view of a tree from a kitchen window, a spade turned to nurture a tomato, a gleeful dash and swing in a playground, or a good stroll down an agreeable sidewalk leaves an urban dweller a moment better.

In ecology as well, a measured ambition has proved resonant over decades. In sharp contrast to the political bombast of the contemporary native plant advocates of the Prairie School, Elsa Rehmann's subtle discussion of ecological plant groupings, exemplified here in a reprint of one of her own articles, was a question of science and practicality, not patriotism. There is no wincing at racist or jingoistic allusions when reading her still eminently applicable principles.[2] She did not hope to make everyone an ideal American by her planting design. She simply proposed that the regional ecology was a valid yardstick for making decisions about the landscape — two generations before Ian McHarg's landmark *Design with Nature*.[3]

If women seemed to drop out of their hard-earned place in the postwar era, the famous rigidity of the period's gender demarcation certainly played its part. But one might question whether the grand scale vision of modernist design and its extraordinarily ambitious social agenda might also have left little place for the kind of design where women had made their mark. The modernist "universal man" and totalizing "functional" solutions swept away the detailed, nuanced, and faceted in design. Modernist design demonstrated a benighted lack of understanding of life as it is ordinarily experienced and lived, notoriously exemplified by the horrifying public housing highrise surrounded by an unclaimable sea of green. Small wonder that the first to burst the universal functionalist bubble was a woman, Jane Jacobs, whose landmark 1961 book, *The Death and Life of Great American Cities* made its case by noticing the particularized, small scale, everyday humanity of assorted and varied urban neighborhoods, judged anathema by the modernists.[4]

As the essays on the contemporary landscape demonstrate, the postwar city of large expanse and suburban extension formed a sphere of experience that continues to resist a feminist recasting of women in the city. The gendered use of urban open space, the globalizing suburban experience, and the supposedly reformed suburbia of New Urbanism demonstrate the hold of the domestic, or at least the domestic imagination, on how cities are built and experienced. Discussions of perception and gender inevitably confront how biology and culture interact in the formation of gender, whether the pull of the domestic can be obviated by a feminist culture in which women have a free rein of place or whether the domestic pulls in a genetically predetermined direction.

The last two essays, in a sense, recasts that discussion and exults the domestic art and the ecological as sources of strength rather than feminized weakness. The literal piecing of quilts presents a spectacular artifact and eloquent metaphor for how women might approach a gendered landscape, erotic and ecological fecundity included, from a point of power and not oppression. In many ways the final essay, by Sally Schauman, proposes an evolution of the stance that gave the early practitioners their central place in landscape architecture — integrative, inclusive, and closely observed.

At the conference, Cornelia Oberlander, a distinguished landscape architect working in Vancouver, presented a project embodying Schauman's proposal. The C. K. Choi Institute of Asian research at the University of British Columbia was an intensely collaborative process between women in allied design professions (architecture, landscape architecture, engineering, and construction) that carried through sustainable and site specific design at every level. The designers carefully devised a system in which building materials, energy consumption, water management, and regional plant materials produced an ecologically assimilated built environment. The long established Oberlander presented the collaboration as an opportunity arising out of like-minded mutuality between women professionals.

We hope this book revives a discussion about gender and the environment in general, and about gender and landscape architecture in particular. Frankly, we sense that it is a little out of fashion. The book does not deal with contemporary women practitioners at the forefront of the profession, such as Kathryn Gustafson and Martha Schwartz. Their position seems unassailable, but then again, so did Marjorie Sewall Cautley's. The field, conceptual and literal, is still shared uneasily and provisionally.

This book has come together because of our willing and most able contributors. Their inspired, insightful, and engaging presentations at the Century of Women conference spurred us to get their efforts in print. We are especially grateful for their work and patience through the publication process. We owe a special thanks to Kenneth Marrota for his careful review of the manuscript and invaluable editorial consultation and to contributor Terry L. Clements who kept an eye out for an interested publisher. The Department of Landscape Architecture and Environmental Planning of the University of California, Berkeley provided consistent support in preparing the conference and pursuit of publication. The very proficient research assistants Crystal Gaudio, Kirsten Negus and Heather Clauss helped keep this project on track. Two generous endowments to the department provided essential support for this book — the Beatrix Jones Farrand Fund and the Geraldine Knight Scott Fund — both the legacy of women in landscape architecture. Needless to say, we hope they will be pleased.

Notes

1. Quoted in Balmori, Diana Balmori, "Beatrix Farrand at Dumbarton Oaks: The Design Process of a Garden," in *Beatrix Jones Farrand: Fifty Years of American Landscape Architecture*, ed. Diane Kostial McGuire and Lois Fern, (Washington DC: Dumbarton Oaks, 1982), 109. It presages Virginia Woolf's famous 1928 address at Oxford warning that women writers "must have money and a room of one's own." Virginia Woolf, *A Room of One's Own*, http://ebooks.adelaide.edu.au/w/woolf/virginia/w91r/, Section 1.
2. See David Egan and William H. Tischler, "Jens Jensen, Native Plants, and the Concept of Nordic Superiority," *Landscape Journal* 18, no. 1 (1999) 11–29.
3. Ian McHarg, *Design with Nature* (Garden City, NY: Doubleday/Natural History Press, 1969)
4. Jane Jacobs, *The Death and Life of Great American Cities* (New York: Random House, 1961).

Bibliography

Balmori, Diana. "Beatrix Farrand at Dumbarton Oaks: The Design Process of a Garden." In *Beatrix Jones Farrand: Fifty years of American Landscape Architecture*, edited by Diane Kostial McGuire and Lois Fern, 97–124. Washington DC: Dumbarton Oaks, 1982.
Egan, David and William H. Tischler. "Jens Jensen, Native Plants, and the Concept of Nordic Superiority." *Landscape Journal* 18, no. 1 (1999): 11–29.
Jacobs, Jane. *The Death and Life of Great American Cities*. New York: Random House, 1961.
McHarg, Ian. *Design with Nature*. Garden City, NY: Doubleday/Natural History Press, 1969)
Woolf, Virginia. *A Room of One's Own*. http://ebooks.adelaide.edu.au/w/woolf/virginia/w91r/.

Chapter 1

Gender and the History of Landscape Architecture, 1875–1975

David C. Streatfield

Introduction

The role of women in the art and profession of landscape architecture has been neglected in its major literature. While scholars have examined the work of individual women landscape architects there is no comprehensive analysis of how gender has affected women in the art of landscape architecture. This essay is an attempt to fill this serious *lacuna* in the scholarly literature. It is also intended to serve as an introductory framework for the essays in this volume that explore specific themes and the work of individual landscape designers in far greater depth.

The history of landscape architecture, from the earliest societies in Mesopotamia and Egypt to the present, has been presented as narratives of landscape designs created by a pantheon of heroic male figures.[1] Each narrative assumes an unquestioned patriarchal paradigm of male power relationships that almost completely excludes any consideration of the various roles played by women.[2] Thus these histories exclude any mention of women in the past who were important patrons of landscape art, plant collectors, civic activists, and writers. This biased view also ignores the fact that prior to World War II, American women landscape architects were regarded in some quarters as superior to their male peers in one of the relatively few professions accessible to women.[3]

Heath Schenker has called for a new feminist history of landscape architecture to redress these biases and interpret the role women have played in this art as patrons, authors, activists and designers. This essay re-examines women's roles in landscape architecture by synthesizing the work of scholars from a number of fields. It presents a history of landscape architecture from 1875 to 1975 as a practice and discipline situated within a society governed by gender and class.[4] It also emphasizes that the role of women landscape architects must be understood within a context of patronage, civic engagement, and dissemination of women's landscape design ideas through writing in popular and academic journals. Within a chronological framework of periods, the essay discusses the situation of women in society related to the roles women played in the principal activities of landscape architecture. Thus this analytical narrative has the central goal of re-examining the role of gender and class in American landscape architecture within a broad set of social impulses.

Women and the Male Public Realm: 19th Century America

By the end of the 19th century the social roles of men and women were classified into separate public (male) and private (female) realms. Male dominance of the public realm was exercised through property ownership, capital accumulation, control of professions, and exclusive access to public commissions. Lack of suffrage automatically excluded women from public life and instead it was generally accepted that they reigned as moral guardians over the private domestic realm.[5] Significantly the garden was considered an important part of the domestic sphere primed by an array of books on garden design and horticulture — some even advocating the garden as a place of women's political expression and proprietorial rights.[6]

In the last quarter of the century, women began to intrude into this gendered society through the access by upper class women to higher education. From the 1860s onwards a group of well-educated and morally concerned upper class "new women" entered society from recently established women's colleges. They channeled a burgeoning sense of public responsibility into work in settlement houses, and membership in social clubs. However, the full impact of the "new women" was not evident until early in the twentieth century.

Control of the domestic domain of the garden consequently involved women in design. In both Europe and America, garden design was indelibly shaped by the work of English garden designer and author Gertrude Jekyll. Jekyll transformed the nature of gardens with her sensitive designs and discussion of structural details, and proto-ecological planting based on the consideration of exposure, soils and microclimate. Her numerous books inspired twentieth century American landscape designers including Beatrix Farrand, Ellen Shipman, Marion Coffin, and Florence Bell Robinson.[7]

In the second half of the nineteenth century the character of the public urban realm was selectively mitigated by members of the new but very small profession of landscape architecture led by Frederick Law Olmsted.[8] Olmsted's great contribution to the development of American cities was to advocate genteel and rather conservative reform based on the essential presence of nature in the city. Concern over issues of access to nature, public morality, health and taste were resolved by the insertion into existing cities of naturalistic parks, park-systems, civic spaces, subdivisions, and private institutions as independent spaces. All of these comprehensively designed and engineered naturalistic landscapes were intended to evoke images of pastoral nature that would become an uplifting corrective to the banal gridiron geometries and ugliness of industrial cities.[9] Though for the most part designed by men, two women participated in this formative phase of landscape architecture: Annette McCrea, the self-proclaimed first woman landscape architect, and Elizabeth Bullard, who with Olmsted's approval, offered to take over her father's role as inspector of Prospect Park and went on to design a number of public landscapes.[10]

Also during this period the architectural writer and critic, Mrs. Schuyler Van Rensselaer, played a critical role in publicizing the nascent profession of landscape architecture in her book *Art Out-of-Doors. Hints on Good Taste in Gardening*. She argued that landscape architecture, or landscape gardening, as it was also known, was an art of comparable aesthetic significance to architecture, painting and sculpture.[11]

The Public Good and the Private Garden: 1900–1920

America became a world power in the first two decades of the twentieth century, exuding a buoyant and exuberant optimism tempered by the systematic and progressive expansion of government. This era also marked the initial entrance of women into the public realm. In addition to women's traditional and subservient roles in domestic service, middle and upper class women sponsored a range of community-oriented municipal improvements derived from the moralizing work of protecting the domestic sphere. Women also began to enter teaching, nursing, librarianship, and social work, which were the only professions considered appropriate for middle class women. Upper class women ventured into the design professions of landscape architecture and architecture. Between 1870 and 1930 the number of professional women was proportionately twice that of women in the overall work force. In 1890 women formed about 17.5 percent of the work force, while 36 percent of all professional individuals were women.[12]

At the beginning of the century the improvement of American cities became a major concern for both men and women. In many major cities prominent businessmen supported bold and grandiloquent City Beautiful proposals for remaking cities and entire regions, subscribing to the rather naive assumption that physically beautiful cities would promote improved civility and eradicate most social problems. These ambitious proposals were resoundingly defeated at the ballot box and survive only as ephemeral dreams rendered in exquisitely drawn plans and grandiose perspectival vistas.[13] Yet they continue to be the central focus of scholarly accounts of the City Beautiful, while the far more subtle and successful interventions initiated by women's clubs have only recently been the subject of scholarly examination.[14] (See Lawson Chapter 3 of this text.)

Women sought to engage in a dialog over civic issues by arguing that their domestic roles should be extended into the municipal realm, their mission being "City Clean, City Sanitary, and City Beautiful."[15] A considerable number of women participated in the General Federation of Women's Clubs, which had 800,000 members in over 495 affiliated groups.[16] Unlike the ambitious City Beautiful projects, driven by aesthetics, women's clubs sponsored relatively modest projects that focused on improving the quality of daily community life. These included schoolyards, planting street trees, building field houses, developing playgrounds, and sponsoring municipal art projects. In addition, the women's clubs addressed issues of public health, child welfare and education, recreation, improved tenement housing for all races, the eradication of billboards, and civic planning. The health, conservation, and other environmental design issues of suburban and rural landscapes became the mission of the Garden Club of America, founded in 1912, and the various state garden clubs.

Collectively the work of these domestic feminists was modest, but because of its modesty, a very popular progressive movement for change. Daphne Spain claims that the volunteer efforts of these new municipal and social clubs were not only very successful agents of change, but that their redemptive nature "saved" American cities.[17] However, these critical female contributions to the improved health of the urban and rural environment continue to be largely unrecognized, overshadowed by the important achievements of the suffrage movement.

The development of landscape architecture as a profession coincided with the rise of the City Beautiful movement. As stated in the introductory chapter, landscape architecture became an organized profession with the establishment in 1899 of the American Association of Landscape Architects by eleven founding members with Miss Beatrix Jones (later Farrand), as the only woman. This was somewhat surprising since Olmsted had dismissed her "as one said to dabble in landscape gardening," a negative remark intended as a rebuke of both the world of ladies and the amateur tradition.[18] Like most new professions this organization established implicit boundaries via university education and gender discrimination. Both of these conditions limited the entry of women. Women confronted considerable obstacles including social ostracism by their families, university departments closed to females with the exception of MIT, Cornell, Illinois and the University of California, Berkeley, and very few professional firms willing to hire women because of the widely held beliefs that female presence would adversely affect office morale and women possessed constitutions incapable of directing workmen on the job.[19]

These roadblocks quickly produced alternative schools for women such as the Lowthorpe School at Groton, Massachusetts, the Pennsylvania School of Horticulture at Ambler, Pennsylvania, and the Cambridge School, Cambridge Massachusetts. The latter was very successful and was later described by Henry Frost, one of its founders, as an accident in which they had been caught up by chance "in a small eddy of a greater movement in which women were beginning to demand equal rights with their brothers."[20]

The importance of horticulture in the curricula of the first two programs tended to direct women toward supervision of nurseries, estate management, and as teachers of gardening. In practice many Lowthorpe graduates developed successful careers as practicing landscape architects. This was in marked contrast to the Cambridge School's strong emphasis upon landscape architecture as a profession of design, and the integration of landscape architecture and architecture without any professional squabbling. Thus the school's graduates exhibited a notable architectonic approach in garden design and architecture, and architects such as Eleanor Raymond displayed strong abilities in garden design.[21] Frost predicted that in both professions women would work in "domestic fields," since they "are more likely to be commissioned by individ-

Beatrix Jones Farrand, one of eleven founding members of the American Society of Landscape Architects (Beatrix Farrand Collection [1955 – 2], Environmental Design Archives, University of California, Berkeley).

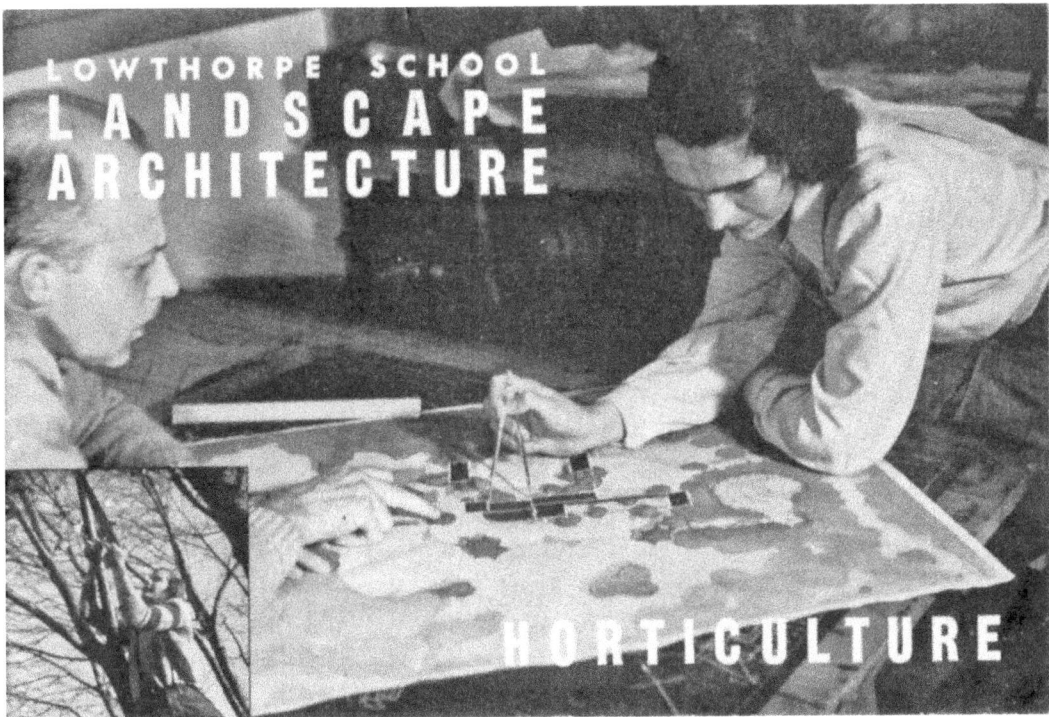

Cover of a 1920s brochure for the Lowthorpe School (Wikimedia Commons).

uals than by corporations and organizations."[22] He also observed that unlike the choice women made in the nineteenth century *between* marriage and lowly work his students *sought* both to marry and have a professional life.[23]

The women that enrolled in landscape architecture programs came from well-to-do families and were usually well connected socially. As Beatrix Jones Farrand said, "I do not know of any of the women who are considered to be successful landscape gardeners who have not had some means of their own assured to start with. At present I do not think there is an opportunity for many or few women who depend upon it entirely for their support."[24]

Private instruction was another career path. Beatrix Jones gained an extensive knowledge of plants through rigorous training by Charles Sprague Sargent, who had also instructed the critic Mariana Griswold Van Rensselaer. Sargent also encouraged Jones to embark upon an extensive program of travel.[25] Charles Adams Platt taught Ellen Shipman the fundamental principles of landscape design, which enabled her to become a consultant on many of his large garden commissions.[26]

A small number of men supported women by hiring them in their offices; Warren Manning hired Marjorie Cautley and Helen Bullard, Fletcher Steele hired Rose Greely, and John Nolen hired Elizabeth Strange.[27]

But it was female firms, such as those of Beatrix Farrand, Ellen Biddle Shipman, and Marion Coffin who consciously hired only women, who provided the necessary apprenticeship and mentoring that occurs after the completion of formal education. Most female firms were located in eastern cities. Florence Yoch was the first woman to open an office on the west coast.[28]

The new profession was given a most ambitious agenda by President Charles Eliot of

Harvard: "The profession of landscape architecture is going to be — indeed, it already is — the most direct professional contribution to the improvement of the human environment in the twentieth century."[29] Though the profession remained largely hidden and misunderstood by the general public during most of the twentieth century, the range of commissions undertaken by landscape architects was formidable.

Landscape architects participated collaboratively on the grandiose and unrealized City Beautiful dreams. They also worked far more productively on realizing more modest urban projects such as playgrounds, civic spaces, housing, subdivisions, parks, park-systems, cemeteries, railroad grounds, university and college campuses, as well as gardens and lavish estates. The profession was well equipped to plan and design this broad range of commissions. Indeed, since there was no separate planning profession, landscape architecture was responsible for all major design and physical planning in the first two decades of the century.

Landscape architecture firms varied considerably in size and focus. Larger firms such as the Olmsted Brothers of Brookline, Massachusetts, and Hare and Hare, of Kansas City accepted the full range of commissions, while smaller firms often specialized in a single type of practice. Women landscape architects were generally excluded from such broad general practices. Their firms concentrated on the design of large gardens and estates.[30]

Low taxes and wages created ideal conditions for creating lavish gardens and estates in the suburbs lying outside major cities such as Lake Forest, Illinois (Chicago), Grosse Pointe, Michigan (Detroit), Long Island, New York (New York City), and the Main Line (Philadelphia, Pennsylvania). Clients were second-generation old moneyed families and newly enriched captains of industry who sought social re-assurance in residing in settings consciously modeled on those of European aristocrats. Designs often deliberately recalled European historic styles.

Since most women landscape architects came from upper class families, they moved easily in their clients' milieu, often staying with them for the duration of a job and maintaining friendships after the garden was completed. Many women obtained commissions on a referral basis through family connections. While some women, such as Marion Coffin and Ellen Shipman, practiced in this profession from financial necessity, others likely managed to live as genteel landscape architects in circumstances that were modestly equivalent to their clients.[31]

Women were particularly adept at garden design. Influenced by Gertrude Jekyll's numerous books they orchestrated flower borders and carefully composed shrubberies and wooded areas according to her carefully articulated aesthetic theories on color and the appropriate use of plants in differing settings. So skilled were women at planting design that a general perception arose that they were not as competent in coping with the grading, engineering and the structural aspects of landscape architecture.

In addition to large gardens, requiring the services of numerous gardeners, women also designed small gardens. They were thus particularly sensitive to the need for providing individuals of modest means with advice on garden design and planting by writing articles in the major shelter magazines, such as *House Beautiful, House and Garden,* and *Country Life in America,* and in books.[32] One of the most prolific of these authors was Mrs. Francis King, a friend of Jekyll, who wrote solely for the amateur but also directed her readers to seek out professional landscape architects. Thus these publications advertised the work of women landscape architects and disseminated design principles by making a clear linkage between large estate gardens and small gardens. Grace Tabor and Rose Standish Nichols wrote pioneering works on garden history and historic garden styles to satisfy scholarly readers. Alice Morse Earle's garden history writing is notable for her pioneering use of primary sources.[33]

Despite well-honed skills in landscape design women were not successful in obtaining public commissions and limited their public work to theater sets, playgrounds and other design commissions for women's clubs. This can be attributed to the exclusion of women from the urban power networks that controlled the patronage of urban landscape commissions. John Nolen observed, "Public prejudice would operate against women's being trusted with public work."[34]

Clubs, Estates, Patrons, and the Domestic Landscape: 1920–1929

The expansive laissez-faire character of the 1920s was not accompanied by a corresponding reduction of restraints on working women. Despite attaining suffrage in 1920 there was no marked increase in the female presence in civic affairs. Instead women devoted themselves to the traditional domestic concerns of marriage and motherhood. The early feminist Suzanne La Follette advocated withdrawal by women from collective civic action to focus on a working career on the grounds that true sexual equality could only be based upon economic independence. This new focus became evident after World War I, when 25 percent of women entered the workforce, and with an increase in the population, this meant that unprecedented numbers of women participated directly in a growing economy. More middle class women worked in white-collar jobs and more educated women entered the work force often combining marriage and careers in "women's professions."[35]

Women continued to promote landscape improvements through voluntary work in social clubs. A notable example of the effectiveness of this is the work of Pearl Chase who directed the Plans and Planting Committee of the Community Arts Association of Santa Barbara, California, from 1927 until her death in 1979. This largely one-woman committee was involved in virtually every aspect of local community planning and conservation throughout California. Her work in the national Better Homes program received the highest honor awards for seventeen years.[36] Elsewhere, women worked for landscape improvement in the numerous garden clubs, raising awareness of the garden as designed space through regular lectures and visits to professionally designed estates, and serving as design exemplars for small gardens.

This became an important part of life in affluent communities, such as Santa Barbara, California, which had an unusually large number of fine estates. In more rural regions the garden clubs were also active in sponsoring beautification projects and in historic garden restoration, most notably in Virginia.[37]

The formation of the American Institute of Planners in 1917 changed the practice of landscape architecture in the 1920s. Many landscape architects entered the planning profession and concentrated exclusively on this type of practice, although henceforward it moved away from physical planning and became increasingly dominated by the formulation of social and economic policies. The major planning projects of the 1920s included the new towns of Palos Verdes, California, Longview, Washington, and Mariemont, Ohio, the latter being sponsored by Mary Emery, a rich woman who wished to build a model community for workers. The Bronx River Parkway instituted new standards for the design of limited access highways, which in many ways anticipated the interstate highway system.[38] The design of Jones Beach State Park on Long Island redefined the park as a place designed for physical recreation by families rather than a transcendental and uplifting encounter with nature. Its liberal provision of swimming pools, dressing rooms, child-care facilities, and restaurants was comparable to those of a private club.[39]

In the early 1920s the newly founded Garden Club of Virginia initiated a new type of landscape practice in funding the garden restoration of Kenmore, the home of Mary Washington, the first of a series of such historic projects which continued on through the 1950s. Rudy Favretti claims that, "No other volunteer organization has consistently raised funds for a span of more than sixty years to restore so many important landscapes."[40] Together with the restoration of the colonial city of Williamsburg at the end of the twenties this club established garden restoration as a new and major type of landscape practice. In Georgia, the Athens Garden Club played a major role in supporting conservation and beautification projects in that region. In addition, it supported the work of the new Department of Landscape Architecture at the University of Georgia.[41]

A number of scholars have described the 1920s as a golden age of garden design.[42] Fletcher Steele, who believed passionately that landscape architecture was an art, celebrated garden design as the only form of landscape design in which art could be attained.[43]

This decade of prosperity enabled a marked increase in the number of estates. By the end of the decade landscape architecture was recognized as an art and profession in which women were more visible than ever. Women headed eleven landscape firms in New York. In 1929 Elizabeth Lord and Edith Schryver opened the first female firm of landscape architects in the Pacific Northwest. Women were now welcome in the profession and the older opposition to women working in offices began to break down. The third National Conference on Instruction in Landscape Architecture in 1922 recommended that women and men work in the same rather than in segregated drafting rooms. However, it also recommended that the study of stenography would be especially useful in helping women to work in the office.[44] But despite this improvement only a few women taught in schools, and usually only as part-time lecturers.

The legacy of the 1920s estates gave women a higher profile as designers than ever before. Between 1929 and 1936 women's superior abilities in estate and garden design were recognized by the Architectural League of New York, which awarded women three out of a total of eleven of its Gold Medals for landscape architecture.

The stylistic eclecticism of the previous decades continued to guide the design of estate gardens, women designers tending to rely on superior planting design to create spaces and wooded landscapes rather than assertive architectural detailing. Only in the Prairie style gardens of Jens Jensen and Ossian Simonds was there a conscious use of native plants, which underscores the pioneering nature of Elsa Rehmann and Edith Roberts' book *American Plants for American Gardens* published in 1929, ten years before Jensen's better known *Siftings*.[45]

Women landscape architects also continued to address the problem of designing smaller gardens both in design commissions and in publications. The major shelter magazines regularly published photographs of estates and gardens designed by women landscape architects as well as articles by women landscape designers. The fine photography in these articles by accomplished women photographers such as Mattie Edwards Hewitt, Frances Benjamin Johnson and Jessie Tarbox Beals was an important mechanism for supporting women designers. The designers in turn became patrons by commissioning photographs of their work.[46]

The successful design of estate gardens frequently involved sophisticated women clients who knew what they wanted from extensive travel and study of art. For over three decades

Mabel Choate was a sympathetic patron for Fletcher Steele, who was considered a harbinger of modernist design as well as an exquisite designer in eclectic modes. Mildred Bliss, advised by Beatrix Farrand, became a knowledgeable collector of books on garden history. She insisted that Farrand incorporate into her garden at Dumbarton Oaks "a wealth of decorative architectural detail and ornament available to the gardener," and this produced an unrivalled masterpiece of American landscape art. Within a forested setting in coastal Maine Abby Aldrich Rockefeller commissioned a serene Spirit Walk using native ground cover plants as a setting for Korean figures at The Eyrie. On the west coast, Florence Bixby and her sister-in-law Susanna Bixby Bryant pioneered the use of native Californian plants in their gardens by consulting appropriate experts.[47] Some garden patrons were so confident of their expertise that they designed their own gardens. Mrs. Oakleigh Thorne designed and laid out her splendid re-interpretation of the Farnese Casino garden at Caprarola at "Las Tejas," Montecito. Louise du Pont Crowninshield, together with her husband Frank, designed one of the most original gardens of the decade at Eleutherian Mills. Within the ruins of the original du Pont gunpowder plant on Brandywine Creek, Delaware, they flooded basements and brought in columns, and balustrades. At Reynolda in North Carolina Catherine Smith Reynolds envisioned and commissioned an entire country estate.[48]

Differences between the sensibilities of male and female patrons played out in various ways in client–designer relationships. Mrs. Harry Bauer interviewed six prominent male and female landscape architects to design her Pasadena garden before deciding that Katherine Bashford had the

The Spirit Walk at The Eyrie, the estate of Abby Aldrich Rockefeller. The design was by Beatrix Jones Farrand (photograph by the author).

most sympathetic temperament. A. E. Hanson always worked with his female clients, while his assistant Geraldine Knight was deputed to work with male clients such as Harold Lloyd.[49]

The eclectic design of estate gardens often necessitated European travel to study appropriate historic precedents. Women designers of the period have left careful records in notebooks with annotated sketches, photographs and measured drawings of details. Some purchased urns and other garden ornaments that were then used as models for reproduction. Other designers such as Beatrix Farrand made reference to historic precedents through the careful study of her extensive collection of historic garden prints, photographs, drawings and books of garden history.[50]

Once the gardens were completed these designers frequently continued to oversee their designs by hiring the gardeners and supervising the garden management on a yearly basis. Surviving examples by Beatrix Farrand and Florence Yoch confirm that this was frequently accompanied by a detailed report establishing the design intent and appropriate ways of maintenance over time.[51]

These estate gardens have been castigated by many landscape historians as examples of "eclectic design." The implied derogatory criticism belies how confident women designers displayed innovation and creativity in their designs. They moved away from a highly derivative character to an aesthetic that was original and new. Marion Coffin's designs, while largely governed by the use of axial organization, are notable for a bold use of color, and the use of wildflowers and woodland plantings to provide subtle transitions from formal to naturalistic areas. Florence Yoch's designs for smaller gardens exhibit the influence of her careful study of small vernacular gardens. Ellen Shipman's designs are devoid of any adherence to particular stylistic character.[52]

Critical social agendas lay behind women's advocacy of thoughtfully designed small gardens. Women landscape architects promoted the civic value of well designed small gardens through lectures and publications for garden clubs, shelter magazines, professional journals and periodicals. In their writing and designs Martha Brookes Hutcheson, Annette Hoyt Flanders and Marjorie Sewell Cautley demonstrated that well-designed domestic landscapes would improve American culture and the lives of American citizens.[53] They believed that gardens were important not only as private spaces but as critical elements of the larger perceived public landscape and that home grounds were therefore critical elements in all communities.

Women landscape architects continued to be supported by firms like Beatrix Farrand, Ellen Shipman, Marion Coffin and Annette Hoyt Flanders that were staffed only with women and by a small number of men who hired women. Fletcher Steele hired Rose Nichols and generously loaned his library to the Cambridge School. A. E. Hanson, a former nurseryman who became a landscape designer, hired several women to work in his large southern Californian firm.[54] Jens Jensen hired Ruth Dean and Genevieve Gillette, although the latter's secretarial role in his office appears to be a classic instance of gender discrimination. However, Jensen's strong promotion of new state parks in Wisconsin later inspired her tireless work creating state parks in Michigan.

Women were not prolific practitioners in the public realm. Beatrix Farrand was involved for over thirty years in the design of courtyards at Yale and Princeton Universities, and Oberlin College. Marion Coffin worked at the University of Delaware, and Florence Yoch designed the eastern portion of the California Institute of Technology campus in Pasadena. Helen Dillon's work on a range of public commissions in Georgia, culminating in her becoming the city landscape architect of Sumter Georgia, and Caroline Donovan's creation of the Department of Conservation in the Division of Forestry in Louisiana are examples of women who were able to practice successfully in the public realm.[55] But it was Marjorie Sewell Cautley who through her publications was the best known woman practitioner outside the world of the private estate. As discussed in Chapter 10, her designs for Sunnyside Gardens, Phipps Gardens Apartments and Radburn demonstrate a strong commitment to the needs of the middle and lower-middle classes and the more radical communitarian ideals of the Regional Planning Association of New York.

Advocacy and Innovation: The Depression and the New Deal, 1929–1941

For women in the labor force the depression years were especially unkind. In a time of national hardship women were easily discarded. A primary goal of the Roosevelt Administration's approach to the disastrous economic consequences of the national depression was to keep as many men employed as possible. Consequently the federal government refused to employ more than a single wage earner from one family. A Gallup poll found 82 percent of respondents disapproved of women working when their husbands had work. By 1940 under 25 percent of the work force was female.[56]

However, women continued their volunteer advocacy; women aggressively promoted the passage of the Wagner-Steagall Act. This act affirmed the responsibility of the Federal government to provide housing for the poor since the private sector was clearly unwilling and incapable of doing this.[57]

Not surprisingly, the practice of landscape architecture was profoundly re-shaped during the Depression. Many firms went out of business and their partners and employees sought work in the newly established federal agencies, where their success depended on the services of landscape architects. The achievements of New Deal agencies employing landscape architects are most impressive. Agencies such as the Works Progress Administration, the Civilian Conservation Corps, the Resettlement Administration, and the Farm Security Administration were instrumental in providing new parks, recreational facilities, new towns, housing for migrant farm workers, and much needed management of the vast lands in the National Forests and Parks.[58] This was an unparalleled opportunity for the profession since landscape architects were fundamental to the success of these New Deal projects.

Collectively the creation of new state parks, state park systems, the Blue Ridge Parkway, the Tennessee Valley Authority, and the new towns of the Resettlement Administration are powerful demonstrations of how landscape design improved the lives of large numbers of desperate Americans. The designs were conservative in nature, being simple transitions from the era of historicist estate gardens rendered in traditional materials with superb handcraftsmanship. Built to last, these designs were superlative demonstrations of American craft traditions that, in the case of the Civilian Conservation Corps, were consciously passed on to the next generation. Only in the temporary and permanent communities built by the Farm Security Administration were modernist ideas of planning and design employed to create instant communities intended to alleviate the lot of poor migrant and permanent farm workers.[59]

Women landscape architects were largely excluded from the work of these agencies. However, the Civilian Conservation Corps retained a few women as supervising landscape engineers; Marjorie Cautley supervised no less than ten camps in New Hampshire.[60] Several women landscape architects worked for the Tennessee Valley Authority and Helen Swift worked with Gilmore Clark on playgrounds for the New York City Department of Parks, under the direction of Robert Moses, developing a rehabilitation program for its city parks.[61]

Genevieve Gillette was hired to design the experimental community of Westacres, a housing community sponsored by Couzens, the Federal Emergency Relief Administration, and Oakland Housing, Incorporated, to explore whether a non-profit organization could successfully build affordable homes for average industrial workers. Gillette's design provided generously sized gardens so that each family could raise its own fruits, vegetables, and poultry.[62]

Outside these government programs some female firms continued to design gardens, although the economic conditions inevitably constricted their scale, which in turn led to innovation. Florence Yoch designed gardens, albeit on a considerably reduced scale, for members of the movie industry who still had the means to be patrons because of the continued popularity of the movies. George Cukor's garden was so constrained by topography that Yoch was forced to depart from her previous historically inspired designs to produce a design that anticipated modernist ideas. This entree into the world of movies resulted in her being commissioned to design sets for films, including *Romeo and Juliet, How Green Was My Valley, The Garden of Allah*, and *Gone with the Wind*.[63]

Annette Hoyt Flanders broke away from stylistic eclecticism in a design for a modernist garden sponsored by *Good Housekeeping* at the Chicago World's Fair in 1934. She designed two very simple abstract gardens using a vocabulary of clipped hedges and fountains devoid of historicist architectural features on a series of shallow terraces.[64]

Flanders' designs anticipated modernist transformation by the end of the decade. Almost simultaneously Thomas Church and three Harvard graduate students created the first modernist designs that broke away completely from stylistic precedents, inspired by the abstract work of European sculptors, painters and garden designers and by the presence at Harvard of Walter Gropius, the former head of he Bauhaus School at Dessau. Their designs employed abstract spatial forms with new materials, such as concrete, asbestos cement, plastics, and light-weight steel.[65]

For decades landscape architecture had been presented to the public in books and articles in the major shelter magazines. With the modernist movement, museums came to play a significant role and Dr. Grace Morley McCann, Director of the San Francisco Museum of Modern Art, pioneered the presentation of completed modern work in photographs and models in a series of exhibitions held in 1937, 1948, 1949 and 1958. However, it was not until the later exhibitions that any designs by women landscape architects were included.[66]

New scholarship on American gardens occurred during the depression. The Garden Club of Georgia published *History of Georgia Gardens 1750–1933* and Alice Lockwood's monumental *Gardens of Colony and State* was the first survey undertaken of national garden history.[67]

By 1940, women landscape architects began to turn away from garden design to larger concerns. Henry Frost wrote in 1941 that women at the Cambridge School were more interested "in housing than in houses ... community centers for the masses rather than in neighborhood clubs for the elect; in regional planning more than in estate planning; in social aspects of her profession more than in private commissions."[68] In the same year a survey conducted by Dean Walter Hudnut of Harvard and Walter Gropius presciently declared that the future lay in public work in parks and recreational areas and regional planning and not in the realm of private estates.[69]

Most of the older women landscape architects made the transition to public work successfully, especially those who had received formal training. However, Ellen Biddle Shipman, who had no training in site planning, found that her practice wound down, and she closed her office in 1947. By contrast, the distinguished garden designer, Katherine Bashford was involved in the design of four USHA public housing projects in Los Angeles. Her finest housing project was Baldwin Hills, arguably the finest "superblock" development in the country.[70]

Opening New Doors: The War Years, 1942–1945

If the Depression was a bleak period for working American women the succeeding war years were the exact reverse. Women were no longer treated as intruders in the labor force but were welcomed, "Rosie the Riveter" being the most conspicuous symbol of the working presence of women in the war effort. With all able-bodied men serving in the armed services, it was a matter of national pride and necessity that everyone, including women, and older men unable to serve because of age or reduced abilities, should contribute to a variety of defense activities at home.[71] Eight million women worked during the war.

The disruption of the war opened some closed doors for women. Geraldine Knight Scott was the first woman to be hired by the Los Angeles Regional Planning Authority. Here she designed low-income housing projects and parks. During the war many departments of landscape architecture closed. The Cambridge School closed permanently in 1942. But Harvard University began to admit women, and remained open during the war for women, and a few men, foreign students, and many men from the military seeking instruction in camouflage. In 1944 Cornelia Oberlander, who later became the foremost landscape architect in Canada, was one of the first women to receive a BLA degree from Harvard. At the end of the war the Lowthorpe School closed and was taken over by the Rhode Island School of Design.

In the armed services women provided valuable assistance in support units as nurses, drivers and mechanics, and landscape support in units doing camouflage design, as well as making models, mapping, and detailed design for emergency military housing units, although this allowed little opportunity for more than the most basic site planning.[72]

Geraldine Knight Scott. After working on California estates in the pre-war years, Scott was the first woman hired by the Los Angeles Regional Planning Authority to design wartime housing developments (Geraldine Knight Scott Collection [2000–3], Environmental Design Archives, University of California, Berkeley).

Education, Firms, and Being in the Workforce: The Postwar Era, 1945–1960

Unlike European countries, America emerged from World War II completely unscathed, rich and buoyant. But in the war's immediate aftermath women had difficulty finding work. By 1946 two million women lost their jobs to make way for returning servicemen. A leaflet of an electrical workers' local expressed a widely shared position, "let's keep the single girl on the job and put the married woman back in the kitchen."[73] Despite such negative views, working women became a fixture of middle class life. Before the war, only one out of four women over the age of 16 worked. But by 1960 two out of five women held jobs.

Socially, the 1950s was a period of explosive population growth, characterized by an abnormally high birthrate and an expanding middle class. By 1960 married women made up over half of the female work force. The largest segment of new women workers in the 1950s were in their 40s or older. The new woman worker was also more likely to be a mother. At the beginning of the post-war period only one out of four workforce women had children between the ages of four and seventeen. By the end of the 1960s over half of all mothers with school age children were working.[74]

This population explosion resulted in an exodus to the suburbs. During the 1950s two-thirds of the growth occurred in sprawling low-density suburbs made possible by low-interest mortgages, veteran benefits, cheap land and the new system of federal freeways. Nominally a military road program, these new highways became much used transportation links. The focus of these new landscapes was often new corporate headquarters on large campuses, surrounded by housing subdivisions, large regional shopping centers, and low-density business parks.[75]

During this period more women entered the profession, which had changed in significant ways. The design of large estates had vanished. Despite the broad recognition of women's success in this arena few were elected as Fellows of the ASLA or as local or national officers. Katherine Bashford served as Secretary of the Southern California Chapter in 1938 and Ruth Shellhorn became President in 1948.

The appearance of large multi-disciplinary firms with a national and international scope is really a phenomenon of the 1960s. But it was anticipated by firms such as Eckbo, Royston and Williams, and the larger successor firms of Eckbo, Dean, Austin and Williams, and Royston Hanamoto, Beck and Alley, in the San Francisco Bay area and Sasaki and Associates in Boston, and Sasaki Strong in Canada. In 1958 Carol Johnson founded Carol Johnson and Associates the first medium-sized firm headed by a woman. Women seeking an independent practice did so in small offices.

The GI Bill enabled returning veterans to go to college to obtain the professional education that would allow them to enter the work force. Enrollment in departments of landscape architecture rose, and women experienced greatly reduced difficulty in gaining admission, but it is not until the 1970s that the number of female students began to reach parity with men. There were few full-time women faculty, most women teachers being part-time lecturers. Previous low female enrollment in departments is reflected in the fact that it was not until the late 1950s that women began to be hired in larger firms.

The immediate postwar decades saw the continued presence of gardens at the center of practice both as created space and as a conceptual model for larger designs. Gardens were now conceived as intensively used private spaces divided into four spatial zones for entertaining, sport, children's play, and service.[76] This new framing of the garden as an integrated private domain resulted in a physical turning away from the local community with small entry spaces, and parking areas or garages presenting an anonymous face to the world.

This new privatization of the garden by largely male designers also reflected a lack of interest in the role of the small garden as a critical element in building a sense of community. By contrast, women landscape designers believed that the small gardens were important both as private domestic spaces and public spaces of community engagement; Elizabeth Lord and Edith Schryver continued to reiterate this concern in radio talks in Oregon.[77]

For Garrett Eckbo the new abstract garden, built with new materials, was a powerful assertion of modernity that also served as a conceptual basis for the design of the larger landscape. He believed that the garden was not only a critical place of experimentation but could also serve as the universal model for landscape design.[78] Unintentionally, landscape modernity became a style, despite Christopher Tunnard's assertion that the "the true style of the twentieth century is no style at all."[79] The architectonic nature of modernist gardens served to diminish and marginalize earlier conceptions of landscape art that acknowledged and embraced nature.

However, older landscape designers were motivated by very different concerns. Florence Yoch's work in the 1940s and 1950s was motivated by the qualities of "permanence, durability, quiet, space, light and shade" which she realized in simpler and more abstract designs.[80] In the Pacific Northwest, Lord and Schryver continued to use the detailing and simple cross-axial spatial organization combined with the very subtle planting design associated with Ellen Shipman.[81] Thomas Church, whose firm designed the iconic Donnell garden on a Sonoma cattle ranch in 1948, was more concerned with satisfying his clients' needs as outdoor living places than making theoretical statements, as the title of his book *Gardens Are For People* suggests.[82] The clients of these three designers were rich but politically conservative businessmen and their wives. Thus it is not surprising that their designs are restrained compared with those of Eckbo and his younger peers, who treated each design as a further opportunity for experimentation.

Design restraint also typified the work of a group of less well known west coast women's firms, including Florence and Walter Gerke of Portland, John and Carol Grant of Seattle, Harriet Wimmer of San Diego, and Imlay and Scott of San Mateo. Marie Harbeck Berger is better known, since her work appeared more frequently in *House Beautiful*, including a Pace-Setter House design. Berger practiced in Texas, with great success, creating finely detailed and restrained abstract designs.[83] These firms also designed low-density business parks, medical institutions, health facilities, parks, and playgrounds and other projects. Here the transition from the domestic world of the private garden to the public realm could be made seamlessly.

The larger firms of the 1950s undertook the design of larger and more complex projects such as suburban shopping centers, industrial and business parks, and housing developments. The exact role of women in these larger firms is difficult to discern. Further research is necessary to understand the complex and often subtle relations in larger offices between male superiors and women. Women were certainly present but according to published designs were largely invisible to the outside world. Ronda Skubi's study of twelve west coast women landscape architects provides some insight into this problem.[84] Credit in publications was invariably given to the firm or the partner in charge, when in fact a team had created the design. The ethical issues of crediting responsibility have never been satisfactorily resolved and this further complicates the already obscure role of women in the profession.

The case of the talented Jean Walton in the firm of Lawrence Halprin and Associates is typical. An extremely skilled plantswoman, Walton's contributions to the firm's larger projects were absolutely essential and invaluable. All of Halprin's projects are most beautifully planted, yet Walton was never given credit for her contribution to each project. This was due in part to her rather retiring nature.[85] But determining the relative contributions in collaborative teams in large firms was problematic in other professions such as architecture and planning. Neither Natalie de Blois's contributions to major Skidmore, Owings, and Merrill projects were ever publicly acknowledged, nor was the invaluable site planning of Dorothy Hussey. Patricia Carlisle, a partner in the firm of Royston, Hanamoto, Beck and Alley, is neither mentioned specifically in credits nor included in the firm's name.[86]

Very small firms run by women continued, and in some cases flourished, although few received national recognition. Ruth Shellhorn, of Redondo Beach, California, and Barbara Fealy, of Portland, Oregon, typify one-woman firms run from their homes. Shellhorn had worked briefly for Florence Yoch in the mid 1930s and successfully continued Yoch's meticulous detailing, rigorous supervision, and long-term management into the postwar period in a successful series of designs for office buildings, shopping centers, schools and larger gardens in Pasadena and west Los Angeles. She first attained regional prominence when she was brought in at the end of the design development phase of the Bullocks Pasadena department store to design the parking lot and a series of small garden entry courts. The high profitability of this store, which was attributed to her work, was so conspicuous that she was hired for each of the firm's subsequent stores. Equally notable were her designs for the Fashion Square regional shopping centers throughout the Los Angeles basin. In these she skillfully employed trees to organize large room-like spaces in the parking areas into places of distinct identity. Shellhorn always insisted on being retained to supervise the yearly maintenance following a project's completion.[87]

Shellhorn was also brought in at a late stage of design development to "save" Disneyland. She refined and clarified the poor site planning and contributed skilled tree planting. These critical design interventions were fundamental to the success of this amusement park in handling large crowds, but are largely invisible design interventions.[88]

From her basement office Barbara Fealy combined a practice of garden design and institutional planning with voluntary planning work in suburban Portland. This enabled her to combine the roles of wife and mother with those of a busy practice for several years without her husband realizing that she was contributing more to the family's annual income than he was. Her understated and beautifully detailed garden designs attracted the developer John Gray, who selected her as the landscape architect for Salishan, the large coastal resort at Gleneden Beach, Oregon. This is notable as a work of conservation and for Fealy's insistence on using and celebrating native plants. Indeed, her native plant orders were so extensive that new nurseries were established.[89]

Extending and Expanding in the Landscape: 1960–1975

This period was a time of significant change for American society. In 1960, 30 percent of workingwomen were married. By 1970 this figure had risen to 40 percent, and by 1980 over 50 percent of women who worked were married. The median age was 41. These figures mask what Nancy Woloch has called a "precarious balance" for women. More women were working but the birthrate was declining and the divorce rate increased dramatically.[90] This erosion of traditional female roles was accompanied by the rise of feminism. The ballooning population increase also resulted in expanding college enrollments.

As Nancy Woloch states, the working mother as "New Woman" of the 1960s was accompanied by the "Educated Daughter." Woloch points out that unlike the conservative college experiences of prior generations of women, the colleges in the 1960s were remarkably egalitarian and became a breeding ground for social activism and a constituency for a new feminism.[91]

The 1960s was a tempestuous decade riled with concerns over civil rights, the Women's Movement, affirmative action, and the Vietnam War. College women participated in all of these activities with sit-ins to draw attention to what many saw as the hypocrisy of traditional societal values.

Two women authors profoundly shifted American environmental values: Jane Jacobs' *The Life and Death of American Cities*, and Rachel Carson's *Silent Spring*. Jacobs provided a critique of the urban renewal programs and pointed to the vibrant values of traditional community life on streets. Carson's critique of the widespread use of chemical fertilizer was written as an impassioned plea to understand the complexity of natural systems. But it was not until the end of the decade that the health of the environment began to be addressed by federal laws including the National Environmental Policy Act, the Endangered Species Act, the Coastal Zone Management Act and the Toxic Substances Act.

The new social roles played by women at this time tended to diminish opportunities for the older tradition of civic engagement in the environment. A conspicuous exception is the creation of the Save the San Francisco Bay Association in 1961 by three faculty wives at the University of California, one of whom was the mother of the noted Olmsted scholar Charles Capen McLoughlin. Appalled by the city of Berkeley's proposal to fill a large section of waterfront, they created this lobbying organization as a non-elitist body with minimal annual dues. This enabled it to function as a representation of the widest possible range of interests in the community. Its objective was to achieve new legislation at the federal, state and local levels to protect the bay. It proved to be a splendid exemplar of a thoroughly democratic and highly effective grassroots environmental organization.

A national example is provided by the dedicated work of Lady Bird Johnson. While she was in the White House she created the *Society for a More Beautiful Capital*. Working closely with the American Association of Nurserymen she worked tirelessly to establish programs protecting wildflowers and their planting along highways. She promoted the Highway Beautification Act, which led to the dismantling of billboards. In the early 1980s, with the actress Helen Hayes, she founded the National Wildflower Research Center in Austin, Texas. This later became the Lady Bird Johnson Wildflower Center, which is dedicated to the protection and conservation of North American native plants. The gardens and structures of the center are a model of resource conservation.

Community gardens were developed during this period as an alternative to large scale industrial farming. The work of the Green Guerillas in New York at the Bowery Houston Community Farm influenced many other communities by demonstrating the value of small productive gardens as a way of building community. The tireless advocacy of Elizabeth Christy is notable as an example of community building.[92]

By the 1970s women had achieved parity in student enrollment in departments of landscape architecture. However, at the same time, out of 350 women teaching in the field only 9 had full-time tenured positions. As recently as 1979 the faculty of University of Georgia, with over twenty men, hired their first full-time woman. A sign of the growing importance of women in the academy was the number of women appointed as departmental chairs; Sally Schauman in 1980 at the University of Washington; Anne Spirn in 1986 at the University of Pennsylvania, and Linda Jewell in 1987 at Harvard University.

During the 1960s a new focus on urban, environmental and behavioral issues dramatically re-shaped education. While Jane Jacobs and Rachel Carson's books, together with Ian McHarg's book *Design with Nature*, were all published in the 1960s their effect on landscape architectural education did not become apparent until the 1970s.

Ian McHarg pioneered a new approach to landscape planning. McHarg believed passionately in the abilities of natural scientists to provide a rational basis for understanding the complex physical and biological systems of the landscape. Through a systematic use of overlay maps he created a method of evaluating the potential of large areas for development. This analytical method was based upon scientific research and research now asserted a new place in the work of academic landscape architects as the field sought respectability within the academy.

Attention to how people used space became a major focus for scholars who used behavioral research techniques. In her study of Easter Hill Village, Richmond, California, Clare Cooper Marcus, a planner-geographer, discovered that this project, in spite of receiving numerous professional design and planning awards, was not viewed favorably by the low-income families who lived there. From this and similar studies of other projects she came to the realization that designer's values do not always coincide with those of the populations for whom they design. Design decisions made at a micro scale, sometimes insufficiently studied by designers, are often of considerable concern to the users.

These new developments in the education of landscape architects were intended to better prepare students for a considerably expanded range of design challenges. During the 1960s landscape architects were involved in the design of large-scale housing projects, urban renewal projects, regional plans, and open space systems. New technical and design issues such as large complex roof gardens were addressed in projects such as Freeway Park, Seattle, designed by Angela Danadjieva in the office of Lawrence Halprin and Associates, and Robson Square, Vancouver, Canada, designed by Cornelia Oberlander. Both are notable for the introduction of nature into high-density urban sites.

The conservation of natural areas had never played a major role in landscape architecture by women. However, it became the major focus of Genevieve Gillette's practice in Michigan, in ways that resembled that of her mentor and former employer Jens Jensen. She played a leadership role in enlarging the large Michigan state park system through her work with the Michigan State Parks Association of which she was President for ten years. This organization lobbied state legislators and she would telephone politicians directly, introducing herself as "the lady in the hat." In 1961 she successfully persuaded the governor to allocate $100 million for parks.

In 1964 State Senator Philip Hart invited her to Washington to help with a land and water bill and legislation to establish the Sleeping Bear Dunes and Picture Rocks as national seashores. Gillette lobbied for both and later developed plans for both areas. The establishment of Sleeping Bear Dunes National Seashore was her crowning achievement. According to Native American legend the largest moving sand dune in the world represents a sleeping mother bear whose twin cubs are swimming ashore.

Later she was asked to serve on a citizen's committee to advise the President's Council on Recreation and Natural Beauty. An outcome of this was her advocacy of scenic roads, the use of native plants and the regulation of billboards, all ideas she credited to Jensen.

Gillette resolutely refused to accept a penny for any of her volunteer activities. At her death she was celebrated for the persistent way in which she had haunted lobbyists, legislators, and governors with a strong, almost evangelistic, fervor.

Landscape and garden history were accorded little importance in landscape architecture departments until the Olmsted Exhibition created at Harvard University in 1963–1964, and the lectures of J.B. Jackson at Harvard and Berkeley in the 1960s. In 1971, Elisabeth Blair MacDougall was appointed Director of the Landscape Architecture Studies program at Dumbarton Oaks and initiated a series of colloquia on garden and landscape history, which placed the study of the designed landscape on a sound scholarly basis. Her own example as a scholar of Renaissance gardens undoubtedly inspired several younger woman scholars, such as Claudia Lazzaro, Mirka Benes, Dianne Harris and Thaïsa Way.

It was not until the 1970s that women began to play more prominent national roles in the ASLA Edith Henderson became vice president in 1971 and Darwina Neal became the first woman president in 1981. This differs markedly from Great Britain, where Sylvia Crowe, Brenda Colvin and Lady Allen of Hurtwood played leading roles in the Landscape Institute from its inception in the 1920s.

Conclusions

The exploratory nature of this chapter by necessity cannot lead to firm conclusions. It certainly suggests areas where further research needs to be undertaken to attain a clearer understanding of how gender has shaped landscape architecture as an art and practice. However, it can be stated clearly that World War II acts as a watershed, separating eras of strong gender discrimination from the postwar period in which some barriers have been lifted and women are recognized among the leaders of landscape architecture.

In the prewar eras women were largely excluded from professional programs, positions of power in public commissions and councils, as well as from positions of influence in major professional organizations. This gender discrimination forced women to operate as landscape architects in a network of relationships quite different from their male peers. Landscape architecture as a new profession consciously sought parity with related older professions, such as architecture and engineering, which were run like exclusive men's clubs, entry being controlled by formal university education. Since women were only admitted to one Ivy League institution and a small number of public universities, alternative women's programs became necessary. The Cambridge School program not only provided the most convincing proof of the argument that gender does not determine design ability but it also provided proof of the virtues of integrating architecture and landscape design.

Diane McGuire has written of the ASLA at that time, "If one were not a white, male, eastern college graduate, the atmosphere was quite chilly." One consequence of this was the organization's strong emphasis upon public work, and lack of emphasis upon estate and garden design. Thus, women landscape architects operated differently from their male peers, resorting to different support mechanisms and working almost entirely in the residential realm.

A striking aspect of this period is the strong connection between women in civic organizations and professional designers. This enabled women to make major contributions in estate garden design and civic engagement, most notably in their advocacy of small gardens as critical elements of communities. It is therefore particularly regrettable that some scholars, reflecting the political and ideological values of later generations, have disparaged or simply left out any discussion of this body of work, arguing that it has no obvious relevance to the succeeding modernist movement. Lavish estate design was certainly a form of conspicuous elite consumption, epitomizing a retreat from broader social and environmental concerns. But this shift in values is socially significant and to completely omit any discussion of it is unnecessarily trivializing, and reveals more about the ideological beliefs of the author(s) than being a true analysis of the past.

Class was also an important characteristic of these earlier eras. The members of the social clubs and women landscape architects, with few exceptions, came from upper class families and were generally well educated. This ensured easy communication between female patrons and female designers who were social equals. This rather closed social structure did not change significantly until after World War II, when many women from middle class families entered the profession. In recent decades, class has not been particularly important.

After World War II massive societal changes affected professional practice in landscape architecture. More women worked and many more women attended colleges and universities. The need for private women's schools evaporated. Women began to assume office in the ASLA. A level of parity was achieved in departments of landscape architecture and many women have become leading scholars.

Women have made major contributions in published public projects. Yet their role in the ubiquitous large multi-discipline firms with national and international clienteles is hard to discern. Examples cited in the essay raise questions about how design teams really work, in terms of organizational structure and responsibility. Further research is needed to determine the exact contribution made by women in these teams.

Finally, it is clear that the history of gender in landscape architecture involves considering the roles played by women as patron, social and civic activist, popular and academic writer, as well as landscape designer. Most landscape histories have ignored the important contributions of women. They have concentrated on the individual designer and formal and aesthetic issues to create a parade of Great Men. It would certainly be easy to create an equivalent parade of Great Women, as this essay suggests. Women are just as capable as men in creating uplifting and sensitive designs. But the history of women in landscape architecture in the first seventy-five years of the twentieth century must be placed in a broad social and cultural context of community and environmental concerns. Viewed in this way women landscape architects can be celebrated as agents of social change, and for their highly developed creativity and willingness to approach broader issues of community life not just from a system of aesthetic values alone. These important contributions rest on a deep and sensitive commitment to understanding the nature of place and habitability and an understanding that landscape architecture is a social art.

Notes

1. Norman T. Newton, *Design on the Land: Development of Landscape Architecture* (Cambridge, MA: Belknap Press of Harvard University Press 1971); George B. Tobey, *The History of Landscape Architecture: The Relationship of People to the Environment* (New York: Elsevier, 1973); Geoffrey and Susan Jellicoe, *The Landscape of Man: Shaping the Environment from Prehistory to the Present Day* (New York: Mayflower Books, 1975); William Mann, *Landscape Architecture: An Illustrated History in Timelines, Site Plans and Biography* (New edition, New York: John Wiley and Sons, 1993); Marc Treib, ed., *Modern Landscape Architecture: A Critical Review* (Cambridge, MA: MIT Press, 1993); Peter Walker and Melanie Simo, *Invisible Gardens: The Search for Modernism in the American Landscape* (Cambridge, MA: MIT Press, 1994); Elizabeth Barlow Rogers, *Landscape Design: A Cultural and Architectural History of Landscape Architecture* (New York: Harry Abrams, 2001).

2. Heath Massey Schenker, "Feminist Interventions in the Histories of Landscape Architecture," *Landscape Journal* 13, no. 2 (1994): 106–112.

3. "Women Take Lead in Landscape Art; Field is Dominated by a Group of Brilliant Designers of Horticultural Vista," *New York Times*, 13 March 1935, 83.

4. Schenker, "Feminist Interventions," 111–112; Thaïsa Way, *Unbounded Practice. Women and Landscape Architecture in the Early Twentieth Century* (Charlottesville: University of Virginia Press, 2009).

5. Nancy Woloch, *Women and the American Experience* (New York: Alfred Knopf, Inc., 1984), 271; Karen J. Blair, *The Clubwoman as Feminist: True Womanhood Redefined, 1868–1914* (New York: Holmes and Meier Publishers, Inc., 1980)

6. Dianne Harris, "Cultivating Power: The Language of Feminism In Women's Garden Literature, 1870–1920," *Landscape Journal* 13, no. 2 (1994): 113–123.

7. For Gertrude Jekyll see Jane Brown, *Gardens of A Golden Afternoon: The Story of a Partnership, Edwin Lutyens and Gertrude Jekyll* (London: A. Lane, 1982).

8. David Schuyler, *The New Urban Landscape: The Redefinition of City Form in Nineteenth Century America* (Baltimore: Johns Hopkins University Press, 1986).

9. Jon A. Peterson, "Frederick Law Olmsted, Sr., and Frederick Law Olmsted, Jr.: The Visionary and the Professional," in *Planning the Twentieth-Century American City*, ed. Mary Corbin Sies and Christopher Silver (Baltimore and London: Johns Hopkins University Press, 1996), 39–54.

10. Amy Brown, "Elizabeth J. Bullard," in *Pioneers of American Landscape Design*, ed. Charles A. Birnbaum and Robin Karson (New York: McGraw-Hill, 2000), 37–39.

11. Mrs. Schuyler Van Rensselaer, *Art Out-of-Doors: Hints on Good Taste in Gardening* (New York: Charles Scribner's Sons, 1893), 3.

12. Woloch, *Women and the American Experience*, 235.

13. Peterson, "The City Beautiful. Forgotten Origins and Lost Meanings," *Journal of Urban History* 2, no. 4 (1976): 415–434; William H. Wilson, *The City Beautiful Movement* (Baltimore: Johns Hopkins University Press, 1989).

14. Mary Beard, *Woman's Work in Municipalities* (New York and London: D. Appleton and Co., 1915); Blair, *The Clubwoman as Feminist*; Eugenie Ladner Birch, "From Civic Worker to City Planner: Women and Planning, 1890–1980," in *The American Planner Biographies and Recollections*, ed. Donald A. Krueckeberg (New York: Methuen, 1983), 396–427.

15. Birch, "From Civic Worker to City Planner," 399.

16. Woloch, *Women and the American Experience*, 290.

17. Daphne Spain, *How Women Saved the City* (Minneapolis and London: University of Minneapolis, 2001).

18. Dorothy May Anderson, *Women, Design, and the Cambridge School* (West Lafayette, IN: PDA Publishers Corp., 1980), 20.

19. See Leslie Rose Close, "Introduction: A History of Women in Landscape Architecture," in *The Gardens of Ellen Biddle Shipman*, ed. Judith B. Tankard (Sagaponack, NY: Sagapress, 1996), xv–xvi.

20. Doris Cole, *From Tipi to Skyscraper: A History of Women in Architecture* (New York: George Braziller, 1973), 80.

21. Cole, *From Tipi to Skyscraper*, 94–96; Susan Torre, ed., *Women in Architecture: A Historic and Contemporary Perspective* (New York: Whitney Library of Design, Watson-Gupthill, 1977), 106.

22. Cole, *From Tipi to Skyscraper*, 81.

23. *Ibid.*, 83.

24. Mary Bronson Hartt, "Women and the Art of Landscape Gardening," *Outlook* 88 (March 28, 1908): 694–704.

25. Judith B. Tankard, *Beatrix Farrand: Private gardens, Public Landscapes* (New York: Monacelli Press, 2009), 19–25.

26. Tankard, *The Gardens of Ellen Biddle Shipman*, 29–31.

27. Robin Karson, "Warren Manning," in *Pioneers of American Landscape Design*, ed. Birnbaum and Karson, 237; Joane Seall Lawson, "Rose Ishbel Greely," in *Shaping the American Landscape: New Profiles From the American Landscape Design Project*, ed. Charles A. Birnbaum and Stephanie S. Foell (Charlottesville: University of Virginia Press, 2009), 143–144; Daniel Krall, "Elizabeth Leonard Strang," in *Shaping the American Landscape*, ed. Birnbaum and Foell, 338–339.

28. Close, "Introduction: A History of Women in Landscape Architecture," xvi; Birnbaum and Karson, *Pioneers of American Landscape Design*, 47–48, 144; James Yoch, *Landscaping the American Dream: the Gardens and Film Sets of Florence Yoch 1890–1972* (New York: Harry N. Abrams, 1989).

29. Quoted in Melanie L. Simo, *The Coalescing of Different Forces and Ideas: A History of Landscape Architecture at Harvard* (Cambridge, MA: Graduate School of Design, 2000), 2.

30. Peterson, "Frederick Law Olmsted, Sr., and Frederick Law Olmsted, Jr.," 47–53; Louise Shelton, *Beautiful Gardens in America* (New York: Charles Scribner's Sons, 1915); Barr Ferree, *American Estates and Gardens* (New York: Munn, 1904); Mac Griswold and Eleanor Weller, *The Golden Age of American Gardens: Proud Owners, Private Estates 1890–1940* (New York: Harry N. Abrams, 1991).

31. Yoch, *Landscaping the American Dream*, 157–178.

32. Helen Rutherford Ely, *A Woman's Hardy Garden* (New York: Macmillan, 1903); Helen Rutherford Ely, *The Practical Flower Garden* (New York: Macmillan, 1911); Ruth Dean, *The Livable House, Its Garden* (New York: Moffat Yard, 1917); Martha Brookes Hutcheson, *The Spirit of the Garden* (Boston: Atlantic Monthly Press, 1923); Marion Coffin, *Trees and Shrubs for Landscape Effects* (New York: Charles Scribner's Sons, 1940).

33. Frances King, *The Well Considered Garden* (New York: Scribner, 1915); Frances King, *Pages From A Garden Notebook* (New York: C. Scribner's Sons, 1921); Frances King, *Variety in the Little Garden* (Boston: Atlantic Monthly Press, 1923); Frances King, *The Beginner's Garden* (New York and London: Charles Scribner's Son, 1927); Frances King, *From a New Garden* (New York: A.A. Knopf, 1930); Grace Tabor, *Old-Fashioned Gardening* (New York: McBride, Nast, 1913); Rose Standish Nichols, *English Pleasure Gardens* (New York: Macmillan, 1902); Rose Standish Nichols, *Spanish and Portuguese Gardens* (Boston; Houghton Mifflin, 1924); Rose Standish Nichols, *Italian Pleasure Gardens* (New York: Dodd, Mead, 1928); Alice Morse Earle, *Old Time Gardens Newly Set Forth: A Book of the Sweet O' the Year* (New York: Macmillan, 1901).

34. Quoted in Hartt, "Women and the Art of Landscape Gardening," 699.

35. Woloch, *Women and the American Experience*, 388, 406; Birch, "From Civic Worker to City Planner," 405.

36. Rosanne Marie Barker, "Small Town Progressivism: Pearl Chase and Female Activism in Santa Barbara 1900–1929," Ph.D. Diss., University of California, Santa Barbara, 1994; Pearl Chase, "Bernhard Hoffmann–Community Builder," *Noticias* 5 (Summer 1959): 15–24.

37. Weller and Griswold, *The Golden Age of American Gardens*, 311–353. Catherine Howett, "*Grounding Memory and Identity*," Garden Club Projects Documenting Historic Landscape Traditions of the American South," in *Designing with Culture: Claiming America's Landscape Heritage*, ed. Charles A. Birnbaum and Mary V. Hughes, (Charlottesville: University of Virginia Press, 2005), 19–38.

38. Jay Downer, "The Bronx River Parkway," in *Proceedings of the Ninth National Conference on City Planning* (New York: Douglas McMurtrie, 1917).

39. "Jones Beach State Park, Long Island, New York," *Architecture* 70 (July 1934): 23–30.

40. Howett, "*Grounding Memory and Identity*," 29.

41. Charles A. Birnbaum and Mary V. Hughes, "Introduction: Landscape Preservation in Context," in *Designing With Culture*, ed. Birnbaum and Hughes, 5, 26–27.

42. Mac Griswold and Eleanor Weller, *The Golden Age of American Gardens*; David Gebhard and Sheila Lynds, eds., *An Arcadian Landscape: The California Gardens of A. E. Hanson, 1920–1932* (Los Angeles: Hennessey and Ingalls, 1985), 25.

43. Fletcher Steele, "Landscape Design of the Future," *Landscape Architecture* 22 (July 1932): 299–302.

44. Ronda Skubi, "Women in Landscape Architecture" (undergraduate thesis, Department of Landscape Architecture, University of Washington, 1975), 4. I take considerable pride in having proposed Ronda Skubi's research topic and in supervising its completion.

45. Edith Roberts and Elsa Rehmann, *American Plants for American Gardens* (1929; reprint, Athens: University of Georgia Press, 1996); Jens Jensen, *Siftings* (Baltimore: Johns Hopkins University Press, 1990).

46. Leslie Rose Close, *Portrait of an Era in Landscape Architecture: The Photographs of Mattie Edwards Hewitt*, Exhibition Catalog (New York: Wave Hill, 1983).

47. Mildred Bliss, "Beatrix Jones Farrand, 1872–1959," Manuscript, Dumbarton Oaks Research Library, Washington, D.C., 1960; Tankard, *Beatrix Farrand*, 116–121; David C. Streatfield, *California Gardens: Creating A New Eden* (New York: Abbeville Press, 1994), 161–168; Lee W. Lenz, *The Rancho Santa Botanic Garden: The First Fifty Years 1927–1977* (Claremont, CA: Rancho Santa Ana Botanic Garden, 1977), 15–55.

48. Weller and Griswold, *The Golden Age of American Gardens*, 327–328, 142–143; Catherine M. Howett, *A World of Her Own Making: Katherine Smith Reynolds and the Landscape of Reynolda* (Amherst: University of Massachusetts Press, 2007).

49. Author's interview of Mrs. Harry Bauer, Pasadena, February, 1976; Author's interview of Geraldine Knight Scott, Berkeley, March, 1974.

50. Yoch, *Landscaping the American Dream*, 205–216; Eleanor M. McPeck, "A Biographical Note and a Consideration of Four Major Gardens," in *Beatrix Farrand's American Landscapes Her Gardens and Campuses*, ed. Diana Balmori, Diane Kostial McGuire, and Eleanor M. McPeck (Sagaponack, NY: Sagapress, 1985), 20.

51. Diane Kostial McGuire, ed., *Beatrix Farrand's Plant Book for Dumbarton Oaks* (Washington: Dumbarton Oaks, Trustees for Harvard University, 1980); Yoch, *Landscaping the American Dream*, 205–216.

52. Yoch, *Landscaping the American Dream*, 15–17, 42–46, 49–50, 60–61; Robin Karson, "Marion Coffin," in *A Genius for Place: American Landscapes of the Country Place Era*, ed. Robin S. Karson (Amherst: University of Massachusetts Press, 2007), 181–194; Tankard, *The Gardens of Ellen Biddle Shipman*, 47–72.

53. Thaïsa Way, "Early Social Agendas of Women in Landscape Architecture," *Landscape Journal* 25, no. 2 (2006): 187–204; Martha Brookes Hutcheson, *The Spirit of the Garden* (Boston: Atlantic Monthly Press, 1923).

54. Author's interview of Geraldine Knight Scott, Berkeley, March 1974.

55. Tankard, *Beatrix Farrand*, 158–171; Yoch, *Landscaping the American Dream*, 151–155; Virginia Lopez Begg, "Julia Lester Dillon," in *Shaping the American Landscape*, ed. Birnbaum and Foell, 76–77; Karen Cole, "Caroline Corneos Dormon," 77–79.

56. Woloch, *Women and the American Experience*, 461; Birch, "From Civic Worker to City Planner: Women and Planning, 1890–1980," 413.

57. Eugenie Ladner Birch, "Woman-Made America: The Case of Early Public Housing Policy," in *The American Planner*, 149–175.

58. Phoebe Cutler, *The Public Landscape of the New Deal* (New Haven and London: Yale University Press, 1985).

59. Dorothee Imbert, "The Art of Social Landscape Design," in *Garrett Eckbo: Landscapes for Living,* ed. Marc Treib (Berkeley: University of California Press, 1997), 115–143.

60. Nell Walter, "Marjorie Sewell Cautley," in *Pioneers of American Landscape Design*, ed. Birnbaum and Karson, 49.

61. Melanie Marchio, "Helen Swift Jones," in *Shaping the American Landscape*, ed. Birnbaum and Foell, 161.

62. Miriam E. Rutz, "Genevieve Gillette: From Thrift Gardens to National Parks," in *Midwestern Landscape Architecture*, ed. by William H. Tishler (Urbana and Chicago: University of Illinois Press, 2000), 215–230.

63. Yoch, *Landscaping the American Dream*, 93–108.

64. Patricia L. Filzen, "Annette Hoyt Flanders. From Beaux Arts to Modernism," in *Midwestern Landscape Architecture*, ed. Tishler, 241–242; Way, *Unbounded Practice*, 210–212.

65. Treib, ed. *Modern Landscape Architecture*, 36–67; 206–210.

66. Grace Morey, *Contemporary Landscape Architecture and Its Sources,* exhibition catalogue, February 12–March 22, 1937 (San Francisco: San Francisco Museum of Art, 1937); *Landscape Design,* exhibition catalogue (San Francisco: San Francisco Museum of Art and the Association of Landscape Architects, 1948); R. Burton Litton, ed., *Landscape Architecture 1958,* exhibition catalogue (San Francisco: San Francisco Museum of Art, 1958).

67. Loraine Meeks, Hattie C. Rainwater, Florence Nesbit Mayne, P. Thornton Mayne, *Garden History of Georgia* (Atlanta: Garden Club of Georgia, 1933); Alice G.B. Lockwood, ed., *Gardens of Colony and State; Gardens and Gardening of the American Colonies and of the Republic before 1840* (New York, C. Scribner's Sons, 1934).

68. Cole, *From Tipi to Skyscraper*, 97.

69. Simo, *The Coalescing of Different Forces and Ideas*, 34.

70. Caroline Doepke Benett, "Katherine Emilie Bashord," in *Shaping the American Landscape,* ed. Birnbaum and Foell, 12–14.

71. Woloch, *Women and the American Experience*, 461–469.

72. Anderson, *Women, Design and the Cambridge School*, 164; Author's interview of Geraldine Knight Scott, March 1974, Berkeley, California; Armistead Fitzhugh, "Camouflage: Adaptation of Basic Principles of Landscape Architecture," *Landscape Architecture* 34 (July 1941): 119–123.

73. Woloch, *Women and the American Experience*, 467.

74. *Ibid.*, 500.

75. Louise Mozingo, "The Corporate Estate in the USA, 1954–64: 'thoroughly modern in concept but down to earth and rugged,'" *Studies in the History of Gardens and Designed Landscapes* 20, no. 1 (2000): 25–56.

76. David C. Streatfield, "Modernist Gardens 'On the Edge of the World,'" in *Masters of American Garden Design III: The Modern Garden in Europe and the United States: Proceedings of the Garden Conservancy Symposium held March 12, 1993 at the Paine Webber Building in New York*, ed. Robin Karson (Cold Spring, New York: The Garden Conservancy, 1994), 43–57.

77. Kenneth J. Helphand, "Elizabeth Lord, Edith Schryver," in *Pioneers of American Landscape Design*, by Birnbaum and Karson, 228–230.

78. David C. Streatfield, "Introduction," in *Landscape for Living*, by Garrett Eckbo, (1950; Reprint Amherst: University of Massachusetts Press, 2008).

79. Christopher Tunnard, "Modern Gardens for Modern Houses: Reflections on Current Trends in Landscape Design," *Landscape Architecture* 32 (January 1942), 60.

80. Streatfield, *California Gardens*, 196.

81. Helphand, "Elizabeth Lord, Edith Schryver," 228–230.

82. Thomas D. Church, Grace Hall, Michael Laurie, eds., *Gardens Are for People* (Berkeley: University of California Press, 1995).

83. J. E. Howland, "Marie and Arthur Berger: A Tribute," *Landscape Architecture* 54 (July 1964): 266–270.

84. Skubi, *Women in Landscape Architecture*, 85–90, 138–154, 158–161, 199–201, 236–250.

85. *Ibid.*, 85–90;

86. Torre, *Women in Architecture*, 111–114; Birch, "From Civic Worker to City Planner," 112–114; Skubi, "Women in Landscape Architecture," 82, 158–161, 199–201.

87. Author's interview of Ruth Shellhorn, Redondo Beach, February 1974.

88. Ruth Shellhorn, "Disneyland: Dream Built in One Year Through Teamwork of Many Artists," *Landscape Architecture* 46 (April, 1956): 125–136.

89. Author's interview of Barbara Fealy, Portland, Oregon, July 1990; Skubi, *Women in Landscape Architecture*, 173–184: Kathleen McCormick, "More Than a Picture on the Wall: Grand Dame of Landscape Architecture," *Landscape Architecture* 83 (February 1993): 48–51.

90. Woloch, *Women and the American Experience*, 505.
91. *Ibid.*, 505–506.
92. Donald Loggins, "Elizabeth (Liz) Christy," in *Shaping the American Landscape*, ed. Birnbaum and Foell, 50–51.

Bibliography

Anderson, Dorothy May. *Women, Design, and the Cambridge School*. West Lafayette, IN: PDA Publishers Corp., 1980.

Barker, Rosanne Marie. "Small Town Progressivism: Pearl Chase and Female Activism in Santa Barbara 1900–1929." Ph.D. diss., University of California, Santa Barbara, 1994.

Barr, Ferree. *American Estates and Gardens*. New York: Munn, 1904.

Beard, Mary. *Woman's Work in Municipalities*. New York: D. Appleton, 1915.

Begg, Virginia Lopez. "Julia Lester Dillon." In *Shaping the American Landscape: New Profiles from the Pioneers of American Landscape Design Project*, edited by Charles A. Birnbaum and Stephanie S. Foell, 76–77. Charlottesville: University of Virginia Press, 2009.

Benett, Caroline Doepke. "Katherine Emilie Bashord." In *Shaping the American Landscape: New Profiles from the Pioneers of American Landscape Design Project*, edited by Charles A Birnbaum and Stephanie S. Foell, 12–14. Charlottesville: University of Virginia Press, 2009.

Birch, Eugenie Ladner. "From Civic Worker to City Planner: Women and Planning, 1890–1980." In *The American Planner Biographies and Recollections*, edited by Donald A. Krueckeberg, 396–427. New York: Methuen, 1983.

Birnbaum, Charles A. and Mary V. Hughes. *Design with Culture: Claiming America's Landscape Heritage*. Charlottesville: University of Virginia Press, 2005.

Blair, Karen J. *The Clubwoman as Feminist: True Womanhood Redefined, 1868–1914*. New York: Holmes and Meier, 1980.

Bliss, Mildred. "Beatrix Jones Farrand, 1872–1959." Unpublished manuscript, Dumbarton Oaks Research Library, Washington, D.C., 1960.

Brown, Amy. "Elizabeth J. Bullard." In *Pioneers of American Landscape Design*, edited by Charles A. Birnbaum and Robin Karson, 37–39. New York: McGraw-Hill, 2000.

Brown, Jane. *Gardens of a Golden Afternoon. The Story of a Partnership. Edwin Lutyens and Gertrude Jekyll*. London: A. Lane, 1982.

Chase, Pearl. "Bernhard Hoffmann — Community Builder." *Noticias* 5 (Summer 1959): 15–24.

Church, Thomas D., Grace Hall, and Michael Laurie, eds. *Gardens Are for People*. Berkeley: University of California Press, 1995.

Close, Leslie Rose. "Introduction: A History of Women in Landscape Architecture." In *The Gardens of Ellen Biddle Shipman*, by Judith B. Tankard, xv–xvi. Sagaponack, NY: Sagapress, 1996.

_____. *Portrait of an Era in Landscape Architecture; The Photographs of Mattie Edwards Hewitt*. Exhibition Catalog. New York: Wave Hill, 1983.

Coffin, Marion. *Trees and Shrubs for Landscape Effects*. New York: Charles Scribner's Sons, 1940.

Cole, Doris. *From Tipi to Skyscraper: A History of Women in Architecture*, New York: George Braziller, 1973.

Cutler, Phoebe. *The Public Landscape of the New Deal*. New Haven: Yale University Press, 1985.

Dean, Ruth. *The Livable House, Its Garden*. New York: Moffat Yard, 1917.

Downer, Jay. "The Bronx River Parkway." In *Proceedings of the Ninth National Conference on City Planning*. New York: Douglas McMurtrie, 1917.

Earle, Alice Morse. *Old Time Gardens Newly Set Forth: A Book of the Sweet O' the Year*. New York: Macmillan, 1901.

Ely, Helen Rutherford. *The Practical Flower Garden*. New York: Macmillan, 1911.

_____. *A Woman's Hardy Garden*. New York: Macmillan, 1903.

Filzen, Patricia L. "Annette Hoyt Flanders: From Beaux Arts to Modernism." In *Midwestern Landscape Architecture*, edited by William H. Tishler, 231–242. Urbana and Chicago: University of Illinois Press, 2000.

Fitzhugh, Armistead. "Camouflage: Adaptation of Basic Principles of Landscape Architecture." *Landscape Architecture* 34 (July 1941): 119–123.

Gebhard, David, and Sheila Lynds, eds. *An Arcadian Landscape; the California Gardens of A. E. Hanson, 1920–1932*. Los Angeles: Hennessey and Ingalls, 1985.

Griswold, Mac, and Eleanor Weller. *The Golden Age of American Gardens. Proud Owners, Private Estates 1890–1940.* New York: Harry N. Abrams, 1991.

Hartt, Mary Bronson. "Women and the Art of Landscape Gardening." *Outlook.* 88 (March 28, 1908): 695–704.

Harris, Dianne. "Cultivating Power: The Language of Feminism in Women's Garden Literature, 1870–1920." *Landscape Journal* 13, no. 2 (1994): 113–123.

Helphand, Kenneth J. "Elizabeth Lord, Edith Schryver," In *Pioneers of American Landscape Design,* edited by Charles A. Birnbaum and Robin S. Karson, 228–230. New York: McGraw-Hill, 2000.

Howett, Catherine. "Grounding Memory and Identity: Garden Club Projects Documenting Historic Landscape Traditions of the American South." In *Designing with Culture: Claiming America's Landscape Heritage,* edited by Charles A. Birnbaum and Mary V. Hughes, 19–38. Charlottesville: University of Virginia Press, 2005.

_____. *A World of Her Own Making: Katherine Smith Reynolds and the Landscape of Reynolda.* Amherst: University of Massachusetts Press, 2007.

Howland, J. E. "Marie and Arthur Berger: A Tribute." *Landscape Architecture* 54 (July 1964): 266–270.

Hutcheson, Martha Brookes. *The Spirit of the Garden.* Boston: Atlantic Monthly Press, 1923.

Imbert, Dorothee. "The Art of Social Landscape Design." In *Garrett Eckbo: Landscapes for Living,* edited by Marc Treib, 115–143. Berkeley: University of California Press, 1997.

Jellicoe, Geoffrey and Susan Jellicoe. *The Landscape of Man: Shaping the Environment from Prehistory to the Present Day.* New York: Mayflower Books, 1975.

Jensen, Jens. *Siftings.* Baltimore: Johns Hopkins University Press, 1990.

"Jones Beach State Park, Long Island, New York," *Architecture* 70 (July 1934): 23–30.

Karson, Robin. "Marion Coffin." In *A Genius for Place: American Landscapes of the Country Place Era.* Amherst: University of Massachusetts Press, 2007.

_____. "Warren Manning." In *Pioneers of American Landscape Design* edited by Charles A. Birnbaum and Robin S. Karson, 137. New York: McGraw-Hill, 2000.

King, Frances. *The Beginner's Garden.* New York: Charles Scribner's Son, 1927.

_____. *From a New Garden.* New York: A.A. Knopf, 1930.

_____. *Pages from a Garden Notebook.* New York: C. Scribner's Sons, 1921.

_____. *Variety in the Little Garden.* Boston: Atlantic Monthly Press, 1923.

_____. *The Well Considered Garden.* New York: Scribner, 1915.

Krall, Daniel. "Elizabeth Leonard Strang." In *Shaping the American Landscape: New Profiles from the American Landscape Design Project,* edited by Charles A. Birnbaum and Stephanie S. Foell, 338–339. Charlottesville: University of Virginia Press, 2009.

Landscape Design. Exhibition catalogue. San Francisco: San Francisco Museum of Art and Association of Landscape Architects, San Francisco Region, 1948.

Lawson, Joane Seall. "Rose Ishbel Greely," in *Shaping the American Landscape: New Profiles From the American Landscape Design Project,* edited by Charles A. Birnbaum and Stephanie S. Foell, 143–144. Charlottesville: University of Virginia Press, 2009.

Lenz, Lee W. *The Rancho Santa Botanic Garden: The First Fifty Years 1927–1977.* Claremont, CA: Rancho Santa Ana Botanic Garden, 1977.

Litton, R. Burton, ed. *Landscape Architecture 1958.* San Francisco: San Francisco Museum of Art and American Society of Landscape Architects, 1958.

Lockwood, Alice G.B., ed. *Gardens of Colony and State: Gardens and Gardening of the American Colonies and of the Republic before 1840.* New York: C. Scribner's Sons, 1934.

Loggins, Donald. "Elizabeth (Liz) Christy." In *Shaping the American Landscape: New Profiles from the Pioneers of American Landscape Design Project,* edited by Charles A. Birnbaum and Stephanie S. Foell, 50–51. Charlottesville: University of Virginia Press, 2009.

Mann, William. *Landscape Architecture: An Illustrated History in Timelines, Site Plans and Biography.* New York: John Wiley and Sons, 1993.

Marchio, Melanie. "Helen Swift Jones." In *Shaping the American Landscape: New Profiles from the Pioneers of American Landscape Design Project,* edited by Charles A. Birnbaum and Stephanie S. Foell, 76–77. Charlottesville: University of Virginia Press, 2009.

McCormick, Kathleen. "More Than a Picture on the Wall: Grand Dame of Landscape Architecture." *Landscape Architecture* 83 (February 1993): 48–51.

McGuire, Diane Kostial, ed. *Beatrix Farrand's Plant Book for Dumbarton Oaks.* Washington: Dumbarton Oaks, Trustees for Harvard University, 1980.

McPeck, Eleanor M. "A Biographical Note and a Consideration of Four Major Gardens." In *Beatrix*

Farrand's American Landscapes: Her Gardens and Campuses, edited by Diana Balmori, Diane Kostial McGuire, and Eleanor M. McPeck, 17–32. Sagaponack, NY: Sagapress, 1985.

Meeks, Loraine, Hattie C. Rainwater, Florence Nesbit Mayne, and P. Thornton Mayne. *Garden History of Georgia.* Atlanta: Garden Club of Georgia, 1933.

Morley, Grace, ed. *Contemporary Landscape Architecture and Its Sources.* Exhibition catalogue, February 12–March 22. San Francisco: San Francisco Museum of Art, 1937.

Mozingo, Louise. "The Corporate Estate in the USA, 1954–64: 'thoroughly modern in concept but down to earth and rugged.'" *Studies in the History of Gardens and Designed Landscapes* 20, no. 1 (2000): 25–56.

Newton, Norman T., *Design on the Land: Development of Landscape Architecture.* Cambridge, MA: Belknap Press of Harvard University Press, 1971.

Nichols, Rose Standish. *English Pleasure Gardens.* New York: Macmillan, 1902.

_____. *Italian Pleasure Gardens.* New York: Dodd, Mead, 1928.

_____. *Spanish and Portuguese Gardens.* Boston: Houghton Mifflin, 1924.

Petersen, Anne. "Women Take Lead in Landscape Art." *New York Times* March 13, 1935, 83.

Peterson, Jon A. "The City Beautiful: Forgotten Origins and Lost Meanings," *Journal of Urban History* 2, no. 4 (1976): 415–434.

_____. "Frederick Law Olmsted, Sr., and Frederick Law Olmsted, Jr.: The Visionary and the Professional." In *Planning the Twentieth-Century American City,* edited by Mary Corbin Sies and Christopher Silver, 39–54. Baltimore: Johns Hopkins University Press, 1996.

Roberts, Edith and Elsa Rehmann. *American Plants for American Gardens.* 1929. Reprint Athens: University of Georgia Press, 1996.

Rogers, Elizabeth Barlow. *Landscape Design: A Cultural and Architectural History of Landscape Architecture.* New York: Harry Abrams, 2001.

Rutz, Miriam E. "Genevieve Gillette: From Thrift Gardens to National Parks." In *Midwestern Landscape Architecture,* edited by William H. Tishler, 215–230. Urbana and Chicago: University of Illinois Press, 2000.

Schenker, Heath Massey. "Feminist Interventions in the Histories of Landscape Architecture." *Landscape Journal* 13, no. 2 (1994): 106–112.

Schuyler, David. *The New Urban Landscape. The Redefinition of City Form in Nineteenth Century America,* Baltimore: Johns Hopkins University Press, 1986.

Shellhorn, Ruth. "Disneyland: Dream Built in One Year through Teamwork of Many Artists." *Landscape Architecture* 46 (April 1956): 125–136.

Shelton, Louise. *Beautiful Gardens in America.* New York: Charles Scribner's Sons, 1915.

Simo, Melanie L. *The Coalescing of Different Forces and Ideas: A History of Landscape Architecture at Harvard.* Cambridge: Harvard University Graduate School of Design, 2000.

Skubi, Ronda. "Women in Landscape Architecture." Undergraduate thesis, Department of Landscape Architecture, University of Washington, 1975.

Spain, Daphne. *How Women Saved the City.* Minneapolis and London: University of Minneapolis, 2001.

Steele, Fletcher. "Landscape Design of the Future." *Landscape Architecture* 22 (July 1932): 299–302.

Streatfield, David C. "Introduction." In *Landscape for Living,* by Garrett Eckbo, 1950. Reprint. Amherst: University of Massachusetts Press, 2008.

_____. *California Gardens: Creating a New Eden.* New York: Abbeville Press, 1994.

_____. "Modernist Gardens 'On the Edge of the World,'" in *Masters of American Garden Design III: The Modern Garden in Europe and the United States: Proceedings of the Garden Conservancy Symposium, March 12,1993 at the Paine Webber Building in New York,* edited by Robin Karson, 43–57. Cold Spring, New York: Garden Conservancy, 1994.

Tabor, Grace. *Old-Fashioned Gardening.* New York: McBride, Nast, 1913

Tankard, Judith B. *Beatrix Farrand: Private gardens, Public Landscapes.* New York: Monacelli Press, 2009.

_____. *The Gardens of Ellen Biddle Shipman.* Sagaponack, NY: Sagapress in association with the Library of American Landscape History, 1996.

Tobey, George B. *The History of Landscape Architecture: The Relationship of People to the Environment.* New York: Elsevier, 1973.

Torre, Susan, ed. *Women in Architecture: A Historic and Contemporary Perspective.* New York: Whitney Library of Design, Watson-Gupthill, 1977.

Treib, Marc, ed. *Modern Landscape Architecture: A Critical Review.* Cambridge, MA: MIT Press, 1993.

Tunnard, Christopher. "Modern Gardens for Modern Houses. Reflections on Current Trends in Landscape Design." *Landscape Architecture* 32 (January 1942): 60.

Van Rensselaer, Mariana Griswold (Mrs. Schuyler). *Art Out-of-Doors: Hints on Good Taste in Gardening.* New York: Charles Scribner's Sons, 1893.

Walker, Peter, and Melanie Simo. *Invisible Gardens: The Search for Modernism in the American Landscape.* Cambridge, MA: MIT Press, 1994.

Walter, Nell. "Marjorie Sewell Cautley," In *Pioneers of American Landscape Design*, edited by Charles A. Birnbaum and Robin Karson, 49. New York: McGraw-Hill, 2000.

Way, Thaïsa. "Early Social Agendas of women in landscape architecture," *Landscape Journal* 25, no. 2 (2006): 187–204.

_____. *Unbounded Practice. Women and Landscape Architecture in the Early Twentieth Century.* Charlottesville: University of Virginia Press, 2009.

Wilson, Joanne Seale. "Greely, Rose Ishbel" in *Pioneers of American Landscape Design* edited by Charles A Birnbaum and Robin S Karson, 143–44. New York: McGraw-Hill, 2000.

Wilson, William H. *The City Beautiful Movement.* Baltimore: Johns Hopkins University Press, 1989.

Woloch, Nancy. *Women and the American Experience.* New York: Alfred A. Knopf, 1984.

Yoch, James. *Landscaping the American Dream: The Gardens and Film Sets of Florence Yoch 1890–1972.* New York: Harry N. Abrams, 1989.

Chapter 2

Where Are the Women in Landscape Architecture?

TERRY L. CLEMENTS

After years of consciously avoiding and ignoring gender issues in landscape architecture and refusing to discuss eco-feminism, a new graduate student asked a question that challenged me to reconsider my stance. She asked about the historic and current status of women in landscape architecture, not as a point of feminist critique but as a factual representation. Although I have been actively involved in the profession for over twenty years, I did not know. However, my curiosity was piqued.

Over the last three decades, symposia, lectures and committees supported by the American Society of Landscape Architecture (ASLA), the Council of Educators of Landscape Architecture (CELA) and academic institutions have addressed women's contributions in landscape architecture and related issues of the designed environment. However, little of this discourse and scholarship has been published or compiled in accessible formats. Few available publications chronicle or highlight where women are within the discipline of landscape architecture today.

This chapter provides a timeline, a short historical narrative, and recent statistics of women's accomplishments within the practice of landscape architecture in the United States. The timeline and historical narrative draws from numerous sources and provides a historical review summarizing the context of women in professional practice as well as significant milestones and contextual events. The statistical analysis demonstrates where women who are licensed to practice landscape architecture stand in relationship to one another and to male practitioners in 1997.

This chapter also indicates where additional research may be useful in understanding the historical contributions of women in practice, their current status and areas of significant contributions, as well as trends and future directions. Women have made significant contributions in built works, community participation, planning and design, policy and planning, landscape architecture theory, academic program development and direction, and within professional organizations. This chapter is an attempt to bring forward and continue discussions and scholarship relative to women landscape architects as we begin the twenty-first century.

Timeline

Where were the Women in Landscape Architecture?

An abbreviated timeline

1870s

- 1870 *Handbook of Landscape Gardening* published
- 1871 University of Illinois offers instruction in garden design for ladies and gentlemen
- 1872 Yellowstone National Park established
- Anna Warner publishes *Miss Tiller's Vegtable Garden and the Money She Made By It*, and includes lessons in business, accounting and customer relations

1880s

1890s

- 1893 Marianna Griswold Van Rennselaer publishes *Art Out-of-doors Hints on Good Taste in Gardening*
- 1895 Beatrix Jones (later Farrand) opens practice in New York
- 1898 Biltmore School of Forestry established
- 1899 American Society of Landscape Architects founded; ten men, one woman (Beatrix Jones Farrand founding member, Elizabeth Bullard joins later in the year)

1900s

- 1900 Harvard offers first degree program in landscape architecture (no women allowed until 1942)
- 1901 Lowthorpe School of Landscape Architecture, Gardening and Horticulture for Women opens
- 13% of ASLA members are women
- 1902 City Planning emerges under realm of landscape architecture
- 1904 Edith Wharton publishes *Italian Villas and Their Gardens*
- Marian Cruger Coffin graduates as a "special student" from the landscape architecture program at Massachusetts Institute of Technology

1910s

- 1910 Louise Bush-Brown opens and heads the Pennsylvania School of Horticulture for Women opens in Ambler (now part of Temple University)
- Theodora Kimball appointed the first librarian for the landscape architecture and city planning departments at Harvard University; co-founded *Landscape Architecture Quarterly* (today known as *Landscape Architecture Magazine*) and co-authored *An Introduction to the Study of Landscape Design* (1917)
- 1912 Marian Cruger Coffin begins professional career
- 1913 Secretary of ASLA states, "It is a mistake to encourage women to enter the Society."

Country Place Era

City Beautiful Movement

Public Park Movement

The vertical era bars (left to right): Country Place Era | City Beautiful Movement | Recreation and State Parks Era | Modernism... | Highway... | Public Works

- 1913   University of California, Berkeley establishes landscape architecture program
- 1914   Annette Hoyt Flanders opens own practice
- 1915   First instruction at what would become the Cambridge School of Architectural and Landscape Design for Women in Cambridge, Massachusetts
- Ruth Bramley Dean sets up firm in New York City, work respects ecology and uses native plants
- 3% of ASLA membership are women
- 1916   National Park Service established
- 1918   Florence Yoch opens practice in Southern California (Lucille Council becomes partner in 1925)

1920s

- 1920   Council of Educators of Landscape Architecture (CELA) founded; 16 institutions
- 1921   CELA resolution (no. 6 of 6) calls upon co-ed institutions to give equal encouragement to men and women who plan to seriously pursue the profession
- Beatrix Jones Farrand begins work at Dumbarton Oaks
- 1923   Garden Club of America founded
- Harvard offers Masters Degree in Landscape Architecture with a major in City Planning; City Planning becomes seperate degree program in 1929
- 1926   Booklet entitled "Women in Architecture and Landscape Architecture" reitereated known problems and prejudices about women professials
- 1928   Restoration of Colonial Williamsburg begins
- Marian Cruger Coffin begins design of Winterthur
- 1929   Elizabeth Lord and Edith Schryver establish first woman run firm in Pacific Northwest
- Ruth Bramley Dean is first woman awarded Architecture League of New York's Gold Medal for Landscape Architecture
- City planning moves out of realm of lanscape architecture and emerges as a separate profession
- Elsa Rehmann and Edith Roberts publish *American Plants for American Gardens*

1930s

- 1930   Marion Cruger Coffin recieves Gold Medal of the Architectural League of New York
- 1931   V. Ethelwyn Harrison is the first woman elected as ASLA chapter secretary (Ohio Michigan Chapter)
- 1933   Jane Silverstein Ries establishes own firm; is the first female landscape architect in Colorado
- Tennessee Valley Authority enacted

The following events are shown along vertical timeline bars labeled (left to right): **Modernism in Landscape Design**, **Highway and Interstate Expansion**, **New Deal Era**, **National Parks and Public Works**.

1933   Elsa Rehmann writes first *Landscape Architecture Magazine* article on designing on an ecological basis

Annette Hoyt Flanders designs modern garden for "A Century of Progress" exhibition at Chicago's World's Fair

13% of ASLA members are women (40 women members), 50% of chapter secretaries are women

1934   Martha Brooks Hutcheson is the first woman elected as Fellow of ASLA

1935   Marjorie Sewell Cautley appointed landscape consultant to New Hampshire to oversee ten CCC state park projects

1936   G. Lester Rowntree promotes native plants in *Hardy Californians*

1937   San Francisco Museum of Art exhibition, "Contemporary Landscape Architecture" features work by women and men

1939   Margherita Tarr works as landscape architect with Iowa State Extension, later becoming Extension Landscape Architect (1946-69)

Katherine Bashford elected president of the Southern California Chapter ASLA

1940s

1940   Beatrix Jones Farrand retires

Florence Bell Robinson publishes *Planting Design*

1941   19% of ASLA members are women

First *Landscape Architecture Magazine* article dealing specifically with social responsibility of designers toward underprivileged and disadvantaged people

1942   Cambridge School closes, Harvard accepts women into landscape architecture program and Cornelia Oberlander graduates (1944)

Geraldine Knight Scott is the first woman hired by the Los Angeles Regional Planning Authority

1943   Dean Gilmore D. Clark (Cornell University) states, "the only way in which the profession may grow and prosper
well-trained and talented young men and women"

Maude Sargent, Lucile Teeter Kissack and Jane Silverstein Reis are among women landscape architects entering military service during World War II

Margaret Winters works with Army Corps of Engineers on airfields and urban sites

1945   Lowthorpe School becomes part of Rhode Island School of Design and co-educational, headed by Elizabeth Pattee

1947   Ruth Shellhorn original member and first landscape architect of the Disneyland design team

1948   National Trust for Historic Preservation established

First *Landscape Architecture Magazine* article published calling for post-construction evaluations

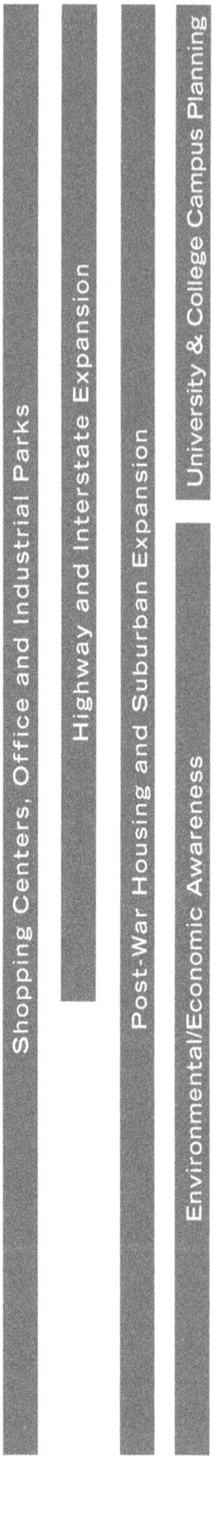

1950s

- 1953   Dorothea K. Harrison is the first woman president of an ASLA chapter, Boston Society of Landscape Architects; is first woman elected as ASLA Trustee in 1954

- 1954   Harriett B. Wimmer becomes San Diego's first woman landscape architect in commercial practice; is founding member and chair of San Diego Chapter of ASLA (1955-56)

- 1956   Genevieve Gillette (the first woman graduate of landscape architecture from Michigan Agricultural College, 1920) is instrumental in establishing Sleeping Bear Dunes (1956) and Pictured Rocks (1972) as National Lakeshores

- 1957   May Theilgaard Watts publishes *Reading the Landscape: an adventure in ecology* and intertwines human and natural history

- 1959   Carol R. Johnson starts own firm to do mainstream landscape architecture. In 1963 she starts to hire men and women "the best she can find."

1960s

- 1961   Rachel Carson publishes *Silent Spring*

- Jane Jacobs publishes *The Death and Life of Great American Cities*

- 1963   First Lady Bird Johnson promotes "A More Beautiful Capital," and expands her program to include the entire nation

- Clean Air Act passes

- 1964   National Park Service cited as largest single employer of landscape architects

- 1965   Angela Danadijeva and L. Halprin design the Ira Keller Fountain (Auditorium Forecourt) in Portland, Oregon

- Land and Water Conservation Fund established

- 1968   18 accredited programs of landscape architecture in North America

1970s

- 1970   National Environmental Policy Act signed, Environmental Protection Agency established

- 1972   Fein Report on education and profession's future published

- Elizabeth Blair MacDougall becomes the first Director of Studies in Landscape Architecture at Dumbarton Oaks

- 28 accredited landscape architecture programs in North America; no full-time female faculty are landscape architects

- ASLA study reveals more women needed to teach, only 6% of ASLA membership are women

- Title IX of the Education Amendment passes

- 1973   Report written for ASLA generalized that female students do not take criticism as well as male students

- Sally Schauman hired in the first Landscape Architecture Section of the Soil Conservation Service

Vertical sidebar labels (left margin, bottom to top):

Shopping Centers, Office and Industrial Parks

Highway and Interstate Expansion

Post-War Housing and Suburban Expansion

University & College Campus Planning

Environmental/Economic Awareness

1974	University of Minnesota awards degrees to their first women landscape architecture graduates
	Edith Henderson is elected vice-President of ASLA75 becomes the first woman officer 75 years after its founding
1975	9 full-time women faculty at the graduate level, despite 30% of graduate students are female
	Carol Franklin and Leslie Sauer establish Andropogon to bring ecological perspective to problem-solving in landscape architecture
	Clare Cooper Marcus establishes primacy of project post-occupancy evaluation with users in mind at Easter Hill Village, California
	Pamela Burton's new firm specializes in urban design and master planning for institutional, commercial and civic clients
	Angela Danadjieva and L. Halprin design Freeway Park; Mai Arbegast serves as planting consultant
1976	ASLA holds first workshop especially for women
1978	Bagel Garden by Martha Schwartz
	50% of landscape architecture programs have no women faculty despite there being over 500 women MLA graduates in four years
	Rachel Kaplan co-authors *Humanscape: Environments for People*, and later *With People in Mind* (1998)
1979	ASLA publishes report on gender issues in *Landscape Architecture Magazine*
	Three Mile Island disaster

1980s

1980	Linda Jewell begins series of articles on construction materials for *Landscape Architecture Magazine* (1980-1987)
	Sally Schauman appointed Chair of the Landscape Architecture program at the University of Washington
1982	13% of ASLA members are women
	Maya Lin designs the Vietnam Veterans Memorial, Washington, D.C.
	Patricia O'Donnell leads historic preservation to include parks and landscapes
1983	Darwina Neal becomes the first woman president of ASLA
	Becca Hanson starts Portico Group in Seattle, a computer literate studio practice focused on zoos and aquariums
1984	20% of ASLA members are women
	Elizabeth Plater-Zyberk and A. Duany design Seaside, Florida and spark the New Urbanist Movement

Historic and Cultural Preservation

Community Participation

Environmental/Economic Awareness

New Urbanism

Historic...

Community...

- Anne Whiston Spirn publishes *Granite Garden: urban nature and human design*, changes discussion of nature to include urban nature

- 1986   Joanna Dougherty is the first female Fellow in Landscape Architecture at the American Academy in Rome (program opened for women in 1947)

- 1988   Dame Sylvia Crowe is the first woman recepient of ASLA Medal

- 1989   Lauren G. Meier starts the Historic Landscape Initiative at the National Park Service

1990s

- Marni Barnes, Joanne Westphal and Nancy Gerlach-Spriggs combine landscape architecture and healthcare degrees

- 1992   Martha Schwartz first female Resident in Landscape Architecture at American Academy in Rome

- Robin Karson becomes first director of Library of American Landscape History

- 1993   Juanita Scherer-Swink becomes first landscape architect appointed to North Carolina Triangle Transit Authority

- Catherine Brown co-founds Congress of New Urbanism

- Leslie Kerr is the first woman to receive ASLA's LaGasse Medal

- 1994   Deborah Dalton is the first woman landscape architect to serve as college dean, University of Oklahoma

- 1995   *Landscape Architecture Magazine* runs feature article entitled, "Women and the Profession"

- Julie Bargmann's collaborative Vintondale Colliery Park Reclamation project reclaims the history and natural resources of a coal town

- 1997   26% of registered landscape architects are women

- Clare Cooper Marcus and Marni Barnes publish *Healing Gardens: Therapeutic Benefits and Design*

- 1998   25% of ASLA members are women; 9.3% (68 total) of the 724 ASLA Fellows are women

- Carol R. Johnson receives the ASLA Medal

- 1999   Janice C. Schach serves as fifth female president of ASLA

2000s

- 2000   Presidents of the Council of Educators of Landcape Architects, American Society of Landscape Architects, and Canadian Society of Landscape Architects, and the executive director of Landcape Architecture Foundation are all women.

- Meg Calkins and Elizabeth Gourley begin writing a series of articles on construction materials and detailing for *Landscape Architecture Magazine*

The Garden Rediscovered

Environmental/Ecological Design and Planning

New Urbanism

Landscape Urbanism

Historical Context

Donna Palmer's 1976 study, "An Overview of the Trends, Eras, and Values of Landscape Architecture in America from 1910 to the Present with an Emphasis on the Contributions of Women to the Profession," identified distinct eras and trends within the American landscape architecture profession as seen through a content analysis of *Landscape Architecture Magazine*.[1] Women actively participated in each era, as either designers, planners, community activists or clients.

1870–1910	Public Park Movement
1893–1929	City Beautiful Movement
1890–1930	Country Place Era
1930–1940	National Park Service and Public Works Era
1933–1942	New Town Era
1945–1953	Post-war Housing and Subdivision Expansion
1939–1959	Highway and Interstate Expansion
1966–1970s	Environmental/Ecological Awareness

During the late 1800s, very few middle-income women actively worked outside the home. Women's roles were primarily limited to development and maintenance of domestic environments for their husbands and families. Only those who had economic means and were able to transcend prevailing attitudes denying women's ability to function in the business world were able to attain the necessary education, background and experience to practice landscape architecture.

Early female practitioners of landscape architecture, such as Beatrix Jones Farrand and Ellen McGowan Shipman, followed the general direction of the emerging profession. Both men and women preferred residential work, particularly large country estates, before 1930. Both generally avoided public works such as courthouses, public schools and banks.[2] This was also true in architecture, where architects preferred to leave the design of factories and other places of work to engineers.[3] By 1899, small numbers of women were involved in landscape architecture, primarily as plantswomen and as consultant landscape gardeners for private residential properties.[4]

In the early twentieth century, women were denied access to academic institutions offering landscape architecture degree programs. Prevailing attitudes in the United States neither acknowledged nor accepted the need or desire for further education for women, except as it pertained to improving domestic environments. This limitation to domestic areas soon provided an access for women to study landscape architecture and architecture. In the early 1900s three schools opened specifically to train women in domestic landscape architecture. In 1901, the Lowthorpe School of Landscape Architecture, Gardening and Horticulture for Women opened in Groton, Massachusetts. In 1910, the Pennsylvania School of Horticulture for Women in Ambler, Pennsylvania began to offer a two-year degree in Horticulture. In 1915, instruction in landscape architecture began at what would become the Cambridge School of Architectural and Landscape Design for Women in Cambridge, Massachusetts.

Initially women's academic studies in landscape architecture focused on such domestic landscapes as small cottages and individual residential properties. Educators thought that women's professional work at this scale would not compromise their important personal expectations of marriage and motherhood and would allow them reasonable freedom to pursue free-lance practices as their family obligations might allow them.

Although the Cambridge and Lowthorpe Schools focused on domestic applications, they demanded complete training in landscape architecture. Henry Frost and William Sears, instructors at the Cambridge School of Domestic Architecture and Landscape Architecture (earlier school title), published a 1928 pamphlet stressing the necessity of complete and adequate training in all branches of the profession, whatever special or limited fields of work might be later chosen. In the 1920s an adequate education consisted of: (1) a regular four-year course at a good college, (2) three years' graduate work in landscape architecture, and (3) a trip abroad.[5]

During the 1920s and 30s, women were honing their skills designing domestic environments on both coasts of the United States. During the Great Depression and later during the great housing shortage of the 1940s, the general practice of landscape architecture, traditionally dominated by men, including public parks, large estates and town planning, moved toward residential design and community design. Men began to compete with women in areas where women were extraordinarily better prepared. Women's education and professional practice had trained them well in garden and yard planning, and in planting design.

Educational opportunities for women diminished even as graduates established themselves in private practice during the 1930s and 40s. When the Cambridge School closed in 1942, over 500 women had participated in the degree program. Shortly afterwards the Lowthorpe School closed. It later reopened as the Lowthorpe School of Landscape Architecture at the Rhode Island School of Design. With the return of the American GIs after World War II and the strength of the GI Bill, American values were refined and strengthened around a preconceived notion that women's primary roles existed within the domestic realm. Women were not encouraged to be involved in the design and construction of any public project, nor within the declining number of large private projects. The relative percentage of women practicing landscape architecture compared to the percent of men in practice diminished and did not grow again until the 1960s.

Societal and cultural conditions changed in the 1960s, allowing and encouraging women and men to become involved in improving the health and condition of the landscape as an environment for living. Rachel Carson's book *Silent Spring*, published in 1961, shocked the nation from its public apathy toward the environment. Jane Jacobs' book, *The Death and Life of Great American Cities* (1961), also challenged people to address the positive qualities of urban life. The environmental movement and concerns about urban conditions took shape around domestic health issues at the same time that universities developed a number of new landscape architecture programs. With these increased educational offerings women rediscovered the profession of landscape architecture and its potential role to improve the environment. They also discovered that they were no longer excluded or blatantly discouraged from enrolling. Women re-entered the profession as its breadth grew to include the newly defined scale of environmental impacts, and as developing regional landscape management principles were tied to a greater understanding and incorporation of natural sciences and ecological systems. Since the 1980s, women have played an increasingly vital and visible role in the design, planning and management of the built environment.

With relatively little difficulty, where women practiced, what they practiced, and the extent of their contributions can be traced up to the 1970s. Reviewing the last forty years is more difficult, in part because it is fairly recent for a reflective historical review, but also because so many women entered the profession after 1970. However, this is the place to start answering my graduate student's simple question, "where are the women in landscape architecture today?"

The Status of Women in Landscape Architecture at the Beginning of the Twenty-first Century

In 1997, The Council of Landscape Architecture Registration Boards (CLARB) conducted a task analysis of current landscape architectural practice from licensed landscape architects in North America.[6] Demographic and other background information from this data set provides the basis for an analysis of women practicing landscape architecture including: academic experience, years of practice, areas of practice, type of organization and position within the organization.[7] This analysis attempts to replace anecdotal accounts of women in practice with substantiated data verifying and disproving prevailing views of the roles women hold in contemporary practice. It is time women's activities and impacts are noted, evaluated and celebrated within the larger practice of landscape architecture in the United States.

Survey recipients were drawn from a CLARB database of registered landscape architects representing each state of the United States and each province of Canada. Twenty-two point two percent of the respondents were women. This is less than the female to male ratio of ASLA membership reported in 1999 (26:74), and of overall student enrollments in accredited landscape architecture degree programs in the United States during the 1990s (34.4:65.6).[8] The differences may reflect the longer duration of practice and the length of time it takes for those desiring licensure to attain it after receiving a degree. In effect, it takes some time for the increased enrollments of women to show up in the ranks of licensed practitioners. The demographic data and background information collected with that data set provides the basis of the following report on the status of women in landscape architecture at the beginning of the twenty-first century.

So where are the women, and men, in landscape architecture at the beginning of the twenty-first century?

Geographic Distribution and Primary Practice Context

In the United States, 14.9 percent of all licensed practitioners hold a California license, the highest representation of landscape architects in any state. 30.1 percent of these are women. The second highest population of licensed practitioners is in Texas, where 23.1 percent are women. The percentages of women holding licenses to practice in New Mexico and Wyoming are 57.9 percent and 60 percent, quite above the expected range of 22 to 27 percent, an equitable representation based upon the ratio of participation in the study. However, less than 1 percent of the practitioners in the U.S. hold licenses to practice in either of these states, making the actual number of women practicing there quite low.

Respondents were asked to select their primary practice context: urban, suburban, rural or wilderness. Based upon the content of the profession's primary built practice publications, *Landscape Architecture Magazine* and *Landscape Architect and Specifier News*, it was not unexpected that of these four contexts, most women and men describe their primary context as either urban or suburban. The overall percents of rural and wilderness practices

Licensed Practitioners in the United States

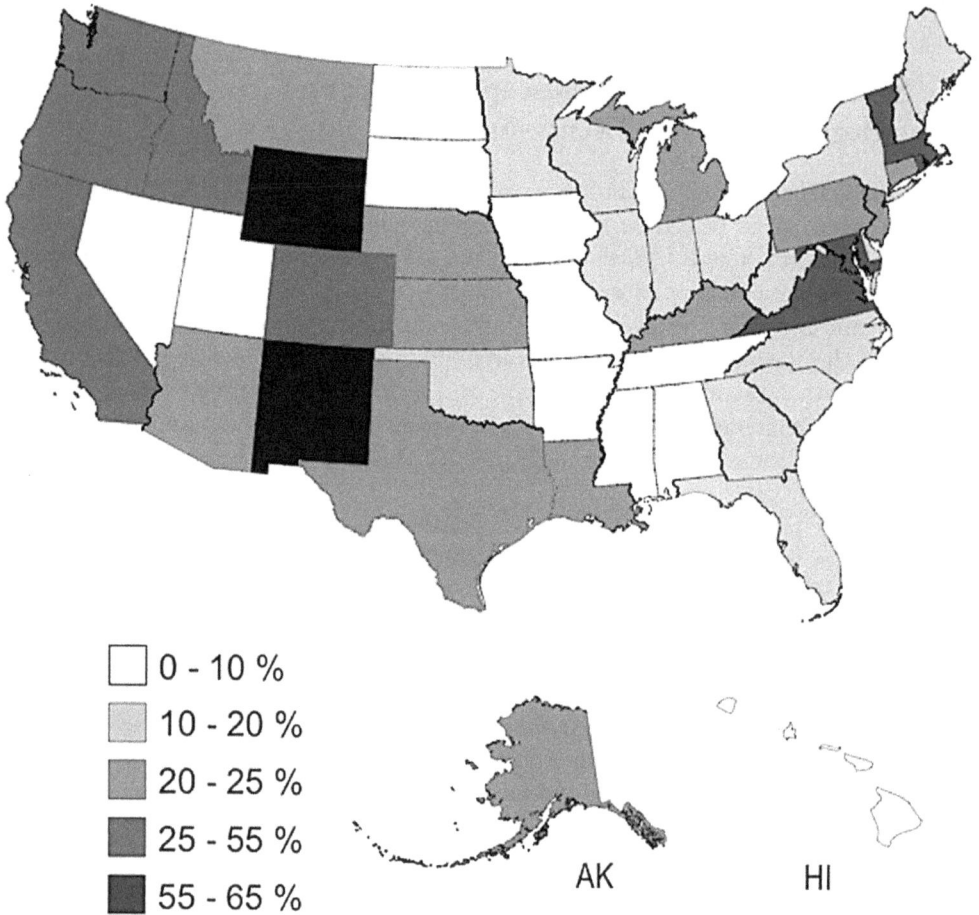

Of the licensed practitioners surveyed in 1997: 78 percent men, 22 percent women. These numbers are similar to a breakdown of the percentage of men and women enrolled in landscape architecture degree granting programs during the last half of the 1990s, as well as that of ASLA membership during the same time frame.

are quite low. Women and men are relatively equitably represented across three of these contexts once the 22:78 gender ratio is considered. Intriguingly, the percent of female wilderness practitioners is 35 percent, significantly above the expected range. This may relate to the greater amount of wilderness practice within the federal government. A higher percentage of the licensed female landscape architects are employed by the federal government than males. This may be a result of more aggressive diversity hiring programs in federal agencies. While local governments have also hired a high percent of women, state governments employ more men than an equitable gender ratio distribution would infer. Another practice context distinction is the dominance of men practicing in suburban locations in relation to the proportion of men in practice. Of licensed men in practice, 16 percent more men practice primarily in suburban areas than in urban areas. For women the difference is 7 percent.

Number of Respondents

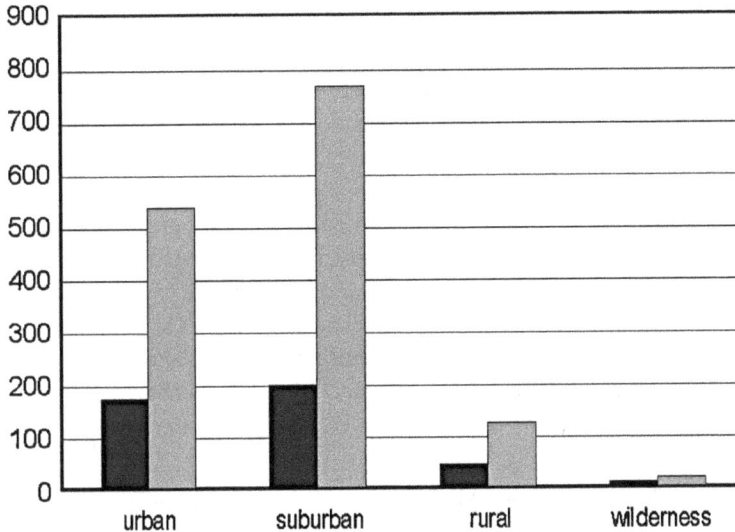

Percentage of Practitioners by Gender

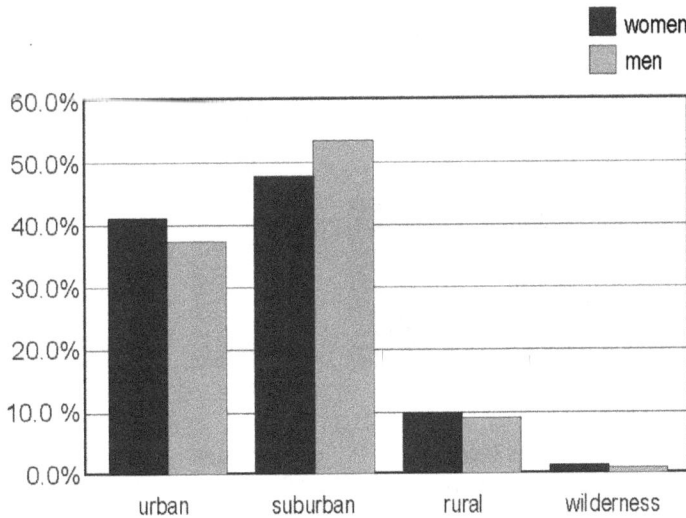

Primary Practice Context. Based upon the content of the profession's publications, it was not unexpected that the primary practice contexts for both women and men would be urban and suburban. Considering the 22:78 ratio of women to men in practice, women and men are relatively evenly represented across three of four practice contexts. The exceptions where the ratio differs is in wilderness practice, as women represent 35 percent of practitioners. Another distinction shown in the percent of practitioners by gender chart is a higher percentage of women in practice practicing in rural and wilderness areas than their male counterparts. This may be influenced by the greater percentage of women in practice who work in local and federal government positions, as well as a higher percentage of women who practice in non-traditional firm types. A third distinction is the dominance of men practicing in suburban locations in relation to the proportion of men in practice. Of men in practice, 16 percent more men practice in suburban areas than in urban areas. For women the difference is 7 percent.

Academic Experience

As the number of accredited landscape architecture programs increased during the 1970's, so did the number of women enrolling in them. 91.3 percent of the women respondents have a degree in landscape architecture. Of these, 56.8 percent hold an undergraduate degree in landscape architecture as their highest degree, 40 percent hold a masters in Landscape Architecture (MLA) as their highest degree, and 0.9 percent achieved a doctorate. In comparison, 68.6 percent of male respondents' highest degree is an undergraduate degree in landscape architecture, 27.2 percent hold an MLA and 1.6 percent attained a doctorate. The CLARB study does not distinguish between first and second professional masters degrees. However, comparisons between age and years providing landscape architecture services indicates that a higher percentage of women than men are attaining a first professional masters degree. Analysis of enrollments during the 1990s shows slightly more women than men in the masters degree programs (52.8:47.2). The low showing of licensed professionals with Ph.D.s may indicate that Ph.D. holders pursued alternate career paths relative

Highest Degree Held by Licensed Practitioners

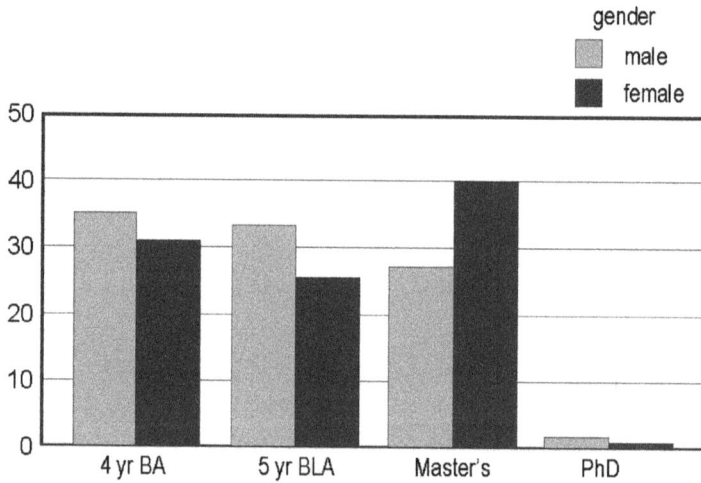

Highest degrees held	women	men	over-all
Landscape Architecture	84.6%	84.3%	84.4%
Plant and Soil Science	2.5%	1.9%	2.0%
Planning	2.3%	3.1%	3.0%
Architecture	1.6%	2.7%	2.4%
Art	1.6%	0.3%	0.6%
Engineering	0.9%	1.0%	1.0%
Forestry/Natural Resources	0.5%	0.5%	0.5%
Geography	0.5%	0.3%	0.3%
Other	5.5%	5.8%	5.7%

Of licensed practitioners, 91 percent of women and 90 percent of men hold landscape architecture degrees. 33 percent stated that their current position did not require them to be registered, although all stated that they are providing landscape architecture services.

to the need to attain licensure. The actual number of people holding Ph.D.s is growing. This trend should continue as universities are now stressing the degree's value as a condition of employment for teaching and research faculty.

Experiences in Professional Practice

While the number of licensed women landscape architects remains relatively small in comparison to the number of men, the percentage of women entering the profession and attaining licensure is growing, whereas the overall percentage of men attaining licensure relative to the number of men in practice is declining. A number of hypotheses can be raised and need further investigation before we understand why this distinction exists or its potential impacts. It may indicate a trend toward more women practicing per capita. Or, it may indicate that the actual number of men continuing to practice is so large that a greater number of newly licensed males is needed to see a shift from more established to newer practitioners. In the current litigious business climate it is unlikely that the decline in the relative percentage of licensed male is related to a lack of desirability for licensure. It may also reflect the higher percentage of women who are sole practitioners or sole-owners of smaller firms. In most states, business owners need a license in order to use the title *landscape architect* or the term *landscape architecture*. A license also demonstrates the firm's credentials to practice. Twenty percent of women hold licenses in multiple state jurisdictions.

Women entered practice over a much wider distribution of ages than men. At least 52 percent of licensed female practitioners began their careers later than one might expect. They did not begin or continually pursue their professional careers by attaining an undergraduate degree and working immediately after completing high school. Female practitioners may have delayed or taken a leave from their careers for family reasons, a factor noted by Nassauer and Arnold's 1983 study.[9] Others entered landscape architecture after changing their initial career direction. A significant number of female graduate students are considered re-entry students, having returned or started to pursue a degree after reaching their thirtieth birthday. Between 56 percent and 65 percent of women 55 to 65 years of age in 1997 began their landscape architecture careers after turning forty. Of women between 45 and 54, fewer than 54 percent began offering landscape architecture services during their twenties. Women were following a different career track. How it affected their available employment options and chosen career directions has not been studied, yet.

In 1997 the average female landscape architect had provided landscape architecture services for 13.5 years; the average male had been in the business for 17.7 years. (See Chart: Number of Years Offering Landscape Architectural Services.) Only 6.7 percent of the practitioners licensed before 1978 were female. By 1993, 31 percent of licensed landscape architects were women. The dramatic increase in the number of licensed women practitioners who entered the profession between 1976 and 1986 corresponds to the increasing number of degree granting programs at a time when the environmental movement was gaining momentum and during continued activism within the women's movement.

As with men, a vast majority of women (70.2 percent) are in private practice. 21.1 percent of licensed women work in public practice, 2.1 percent in academia, and 6.7 percent in other areas. Of these, 21.3 percent work in multi-disciplinary organizations, 0.5 percent in industry or commerce, and 9.4 percent in design-build. Employment in Exclusively Landscape Architecture Firms is the preferred employment for all age groups of women.[10]

Age distribution of licensed women landscape architects
across types of professional firms

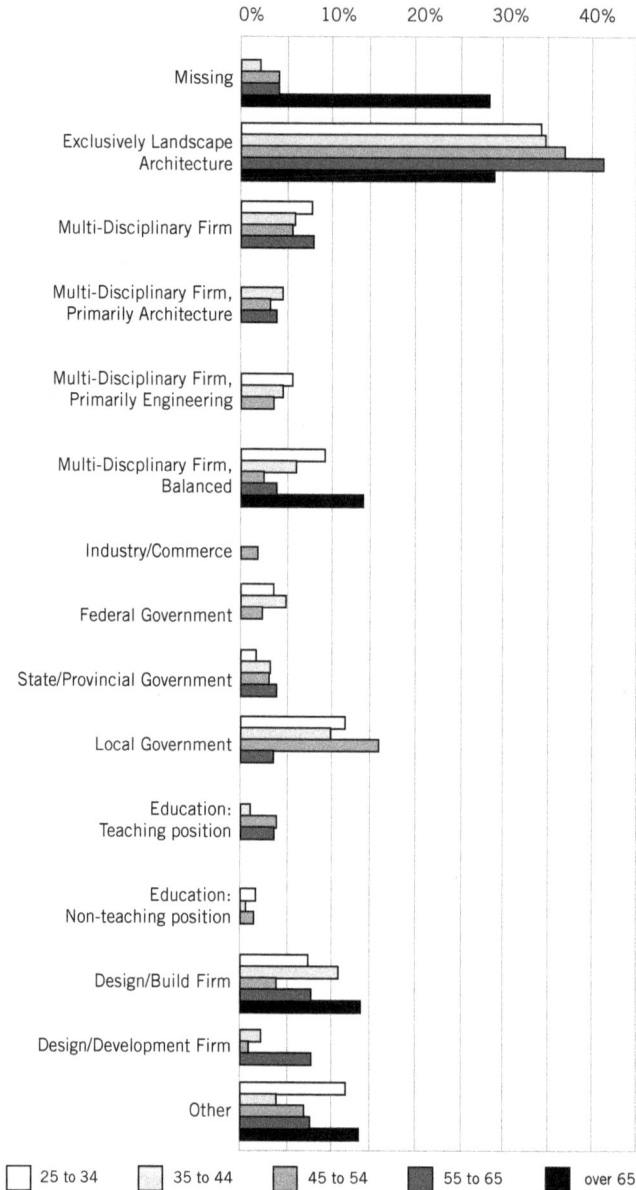

| | 25 to 34 | | 35 to 44 | | 45 to 54 | | 55 to 65 | | over 65 |

Age Distribution: across types of professional organizations-Employment in exclusively land-scape architecture firms is the preferred employment for all age groups of women. Women 45–54 years of age are the only group represented by more than 15 percent in any other employment area (Local Government). Women over 65 comprise the only group having over 14 percent representation in three areas (Balanced Multi-Disciplinary, Design-Build, and Others). It should be noted that women are not represented in Industry/Commerce, and only women 55–65 are seen in Design/Development firms. Women 55–65 are not well-represented in federal government or Primarily Engineering firms. Women 35–44 are not well-positioned in education, whether teaching or non-teaching. Women 25–34 are relatively well-distributed across most areas.

Age of Women Related to Professional Positions Held

☐ 25 to 34   ☐ 35 to 44   ▨ 45 to 54   ▨ 55 to 65   ■ over 65

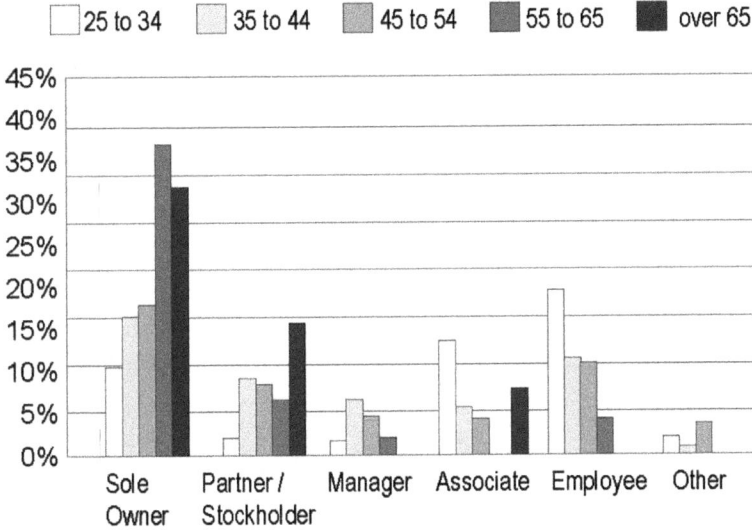

Positions Held Related to Years
Providing Landscape Architectural Services

■ Sole Owner   ▨ Associate
▨ Partner/Stockholder   ▨ Employee
▨ Manager   ☐ Other

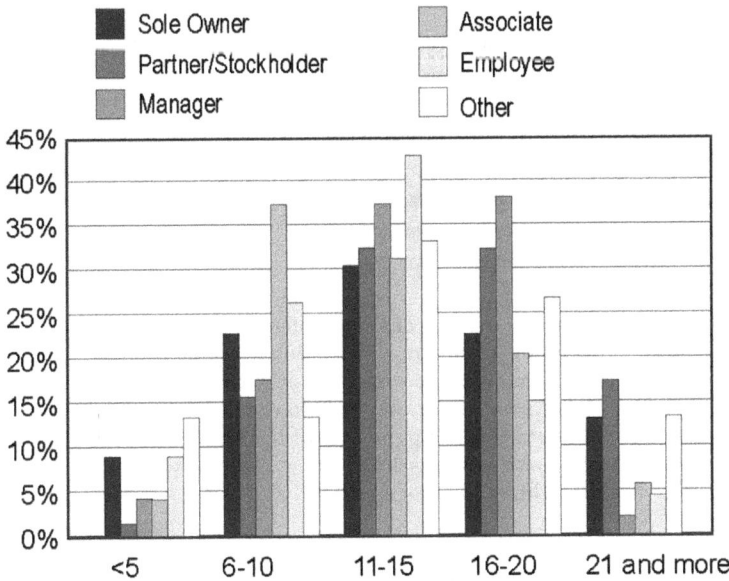

Significant numbers of women are skipping partner/stockholder and manager positions and moving toward sole ownership, 20 percent before turning 35. Anecdotal accounts still have women working off their kitchen tables or as a hobby. However, over 23 percent of sole owners have annual project construction costs between $1 and 5 million. Since the 1910s, domestic landscape architecture and architecture have been viewed as acceptable practices for women as this scale of work was thought not to compromise their important personal expectations of marriage and motherhood and would allow them reasonable freedom to free-lance around their family obligations.

Age of Women Related to Years Providing
Landscape Architectural Services

☐ 25 to 34   ☐ 35 to 44   ■ 45 to 54   ■ 55 to 65   ■ over 65

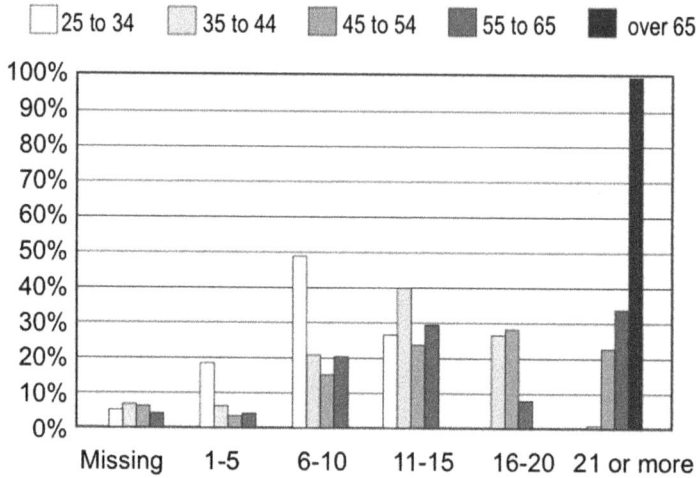

Of the women 55 to 65 years of age:
~ between 56 and 65% began their landscape architecture careers after turning forty.

Of the women 45 to 54 years of age:
~ between 3.7 and 20% began after turning forty,
~ between 46 and 76% began after turning thirty,
~ less than 54% started during their twenties.

Of the women 35 to 44 years of age:
~ as few as 6.4% began after turning forty,
~ as many as 71% began after turning thirty.

This chart indicates that at least 52 percent of licensed female practitioners began their careers later than a perceived expectation to begin a professional career directly after attaining an undergraduate degree. Female practitioners may have delayed their careers for family (a contributing factor noted in earlier surveys) or they may have entered after changing their career direction. This is also seen in data reviewing the ages of female masters degree students. A significant number of female graduate students are re-entry students (those that have returned to pursue a degree after reaching thirty years of age).

Interestingly, most women either work for themselves or in firms employing less than six people. While this may seem to corroborate anecdotes that women's contributions to the field are smaller, and less serious or important than men's, a number of men also work in smaller firms. Many of the male stars of landscape architecture worked in smaller firms before the firm merger movement of the 1990s and continuing today.

One quarter of all the women surveyed work for and by themselves, while another 27.6 percent work in firms employing between two and five people. Relatively few women, less than 27 percent, work for mid-sized firms employing between 6 and 50 people. Twenty point nine percent of women work in firms employing over 50 people. A high percent of women working in large firms (61.1 percent) describe themselves as employees rather than as owners, stockholders, partners, managers or associates. Indeed no women surveyed owned a firm with more than 20 employees. Only 2.3 percent of women in large firms were partners or stockholders. Of the women employed in larger firms, 18.1 percent were managers and 16.4 percent were associates. Tracking the careers of women who entered practice in the late seventies and early eighties, we would expect to see more women represented in the higher administrative and ownership levels of these firms, if they were to follow the model established by their male colleagues. The majority of women held the lowest positions within

Firm Description: Type of Professional Organization

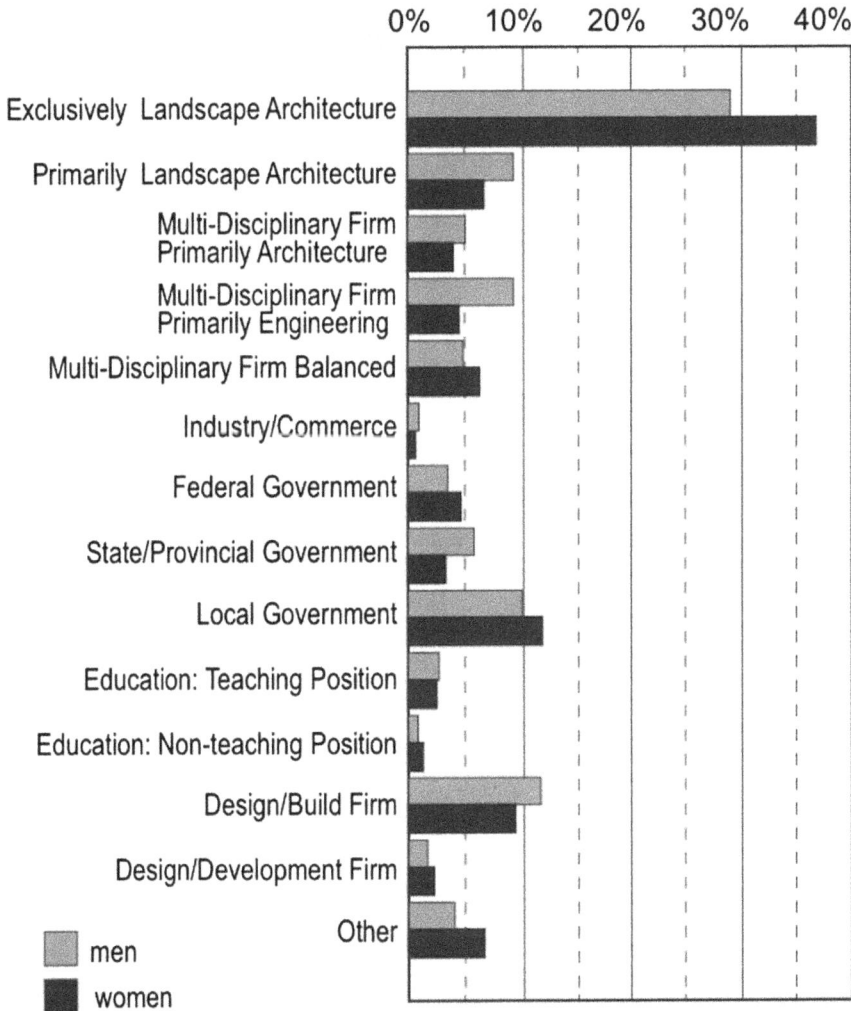

While the total number of women practicing landscape architecture is significantly less than that of men, women are proportionately more likely to be working in an exclusively landscape architecture firm or a balanced multi-disciplinary firm than men. They are also well represented in public practice for either the federal or local governments. This is not the case for state government positions. This may represent more aggressive equal opportunity hiring at the federal level, and historically strong community activism by women at the local government level.

Number of Respondents Per Position

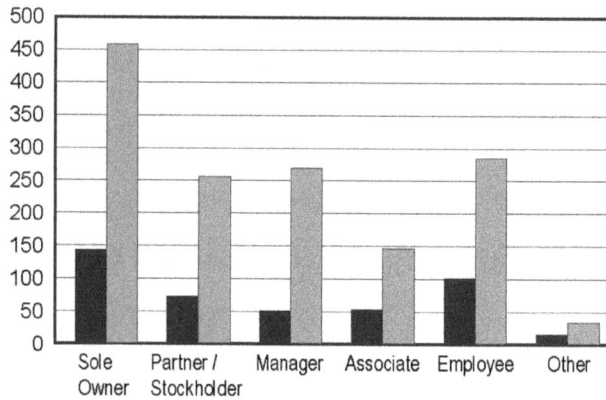

Percentage of Women and Men Relative to Positions

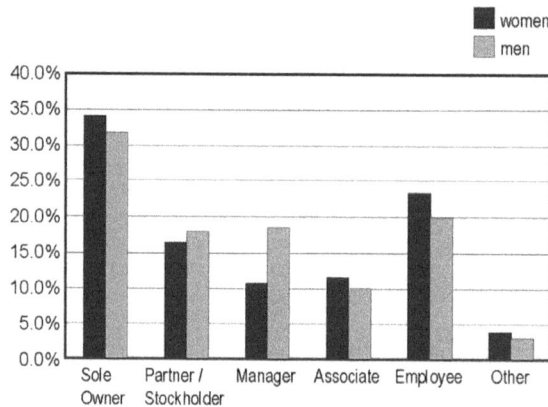

Proportion of licensed women employed in each firm size to licensed women practicing.

Percent	# people in firm
25.4%	One
27.6%	2 to 5
7.6%	6 to 10
9.6%	11 to 20
8.9%	21 to 50
5.9%	51 to 100
15.0%	over 100

Professional Positions Held within Firms. The number of women and men employed in each position closely reflects the ratio of women to men over-all (22:78), except in manager positions (14:86). This may relate to the relatively low percent of women practicing who work in mid-sized and large firms, those most likely to include managers within the office hierarchy. The distribution of each gender represented within office hierarchy raises another question about gender differences in mid-career positions. When compared to the age of individual female practitioners, there is a higher percentage of women maintaining sole ownership after only 6 to 10 years of practice than seen in a similar analysis of men. There are also a significantly higher proportion of women in employee positions with between 6 and 15 years of offering landscape architectural services.

the largest firms. The expected representation of women to men (22:78) does not exist in any comparison between employment position and firm size. A significant number of women appear to be by-stepping partner/stockholder and manager positions and moving toward sole ownership. 20 percent of women became sole owners before turning thirty-five. Thirty percent of women between 35 and 44 are already sole owners, significantly more than men

Number Respondents Per Years of Practice

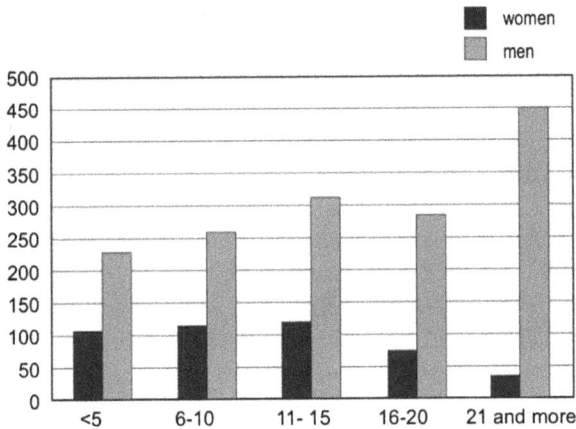

Percentage of Women and Men Relative to Years of Practice

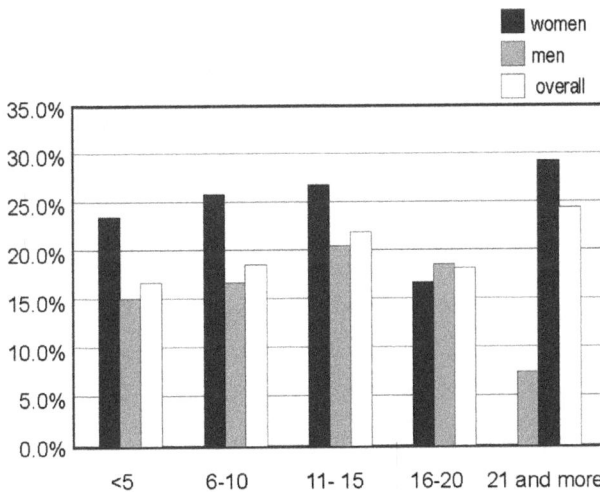

Number of Years Offering Landscape Architectural Services Related to Gender. A comparison between these two charts demonstrates the 76 percent dominance of male practitioners in landscape architecture. The top chart highlights a senior male work force. The charts also demonstrate a dramatic increase in the number of licensed women practitioners who entered the profession between 1976 and 1986. This corresponds to the increasing number of accredited degree programs in landscape architecture at a time when the environmental movement was gaining momentum and a continued national activism of the women's movement. It is also interesting to note an over-all decline rather than increase of licensed practitioners in each five-year period since 1986.

in the same age group. The data set does not reveal why so many women find sole ownership a preferable practice option.

Anecdotal accounts still have women working off their kitchen tables or as a hobby. Since the 1910s, domestic landscape architecture has been viewed as an acceptable activity for women as long as the scale of work does not compromise expectations of marriage and motherhood. A large number of female sole owners are working without full-time employee support. 8.4 percent of sole owners run a two to five person firm. A similar percentage of men (31.5 percent) are also sole owners. Little anecdotal commentary questions the merits of work conducted by male sole owners. Women's work is increasingly growing in scale and scope, as well as in recognition. Further research is needed to determine whether women's work and expertise is being recognized by peers, as well as within practice.

Thoughts on Women in Practice

My curiosity has not been satisfied yet. The survey conducted by CLARB was limited to licensed practitioners. It is not feasible to make declarations about the direction of women's practice in landscape architecture from this set of statistical correlations or as a result of reviewing the historical timeline or narrative. Surveys conducted by the ASLA were limited to ASLA membership. But what of women educated in landscape architecture who choose a career path that did not need licensure? What of women who chose not to pursue membership in the ASLA? The CLARB survey showed over 30 percent of those surveyed did not need licensure to do their work. Little has been done to document what women have done after receiving a degree in landscape architecture. Did many aspire to traditional prac-

Age of Licensed Practitioners of Landscape Architecture

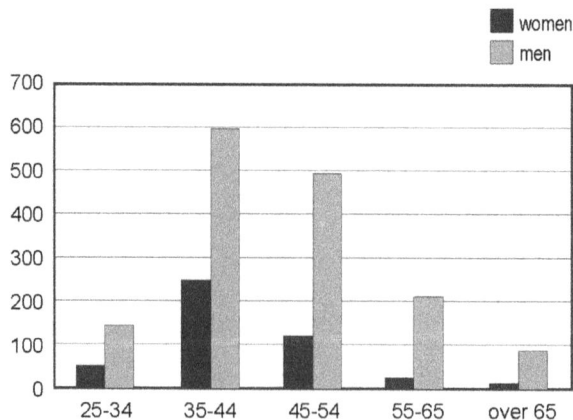

While the number of women licensed as landscape architects remains relatively small in comparison to the number of men, the percentage of women entering the profession and attaining licensure is growing faster. The relatively few women over 54 years of age may be partially explained by a societal reluctance to encourage women to enter design and building professions before the mid–1970s. As the environmental movement grew during the 1960s, the number of accredited landscape architecture programs grew, particularly in the mid-west and on the west coast. Women began to have a significant presence even within the traditionally male dominated programs during the 1970s.

tice roles in private or public institutions? Why did they choose landscape architecture as a degree program? What were their aspirations or motivations? What are their aspirations/motivations today? Did some use their education in pursuing non-traditional practices? What have women graduates done and where did they do it? What do they think of what they've accomplished? These questions remain unanswered. Future analysis of the CLARB data set of licensed landscape architects alongside a new survey of women graduates of landscape architecture programs from across the United States should reveal general trends of women in practice, their range of practice, and a better sense for the range of their contributions.

Notes

1. Donna Palmer, "An Overview of the Trends, Eras, and Values of Landscape Architecture in America from 1910 to the Present with an Emphasis on the Contributions of Women to the Profession." (Master's thesis, Landscape Architecture, College of Design, North Carolina State University, 1976).

2. Dorothy May Anderson, "Women's Breakthrough via the Cambridge School," *Landscape Architecture* 68 (March 1978): 148.

3. Joseph Sherman, "Architecture is 90 percent business, 10 percent art," *Smithsonian*, September 1994, 48–59.

4. Many of these women are included in *Pioneers of American Landscape Design* and *Pioneers of American Landscape Design II*.

5. Henry Atherton Frost and William R. Sears, *Women in Architecture and Landscape Architecture: A Study for the Institute for the Co-ordination of Women's Interests* (Northampton, MA: Smith College, 1928).

6. Council of Landscape Architecture Registration Boards (CLARB), *The Practice of Landscape Architecture: A Study of Activities and Knowledge Areas for the Licensed Landscape Architect* (Fairfax, VA: Council of Landscape Architecture Registration Boards, 1998). The survey had 1849 respondents, 22.3 percent women (n=412) and 77.7 percent men (n=1437). Certain states and provinces were over sampled based on low anticipated returns from those areas because of low numbers of registered landscape architects. CLARB graciously provided access to their data set for use in this study.

7. Terry Clements, "Where They've Been and A Preliminary Investigation to Disclose Where the Women in Landscape Architecture Are Today," (paper presented at the Council of Educators of Landscape Architecture/American Society of Landscape Architects Annual Conference, Boston, 1999).

8. Enrollment figure drawn from Landscape Architectural Accreditation Board, Annual Report Statistics: 1991–1992 to 1996–1997, Compilation provided by Council of Landscape Architecture Registration Boards, January 1999.

9. Joan Iverson Nassauer and Karen Arnold, *The National Survey of Career Patterns among Women in Landscape Architecture* (Washington, DC: American Society of Landscape Architects, 1983).

10. There were fourteen types of professional organizations included in the survey's organization data field: Exclusively landscape architecture, Multi-disciplinary primarily landscape architecture, Multi-disciplinary primarily architecture, Multi-disciplinary primarily engineering, Multi-disciplinary balanced, Industry/Commerce, Federal Government, State/Provincial Government, Local Government, Education: Teaching, Education: Non-teaching, Design/Build Firm, Design/Development, and Other.

Bibliography

American Society of Landscape Architecture. *A Map of the Territory: Survey Data on the Size, Scope, and Direction of Landscape Architecture Practice.* Washington DC: The American Society of Landscape Architecture, 1997.

Anderson, Dorothy May. "Women's Breakthrough via the Cambridge School." *Landscape Architecture* 68 (March 1978): 148.

_____. *Women, Design, and the Cambridge School.* West Lafayette, IN: PDA Publishers Corporation, 1980.

Birnbaum, Charles A., and Lisa E. Crowder, eds. *Pioneers of American Landscape Design: an Annotated Bibliography.* Washington, DC: Government Printing Office, U. S. Department of the Interior National Park Service, Cultural Resources, 1993.

Birnbaum, Charles A,. and Julie Fix, eds. *Pioneers of American Landscape Design II: an Annotated Bibliography.* Washington, DC: Government Printing Office, U. S. Department of the Interior National Park Service, Cultural Resources, 1995.

Brown, Catherine R. *Women and the Land: A Biographical Survey of Women who have Contributed to the Development of Landscape Architecture in the United States.* Preliminary Working Paper, Morgan State University. Baltimore, 1979.

Carter, Elizabeth, and Anne Pietro. *A Selected and Annotated Bibliography on Women in Landscape Architecture.* Unpublished manuscript, Department of Landscape Architecture, California State Polytechnic University, Pomona, March 15, 1990.

Clements, Terry. "Where They've Been and a Preliminary Investigation to Disclose Where the Women in Landscape Architecture Are Today." Paper presented at the Council of Educators of Landscape Architecture/American Society of Landscape Architects Annual Conference, Boston, 1999.

Council of Landscape Architectural Registration Boards. *The Practice of Landscape Architecture: A Study of Activities and Knowledge Areas for the Licensed Landscape Architect.* Fairfax, VA: Council of Landscape Architectural Registration Boards, 1998.

Floyd, Margaret Henderson, ed. *Architectural Education and Boston: Centennial Publication of the Boston Architectural Center 1889–1989.* Boston: Boston Architectural Center, 1989.

Frost, Henry Atherton, and William R. Sears. *Women in Architecture and Landscape Architecture: A Study for the Institute for the Co-ordination of Women's Interests.* Northampton, MA: Smith College, 1928.

Furr, Mary Pope. "'The purpose ... is to train women': the Academic Program of the Cambridge School of Architecture and Landscape Architecture, 1915–1942." Master of Architectural History Thesis, School of Architecture, University of Virginia, 1995.

Harris, Charles. "The Once-Lonely Turf: New Directions for Landscape Architecture at Harvard from 1958 to 1970." In *Architectural Education and Boston: Centennial Publication of the Boston Architectural Center 1889–1989*, edited by Margaret Henderson Floyd, 63–85. Boston: Boston Architectural Center, 1989.

Lowthorpe School. *Lowthorpe: A School of Landscape Architecture for Women.* Groton, MA: Lowthorpe School, 1925.

Mann, William A. *Landscape Architecture: an Illustrated History in Timelines, Site Plans, and Biography.* New York: John Wiley & Sons, 1993.

Nassauer, Joan Iverson, and Karen Arnold. *The National Survey of Career Patterns Among Women in Landscape Architecture.* Washington, DC: American Society of Landscape Architecture, 1983.

Newton, Norman T. *Design on the Land: the development of Landscape Architecture.* Cambridge, MA: Belknap Press of Harvard University Press, 1971.

Palmer, Donna. "An Overview of the Trends, Eras, and Values of Landscape Architecture in America from 1910 to the Present with an Emphasis on the Contributions of Women to the Profession." Master's thesis, Landscape Architecture, College of Design, North Carolina State University, 1976.

Rutz, Miriam Easton, ed. *Proceedings of the Symposium Landscapes and Gardens: Women Who Made a Difference*, Michigan State University, June 9–10, 1987.

_____. "Women's Influence on Planning and Design in America: A collection by Miriam E. Rutz" unpublished manuscript and collection of 14 articles. Department of Landscape Architecture, Michigan State University, 1992.

Sherman, Joseph. "Architecture is 90 Percent Business, 10 Percent Art" *Smithsonian.* September 1994, 48–59.

Sievers, Ann H. *Landscape Architects from the Cambridge School.* Northampton, MA: Smith College Museum of Art, 1984.

Zaitzevsky, Cynthia. "Education and Landscape Architecture." *Architectural Education and Boston: centennial publication of the Boston Architectural Center 1889–1989*, edited by Margaret Henderson Floyd, 86–106. Boston: Boston Architectural Center, 1989.

Statistics derived using demographic and practice data from a 1997 survey of licensed practitioners graciously provided by CLARB (Council of Landscape Architecture Registration Boards).

Chapter 3

Women and the Civic Garden Campaigns of the Progressive Era: "A woman has a feeling about dirt which men only pretend to have..."

LAURA J. LAWSON

In his 1902 book, *Constructive and Preventive Philanthropy*, Joseph Lee praised women's contributions to civic improvements, stating, "A woman has a feeling about dirt which men only pretend to have. The reaction which the sight of dirty streets produces in her, when once she has come to look on the matter as being within her sphere, is something of which every head of family has learned to stand in awe."[1] As vice-president of the Massachusetts Civic League, Joseph Lee intended these words to encourage women to continue to improve the health, morality, and aesthetics of their communities. By framing their duty as "municipal housekeeping," women could "come to look on the matter as being within [the woman's] sphere," because it echoed at a community scale the attention to aesthetic, health, and moral development that she gave to the home. In this capacity, women were actively shaping the public landscape through the development of new parks and playgrounds, school gardens, street tree planting, reclaiming vacant lots as gardens, promoting home gardens, and improving institutional grounds.

It is generally accepted in environmental design histories that the professionalization that was occurring at the turn of the century was complemented and supported by a parallel voluntary sphere of improvement societies, garden clubs, and civic associations.[2] This period roughly coincides with the Progressive Era, from 1900 to 1914, which historian Richard Hofstadter describes as "a rather widespread and remarkably good-natured effort of the greater society to achieve some not very clearly specified self-reform."[3] Some of these good-natured efforts engaged reformers in urban planning and environmental design. Faith in environmental determinism — the belief that changes to the physical environment would lead to individual and social betterment — resulted in a range of design solutions to address social concerns about urban expansion, immigration, and changing industry. Civic commissions made up of prominent citizens hired professional designers to create master plans that epitomize the period, such as City Beautiful civic centers, park systems, garden suburbs, and industrial villages. Until the full plans could be realized, however (and they rarely were), incremental acts by civic groups chipped away at the central ideas, working within the context of laissez faire capitalism and philanthropy. Scolars also have effectively argued that this volunteer sphere provided a channel for women's involvement in social and physical planning.[4] Women's voluntary associations promoted and raised funds for civic plans while also initiating local projects to address immediate concerns.

The purpose of this chapter is not to repeat this history but to make particular connections between landscape architecture and the civic garden campaigns that were contributing to the development of the public landscape. If the domain of landscape architecture as a profession was dominated by men, with exclusivity maintained through education, internships, and fraternal connections, civic gardening was an acceptable realm for female activism because of its association with municipal housekeeping, its educational potential, the scale of activism at the household and neighborhood level, and the assumption that such campaigns would serve as catalysts to inspire society towards bigger — therefore professionally produced — plans.

Connections and Boundaries between Landscape Architecture and Civic Gardening

During the Progressive Era, civic gardening was included along with other proposed activities that volunteers and new professionals could initiate to address sanitary, aesthetic, and social concerns of the evolving city. Also called "cooperative gardening" and the "universal gardening movement," civic gardening campaigns were local efforts to encourage beautification of homes, vacant lots, and institutional grounds, particularly schools.[5] In line with the environmental determinist beliefs of the time, advocates considered gardening not only a way to improve the visual character of a neighborhood, but also a means to inspire an avocation associated with greater civic mindedness and moral behavior. The intended beneficiaries — primarily working-class families, immigrants, and children — were reached through garden contests and exhibits, free seed and instruction, and school gardens.

A national model of civic gardening was the campaign in Cleveland. The idea was started in 1896 when the Goodrich House Social Settlement started a flower garden program. The project was based on the theory that if each household committed to gardening, then "the beauty of orderliness and cleanliness would soon assert its supremacy over the disorder, dirt, and debris which so often holds sway in crowded neighborhoods."[6] With school teachers joining the effort, the Home Garden Association was established to develop school gardens and to distribute seeds and information to children for home gardens. Their seed packet program grew into a national project, so that by 1905, they were providing 238,000 seed packets in Cleveland and 151,000 elsewhere. The association provided lectures on famous European gardens and the principles of garden design, held contests, and displayed exhibits. They developed a small park on a vacant lot near the downtown library. After developing many school gardens, the local school board eventually took over responsibility in 1905 and hired Louise Klein Miller as curator of all the district's school gardens, with part of her salary paid for by the Home Garden Association and donations.

As a complement and catalyst for larger landscape projects, public leaders and professional designers encouraged local organizations — irregardless of whether the group was predominantly male, female, or combined — to start garden campaigns. In support of such voluntary campaigns, Edwin Shuey of the American Parks and Outdoor Art Association stated, "It is no reflection upon the value of parks or public gardens to say that the surest

Before and after images of children engaged in the Cleveland garden program. Reprinted from M. Louise Greene, *Among School Gardens* (New York: Russell Sage Foundation, 1910), facing p. 96.

and best method of improving conditions of the masses is to encourage home planting and cultivation of vines and flowers even in the smallest dooryards of the crowded streets."[7] Interestingly, this organization, originally founded in 1897 as a forum for professional designers, shifted its focus to outreach to the general public in order to inspire physical improvements to cities, including school gardens. In his 1901 book, *The Improvement of Towns and Cities*, Charles Mulford Robinson promoted City Beautiful master plans while also suggesting smaller, incremental projects for civic groups, such as planting thoroughfares, nature strips along streets, transit facilities, private residences, vacant lots, and school grounds.[8] In a 1904 *Craftsman* article, landscape architect Warren Manning distinguished between the responsibilities of city officials to make improvements, such as street lights, tree planting, and road repair, and the role of citizen improvement societies to "inaugurate activities of which little is known in their community; such as the improvement of school and home grounds, and the establishment of school gardens and playgrounds."[9] Words such as these encouraged activism around gardening but also attempted to establish boundaries between the roles of professional and volunteer, which were even more pronounced when considered from a gendered perspective.

The public could accept women's participation in civic gardening campaigns because it fell under the umbrella of "municipal housekeeping" that justified women's responsibility for cleaning and protecting the health of the city just as they would their own home. As homemakers, women gardened to create a protective and healthy place to raise children and teach them nature's morality. The garden was part of home life in all its aesthetic, social, and educational dimensions. As Mary Rankin Cranston stated in a 1909 *Craftsman* article, "Just as the interior of a house discloses the inner life of the family, so do the home grounds reflect the family's ideal of the larger, or civic, life. A well-kept, orderly garden indicates a responsible personality, a neglected dooryard is a sign of shiftlessness."[10] If a poor environment reflected and produced inferior people, then the solution was first to put your own garden in order and then to encourage others. Mary Woods, publicist for the General Federation of Women's Clubs, emphasized women's entitlement to improve the public landscape because it was an extension of women's home improvement, stating that "[women] began to realize that the one calling in which they were, as a body, proficient, that of housekeeping and homemaking, had its outdoor as well as its indoor application."[11] Justified on the basis of motherhood, women frequently approached civic gardening and other improvement campaigns as a means to educate children and other families about sanitation, aesthetics, civic duty, and moral behavior. For example, school gardens were intended not only to educate children, but as "radiating centers for civic improvement" that could influence the family and neighborhood.[12]

While advocates like Joseph Lee encouraged this female participation, some designers and public officials were concerned to distinguish their professional responsibilities for civic and neighborhood improvements from women's volunteer work. Even though women were a major audience for his writing, Charles Mulford Robinson protested the association between women and civic work when he stated that "There is nothing effeminate or sentimental about it.... It is vigorous, virile, sane. Altruism is its impulse, but it is older than any altruism of the hour — as old as the dreams and aspirations of men."[13] While the magazine *American City* devoted an entire issue in 1912 to women's civic work — citing exemplary work in garden campaigns along with street improvements, sanitation, noise and smoke abatement programs, development of parks and playgrounds, and land preservation — the editorial introduction included an apologetic plea to the predominantly male readership that women's work was indeed a worthy topic.[14] Fine distinctions were made between the roles of the professional and the volunteer as well as the duties of male and female. These distinctions were reinforced through educational and career opportunities that made it difficult for women to work on the public landscape as professional designers but did provide some parallel paths that were socially acceptable if less prestigious.

Education and Professional Roles Associated with Civic Gardening

The acceptance of municipal housekeeping opened doors for women as both volunteers and "other" professionals. In this context, advanced education for women was justified to provide the "scientific" principles of good household management, to equip women in their roles as formal and informal educators, and to guide civic duty.[15] Educational opportunities in design and horticulture could be opened to women without direct implications for the landscape architecture profession because such training also related to other household and career opportunities. Once a woman received training, her career path could take many different directions — a professional career in landscape architecture or a related field or through volunteerism in civic gardening projects.

During the period from about 1890 to 1914, advanced education and professional opportunities for women expanded, and although landscape architecture was not a common or easy profession for women, it was not entirely closed. While some public and private schools provided training in professional design to women, they often also provided tangential career opportunities in the related fields of gardening, horticulture, and teaching. As early as 1871, the Universities of Illinois and Iowa opened courses in landscape gardening to women, and MIT's landscape architecture program allowed women when it formed in 1899.[16] There were also specialized schools, such as the Lowthorpe School of Landscape Architecture and Horticulture for Women in Groton, Massachusetts, which opened in 1901 a year after Harvard founded its landscape architecture program for men. Founder Mrs. Edward Gilchrist Low did not intend the school to be a finishing school for "ladylike 'accomplishments'" but a school for students "going out into the real world to open real offices and to make real money."[17] The three-year program included two tracks of study — landscape architecture and horticulture. Courses in landscape architecture taught design, construction, and plant material, with such notable instructors as Ellen Biddle Shipman. The horticulture track was intended to train women as garden consultants, horticultural assistants in landscape architecture offices, superintendents of nurseries and greenhouses, and teachers of gardening and horticulture. Located on an estate thirty-five miles from Boston, the program included hands-on training in surveying, gardening, greenhouse production, and arboriculture. During the winter term held in Boston, students attended classes in the School of Architecture at MIT. Another educational opportunity existed at the Pennsylvania School of Horticulture for Women in Ambler, established in 1910 by Jane B. Haines and first under the direction of Elizabeth Leighton Lee and later Louise Bush-Brown, who also co-authored books on landscape design with her landscape-architect husband.[18] The Pennsylvania School of Horticulture for Women was situated on a seventy-one acre farm that included cropland, orchards, vineyard, vegetable and flower gardens, nurseries, greenhouses, hot beds, cold frames, bee colonies, and a poultry plant.

With professional training completed, women who wanted or needed to establish careers in landscape design or horticulture had to devise alternative career paths from their male peers. A general reflection on women's professional opportunities during this period suggests that women had to seek new professional niches that did not directly threaten male professional status. For a woman to pursue a career in landscape architecture, she had to be resourceful, developing strategies such as opening her own firm, focusing on estate design, utilizing social connections, and so on.[19] On the other hand, women could forge alternative entries into design and planning through fields that were more available to women. Scholars of city planning note that the split of physical planning from social planning resulted in new professional outlets for women, such as social work, public health inspectors, playground supervisors, and kindergarten teachers. Other scholars describe the settlement house as a semi-professional outlet for women that assisted neighborhood improvements in sanitation, health, education, and employment. These new professions were available to women in part because they resonated with socially accepted characteristics of femininity and because they were generally not considered high status or well paid. Teaching was the most obvious and available career path for women during this period. In 1900, approximately two-thirds of women in coed schools were in teacher-training programs. By 1920, teachers represented 57 percent of all women professionals. With women representing 88 percent of all elementary school teachers and 62 percent of secondary teachers, they were a majority presence, even if paid less than male teachers and often denied promotions.[20]

Although the connection between landscape architectural training and such careers as social work and teaching may not be readily apparent to us today, civic gardening provided a bridge during the Progressive Era, particularly through women's involvement in the school garden movement.[21] Education reform during this time emphasized nature study and gardening as hands-on learning methods to teach biology, agricultural science, social science, civics, and aesthetics. The school garden movement, which lasted from about 1890 to just after World War I, promoted gardening at schools, in playgrounds and parks, and in children's homes. Starting in 1901 with the George Putnam School in Roxbury, Boston, the idea quickly spread so that by 1906, the USDA estimated that there were over 75,000 school gardens.[22] The national movement received federal endorsement when in 1914 the U.S. Bureau of Education established the Division of Home and School Gardening. Normal schools, teacher's schools, and African American colleges provided classes in gardening as a quasi-scientific teaching method. Universities and private institutions developed summer courses as well. For instance, in the 1910s, the University of California offered summer training for teachers in gardening.[23] Many advocates were optimistic that a specialized career as school garden supervisor/curator would develop; however, the movement dwindled after World War I.

Successful school gardening required that teachers blend art and science with motherliness. While conducting an agricultural lesson, for instance, the teacher was also encouraged to convey the civic and aesthetic capacities of the garden. Assuming that the teacher would be a woman, M. Louise Greene, in her book *Among School Gardens*, stressed that teachers develop strict yet nurturing relationships with the children in the garden, stating that "nowhere does character count more than in the intimacy between children and teachers which the garden fosters."[24] Demonstration and class gardens were located on school grounds, vacant lots, parks, and playgrounds. Although designed primarily for educational efficiency rather than "landscape effect," they often included perennial borders, pergolas, flowerbeds, and complex path systems. For instance, after the superintendent of the Shaw Botanical Garden in St. Louis visited the Doan School garden in Cleveland, he stated, "I

The University of California provided a training program for teachers. The garden was located just west of the President's house on the Berkeley campus. Reprinted from Fred Harvey Bolster, *The High School Garden* (M.S. thesis, University of California, 1913), p. 64 (courtesy University of California).

did not think that it was possible to secure such scientific and artistic results in a school garden."[25] In addition to the demonstration garden, many school programs actively promoted home gardens. Teachers were often expected to visit homes around the neighborhood in order to check on students' home gardens, persuade parental involvement, and encourage other household and neighborhood improvements.

Teaching gardening to children may seem far removed from landscape architecture until we reconsider the educational connections with such programs as the Lowthorpe School. In 1910, when the East Seventh Street School in Los Angeles proposed to start a garden project, the principal hired Merle Smith, who was trained at Lowthorpe. The first garden was a small flower and vegetable garden and expanded to an adjacent vacant lot that had been used as a dump for years. Along with the teacher, the effort involved the city, Board of Education, and several women's groups. The children were enthusiastic as well, with the principal, Mrs. Larkey, reporting that, "Miss Smith does not have to urge the boys to work; they work her."[26] In 1913, it won one of the annual school-garden awards from *Garden Magazine* for the greatest improvement of school grounds.[27]

The Volunteer: Women's Clubs and Civic Gardening

For many women who received advanced education or left professional careers to raise families, women's clubs provided essential intellectual outlets.[28] Women's clubs that estab-

The East Seventh Street School in Los Angeles, 1913 (courtesy Security Pacific National Bank Photograph Collection, Los Angeles Public Library).

lished garden campaigns were part of a larger growth of women's organizations in the second half of the nineteenth century, with objectives ranging from self-improvement to anti-slavery, temperance, moral reform, sanitation, suffrage, and women's protective unions. Clubs provided a social venue, continued women's education through sponsored lectures and programs, and opened avenues for activism in which women developed leadership skills and learned how to organize, lobby, and fundraise. Women's clubs also provided networking opportunities that were very useful to women professionals seeking references and clients.

While a range of clubs participated in civic gardening campaigns, including literary societies, civic improvement clubs, religious associations, and women's auxiliaries to men's clubs, the garden club represented a direct expression of participating women's desire to be involved with gardening, landscape architecture, and horticulture. Garden club membership was primarily female, although there were men's garden clubs and clubs open to both men and women. As described in a 1913 *Garden Magazine* piece by Francis King, garden club membership consisted primarily of upper income groups, since "Gardening at its highest can best be carried on by men and women of high intelligence, taste, experience — and alas, that it must be said — the wherewithal."[29]

National organizations encouraged local clubs to start garden projects and engage in community outreach. For instance, the Greater Federation of Women's Clubs — initially conceived in 1890 as a literary club but expanded to promote civic improvement — produced a circular in 1910 that suggested ways for local clubs to promote home gardens, improve vacant lots and school grounds, and also beautify roads and parks.[30] The National Plant, Fruit and Flower Guild formed in 1893 to distribute donated plants and fruit to hospitals, tenements, kindergartens, and the poor and to encourage poor people to care for plants in their homes. The Garden Club of America, established in 1913, included in its mission statement the goals to "to stimulate the knowledge and love of gardening among amateurs, to share the advantages of association through conferences and correspondence, in this country and abroad; to aid in the protection of native plants and birds; and to encourage civic planting."[31] An organization focused more directly on supporting women's careers in agriculture, horticulture, and related professions was the Women's National Farm and Garden Association, established in 1914, which provided educational opportunities and scholarships, flower shows and exhibits.[32] These national organizations held conferences and published materials to provide "how to" advice and to highlight the successes of various local projects. Unfortunately for later scholars, the information was often anecdotal and lacked specifics as to who was involved, how projects were funded, and how long they lasted.

Women volunteers provided a key resource for civic garden campaigns. Women's clubs organized garden contests and exhibits, provided seeds, and gave demonstrations and lectures. To combat the visual and health eyesores of vacant lots that were a result of land speculation, clubs encouraged adopt-a-lot programs and sponsored contests. In dense neighborhoods where little land was available, they supported dooryard and window-box gardens as a way to add greenery to tenement districts. For instance, in 1908, the New York Branch of the National Plant, Fruit, and Flower Guild facilitated five hundred window-box gardens by selling affordable boxes and providing plant materials. The boxes cost approximately $1.25 to make, but were sold for 25 cents each.[33] Beautification also extended to the development of new parks and playgrounds, plantings around roadways, railroad stations, and institutions, and preservation of scenic, undeveloped areas.

The support given by women's clubs to the school garden movement was fundamental to its success. Frequently, teachers and women's clubs worked collaboratively to start children's garden programs. Club members helped to secure sites, volunteered as instructors, visited children's homes, and often provided supplements to teachers' salaries for their extra work related to gardening. This kind of support was often essential to start projects and show their success so that school boards would eventually take over the responsibility for the gardens. In Washington, D.C., for example, a home garden campaign was started in 1902 by the Civic Center of Washington and the Washington Branch of the National Plant, Flower and Fruit Guild. After a successful first year, officials from the USDA became involved, donating time and land to the project. Ultimately the school district established a district-wide school garden program under the leadership of botany teacher Susan Sipe Albertis, who went on to be a national advocate for school gardens.[34]

Women's clubs also initiated extracurricular children's gardens, such as the Fairview Garden in Yonkers, started in 1903 by the Civic League of Women's Institutions, led by its president, Mary Marshall Butler.[35] This garden expanded so that by 1911 it included a three and one-half acre garden that served six hundred boys and girls. Children mainly grew their own produce to take home, but they also grew flowers that were sent to the New York Flower Mission to be distributed in hospitals and to the poor. The garden won two *Garden Magazine* school garden awards in 1910 for best flower display and best vegetables. Children were trained and supervised by an adult gardener whose salary was paid through donations and the Women's Institute. The ultimate goal was for the garden to be taken over by the school board, although it is unclear if this happened.

As if to placate concerns about women's encroachment on professional design and elite commissions, women's voluntary civic gardening projects were generally described as experimental, local, and temporary. Women's local campaigns were promoted as catalysts to excite local interest that might eventually lead to bigger projects that men with civic stature and professional experience would spearhead.[36] As stated by Richard Watrous, Secretary of the American Civic Association, women and their organizations "have been leaders in organized effort and have enlisted the sympathy and actual cooperation of men and associations of men in their laudable undertakings. Hundreds of cities that have distinguished themselves for notable achievements can point to some society or several societies of women that have been the first inspiration to do things."[37] Successful projects were usually handed over to others once legitimized as effective and worthy of long-term support. Responsibility transferred to the household, to the school district, or to officials and professionals. Thus, women were encouraged yet bounded in their pursuit of environmental activism.

Conclusion

Admittedly, the civic garden campaigns of the Progressive Era did not leave many traces. All that remains are a few grainy pictures and flowery praise in magazines, books, and conference proceedings from that time. As intended, the efforts were temporary or transferred to the responsibility of the home gardener, the school, or the city. Civic garden campaigns were often collaborative efforts that involved various clubs and institutions, so sometimes it is difficult to pinpoint names of individuals or give complete credit to women. However, it is rare to read about a campaign and *not* find an association with a women's club, teacher, or individual woman.

In the encyclopedia of landscape architects, *Pioneers of American Landscape Design,* 31 of the 160 entries are women.[38] Many of the women that are included played some role in the promotion of women's work in civic gardening. For instance, Frances Duncan wrote about gardens and later worked with school gardens in Los Angeles. Mrs. Francis King helped found the Garden Club of America and the Women's National Farm and Garden Association. Beatrix Farrand advised the Garden Club of America. Their biographies reveal various educational and professional routes to landscape architecture. Digging deeper into the training made available at Lowthorpe, Ambler, Hampton Normal and Agricultural Institute, and the many teachers' schools that provided training in design, gardening, and horticulture may reveal individual women who played active roles in the development of the public landscape through civic and school gardening. These might include Louise Klein Miller, who was curator for all school gardens in Cleveland, Ohio, and Ellen Eddy Shaw, children's garden curator at the Brooklyn Botanical Garden and regular writer on school gardens for *Garden Magazine.* Many of these women were not professional landscape architects, but they were advocates and activists for the public landscape. These women — and the teachers and club members who promoted gardening — helped develop actual places as well as an appreciation for landscape that nurtured the amateur, the philanthropist, the future client, and the future landscape architecture professional.

Notes

1. Joseph Lee, *Constructive and Preventive Philanthropy* (New York: Macmillan, 1902), 89.
2. See Jon Peterson, "The City Beautiful Movement: Forgotten Origins and Lost Meanings," *Journal of Urban History* 2, no. 4 (1976): 415–434; Bonj Szczygiel, "'City Beautiful' Revisited: An Analysis of 19th Century Civic Improvement Efforts," *Journal of Urban History* 29, no. 2 (2003): 107–132.

3. Richard Hofstadter, *The Age of Reform: From Bryan to FDR* (New York: Alfred A. Knopf, 1959), 5.

4. See Karen Madsen and John F. Furlong, "Women, Land, Design: Considering Connections," *Landscape Journal* 13, no. 2 (1994): 88–101; For similar perspectives on women in the playground and kindergarten movements, see Suzanne Spencer-Wood, "Turn of the Century Women's Organizations, Urban Design, and the Origin of the American Playground Movement," *Landscape Journal* 13, no. 2 (1994); and Karen Wolk Feinstein, "Kindergartens, Feminism, and the Professionalization of Motherhood," *International Journal of Women's Studies* 3, no. 1 (1980): 28–38.

5. For illustrations of various terms, see Louise Klein Miller, *Children's Gardens for School and Home: A Manual of Cooperative Gardening* (New York: D. Appleton, 1904); "Gardens and the Unemployed," *Craftsman* 27 (March 1915): 708–710.

6. Art Education Society and the Home Garden Association, *Annual Report*, 1904, 29.

7. E. L. Shuey, "Outdoor Art and Workingmen's Homes," *Second Annual Report of the American Parks and Outdoor Art Association* (Chicago: American Parks and Outdoor Art Association, 1898): 112–123. The organization merged with the American League for Civic Improvement in 1904 to form the American Civic Associations. For specific support of children's gardens, see Dick Crosby, *Children's Gardens: Prospectus of the Department, Leaflet No. 1* (New York: American Civic Association, 1904).

8. Charles Mulford Robinson, *The Improvement of Towns and Cities* (New York: G.P. Putnam and Sons, 1901).

9. Warren H. Manning, "The History of Village Improvement in the United States," *Craftsman* 5 (February 1904): 423–432.

10. Mary Rankin Cranston, "The Garden as Civic Asset, And Some Simple Ways of Making It Beautiful," *The Craftsman* 6 (May 1909): 205–210.

11. Mary I. Woods and Percy V. Pennypacker, "Civic Activities of Women's Clubs," *Annals of the American Academy of Political and Social Science* 56 (November 1914): 78–87.

12. Louise Klein Miller, "Civic Aspects of School Gardens," *Nature-Study Review* 8 (February 1912): 74–76.

13. Charles Mulford Robinson, *Modern Civic Art* (New York: G.P. Putnam's Sons, 1904), 27–28.

14. "The Old Order Changeth," *American City* 6 (June 1912): 801–803. Along with Benjamin Marsh, John Nolen, Horace McFarland, and other well-known promoters of urban planning and design, the Board of *American City* included two women — Mrs. Phillip Moore who was president of the General Federation of Women's Clubs, and Mrs. Thomas Scruggs, a child welfare advocate. Also See Mary Ritter Beard, *Woman's Work in Municipalities* (1915; reprinted New York: Arno Press, 1972), 297.

15. See Roberta Wein, "Women's Colleges and Domesticity, 1875–1918," *History of Education Quarterly* 14, no. 1 (1974): 30–48.

16. Madsen and Furlong, "Women, Land, Design," 1994.

17. Richard Kimball, "A Little Visit to Lowthorpe," *House Beautiful* 39 (March 1916): 111–113; Lowthorpe School, *Lowthorpe School* (Groton, MA: Lowthorpe School, 1937).

18. "Back to the Farm," *Illustrated World* 28 (1917): 613.

19. Madsen and Furlong, "Women, Land, Design," 1994.

20. See Jill Conway, "Perspectives on the History of Women's Education in the United States," *History of Education Quarterly* 14, no. 1 (1974): 1–12; Penina Migdal Glazer and Miriam Slater, *Unequal Colleagues: The Entrance of Women into the Professions, 1890–1940* (New Brunswick: Rutgers University Press, 1987). For discussion of planning professions, see Eugenie Ladner Birch, "From Civic Worker to City Planner: Women and Planning, 1890–1980," in *The American Planner,* ed. Donald A. Kruekeberg (New York: Center for Urban Policy Research, 1994), 396–427; Suellen Hoy, "'Municipal Housekeeping': The Role of Women in Improving Urban Sanitation Practices, 1880–1917" in *Pollution and Reform in American Cities, 1870–1930,* ed. Martin V. Melosi (Austin: University of Texas Press, 1980), 154–198; and Susan Marie Wirka, "The City Social Movement," in *Planning the Twentieth-Century American City,* ed. Mary Corbin Sies and Christopher Silver (Baltimore: Johns Hopkins University Press, 1996), 55–75; for settlement house, see Allen Davis, *Spearheads for Reform* (New York: Oxford University Press, 1967).

21. Although these two gardening campaigns are often distinguished from each other, in part because of the intention to institutionalize school gardening into the public school curricula, I consider the two movements as intertwined, especially in regards to the essential role played by women's organizations. See Thomas Bassett, "Reaping the Margins: A Century of Community Gardening in America," *Landscape* 25, no. 2 (1981): 1–8; Laura Lawson, *City Bountiful: A Century of Community Gardening in America* (Berkeley: University of California Press, 2005); Brian Trelstad, "Little Machines in their Gardens: A History of School Gardens in America," *Landscape Journal* 16, no. 2 (1997): 161–73.

22. James Ralph Jewell, *Agricultural Education Including Nature Study and School Gardens,* Bulletin 2, Department of Interior, Bureau of Education (Washington, DC: Government Printing Office, 1907).

23. Fred Harvey Bolster, "The High School Garden," Master's thesis, University of California, 1913.

24. Greene, *Among School Gardens,* 198.

25. Home Garden Association of Cleveland, *Sixth Annual Report* (Home Garden Association, 1905):19.

26. Ellen Eddy Shaw "Organization of Children's Gardens," *Garden Magazine* 20 (January 1915): 202.

27. *Garden Magazine,* first published in 1905 as an outgrowth of *Country Life in America,* encouraged school gardening. From 1909 until at least 1914, the magazine included a monthly section called "Children's Gardens Everywhere," that was written and/or edited by Ellen Eddy Shaw, curator of the children's garden at the Brooklyn Botanical Garden.

28. See Ann Firor Scott, *Natural Allies: Women's Associations in American History* (Urbana: University of Illinois Press, 1992); Karen J. Blair, *The History of American Women's Voluntary Organizations, 1810–1960* (Boston: G.K. Hall and Co., 1989); and Marilyn Gittell and Teresa Shtob, "Changing Women's Roles in Political Volunteerism and Reform in the City," in *Women and the American City,* ed. Catherine R. Stimpson, Elsa Dixler, Martha J. Nelson, and Kathryn Yatrakis (Chicago: University of Chicago Press, 1980), 67–78. For perspectives from the period, see *Women in Public Life: Annals of the American Academy of Political and Social Science,* 56 (November 1914); and a special edition on women's work in the 1910 *Chautaquan.*

29. Mrs. Francis (Louisa Yoemans) King, "Significance of the 'Garden Clubs,'" *Garden Magazine* 17 (April 1913): 186, 188.

30. See Mary I. Woods, *History of the General Federation of Women's Clubs for the First Twenty-two Years of its Organization* (Norwood, MA: Norwood Press, 1912). Karen Blair credits Sarah Decker's presidency, from 1904 to 1908, for the shift to civic reform. See Karen Blair, *The Torchbearers: Women and their Amateur Arts Associations in America, 1890–1930* (Bloomington: Indiana University Press, 1994).

31. Ernestine A Goodman, *Garden Club of America: History 1913–1938* (Philadelphia: Edward Stern, 1938).

32. Martha Nolen, *A History of Woman's National Farm and Garden Association, Incorporated, 1914–1984* (Fremont, Ohio: Lesher Printers, 1985).

33. See Katherine Paul, "Results in New York City," *Garden Magazine* 19 (March 1914): 102; Washington Branch of the National Plant, Fruit, and Flower Guild, *Reports* 1896, 1898, 1902, 1914; Elisabeth Irwin, "The Little Gardens of the East Side: How the Poor Cultivate Window Boxes," *Craftsman* 14 (July 1908): 404–406.

34. Elizabeth Rafter, "Home and Club Gardens: The Story of the Transformation Wrought in Five Hundred Washington Backyards," *Charities* 11 (September 5, 1903): 210–218; Board of Education of the District of Columbia, *Outline of Work: Home Gardening: Graded Schools* (Washington, DC: Press of Gibson Brothers, 1906); National Plant Fruit, and Flower Guild, *Reports* 1896, 1898, 1902, 1914; Susan Sipe, "What Washington School Children Are Doing for the Capital in Gardening," *Nature–Study Review* 12 (April 12, 1912): 179.

35. Mary Marshall Butler, "A New Kind of School Garden," in report, *Compilations and Suggestions on Methods of Teaching Horticulture in Public Schools* (Society of American Florists and Ornamental Horticulturalists, 1906): 10–12. Mrs. A. L. Livermore, *School Gardens: Report of the Fairview Garden School Association, Yonkers, New York* (Yonkers: Fairview Garden School Association, May 1910).

36. See Mary Ritter Beard, *Woman's Work in Municipalities;* Sophonisba Breckinridge, *Women in the Twentieth Century* (1930; reprinted New York: Arno Press, 1972); and Wendy Kaminar, *Women Volunteering: The Pleasure, Pain, and Politics of Unpaid Work from 1830 to Present* (Garden City, New York: Anchor Press, 1984).

37. Richard Watrous, "The American Civic Association," *American City* 1 (October 1909): 59–63.

38. Charles Birnbaum and Robin Karson, eds. *Pioneers of American Landscape Design.* New York: McGraw-Hill, 2000.

Bibliography

Art Education Society and the Home Garden Association, *Annual Report,* 1904.

"Back to the Farm," *Illustrated World* 28 (1917): 613.

Bassett, Thomas. "Reaping the Margins: A Century of Community Gardening in America," *Landscape* 25, no. 2 (1981):1–8.

Beard, Mary Ritter. *Woman's Work in Municipalities.* 1915. Reprinted, New York: Arno Press, 1972.

Birch, Eugenie Ladner. "From Civic Worker to City Planner: Women and Planning, 1890—1980." In *The American Planner,* edited by Donald A. Kruekeberg, 396–427. New York: Center for Urban Policy Research, 1994.

Birnbaum, Charles, and Robin Karson, eds. *Pioneers of American Landscape Design.* New York: McGraw-Hill, 2000.

Blair, Karen J. *The History of American Women's Voluntary Organizations, 1810–1960.* Boston: G.K. Hall, 1989.

_____. *The Torchbearers: Women and their Amateur Arts Associations in America, 1890–1930.* Bloomington: Indiana University Press, 1994.

Board of Education of the District of Columbia. *Outline of Work: Home Gardening: Graded Schools.* Washington, DC: Press of Gibson Brothers, 1906.

Bolster, Fred Harvey. "The High School Garden." Master's thesis, University of California, 1913.

Breckinridge, Sophonisba. *Women in the Twentieth Century: A Study of Their Political, Social and Economic Activities*. 1933. Reprinted, New York: Arno Press, 1972.

Butler, Mary Marshall. "A New Kind of School Garden." In *Compilations and Suggestions on Methods of Teaching Horticulture in Public Schools*, 10–12. Washington, DC: Society of American Florists and Ornamental Horticulturalists, 1906.

Conway, Jill. "Perspectives on the History of Women's Education in the United States," *History of Education Quarterly* 14, no. 1 (1974): 1–12.

Cranston, Mary Rankin. "The Garden as Civic Asset, And Some Simple Ways of Making It Beautiful." *Craftsman* 6 (May 1909): 205–210.

Crosby, Dick. *Children's Gardens: Prospectus of the Department. Leaflet No. 1.* New York: American Civic Association, 1904.

Davis, Allen. *Spearheads for Reform.* New York: Oxford University Press, 1967.

Feinstein, Karen Wolk. "Kindergartens, Feminism, and the Professionalization of Motherhood." *International Journal of Women's Studies* 3, no. 1 (1980): 28–38.

"Gardens and the Unemployed." *Craftsman* 27 (March 1915): 708–710.

Gittell, Marilyn and Teresa Shtob. "Changing Women's Roles in Political Volunteerism and Reform in the City." In *Women and the American City*, edited by Catherine R. Stimpson, Elsa Dixler, Martha J. Nelson, and Kathryn Yatrakis, 67–78. Chicago: University of Chicago Press, 1980.

Glazer, Penina Migdal and Miriam Slater. *Unequal Colleagues: The Entrance of Women into the Professions, 1890–1940.* New Brunswick, NJ: Rutgers University Press, 1987.

Goodman, Ernestine A. and Garden Club of America. *Garden Club of America: History 1913–1938.* Philadelphia: Edward Stern, 1938.

Hofstadter, Richard. *The Age of Reform: From Bryan to FDR.* New York: Alfred A Knopf, 1959.

Home Garden Association of Cleveland. *Sixth Annual Report.* Cleveland: Home Garden Association, 1905.

Hoy, Suellen. "'Municipal Housekeeping': The Role of Women in Improving Urban Sanitation Practices, 1880–1917." In *Pollution and Reform in American Cities, 1870–1930*, edited by Martin V. Melosi, 154–198. Austin: University of Texas Press, 1980.

Irwin, Elisabeth. "The Little Gardens of the East Side: How the Poor Cultivate Window Boxes." *Craftsman* 14 (July 1908): 404–406.

Jewell, James Ralph. *Agricultural Education Including Nature Study and School Gardens, Bulletin 2, Department of Interior, Bureau of Education.* Washington, DC: Government Printing Office, 1907.

Kaminar, Wendy. *Women Volunteering: The Pleasure, Pain, and Politics of Unpaid Work from 1830 to Present.* Garden City, New York: Anchor Press, 1984.

Kimball, Richard. "A Little Visit to Lowthorpe." *House Beautiful* 39 (March 1916): 111–113.

King, Francis (Louisa Yoemans). "Significance of the 'Garden Clubs.'" *Garden Magazine* 17 (April 1913): 186, 188.

Lawson, Laura. *City Bountiful: A Century of Community Gardening in America.* Berkeley: University of California Press, 2005.

Lee, Joseph. *Constructive and Preventive Philanthropy.* New York: Macmillan, 1902.

Livermore, A.L. *School Gardens: Report of the Fairview Garden School Association, Yonkers, New York.* Yonkers: Fairview Garden School Association, 1910.

Lowthorpe School. *Lowthorpe School.* Groton, MA: Lowthorpe School, 1937.

Madsen, Karen and John F. Furlong. "Women, Land, Design: Considering Connections." *Landscape Journal* 13, no. 2 (1994): 88–101.

Manning, Warren H. "The History of Village Improvement in the United States." *Craftsman* 5 (February 1904): 423–432.

Miller, Louise Klein. "Civic Aspects of School Gardens," *Nature–Study Review* 8 (February 1912): 74–76.

_____. *Children's Gardens for School and Home: A Manual of Cooperative Gardening.* New York: D. Appleton Co., 1904.

Nolen, Martha. *A History of Woman's National Farm and Garden Association, Incorporated, 1914–1984.* Fremont, Ohio: Lesher Printers, 1985.

Paul, Katherine. "Results in New York City." *Garden Magazine* 19 (March 1914): 102.

Peterson, Jon. "The City Beautiful Movement: Forgotten Origins and Lost Meanings." *Journal of Urban History* 2, no. 4 (1976): 415–434.

Rafter, Elizabeth. "Home and Club Gardens: The Story of the Transformation Wrought in Five Hundred Washington Backyards." *Charities* 11 (September 5, 1903): 210–218.

Robinson, Charles Mulford. *The Improvement of Towns and Cities.* New York: G.P. Putnam and Sons, 1901.

_____. *Modern Civic Art.* New York: G.P. Putnam's Sons, 1904.

Scott, Ann Firor. *Natural Allies: Women's Associations in American History.* Urbana: University of Illinois Press, 1992.

Shaw, Ellen Eddy. "Organization of Children's Gardens." *Garden Magazine* 20 (January 1915): 202.

Shuey, E. L. "Outdoor Art and Workingmen's Homes." *Second Annual Report of the American Parks and Outdoor Art Association.* Chicago: American Parks and Outdoor Art Association, 1898.

Sipe, Susan. "What Washington School Children Are Doing for the Capital in Gardening." *Nature–Study Review* 12 (April 12, 1912): 179.

Spencer-Wood, Suzanne. "Turn of the Century Women's Organizations, Urban Design, and the Origin of the American Playground Movement." *Landscape Journal* 13, no. 2 (1994): 124–137.

Szczygiel, Bonj. "'City Beautiful' Revisited: An Analysis of 19th Century Civic Improvement Efforts." *Journal of Urban History* 29, no. 2 (2003): 107–132.

"The Old Order Changeth." *American City* 6 (June 1912): 801–803.

Trelstad, Brian. "Little Machines in Their Gardens: A History of School Gardens in America." *Landscape Journal* 16, no. 2 (1997): 161–73.

Washington Branch of the National Plant, Fruit, and Flower Guild. *Reports 1896, 1898, 1902, 1914.*

Watrous, Richard. "The American Civic Association." *American City* 1 (October 1909): 59–63.

Wein, Roberta. "Women's Colleges and Domesticity, 1875–1918." *History of Education Quarterly* 14, no. 1 (1974): 30–48.

Wirka, Susan Marie. "The City Social Movement: Progressive Social Planning and Early Women Reformers." In *Planning the Twentieth-Century American City*, edited by Mary Corbin Sies and Christopher Silver, 55–75. Baltimore: Johns Hopkins University Press, 1996.

Woods, Mary I. and Percy V. Pennypacker. "Civic Activities of Women's Clubs." *Annals of the American Academy of Political and Social Science* 56 (November 1914): 78–87.

_____. *History of the General Federation of Women's Clubs for the First Twenty-two Years of Its Organization.* Norwood, MA: Norwood Press, 1912.

Chapter 4

Cultivating Mind, Body and Spirit: Educating the "New Woman" for Careers in Landscape Architecture

VALENCIA LIBBY

In the 1890s when a young New Yorker named Beatrix Jones chose to pursue a career in "landscape gardening" as landscape architecture was then called, she had to piece together an education which included a year of private tutoring at the Arnold Arboretum in Boston and a few engineering courses at Columbia College in New York. Beatrix Jones opened an office in her home and was fortunate in being able to find her first clients through her family's social connections. She would go on to become a founding member of the American Society of Landscape Architects in 1899 and, despite her lack of a formal education, the profession's most famous female practioner under her married name, Beatrix Jones Farrand.

By 1900 and the beginning of a new century, American women increasingly sought out careers in fields beyond the traditional ones of school teacher, nurse and office clerk. They wanted to enter fields once considered the exclusive domain of men, such as architecture, landscape design and horticulture. Their demand would be met by a limited number of educational institutions, however, several smaller schools were created specifically for women. In Groton, Massachusetts, for example, Mrs. Edward Gilchrist Low established the Lowthorpe School in 1901 to provide women with a two-year program in landscape design or horticulture. Jane B. Haines opened the Pennsylvania School of Horticulture for Women in Ambler, Pennsylvania, in 1910. These schools offered a very different type of learning environment; one in which women taught other women the subject material as well as preparing them to lead lives of economic independence. In the following essay, the personal experiences of two successful professional women — Marion Cruger Coffin and Louise Carter Bush-Brown — will provide a firsthand perspective on the two forms of education available to women in the early decades of the twentieth century.

In 1901 Marian Cruger Coffin entered the landscape architecture program at the Massachusetts Institute of Technology. Coffin considered herself a "pioneer" in the new profession of landscape architecture, but she was not one of the first women to attend MIT nor was she the only woman studying landscape architecture. MIT's policy had been to accept women into any of its programs beginning in 1870, only nine years after the institution opened.[1]

Coffin was one of four women enrolled in the Architecture Course and one of two women studying landscape architecture. In her graduating class of 1904, the college awarded 232 baccalaureate degrees; six of these went to women and three of the women were in Architecture. Coffin, however, did not receive a degree because she had completed the program as a "special student" thoroughly prepared to enter the profession, but ineligible for a degree. This was not unusual at MIT at the time. Under a widely accepted policy, both men and women choosing to enter a profession could enroll as special students. There were 413 special students at MIT in the academic year 1901–1902. Most of them were older students who had spent two years or more in a professional office and were admitted at the discretion of "the Faculty."[2]

Born near New York City in 1876, Marian Cruger Coffin had moved to Boston with her mother in order to prepare herself for a career in a creative field. Regarding her youthful aspirations, Coffin would later admit: "I secretly cherished the idea of being a great artist … but that dream seemed in no way possible of realization … [although] my desire to create beauty was strong, I did not seem to possess talent for music, writing, painting or sculpture, at that time, the only outlet a woman had to express any artistic ability…. My artistic yearnings lay fallow until I realized it was necessary to earn my living."[3] An architect friend suggested she might wish to try landscape gardening, a new field that was open to women. As Coffin lived in the patrician world of the old New York families, she had heard of Beatrix Jones's "novel profession" and on further investigation found out that the most worthwhile course was offered at MIT, so "off I went gaily expecting to be welcomed with open arms."[4]

Guy Lowell (1870–1927), an architect and an 1894 graduate of MIT had just founded the course in landscape architecture; it was a new "Option 3" of the Architectural Course. The requirements were as demanding as those of architecture, except that the landscape students studied horticulture and landscape design. In their final year, they diverged into a separate studio focused on the landscape.[5] Lowell was an able leader of the new program. He was a well-respected architect in Boston with experience in both residential and institutional design. (He would design the Boston Museum of Fine Art in 1908.) He had studied for four years at the Ecole des Beaux-Arts in Paris and was a great admirer of neoclassical design. Despite his reputation, landscape architecture was a short-lived program, discontinued as an undergraduate degree in 1904. The graduate option ended in 1909 due to competition from Harvard, but Harvard did not admit women.[6]

Nevertheless, the MIT program lasted enough to serve Coffin's educational yearning. Martha Brooks Brown, Coffin's predecessor in the landscape architecture program, had found out that this yearning to obtain an education ran deep: "I was fired with the desire to enter the Institute in spite of the fact that at the time, it was considered almost social suicide and distinctly matrimonial suicide, for a woman to enter any profession."[7]

When Coffin arrived at MIT for her entrance interview, she recalled how intimidating "Tech" was "to a young woman who had never gone more than a few months to a regular school [she had been tutored at home], and when it was reluctantly dragged from me that I had only a smattering of algebra and hardly knew the meaning of the word 'geometry,' the authorities turned from me in calm contempt."[8] She was denied admission. It was only due to the special kindness of Professor Chandler, head of the architectural school, to Professor Sargent, director of the Arnold Arboretum, and to Guy Lowell's encouragement that she persevered and by means of "intensive tutoring in mathematics" was able to enter the program as a special student.

What exactly did students at that time study? The first year of college was preparatory, and included courses like Chemistry and English as well as Freehand Drawing and Drafting.

The studio sequence began in the second year. Coffin combined the first two years into one by taking the required courses in geometry, drawing and drafting along with biology and geology. Over the next two years, she completed "Specifications and Working Drawings, Watercolour Rendering, Drawing and Drafting, one studio in basic design, one studio in Landscape Architecture and three in Landscape Design." Unlike the matriculated students, she chose not to take courses in "Surveying, Curves & Earthworks, Structures, Architectural History or Highway Engineering" but tailored a schedule to meet her needs.[9] Later in her career, she relied on her architectural colleague, James M. Scheiner, to work out structural components.

Coffin also studied plants and horticulture at the Arnold Arboretum under the professional staff of Boston's mecca for botanical research. This was one aspect of her education in which she reveled: her firsthand knowledge of woody and herbaceous plants. She was familiar with hundreds of botanical names and able to share the pure joy of learning with a fellow student of horticulture, the young millionaire Henry Francis du Pont of Winterthur, Delaware. Their lifelong friendship and collaboration would result in the design of Winterthur Gardens, one of Coffin's most memorable landscapes. She also utilized her plant knowledge to write her only book, *Trees and Shrubs for Landscape Effects*, published in 1940.

Omitting the pleasure derived from that particular friendship, Coffin would later describe her college experience as follows:

> Those three years ... were one long grind. The first summer I took drafting lessons from an architect. The only break in the long routine of hard work was a trip abroad, another summer, to study continental landscape design in Italy and France. In the drafting rooms and in our classes the four women students of my year (two were studying architecture and we other two landscape) were thrown in all our work in competition with the men. The invasion of their province as well as our specialty (which was a new and untried architectural development) put us on our mettle to prove that we, too, were serious students and competitors. This association with many types of boys and men I found very helpful as we had a fine spirit of camaraderie in the drafting room and many a helping hand was given me at a critical moment, though one had to steel oneself to hear many a severe criticism, which was perhaps even more valuable.[10]

As to making her livelihood after she left MIT: "one expected the world to welcome newly fledged landscape artists, but alas, few people seemed to know what it was all about ... while the idea of taking a woman into an office [in New York where she chose to live] was unheard of. 'My dear young lady, what will you do about supervising the work on the ground? [meaning the men, the rough laborers].' [It] became such a constant and discouraging query that the only thing seemed to be for me to hang out my own shingle and see what I *would* do about it."[11]

Coffin established an office in New York around 1905 and continued to practice until she reached the age of eighty-one. Throughout her long career, she completed approximately fifty large-scale designs for private and public properties as well as many modest designs. She always considered herself a professional, the equal to any architect on the job. She required payment based on the same fee scale as the architects and equal treatment under a contract. Coffin generally employed women in her practice to afford them the apprenticeship she was unable to obtain in the early 1900s. In this sense, and in her ability to manage spatial compositions of refined balance and proportions, her education at MIT had served her well.

In retrospect Coffin claimed that she was more than grateful for "the splendid training in design we were given and three years of such hard work as I fancy few of the schools now insist upon, as well as the patience and enthusiasm of Prof. Jack who guided our steps through an intensive training in plant material." She stated: "We were pioneers, and more-over pioneer women in a new-old profession, and one in which all one's ability to see and interpret beauty out of doors taxed all our resources, and we were determined to show what enthusiasm and hard work could accomplish."[12]

A very different form of vocational education was available at the Pennsylvania School of Horticulture for Women, established in 1910. In September of 1914, Louise Carter of New York arrived by train at the station in Ambler, Pennsylvania. Philadelphia was only eighteen miles away, but it seemed like another world. Carter was amused by "the little rattle trap taxi" that transported her along a rural turnpike with a toll gate and a long, dusty country road that led to her new school. When she reached the stone farmhouse that served as the school's headquarters, she found that she still had to walk another half mile down the road carrying her heavy suitcase to room in a house nearby.[13] Thirteen other young women had enrolled that year to live and work on the small farm called the Pennsylvania School of Horticulture and the small cottage "on campus" that served as the dormitory was full. For the next two years, Louise Carter and her classmates lead "a wholesome country life" as "dirt farmers" in an academic community founded by women, run by women, and financed by women, to provide them with career options in land-based occupations such as horticulture, garden design, estate management, farming and education of the young.[14]

The Pennsylvania School was the inspired idea of Jane Bowne Haines (1869–1937), a member of the distinguished Wistar-Haines family of Quaker Philadelphia, known for their long association with horticultural pursuits. Jane Haines was well educated, having earned both undergraduate (1896) and graduate degrees from Bryn Mawr College; and she had worked as professional librarian for the Library of Congress. She was concerned about the working conditions of women who had to earn their living, and she was determined to do something about it.[15]

Together with a small group of supporters, Haines purchased a 70 acre farm near Ambler in 1910 to set up a school of practical training. She formed a board of trustees, over which she presided until her death in 1937, and had the colonial farmhouse remodeled to provide an office, dining hall, staff quarters and classroom. The board hired a director and one fulltime instructor, both women; and in the winter of 1911, the Pennsylvania School of Horticulture for Women opened its doors to five students.

As "Miss Haines" explained: "Our vision was of a place where earnest women could live and dream, where they should not be expected to do household work, but should give all their time to learning under competent teachers to become competent workers."[16]

When Louise Carter came to Ambler in 1914, life there was pretty rustic. Classes were held on the sunporch of the farmhouse: "There was a long unpainted shelf which consisted of two pine boards placed against the glass windows ... at which we sat while taking our notes, our backs to the instructor who stood in the doorway when lecturing."[17] The following year, the trustees raised enough money to erect a second building to provide a proper class-room, a sitting room with a fireplace and a dormitory on the second floor. Later a design studio was installed under the sloping eaves of the third floor. From modest beginnings, the Pennsylvania School grew slowly and steadily over four decades to become a junior college specializing in horticulture by 1952 and, finally, to merge with Temple University in 1958.

The "Ambler farmerettes," as the students were locally known, studied botany, horti-culture, floriculture, soil chemistry, orchard care, farm management, garden design and book-keeping. They had the option to study beekeeping, farm carpentry, dairy or poultry. Everyone received practical training in the gardens, greenhouses, orchards and fields; two hours out-of-doors for each hour in the classroom. It was a hands-on approach to education intended to develop both the manual skills and the stamina of young women.

Haines had drawn her model from two successful schools of gardening for women in England: the Studley School near Reading and the Swanley School near London. Although the Pennsylvania School was the second of its kind in the United States, as the Lowthorpe School in Groton, Massachusetts, was founded in 1903, the students still felt like pioneers. There was just a spirit about Ambler that Louise Carter later described: "We were venturing into completely new territory for women and we had no way of knowing what opportunities the future might hold for us. But we had enthusiasm for the work and faith and zeal. And we realized that we were blazing a new trail; if we were successful in the positions we held, it would create new opportunities for the students of the future."[18]

The graduates had a variety of job offers. Louise Carter (1897–1973), for example, first worked as an instructor of horticulture for girls in Boston and then in Kentucky. She became an estate manager in Tallahassee, Florida, and a cooperative extension agent. In 1924, she returned to Ambler as the Pennsylvania School's fourth director. One year later, Miss Carter married the landscape architect James Bush-Brown (BLA University of Pennsylvania, MLA Harvard) who taught the school's landscape design course. Louise Carter Bush-Brown reigned supreme over the institution with the trustees' full support for the next twenty-five years.

The landscape design program at the Pennsylvania School began in 1915 when Elizabeth Leighton Lee, considered to be the first female practitioner of landscape architecture in Philadelphia, became director of the school. "Under her skilled guidance" eight students in the Class of 1916 carried out their first design — a small colonial revival garden behind the eighteenth-century farmhouse.[19] From this beginning, landscape design was a popular topic of study. In 1925, the school attracted Markley Stevenson, who had earned a Master of Landscape Architecture at Harvard, to join the faculty and lecture on "the history of gardens and the appreciation of landscape design."[20] The school planned a large formal garden to showcase a collection of hardy perennials. Even Beatrix Jones Farrand was called on to submit design sketches for the garden pavilions, although the final project appears to be that of James Bush-Brown.[21]

In the fall of 1934, James Bush-Brown established the "Preparatory Course for Professional Study in Landscape Architecture," a two-year program leading to a diploma. The first year of study entailed botany, chemistry, design (nine hours per week of freehand drawing, mechanical drafting and the history of gardens), entomology, floriculture, plant materials and rural economy. The second year coursework continued with botany, floriculture, business methods, design (nine hours per week of freehand drawing, landscape construction and planting design), soils, and trees and shrubs. By 1935 graduates of this program were eligible "for admission with advanced credit to the Cambridge School of Domestic and Landscape Architecture."[22] By 1940 the Cambridge School had merged with Smith College to become the Smith College Graduate School of Domestic and Landscape Architecture, but the same policy applied. Several Ambler graduates went on to complete the Cambridge program and become landscape architects.

When Louise Carter Bush-Brown retired in 1952, she had done her best to bring the school through both the Depression and World War II and insure its future as an accredited junior college. But the Pennsylvania School could not survive the cultural and economic changes of postwar America. The men were home, and marriage and motherhood beckoned. New junior colleges and new career opportunities drew away potential students and the staff. The school's fifth director, Jonathon French, and the board of trustees negotiated a merger with Temple University in 1958.

Over the course of almost five decades, the students of the Pennsylvania School of Horticulture for Women proudly shared in the accomplishments of their classmates as many of them went on to set up their own farms, nurseries, landscape design and floral businesses. They became educators, directors of schools, journalists, authors, landscape architects and leaders of public organizations. In a variety of ways, Jane B. Haines and the women of the Pennsylvania School of Horticulture made a lasting contribution to the changing perception and value of women in the workplace. While the formality of an institution such as MIT served the self-motivated young design professional well, it was ultimately an educational model developed for and administered by men. The informality of a small private occupational school such as the Pennsylvania School, established specifically for women, offered much more than career preparation. It provided an environment where young women were instructed in ways to forge their own paths in life with self-confidence and encouraged via a lasting network of mentors and supporters.

Notes

1. See Marilyn A. Bever, "The Women of M.I.T., 1871 to 1941: Who They Were, What They Achieved," (BS thesis, MIT, 1977), 38.
2. Letter from Lois Beattie, staff assistant MIT Archives, to author, September 18, 1985.
3. M.C. Coffin's letter to Clarence Fowler for his article "Three Women in Landscape Architecture," *Cambridge School of Architecture and Landscape Architecture Alumnae Review* 9 (1932):11.
4. *Ibid.*, 11.
5. MIT Catalogue, (1901–1902): 40–42.
6. Letter from Lois Beattie, staff assistant MIT Archives, to author, September 18, 1985; Martha Brookes Hutchinson letter to Clarence Fowler for his article "Three Women in Landscape Architecture," *Cambridge School of Architecture and Landscape Architecture Alumnae Review* 9 (1932): 9.
7. M.C. Coffin's letter to Clarence Fowler for his article "Three Women in Landscape Architecture," *Cambridge School of Architecture and Landscape Architecture Alumnae Review* 9 (1932): 11–12.
8. Copy of Marian C. Coffin's transcript, MIT Archives, 1901–1904; M.C. Coffin's letter to Clarence Fowler for his article "Three Women in Landscape Architecture," *Cambridge School of Architecture and Landscape Architecture Alumnae Review* 9 (1932): 12.
9. *Ibid.*, 12.
10. *Ibid.*
11. Louise Carter Bush-Brown, "Fifty Years Ago," *Pen and Trowel* (alumnae newsletter of Pennsylvania School of Horticulture), Summer, 1964, 4–5, courtesy of Temple University, Ambler College Archives.
12. See Valencia Libby, "Jane Haines' Vision: The Pennsylvania School of Horticulture for Women, 1910–1958," *Journal of the New England Garden History Society* 10 (Fall 2002): 44–52.
13. *Ibid.*, 44.
14. Jane B. Haines, Pennsylvania School of Horticulture fundraising brochure dated 1925, courtesy of Temple University, Ambler College Archives.
15. Bush-Brown, "Fifty Years Ago," 4.
16. *Ibid.*
17. *Ibid.*
18. "Ambler Institution Strikes Strong Position," *Ambler Gazette*, January 22, 1925.
19. This was the conclusion of a research committee to re-create the formal garden, chaired by John F. Collins, Department of Landscape Architecture and Horticulture, Temple University, 1990.
20. *The School Horticulture for Women: A School of Country Life*, prospectus 1934–1935 (Ambler: Pennsylvania School of Horticulture, 1934), courtesy of Temple University, Ambler College Archives.
21. A monthly newsletter, *Wise Acres*, created by the students in 1914, shared both small and large triumphs. Of all the students who attended the School of Horticulture for Women, three individuals stand out for their lifelong contribution to American horticulture and civic service: Louise Carter Bush-Brown (Class of 1916) who together with her husband authored *America's Garden Book* (1939) and founded the Neighborhood Garden Association of Philadelphia, an early model of neighborhood greening and civic improvement; Elizabeth C. Hall

(Class of 1923) who was the research assistant for the ten-volume *New York Botanical Garden Illustrated Encyclopedia of Horticulture*, her work for almost 50 years; and Ernesta Drinker Ballard (Class of 1954) a member of the first board of the National Organization for Women (NOW), civic leader, political activist, horticulturist and executive director of the Pennsylvania Horticultural Society for eighteen years (1963–1981) in which time she transformed it into an engine for urban greening. See Suzanne Sataline's article on Ernesta Drinker Ballard, *Inquirer Magazine* of *The Philadelphia Inquirer*, 12 July 1998.

22. *The School Horticulture for Women: A School of Country Life*, prospectus 1934–1935 (Ambler, PA: Pennsylvania School of Horticulture, 1934), courtesy Temple University, Ambler College Archives.

Bibliography

"Ambler Institution Strikes Strong Position." *Ambler Gazette*, 22 January 1925.

Beattie, Lois. Letter to author from staff assistant Massachusetts Institute of Technology Archives, September 18, 1985.

Bever, Marilyn A. "The Women of M.I.T., 1871 to 1941: Who They Were, What They Achieved." Bachelor of Science thesis, Massachusetts Institute of Technology, 1977.

Bush-Brown, Louise Carter. "Fifty Years Ago." *Pen and Trowel* (alumnae newsletter of Pennsylvania School of Horticulture). Summer, 1964.

Fowler, Clarence. "Three Women in Landscape Architecture." *Cambridge School of Architecture and Landscape Architecture Alumnae Review* 9 (1932): 9–12.

Haines, Jane B. Fundraising brochure Pennsylvania School of Horticulture, 1925. Temple University, Ambler College Archives.

Libby, Valencia. "Jane Haines' Vision: The Pennsylvania School of Horticulture for Women, 1910–1958." *Journal of the New England Garden History Society* 10 (Fall 2002): 44–52.

_____. "Marian C. Coffin (1876–1957): The Landscape Architect and the Lady" and "The Formal Garden at Clayton." *The House and Garden*. Exhibition catalogue, 24–29 and 30–38. Roslyn, NY: Nassau County Museum of Fine Art, 1986.

"Marian C. Coffin." In *Pioneers of American Landscape Design*, edited by Charles Birnbaum and Robin Karson, 64–68. New York: McGraw-Hill 2000.

Massachusetts Institute of Technology Catalogue 1901–1902. Cambridge: Massachusetts Institute of Technology, 1901.

The School Horticulture for Women: A School of Country Life (prospectus 1934–1935). Ambler: Pennsylvania School of Horticulture, 1934.

Chapter 5

Were They Feminists? Men Who Mentored Early Women Landscape Architects

DANIEL W. KRALL

Women who in the last part of the nineteenth and early years of the twentieth century chose to become landscape architects faced an enormous array of obstacles. The relative newness of the profession, lack of schools for training, the general societal attitudes against women working, as well as more immediate criticism from family members, did not suggest a high probability of success. In spite of these and other issues, a set of women persevered and became important individuals in the early years of the profession. While the number of women professionals during this period was never large, it was certainly greater than the number of women in the fields of architecture or engineering. This is surprising when one realizes that the American Institute of Architects was organized in 1857 and at least eight programs of architectural instruction had been established by 1899, the founding date of the American Society of Landscape Architects.

How and why these women were able to enter the profession of landscape architecture continues to be debated. Was it, as one writer suggests, "that a career in gardening and landscape design could be accepted as a logical extension of women's traditional domestic role?"[1] Or was it that women were becoming interested in job opportunities as professionals just as landscape architecture was emerging as a choice? But these possibilities still do not explain how women became such important practitioners and, as Ellen Shipman noted in 1938, emerged as "leaders in the profession."[2] This chapter will argue that in the early years of the landscape architectural profession there was a group of men, however small, that mentored many of these women, and, in doing so, helped promote an extraordinary group of female practitioners that was unique when compared with similar professions. While this may represent only one of the reasons that women emerged as successful professionals, this unusual mentoring by these men, given the times, occurred too often to go unexamined. What follows will be a discussion of some of these individuals and their documented assistance to these women, female practitioners and their acknowledgment of this support, and finally, what these unique relationships suggest in understanding how women emerged and worked as designers in a male-dominated society.

Elizabeth Jane Bullard, generally recognized as the first professional woman landscape architect in this country, no doubt became a landscape architect due to her father's tutelage. Oliver Bullard became acquainted with Frederick Law Olmsted during the Civil War and later worked with him on such sites as Prospect Park and the United States Capitol grounds.

After supervising Olmsted's park work in the city of Bridgeport, Connecticut, Oliver Bullard, with Olmsted's blessing, became the city's first park superintendent. Throughout this period, Elizabeth Bullard was often at her father's side observing and learning his profession. At the time of Mr. Bullard's sudden death in 1890, Elizabeth was undertaking many private landscape projects in Bridgeport. When requested by the City Council to take her father's place, she refused, anticipating the harsh political rivalries that soon enveloped the Bridgeport Parks Department. However, she had received a ringing endorsement from the senior Olmsted who, in reply to the city fathers, said that he had no doubt that she could successfully carry on her father's work. Additionally, he proposed that she be given more authority in the position than would a man, understanding the struggles she would encounter as a female. Elizabeth Bullard did continue her father's private projects including several with the Olmsted firm. She was later chosen the first new, or twelfth, member of the ASLA in the fall of 1899.[3]

Another individual, Charles S. Sargent, was remembered by several early women landscape designers as a mentor. Following an interest in horticulture beginning with his childhood days in Boston, Sargent was appointed the director of the yet undeveloped Arnold Arboretum in 1872, a position he held until his death in 1927. During this period he worked with many young women, his most famous protégé being Beatrix Jones (Farrand) who studied under his direction in the early 1890s. It was with Sargent that Jones learned horticulture, "as an artist would have apprenticed to a master to learn anatomy and the technique of painting."[4] It was Sargent who encouraged the young woman to study landscape gardening, travel widely, and to accept her first professional commissions. One author suggests that "for the rest of her life she regarded knowing Professor Charles Sprague Sargent as the key to her success."[5] Years later she still referred to him as "my old friend and teacher."[6] Marian Coffin also studied horticulture at the Arnold and later acknowledged her appreciation for the encouragement given to her by Professor Sargent.[7]

Perhaps as important as encouraging women to enter the profession of landscape architecture was Sargent's role as editor of *Garden and Forest*, beginning in 1888. As the preeminent periodical in the earliest days of the profession, many of its articles and editorials extolled the possibilities for women in landscape design. One noted:

> A class of practitioners may be advantageously developed who, while not being landscape gardeners in the broadest sense, may yet do much to redeem country and suburban places, from the commonplace look that too many of them now wear. This work may well be done by women. Those who natural tastes induce them to take it up, should prepare themselves for the work by taking such landscape gardening courses as offered, or by study with practicing professionals, and after undertaking work along, should cling to the best traditions and methods of the profession.[8]

This comment did come sometime after Sargent had noted that, "landscape-gardening on a large scale is, after all, a masculine art, and requires a certain manly vigor of treatment, an unhesitating despotism, that the gentler sex deprecate as cruel and unnecessary."[9]

Sargent's son-in-law, architect Guy Lowell, also trained several young women who became leaders in the landscape architectural profession. As the faculty member heading the landscape architecture program established at MIT in 1900, Lowell instructed Marian Coffin, a graduate of the program, as well as Martha Brown (Brookes Hutcheson), Rose Standish Nichols and Mabel Babcock, who each attended the program for differing lengths of time. Here it is somewhat difficult to determine a real sense of Lowell's attitudes. Marian Coffin acknowledged that it was owing to others and "Mr. Lowell's encouragement that I persevered [at MIT]...."[10] However, in her biography of Brown, Rebecca Warren Davidson noted that she left MIT in 1902, "obviously dissatisfied with the curriculum, but she may also have had personal or professional disagreements with Lowell."[11]

Warren Manning, an early employee of Olmsted and a founding member of the ASLA, was also a supporter of women practitioners. Asked at the beginning of the twentieth century what he thought of women entering the profession, Manning replied, "[I see] no reason why there is not the same opening for women here as in nearly every other profession... Women can succeed in this profession only by the same means that men have succeeded, — securing knowledge, skill and experience through years of study and practice in actual work."[12]

Manning was one of the earliest practitioners to hire women in his office. Finding employment was always a critical problem for women and many, such as Coffin and Hutcheson, were forced to open their own offices when they could not find other work. Manning, however, employed two young women from the Cornell program. Marjorie Sewell (Cautley), a 1917 graduate, and Helen E. Bullard, class of 1919, both worked immediately after graduation in Manning's office. Sewell, in fact, received a stellar recommendation from Cornell Professor Ralph Curtis in his reply to an inquiry from Manning. Curtis wrote, "She is already well fitted in landscape planting and is not only greatly interested in her work but is unusually single-minded in her determination to succeed in the profession. She is that keen kind of outdoor student that you enjoy and if there is any work in which you can use her this summer, I am sure you will not make a mistake in trying her out."[13]

Manning also sought out women designers in his later professional work. Unable to please Gertrude Seiberling while designing the English garden at Stan Hywet Hall, the family estate outside Akron, Ohio, Manning requested that she engage Ellen Shipman whom he identified as "one of, if not the very best, flower garden maker" in the country.[14] Shipman was hired, and today the walled garden at the estate is one of the few Shipman sites that has been successfully restored.

Charles Adams Platt, another well-known landscape architect of this period, was certainly recognized for his support of women professionals. Summering in the artist colony at Cornish, New Hampshire, he was so impressed with Ellen Shipman's gardening skills and sense of taste that he encouraged her to become a professional and allowed her to enter his office, where she acquired drafting and rendering skills. Between 1910 and the time she opened her own New York City office in 1920, Shipman collaborated with Platt on several projects that highlighted her garden design ability and introduced her to many future clients. Later Shipman acknowledged "it was working with Charles Platt ... that gave me the foundation for my future knowledge of design."[15] It was also at Cornish that Rose Standish Nichols expressed interest in becoming a landscape architect. "Accordingly," she later wrote, "I wished to study layout from an architect's point of view, so took lessons with my Cornish neighbor, Mr. Charles Platt."[16]

Another individual may represent the ultimate mentor of this period, Henry A. Frost, who served as the only director of the Cambridge School throughout its more than twenty-five years of existence. When a young Katherine Brooks appealed to Professor James Sturgis Pray for admittance to the Harvard landscape architecture program in the fall of 1915, Pray encouraged Frost and landscape architect Bremer Pond to informally tutor the young woman. Trained as an architect, Frost was at first leery of the challenge. But he soon noted that he found Brooks and several young women who had joined her "willing workers, so apt in their ability to understand, that from this time on we welcomed such students ... in fact took them eagerly."[17] By 1928, when Frost co-authored a report on women in landscape architecture, he noted that "women did better work than men in the residential field partly because ... they had a flair for design related to the human scale and partly because they paid more attention to detail."[18] As time went by Frost became more convinced of the quality of his female students and their commitment to their work:

> The professions of architecture and landscape architecture have been, until very recent times, entirely in the hands of men. At present, women are not welcomed in many offices (even) as draughtsmen, and not a few practitioners are sincere in advising women not to attempt either profession. Therefore, a student entering the Cambridge School has to some degree the pioneering instinct [as well as] a modem viewpoint. She must realize that success in a field where men are receiving their training in long-established schools requires for her a training as good [as theirs].... And that with this training, because she is of necessity a pioneer, must go a high enthusiasm and an unusual tenacity of purpose. Our students do not drift into their profession along the lines of least resistance, nor do they drift through this school.[19]

Dorothy May Anderson, in her history of the school, acknowledged, "without exception ... no student left the Cambridge School without a sense of gratitude and lifelong devotion to its Director."[20]

Other men may have also been supportive individuals in the early years of the profession, but documentation is too spotty to be certain. Elizabeth Leonard (Strang), the first female graduate of the Cornell Landscape Art program (1910), worked for brief periods in the offices of Hinchman & Pilat and Ferruccio Vitale before spending two years in the Boston office of well-known city planner John Nolen. She was also befriended by landscape architect Stephen Child, who encouraged her to begin teaching at the Lowthorpe School of Landscape Design for which he served on the board of directors. Child also sponsored her admission to the ASLA as the fourth woman member.[21] Similarly, Annette Hoyt Flanders started her professional practice in 1920 as an associate with Vitale and his partners in New York City.[22] Ruth Dean, beginning in 1910, worked for some time in the office of Jens Jensen while Rose Greely, upon graduating from the Cambridge School in 1920, spent three years in the office of Fletcher Steele.[23]

So what does this rather brief overview reveal regarding these early practitioners and women in the field of landscape architecture? Let me suggest a few points for discussion and additional research. One, that there were several early and well-established male practitioners who encouraged women to become landscape architects. While this support varied and may not have been as vigorous or apparent as one would hope, and in many cases the benefits were as much for the men as for the women, it was unique among design professionals of the period. Second, many of these women who became outstanding designers later acknowledged learning their design skills from these male mentors. Already mentioned was Ellen Shipman's noting her understanding of design from her association with Charles Adams Platt. Similarly, Marian Coffin's biographer observes that while she was his student, Guy Lowell published *American Gardens* (1902)and that Coffin's landscape plans "reflect the influence of Lowell's teaching of Italian Renaissance design principles" which at the time were in stark contrast to the naturalistic style being generated at the nearby Olmsted office.[24] Here the question posed for the researcher is how can design skills and intentions be separated between mentor and student? Is such an undertaking even necessary or desirable?

Third, in discussing the early history of the landscape architecture profession, does this support or mentoring offer an opportunity, not to ascribe differences or highlight discrimination, but to attest to the interaction of men and women that resulted in professionals of outstanding abilities? Is this perhaps one way in which the early practice of landscape architecture was truly unique among the design professions? Unlike the writer who asked, "Why Have There Been No Great Women Artists?" perhaps the question in landscape architecture should be, "Why were there so many outstanding women practitioners in the early years of the profession?"[25] Recent histories have begun to document the lives of some of these women who became important practitioners, worked with major clients, and designed outstanding projects. While I do not suggest that we ignore or minimize the many inequalities suffered by early female practitioners at the hands of male professionals, there may also have been an unusual level of interaction and encouragement among these early landscape architects that was rare and unique for the period. While this must be documented further, I submit that this does suggest a new way of understanding the early years of the profession.

Elizabeth Meyer, in her article, "The Expanded Field of Landscape Architecture," speaks to the problem of seeing the history of the profession as pairs of "either-or." Terms such as "culture and nature," "architecture and landscape architecture," "city and country," "man and nature," and "male and female" are ones most of us have heard and perhaps used in discussing inclusion and exclusion within the profession. But Meyer questions, "Has [this kind] of thinking blinded us from seeing (more) complex webs of interrelationship?"[26] Similarly, Robert Riley, author and former editor of *Landscape Journal*, writes of the problems of such "duality" of terms. The danger, he believes, is "in their use — or misuse." In place of such paradigms, he maintains that we should "set up questions about sex, gender, and landscape in a larger framework of variability and diversity."[27] It is within such a construct, I would argue, that we should acknowledge that the idea of "diversity," and not "duality," best describes an understanding of the relationships just presented.

It is my personal belief that the really tragic and more egregious period in the history of the profession is from the mid 1930s to the 1950s. How did this active and prominent group of female practitioners, noted as leaders in 1938, virtually disappear by midcentury? Some of the reasons are fairly clear. While the Depression years were crippling, the period of World War II was even more difficult for women designers. Certainly the closings of Lowthorpe and the Cambridge School in the 1940s were significant. Other issues, confronting the entire profession, were the changing nature of practice and the increasing focus on planning. But I also wonder if perhaps women practitioners by the 1930s had become so successful that they were seen as threats in an evolving profession with fewer projects and growing issues of job security. Perhaps rather than mentors, men became hard-nosed competitors and women practitioners, always fewer in number, were successfully pushed aside. This hypothesis certainly requires additional investigation. But resolving this question might add even more importance to the early period of the profession and highlight the role of those males who mentored women practitioners.

Landscape architect Helen Bullard was once heard to remark, following a fiery speech by a women's liberation speaker, "I owe my success to the many fine men with whom I have been associated."[28] I believe many early female landscape architects could have echoed this comment. It is sad that by the 1950s there were few women who could express such sentiments. Times had changed, society had changed, and landscape architecture had changed, not to the benefit of the young women interested in pursuing the field as a career. It is just within the last decades that women are once again taking their proper place within the profession. However, as we continue to document the history of landscape architecture in this country, we should not overlook the unusual and unique way in which some male practitioners encouraged and instructed many of the women who became outstanding landscape architects in the early years of the twentieth century.

Notes

1. Leslie R. Close, "Introduction" in *The Gardens of Ellen Biddle Shipman*, by Judith Tankard (New York: Sagapress, 1996), xv.
2. Shipman as quoted by Anne Petersen, "Women Take Lead in Landscape Art," *New York Times*, March 13, 1938, 83.
3. Daniel W. Krall, "The Illusive Miss Bullard: First Professional Woman Landscape Architect," *Landscape Journal* 21, no. 1 (2002): 116–122.
4. Diana Balmori, Diane McGuire, and Eleanor McPeck, *Beatrix Farrand's American Landscapes: Her Gardens and Campuses* (Sagaponack, NY: Sagapress, 1985), 6.
5. Jane Brown, *Beatrix: The Gardening Life of Beatrix Jones Farrand* (New York: Viking Press, 1995), 31.
6. Balmori, McGuire, and McPeck, 169.
7. Nancy Fleming, *Money, Manure & Maintenance* (Weston, MA: Country Place Books, 1995), 11.
8. Quoted by Frances Copley Seavey, "Women as Landscape Gardeners," *Park and Cemetery* 12 (December 1902): 417.
9. Charles S. Sargeant, "Taste Indoors and Out," *Garden and Forest* 5, no. 233 (1892): 373–374.
10. Fleming, 7.
11. Martha Brookes Hutcheson, *The Spirit of the Garden*, reprinted (Amherst: University of Massachusetts Press, 2001). Rebecca Warren Davidson, "Introduction," xiii.
12. Seavey, 416.
13. Ralph Curtis to Warren Manning, 31 March 1917 (Coll. 21/25/137, Box 11). Rare Manuscript Collections, Carl A. Kroch Library, Cornell University, Ithaca, NY.
14. Tankard, 117.
15. *Ibid.*, 29.
16. *Rose Standish Nichols: As We Knew Her* (Boston: Friends of Rose Standish Nichols, 1986), 6.
17. Dorothy May Anderson, *Women, Design and the Cambridge School* (West Lafayette, IN: PDA Publishers Corp, 1980), 16.
18. *Ibid.*, 41.
19. *Ibid.*, 76.
20. *Ibid.*, 79.
21. Daniel W. Krall, "The Landscape Architect as Advocate: The Writings of Elizabeth Leonard Strang," *Journal of New England Garden History Society* 11 (Fall 2003): 12–21.
22. Patricia L. Filzen, "Annette Hoyt Flanders: From Beaux Arts to Modernism," in *Midwestern Landscape Architecture*, ed. William Tishler (Urbana and Chicago: University of Illinois Press, 2000), 231–242.
23. Charles Birnbaum and Robin Karson, eds., *Pioneers of American Landscape Design* (New York: McGraw-Hill, 2000), 79, 144.
24. Fleming, 11.
25. Linda Nochlin, "Why Have There Been No Great Women Artists?" in *Women, Art, and Power* (New York: Harper & Row, 1988), 145.
26. Elizabeth Meyer, "The Expanded Field of Landscape Architecture," in *Ecological Design and Planning*, ed. George F. Thompson and Frederick R. Steiner (New York: John Wiley & Sons, 1997), 45–79.
27. Robert R. Riley, "Gender, Landscape, Culture: Sorting Out Some Questions," *Landscape Journal* 13, no. 2 (1994): 153–163.
28. David Bullard, "Helen Elise Bullard: A Biographical Minute," in the Helen Bullard Collection, Rare Manuscript Collections, Carl A. Kroch Library, Cornell University, Ithaca, NY.

Bibliography

Anderson, Dorothy May. *Women, Design and the Cambridge School.* West Lafayette, IN.: PDA Publishers Corp., 1980.
Balmori, Diana, Diana McGuire, and Eleanor McPeck. *Beatrix Farrand's American Landscapes: Her Gardens and Campuses.* Sagaponack, NY: Sagaponack Press, 1985.
Birbaum, Charles, and Robin Karson, eds. *Pioneers of American Landscape Design.* New York: McGraw-Hill, 2000.

Brown, Jane. *Beatrix: The Gardening Life of Beatrix Jones Farrand.* New York: Viking Press, 1995.

Bullard, David. "Helen Elise Bullard: A Biographical Minute." In the Helen Bullard Collection, Rare and Manuscript Collections, Carl A. Kroch Library, Cornell University, Ithaca, NY.

Close, Leslie R. "Introduction: A History of Women in Landscape Architecture" to *The Gardens of Ellen Biddle Shipman*, by Judith Tankard, xv-xvi. Sagaponack, NY: Sagapress, 1996.

Curtis, Ralph. Letter to Warren Manning, March 13, 1917 (Coll. 21/25/137, Box 11). Rare Manuscript Collections, Carl A. Kroch Library, Cornell University, Ithaca, NY.

Filzen, Patricia L. "Annette Hoyt Flanders: From Beaux Arts to Modernism." In *Midwestern Landscape Architecture*, edited by William Tishler, 231–242. Urbana and Chicago: University of Illinois Press, 2000.

Fleming, Nancy. *Money, Manure & Maintenance.* Weston, MA: Country Place Books, 1995.

Friends of Rose Standish Nichols. *Rose Standish Nichols: As We Knew Her.* Boston: Self-published, 1986.

Hutcheson, Martha Brookes. *The Spirit of the Garden.* 1923; Reprint, Amherst: University of Massachusetts Press, 2001.

Krall, Daniel W. "The Illusive Miss Bullard: First Professional Woman Landscape Architect." *Landscape Journal* 21, no. 1 (2002): 116–122.

_____. "The Landscape Architect as Advocate: The Writings of Elizabeth Leonard Strang." *Journal of New England Garden History Society* 11 (Fall 2003): 12–21.

Meyer, Elizabeth. "The Expanded Field of Landscape Architecture." In *Ecological Design and Planning*, edited by George F. Thompson and Frederick R. Steiner, 45–79. New York: John Wiley & Sons, 1997.

Nochlin, Linda. *Women, Art and Power.* New York: Harper & Row, 1988.

Petersen, Anne. "Women Take Lead in Landscape Art." *New York Times* March 13, 1935, 83.

Riley, Robert R. "Gender, Landscape, Culture: Sorting Out Some Questions." *Landscape Journal* 13, no. 2 (1994): 153–163.

Sargeant, Charles Sprague "Taste Indoors and Out." *Garden and Forest* 5, no. 233 (1892): 373–374.

Seavey, Copley. "Women as Landscape Gardeners." *Park and Cemetery* 12 (December 1902): 417.

Thompson, George F., and Frederick R. Steiner, eds. *Ecological Design and Planning.* New York: John Wiley & Sons, 1997.

Tishler, William, ed. *Midwestern Landscape Architecture.* Urbana and Chicago: University of Illinois Press, 2000.

Chapter 6

Women Take the Lead in Landscape Art

Judith B. Tankard

"Women Take the Lead in Landscape Art," a feature published in *The New York Times* in 1938, profiled trailblazers in the field of landscape architecture.[1] Headlines such as "Field is Dominated by a Group of Brilliant Designers of Horticultural Vistas," "Countrysides Made Over," and "Saga of Feminine Achievement Tells of Miracles on Estates, Parks, and Fair Grounds" attest to the newsworthiness of the topic. In addition to highlighting the achievements of these women, the feature also revealed their struggles for identity as well as some of the obstacles they encountered, such as the social stigma of entering a profession and the practicalities of obtaining training, landing clients, and managing a viable practice. This essay focuses on some of the pioneering women who helped shape the American landscape beginning in the early 1900s. Ellen Shipman, Marian Coffin, Beatrix Farrand, and Martha Brookes Hutcheson are among the most pre-eminent names associated with this era, but there are scores of other important women whose careers remain elusive due to lack of extant gardens, archives, or writings by and about them.

Ellen Shipman summed up the situation for the *Times* in her statement, "before women took hold of the profession, landscape architects were doing cemetery work.... Until women took up landscaping, gardening in this country was at its lowest ebb. The renaissance of the art was due largely to the fact that women, instead of working over their boards, used plants as if they were painting pictures. Today women are at the top of the profession."[2] Recognition for their work, however, was slow to come. Shipman and other "trailblazers" began their professional lives in an era when women were stereotyped as guardians of the home and gardening was considered part of the cult of domesticity. Also, landscape design was considered an elitist profession in the early years, especially among women whose achievements were often marginalized and sometimes invisible.

Magazine articles and books published in the 1910s and 1920s clearly show that sophisticated planting design not only had its place in landscape architecture, but was almost exclusively a woman's domain. The Boston architect Guy Lowell (1870–1927) commented that "a woman will *fuss* with a garden in a way that no man will ever have the patience to do. If necessary she will sit on a campstool and see every individual plant into the ground."[3] The early 1900s saw an explosion of interest in home gardening through the publication of popular books, such as Helena Rutherfurd Ely's *A Woman's Hardy Garden* (1904) and Mabel Osgood Wright's *The Garden You and I* (1906), that were aimed specifically at women to inspire them to channel their excess creativity into gardening. Garden historian Alice Morse Earle's (1851–1911) books, such as *Old-Time Gardens* (1901) and *Sundials and Roses of Yesterday*

Sun Dials and Roses and **Old Time Gardens** (1902) by Alice Morse Earle (author's collection).

Beatrix Farrand (1872–1959), Santa Barbara, California, 1943 (courtesy the Beatrix Farrand Society).

(1902), provided the stylistic underpinnings for Shipman and other female designers of her generation. The old-fashioned gardens that Earle wrote about (now called Colonial Revival gardens) are identified by their geometric, four-square layout, lush perennial borders, and simple architectural embellishments.[4]

In 1893, Mariana Griswold Van Rensselaer's book *Art Out-of-Doors: Hints on Good Taste in Gardening* had brought aristocratic recognition to gardening arts in this country. A highly respected art and architectural critic, Van Rensselaer (1851–1934) defined the landscape gardener as "a gardener, an engineer, and an artist, who like an architect considers beauty and utility together."[5] Her book received a lukewarm review from landscape architect Charles Eliot (1859–1897), a partner in the Olmsted office, who questioned the perceived limitations of her viewpoint. He wrote, "Ever since man became man he has been remodeling the face of the earth, but it is to be regretted that no general account of either the breadth or the depth of the subject is to be found in this book ... good 'out-of-doors' must be founded in rationality, purpose, fitness ... the essentially *virile* and practical nature of the art and profession is ignored."[6] Virility versus femininity in landscape design would dominate the formative years of the profession.

One of the main issues that women had to deal with was one of attitude. As contemporary landscape architect Diane Kostial McGuire has written, Beatrix Farrand (1872–1959) "was spoken of disparagingly at an ASLA [American Society of Landscape Architects] meeting by one of her male colleagues as a woman who had 'a bedroom practice' where she turned out a little work occasionally between cards and tea."[7] In 1894, Frederick Law Olmsted, Sr. (1822–1903), one of the country's foremost landscape architects, dismissed Beatrix Jones (as she was then known) as someone "inclined to dabble in landscape architecture."[8] Today Farrand has achieved legendary status as one of America's premier landscape architects. By setting high professional standards, ranging from successful office management to the donation of her papers to a university archives for use by future generations, Farrand paved the way for other women to follow in her footsteps. Farrand worked for some of the most elite families of the day, including the Rockefellers in Maine and the Blisses at Dumbarton Oaks in Washington, D.C. In addition, the publication of Farrand's *Plant Book for Dumbarton Oaks* is considered a model for enlightened preservation of gardens.

Farrand, who came from a prominent family with many important artistic and social connections, including her aunt Edith Wharton, was able to prepare for her career through travel abroad and private study. One of her most important mentors was Charles Sprague Sargent (1841–1927), founder of the Arnold Arboretum, Boston, who advocated women taking up callings that brought them into the "healthy open air."[9] But what options were available for like-minded women from less genteel families? In 1901, the founding of the Lowthorpe School of Landscape Gardening for Women in Massachusetts signaled the begin-

Mélisande's Allée at Dumbarton Oaks, former estate of Robert and Mildred Bliss, Washington, D.C. (photograph by Richard Cheek).

ning of a new era for training women for careers in gardening arts. The Pennsylvania School of Horticulture for Women followed in 1910, and five years later the Cambridge School for Domestic and Landscape Architecture was founded. Graduates from these institutions provided a talented workforce for the exclusively female-run firms, such as those founded by Farrand and Shipman. Many graduates subsequently established their own firms.

In the early 1900s "landscape gardening" was the preferred term used by women. Farrand, for example, referred to herself as a landscape gardener in the Reptonian sense, not a landscape architect. "A young woman [who] would shrink affrighted from the thought of meddling with anything so ambitious as landscape architecture conceives herself quite capable of mastering the art of landscape gardening," wrote one journalist in 1908.[10] Even by 1916, when an article on the Lowthorpe School appeared in *House Beautiful*, the idea of women taking up landscape gardening as a career was still not regarded seriously. "Perennial borders filled with flowers and girls" and other captions for the article expressed the attitudes of the day regarding working women.[11] "The man in this feminine paradise does not seem to be suffering ... the proper kind of feminism — he leans on his rake while the girls dig the trench" and "at these sloping tables are drawn and rendered to be technical those plans of gardens that look too good to come true" are observations that would not have appeared in an article about the Olmsted office.

In the early 1900s, a stigma about working women persisted. Occupations for a well-brought-up woman from a good, but not wealthy family were restricted to nursing, writing, education, and similar, socially acceptable pursuits. Beatrix Farrand's mother, Mary Cadwalader Jones, was an early advocate of careers for women and wrote articles for *Scribner's Magazine* upon the subject which undoubtedly influenced the direction of her daughter's life. Mrs. Rayne's popular self-help manual of the early 1900s, *What Can a Woman Do?*, had pages of advice for women in the business world, but the professions of architecture and landscape architecture were overlooked, presumably because they were not considered within the established realm of what a women could do at that time. During this era, women from the higher social echelons were often encouraged to channel their excess energy into charitable endeavors. Landscape architect Annette Hoyt Flanders (1887–1946), for example, designed gardens for many years before charging fees for her work.

In 1900, when Martha Brookes Hutcheson (1871–1959) announced her intentions of taking up a career in landscape design and, worse still, wanted to attend the new program at the Massachusetts Institute of Technology to which women were admitted briefly as special students, her family pleaded with her to change her mind about attending a technical school, with its inherent social ostracism — they even offered to send her to Europe and give her a free hand in designing the family property. "I was fired with the desire ... in spite of the fact that it was considered almost social suicide and distinctly matrimonial suicide for a woman to enter any profession," Hutcheson said.[12] She walked around the block three times before she could bring herself to climb "those awful steps" to MIT. Fortunately she did and was able to receive exceptional training in Beaux Arts design and planning principles under the direction of Guy Lowell. But even Lowell did not wholeheartedly encourage women to take up the profession: "don't go into it unless you simply can't keep out," he advised.[13]

Within a year of attending MIT, Hutcheson landed a number of important commissions in the Boston area that confirm her predilection for classically inspired layouts, the result of her training under Lowell at MIT. The Lowthorpe program, in contrast, emphasized planting design and maintenance. Hutcheson is also important for her book, *The Spirit of the Garden* (1923), which was recently hailed as the "first account by a woman practitioner to combine a discussion of design with an extensive visual presentation of her own work."[14] A number of Hutcheson's commissions, including Maudesleigh, the former Frederick Moseley estate in Newburyport, Massachusetts (now Maudsley State Park), and the Longfellow House Garden, in Cambridge, Massachusetts (now a National Park Service property), are undergoing rehabilitation, thanks to an increased awareness of her work.

Marian Cruger Coffin (1876–1957), another exemplar designer in the same league as Hutcheson, also attended MIT as a special student, graduating in the Class of 1904. She was one of only a handful of women to complete the program before it was discontinued a few years later. In speaking about the profession, she told an interviewer, "Unless a woman has capital, or influence, or is able to get into a good office, she is very foolish to take up the profession as a means of support."[15] After finishing their studies, women found that the male-dominated design firms would not hire them, another significant hurdle they encountered. Presumably women disrupted the morale of male workers or were considered unable to prepare construction drawings or supervise field work. "It is hard to get a start," Coffin claimed, "as there is a prejudice in many offices against employing women.... A woman has to solve many problems and learn the ropes entirely by herself, while a man has the advantage of long office training and experience."[16]

Coffin promptly opened up her own office, accepting commissions that can be traced to invaluable family connections, such as the duPont family at Winterthur, where her com-

Maudsley State Park, former Frederick Moseley estate, Newburyport, Massachusetts (photograph Pressley Associates, Landscape Architects).

prehensive scheme involved an exceptional degree of design responsibility, going well beyond the limitations of garden design. Despite a recent biography, an understanding of Coffin's work remains somewhat fragmentary. In addition to Winterthur, Coffin is primarily remembered for two other high profile gardens: Gibraltar, the former Rodney Sharp estate, in Wilmington, Delaware, which has recently been restored, and the former Childs Frick estate on Long Island.

Unlike, Farrand, Hutcheson, and Coffin, all of whom pursued careers as young women, Ellen Shipman (1869–1950) came from another track. In 1910, when she was in her early forties and living in rural New Hampshire, Shipman took up a career to support herself and her children. Her Main Line Philadelphia family reputedly was not thrilled with her decision to take up garden design as a career. Because she was homebound and unable to attend the Lowthorpe School, she trained informally with the country house architect Charles A. Platt (1861–1933). Shipman proved to be an extraordinarily gifted planting artist based on years of hands-on experience in her country garden long before she turned professional, around 1912. After learning the rudiments of design and construction from Platt, she began her legendary collaboration with him, designing lush plantings to harmonize with his classical architectural elements. She soon rose to the top of her profession, specializing in small residential properties that were featured in *House Beautiful* and other magazines. At the heart of her work was her sophisticated plantsmanship and her ability to create simple, yet intimate garden settings. By the early 1920s she was at the peak of her career, managing a New York office with as many as a dozen female employees. Not until the 1930s did she begin to receive larger, more comprehensive commissions, such as Longue Vue Gardens in New Orleans and the terrace gardens at Duke University in North Carolina.[17]

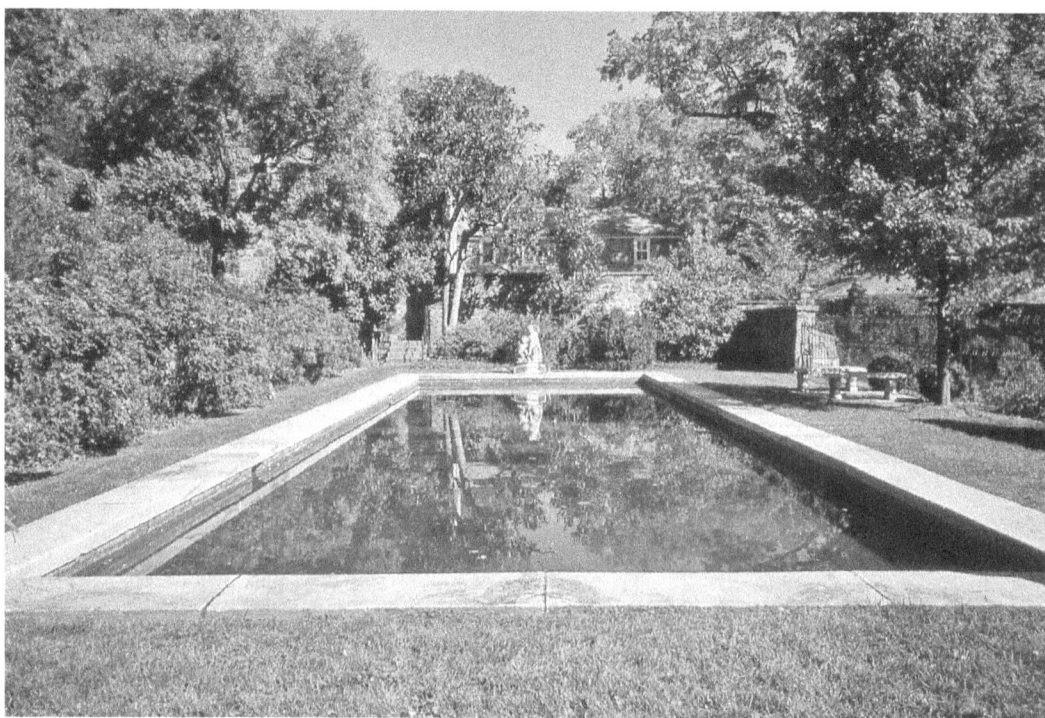

Gibraltar, former Rodney Sharp Estate, Wilmington, Delaware (photograph Judith B Tankard).

On the whole, Shipman's work has not fared as well as Farrand's. Of her 600 commissions (400 more than Farrand, for example), only a handful are in any recognizable form today due to alterations or destruction. She has no equivalent of Farrand's Dumbarton Oaks or Coffin's Winterthur. The rehabilitation of Chatham Manor, Fredericksburg, Virginia (now a National Park Service property), a number of years ago, as well as the walled garden at Stan Hywet Hall, Akron, Ohio, represent the beginnings of awareness of Shipman's significance as a landscape architect. More recently, her gardens at the Cummer Museum of Art and Gardens in Jacksonville, Florida, were rediscovered after lying dormant for decades and replanted with the aid of Shipman's archives held at Cornell University.

Shipman remains somewhat of an anomaly. Unlike Farrand, Hutcheson, and Coffin, she was not affiliated with the prestigious ASLA, as most of her clientele came from the garden club circuit. She was, however, a staunch advocate for women in the profession, once remarking that "There is no profession so suited to [women], so needed and so repaying in every way — nor any that at once give so much of health, wealth and happiness."[18] Her advocacy extended to her nationwide lectures and a bustling New York office, which served as a training ground for scores of young women, mostly recruits from the Lowthorpe School, whom she guided through the practicalities of preparing construction drawings, supervising field work, and running a business. Elizabeth Leonard Strang (1886–1948), one of her earliest

Ellen Shipman (1869–1950), New York, New York, early 1920 (courtesy Nancy A. Streeter).

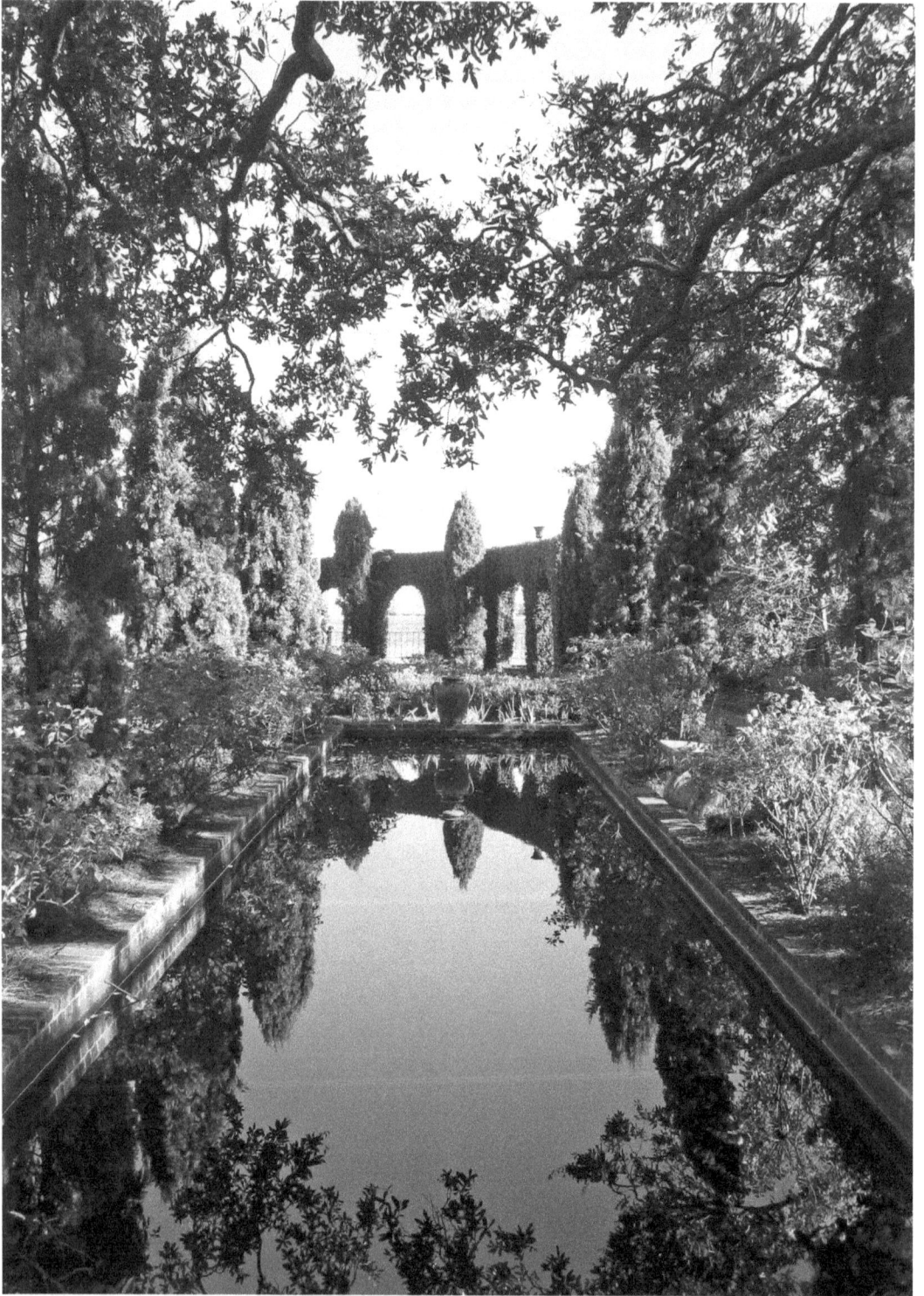

Italian Garden at the Cummer Museum of Art and Gardens, Jacksonville, Florida (photograph by Judith B. Tankard).

recruits, worked in Shipman's office after training at Cornell and later opened her own office specializing in residential garden design. Elizabeth Lord (1887–1976) and her partner, Edith Schryver (1901–1984), who worked in Shipman's office in the mid–1920s, were both Lowthorpe graduates, and in 1929 opened up the first female-managed landscape architectural office on the west coast, in Salem, Oregon.

The careers of countless other women are only now being resurrected from oblivion, but the absence of archives and office records remains the chief obstacle to research. One example is Nellie B. Allen (1869–1961), a graduate of the Lowthorpe program in 1919 who had a brief career based in suburban New York in the 1920s and 1930s. The lack of systematic archives and a paucity of biographical information have significantly hampered an in-depth career profile. A chance discovery of a brief note in a book on the English garden designer Gertrude Jekyll, stating that Allen had visited Munstead Wood (Jekyll's home in England), provided a link to an American landscape architect who was greatly influenced by the English designer. The subsequent discovery that Allen had designed numerous gardens along the east coast instigated a serious investigation of her career; family members produced examples of her Lowthorpe school work, including watercolor renderings and a set of tracings of borders designed by Jekyll.

Like many of her female colleagues, Allen specialized in planting design, especially perennial flower borders, the result of her training at Lowthorpe. Allen's proclivity for English Elizabethan-inspired knot gardens, clipped topiaries, and sophisticated flower borders resulted from her frequent travels to Britain and her meeting with Jekyll. Allen's clients include Frank E. Bliss, Clifford McCall, Anne Morgan and Anne Vanderbilt, and Mrs. Oakleigh Thorne, among others.[19] Allen's career is not unlike those of dozens of women who

"A Persian Garden" by Nellie B. Allen for Lowthrope School, 1919 (author's collection).

never became prominent figures due to family responsibilities, insufficient training, or lack of opportunities.

Although better known than Allen, the Boston-based landscape designer Rose Standish Nichols (1872–1960) remains an equally elusive figure, due mainly to the fact that her work record was inadvertently discarded by family members shortly after her death. With the exception of a collection of vintage slides taken in the 1930s and housed at the Smithsonian Institution, few photographs exist that show her gardens in their heyday and to date no extant plans have been found. Her uncle, the American Renaissance sculptor Augustus Saint-Gaudens (1843–1907), initially pointed Nichols in the direction of garden design in the early 1890s. One of America's earliest female garden designers, Nichols studied briefly at MIT in 1899 and tutored privately with architect Charles Platt, among others. Like Allen, she specialized in the design and planting of small residential gardens.

Her first garden, for her family's summer home in Cornish, New Hampshire, was included in Guy Lowell's book, *American Gardens* (1902), the only garden designed by a woman to be included. Laid out in 1896, when Farrand was just beginning her career and fifteen years before Shipman embarked on hers, the garden showed the promise of a budding career. Nichols's style was formulated on the gardens of England and Italy as well as American Colonial Revival gardens. In all, she designed about 70, but few are extant and little is known about most of them. Most are concentrated in Lake Forest, Illinois, where she collaborated with architects David Adler and Howard Van Doren Shaw, both

Rose Standish Nichols (1872–1960), watercolor by Taylor Greer, 1912 (courtesy Nichols House Museum, Boston). *Right: English Pleasure Gardens* by Rose Standish Nichols (author's collection).

followers of Platt. In these projects, her design responsibilities were confined primarily to plantings alone. In her other commissions, ranging from Santa Barbara and Tucson, to Georgia and the New York-New England area, she sometimes had a greater hand in laying out the entire property.

Nichols is better known as the author of three important books on historic gardens. An astute critic, with an excellent grounding in history based on extensive travels abroad, Nichols was a distinguished garden historian, writing dozens of articles for *House Beautiful* between 1909 and 1930, in addition to three books. While Elizabeth Strang, Ruth Dean, Rose Greely, Louise Payson, and other contemporary garden writers focused on the practicalities of planning and maintenance, Nichols concentrated on historic gardens and trends in garden design, such as Futurist gardens in Germany and modern movement gardens in England. Nichols's first book, *English Pleasure Gardens* (1902), is one of the first comprehensive treatments of the subject, and her later volumes, *Spanish and Portuguese Gardens* (1924) and *Italian Pleasure Gardens* (1928), are both considered standard works on the subject.

These brief profiles offer a representative sampling of some of the female trailblazers who staked out their own turf in the early years of the profession. Some, like Nichols and Shipman, worked as collaborators with male architects and landscape architects, while others, notably Farrand and Coffin, set out to prove that they were quite capable of doing it all. Each one proved that women, too, were leaders in the profession.

Notes

1. Anne Peterson, "Women Take the Lead in Landscape Art," *New York Times*, 13 March 1938.
2. Peterson, "Women Take the Lead in Landscape Art."
3. Quoted in Mary Bronson Hartt, "Women and the Art of Landscape Gardening," *Outlook* 88 (March 28, 1908): 697.
4. Judith B. Tankard, "Ellen Biddle Shipman's Colonial Revival Garden Style," in *Re-creating the American Past: Essays on the Colonial Revival*, edited by Richard Guy Wilson, Shaun Eyring, and Kenny Marotta (Charlottesville, 2006), 67–80.
5. Mrs. Schuyler Van Rensselaer, *Art Out-of-Doors: Hints on Good Taste in Gardening* (New York, 1893), 18.
6. Charles W. Eliot, ed., *Charles Eliot Landscape Architect* (Boston and New York: Houghton Mifflin, 1902), 546–47.
7. Diane Kostial McGuire, "Beatrix Farrand's Contribution to the Art of Landscape Architecture," in *Beatrix Jones Farrand (1872–1959): Fifty Years of American Landscape Architecture*, edited by Diane Kostial McGuire and Lois Fern (Washington, DC: Dumbarton Oaks and the Trustees of Harvard University, 1982), 31.
8. Quoted in Hartt, "Women and the Art of Landscape Gardening," 699.
9. Charles Sprague Sargeant, "Women as Landscape Architects." *Garden and Forest* 5, no. 242 (1892): 482.
10. Quoted in Hartt, "Women and the Art of Landscape Gardening," 697.
11. Richard B. Kimball, "A Little Visit to Lowthorpe," *House Beautiful* (March 1916): 111–13, xxvii.
12. Clarence Fowler, "Three Women in Landscape Architecture," *Alumnae Bulletin of the Cambridge School of Domestic and Landscape Architecture* 4, no. 2 (April 1932).
13. Quoted in Hartt, "Women and the Art of Landscape Gardening," 697.
14. Virginia Lopez Begg, "Martha Brookes Hutcheson," in *Pioneers of American Landscape Design*, edited by Charles A. Birnbaum and Robin S. Karson (New York, 2000), 189.
15. Quoted in Fowler, "Three Women in Landscape Architecture."
16. *Ibid.*
17. Judith B. Tankard, *The Gardens of Ellen Biddle Shipman* (New York: Sagapress/Abrams, 1996).
18. "Professional Opinions," *Lowthorpe School Catalogue* (Groton, MA: Lowthorpe School, 1926).
19. Judith B. Tankard, "Nellie B. Allen," in *Pioneers of American Landscape Design*, 3–6.

Bibliography

Anderson, Dorothy May. *Women, Design, and the Cambridge School.* West Lafayette, IN.: PDA Publishers, 1980.

Balmori, Diana, Diane Kostial McGuire, and Eleanor M. McPeck. *Beatrix Farrand's American Landscapes: Her Gardens and Campuses.* Sagaponack, NY: Sagapress, 1985.

Begg, Virginia Lopez. "Mabel Osgood Wright: The Friendship of Nature and the Commuter's Wife." *Journal of the New England Garden History Society* 5 (1997): 35–41.

Birnbaum, Charles A., ed. *Pioneers of American Landscape Design.* New York: McGraw-Hill, 2000.

_____, and Stephanie S. Foell, eds. *Shaping the American Landscape: new profiles from the pioneers of American landscape design project.* Charlottesville: University of Virginia Press, 2009.

Coffin, Marian Cruger. *Trees and Shrubs for Landscape Effects.* New York: Scribner's, 1940.

Earle, Alice Morse. *Old Time Gardens, Newly Set Forth.* New York: Macmillan, 1901.

Eliot, Charles W., ed. *Charles Eliot Landscape Architect.* Boston and New York: Houghton Mifflin, 1902.

Ely, Helena Rutherfurd. *A Woman's Hardy Garden.* New York: Macmillan, 1903.

Fleming, Nancy. *Money, Manure and Maintenance: Marian Coffin, Pioneer Landscape Architect 1876–1957.* Weston, MA: Country Place Books, 1995.

Gebhard, David, ed. *Accents as Well as Broad Effects: Writings on Architecture, Landscape, and the Environment, 1876–1925 by Mariana Griswold Van Rensselaer.* Berkeley: University of California Press, 1996.

Hartt, Mary Bronson. "Women and the Art of Landscape Gardening." *Outlook.* 88 (March 28, 1908): 695–704.

Hutcheson, Martha Brookes. Introduction by Rebecca Warren Davidson. *The Spirit of the Garden.* 1923. Reprint, Amherst: University of Massachusetts Press, 2001.

Jones, Mary Cadwalader. "Women's Opportunities in Town and Country." In *The Woman's Book: Dealing Practically with Modern Conditions of Home-Life, Self-Support, Educational Opportunities, and Every-Day Life.* New York: Scribner's, 1894.

Kimball, Richard B. "A Little Visit to Lowthorpe." *House Beautiful.* March 1916, 111–13.

Knight, Jane Alison. "An Examination of the History of the Lowthorpe School of Landscape Architecture for Women, Groton, Massachusetts, 1901–1945." Master's thesis, Cornell University, Ithaca, New York, 1986.

Lowthorpe School. *Lowthorpe School Catalogue.* Groton, MA: The Lowthorpe School, 1926.

McGuire, Diane Kostial, ed. *Beatrix Farrand's Plant Book for Dumbarton Oaks.* Washington, DC: Dumbarton Oaks and the Trustees of Harvard University, 1980.

_____, and Lois Fern, eds. *Beatrix Jones Farrand (1872–1959): Fifty Years of American Landscape Architecture.* Washington, DC: Dumbarton Oaks and the Trustees of Harvard University, 1982.

Nichols, Rose Standish. Introduction by Judith B. Tankard. *English Pleasure Gardens.* 1902. Reprint, Boston: David R. Godine, 2003.

Peterson, Anne. "Women Take Lead in Landscape Art." *New York Times* March 13, 1935, 83.

Rayne, Mrs. M. L. *What Can a Woman Do: Or, Her Position in the Business and Literary World.* Petersburgh, NY: Eagle Publishing, 1899.

Sargeant, Charles Sprague. "Women as Landscape Architects." *Garden and Forest* 5, no. 242 (1892): 482.

Tankard, Judith B. *Beatrix Farrand: Private Gardens, Public Landscapes.* New York: Monacelli Press/Random House, 2009.

_____. "Designing Their Turf: Pioneer Women Landscape Designers." *Studies in Decorative Arts/Bard Graduate Center* 8, no. 1 (2000–01): 31–53.

_____. *The Gardens of Ellen Biddle Shipman.* New York: Sagapress/Abrams, 1996.

_____. *A Legacy in Bloom: Celebrating a Century of Gardens at The Cummer.* Jacksonville, FL: Cummer Museum of Art and Gardens, 2008.

_____, and Gilbert, Alma M. *A Place of Beauty: The Artists and Gardens of the Cornish Colony.* Berkeley, CA: Ten Speed Press, 2000.

Van Rensselaer, Mariana (Mrs. Schuyler). *Art Out-of-Doors: Hints on Good Taste in Gardening.* New York: Scribner's, 1893.

Way, Thaïsa. *Unbounded Practice: Women and Landscape Architecture in the Early Twentieth Century.* Charlottesville: University of Virginia Press, 2009.

Zaitzevsky, Cynthia. *Long Island Landscapes and the Women Who Designed Them.* New York: W.W. Norton, 2009.

Chapter 7

"City Beautiful" Revisited: An Analysis of 19th Century Civic Improvement Efforts

Bonj Szczygiel

The City Beautiful Movement is readily recognized by most planners, landscape architects, architects and urban historians as a brief period in the United States in which large-scale planning and design impacted urban development. Most will also recognize it as a relatively short-lived phenomenon in urban history, rising in the late 1890s and beginning to receive severe criticism by 1910. Planning historiography of the period routinely references two general types of activity. The primary, and most publicly heralded, was the link to large scale master planning and design — such as park and boulevard systems planning — requiring the guidance of professionals. The second type of activity was marked by the completion of smaller projects — such as billboard removal and street paving — which, in grand sum, had a far reaching impact on towns large and small, but were grassroots-driven. Additionally, the traditional telling of the City Beautiful story has often combined the efforts of men and women — as if united in step — working collaboratively and using shared methods toward a unified goal of urban beautification.[1]

A review of literature on the movement reveals a peculiar disconnect between not only the two diverse activity types, but also between the respective roles of men and women. For example, the historiography has tended, almost exclusively, to address the large scale planning efforts undertaken by prominent men and aspiring professionals, to the exclusion of the small scale efforts. And, while generally signifying the importance of women within the movement, the documentation has been equally exclusive of their actual work. A possible explanation for the exclusionary nature of the literature is that most, if not all, documentation has been directed along a "gender blind" analysis, suggesting that women's actual contributions were considered of equal value and that, presumably, they were similar in nature to those of their male counterparts. But the fact that this time period was one of significant cultural divisions based on sex differences immediately indicates skepticism about such an approach. The degree to which women were involved in the City Beautiful movement and other urban improvement activities needs to be re-examined under the reality of nineteenth-century gendered cultural opportunities and limitations.

This chapter will examine the historiography of the movement, trace the development of the City Beautiful in comparison to the development of the women's club phenomenon as explored through the General Federation of Women's Clubs, examine the emergence of City Beautiful's national identity as associated with large-scale urban planning efforts, and consider the overall significance of club women's work within the tumultuous rise and fall of City Beautiful.

"City Beautiful" Historiography

In the arena of American urban planning history there has been nothing so evocative and immediately recognizable as the urban form normally associated with the City Beautiful movement: classically-inspired, monumental architecture; wide, tree flanked boulevards and large civic spaces; the grand urban axis punctuated with statuary, or obelisk. The most famous expression of the movement in the United States is the mall and surrounding area in Washington, D.C., along with lesser known achievements in places like Chicago, Kansas City, and Denver. This highly public face of City Beautiful has been clearly, and correctly, associated with white, middle-class, male-dominated leadership who developed particular methods of operation. These included: the reliance on professional opinion in the name of efficiency and beauty; a search for reform by working within the political and economic structures; and belief in the positive effects of behavior modification through environmental improvement. The historiography on the movement also indicates a shared involvement of both men and women. And yet the first two elements of that method of operation would immediately indicate the exclusion of women from meaningful involvement since access to higher education (necessary to obtain professional status) and access to political structures (at a time when most were not allowed suffrage even at state level). These were difficult, if not impossible, obstacles to overcome. The reality of women's position in society then begs the question of exactly to what degree, and in what manner, they were involved in City Beautiful.

In general, historians of the planning professions have relied on a succession of momentous personalities and the occasional revolutionary idea to document the profession's evolution. In *Making the Invisible Visible*, Leonie Sandercock points to that tradition of history writing as one of seeking to document the "official story."[2] She suggests that historiography of planning is very much a product of modernist traditions, which poses certain limitations. Not only does she question the methods used in the past but also the most elemental assumptions made about the profession, including its definition. Who, she asks, has decided what is the proper planning process, and how have planners come to understand what was in the public interest; she even questions, which "public" is being served. By relying on a pantheon of heroes and celebrating their contributions to the exclusion of lesser known figures (such as women and minorities), by painting its history as unproblematic (one of good fighting evil) and by not questioning attitudes and assumptions brought to the job, the official story is, at its very best, incomplete: "The boundaries of planning history are not fixed, not a given. These boundaries shift in relation to the definition of planning and to the historian's purpose. If we define planning as the profession, and its objective as city building, we generate one set of histories. If we define planning as community building, we generate another.... The point is that the writing of histories is not simply a matter of holding a mirror to the past and reporting on what is reflected back. It is always a representation, a textual reconstruction ... shaped by the questions we ask."[3]

This positionality — the historian's lens — helps to understand why the significant books and articles on the history of planning, and in particular that of City Beautiful, sound very similar in celebrating largely predictable people and events. While I believe there is clear value to this approach, one must also recognize the significant omissions. The lens often utilized in the historiography of the City Beautiful movement is that of the "master plan." The key elements unifying these histories was master planning of large urban systems (roads, parks, buildings etc.) as guided by male professionals working with prominent men and public officials. Given women's relative exclusion from such a process, when attempting to understand the role women played in civic improvement, the lens — of necessity — must change.

Women's work was indeed essential for the rise of City Beautiful but they remained firmly apart from the movement's male-driven, professionally-guided methods, operating instead in different modes and places. Women's improvement methods had been developed as early as the mid–1800s and were carried through into the Progressive Era. In contrast, and amid growing criticism of its empty aesthetics and top-heavy decisions made by private individuals and businesses, City Beautiful died a relatively quick death. Rhetoric appeared as early as 1909 from detractors. Calls were heard for a city practical, or a city livable with attention paid to the sociological aspect of poverty. In contrast to its rapid rise and fall, women's club work continued steadily and was sustained, given their methods of smaller scale achievements, through cooperative engagement by all community members. Instead of collaboration toward shared beautification goals implied in the conventional descriptions, men and women acted, for the most part, separately and differently. This is best understood by placing into context the period's rise of professionalism and women's role in nineteenth-

Too many cities are planning magnificent civic centers like this

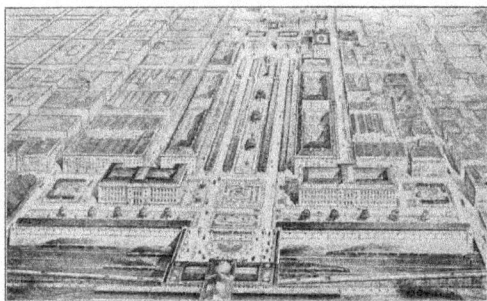

While paying too little attention to present conditions like this

GROUP PLAN OF THE PUBLIC BUILDINGS OF CLEVELAND, OHIO

PLAN FOR FOUNTAIN AT END OF MALL, CLEVELAND, WITH GARDENS, TERRACES, FORMAL TREES AND REFLECTING POOL

THESE WRETCHED DWELLINGS IN CLEVELAND HAVE BEEN CONDEMNED IN THE CAMPAIGN FOR A MORE BEAUTIFUL AND HEALTHFUL CITY

A 1912 commentary on the limitations of City Beautiful. *The American City*, July 1912, pp. 60–561.

century society. Sociologist Anne Witz has put forth a theory that addresses the newly acquired reliance on professionalism in her book, *Professions and Patriarchy*. By relating the rise of the professions to gender, she offers a theory that validates the need for the reconsideration of City Beautiful.

Consider the following address delivered by a male speaker to a 1908 General Federation of Women's Clubs convention held in Boston, regarding the question of how best to accomplish municipal improvement:

> You would not consent, any of you, to have an architect or artist order your dinners or run the servants of your house, and there is no earthly reason why the committees appointed to deal with these municipal improvements should not at once appreciate the fact that in certain points of action they are necessarily ignorant, because they have not been trained, and they shall go to the very best men in the profession, and let the action of these men upon those points be absolutely autocratic.[4]

A sociological framework of "patriarchal capitalism" put forth by Witz is helpful in understanding the actions of both men and women civic improvers, and the above quote. The use of the term patriarchy is not the narrowly defined reference to the power of the head of the household, but a broader reference to gender relations in which men are dominant. According to Witz "[t]o speak of the patriarchal structuring of gender relations is to describe the ways in which male power is institutionalized within different sites of social relations in society."[5] As well, she situates the rise of professionalization within the historical matrix of industrial capitalism. Witz suggests that with an eye toward financial rewards, the newly emerging professions strove to form organizations which would set standards and control the dissemination of knowledge, enabling them to dominate the market. As they standardize and restrict access to their knowledge, they are in a position of controlling the market. As has been observed by other scholars, the process by which occupations were transformed into powerful and rewarding professions occurred independent of women's interests.[6]

Witz has succeeded in mapping out a less androcentric method of discussing a dual framework by moving away from the assumption that to be a professional, at one time, meant to be male. Referring to this as paradigmatic of a particular time in history, and therefore, too rigid to be of much value, Witz prefers to use the phrase "professional projects" as a way to avoid the generic and to cast a more historically-specific frame that would allow discussion of both men's and women's professional experiences. In this case, nineteenth-century men were in a particularly good position to advance. "Professional projects are strategies of occupational closure which seek to establish a monopoly over the provision of skills and competencies in a market for services."[7] One way to obtain occupational closure is to utilize credentialist strategies, educational tactics such as requiring formal education or implementing accreditation standards, or a legalistic tactic such as requiring licensure or registration from the state.[8] Central to the rise of professional projects, then, are these exclusionary tactics. Given this theoretical framework the rise of the City Beautiful movement begins to make sense as diverging from the work undertaken by women volunteers, and begins to offer an explanation of why and how men and women differed in their approaches of civic improvement.

Another important aspect to the patriarchal system has been presented by Keith M. Macdonald in his book *The Sociology of the Professions*. He follows Witz's definition of patriarchy but elaborates that it is a system of behavior rather than a static structure of cause and effect. Indeed, he suggests it is like a language. And, because it has been embedded in our primary socialization in an almost indelible way, its importance has been overlooked. He suggests, "[i]t is for this reason that [patriarchy] is to be found embodied in social institutions (such as the state or the system of economic production), in culture, in social relationships and in language. It is, to change the metaphor, part of the grammar of society and social interaction; it is inherent in the structure of social existence, but unless our attention is drawn to it, we remain unconscious of it ... patriarchy is not merely *like* language; in one respect, it *is* language.[9]

Language is a powerful social tool, especially when it is employed in discursive strategies, as a means to distance the privileged from less privileged, men from women, the professional from non-professionals. Discursive strategies, in this sense, are those words which carry value and the meaning of male superiority. As well, Macdonald concludes, silence is also a type of word usage that can significantly diminish.

What is being suggested here, simply put, is that instead of uniform movement toward shared improvement goals, male experts moved into what had previously been female territory. The program and the language was then modified to suit the new aura of professionalism, and ostensibly, to keep "irregulars" (such as untrained women) from positions of authority. This did not, though, keep the professionals from wanting to enlist women as foot soldiers for the cause, thus explaining the peripheral involvement of women and the historiographic narrative about the importance of their involvement. Having said that, I also do not mean to suggest that women were entirely estranged from the master planning process. Neither is it being suggested that these differing roles were completely forced upon participants; many club women came from the leisure class and would have shared many attitudes with their well-to-do husbands. Indeed, club women may have felt a common cause with their male counterparts, which helps to explain a loose association with City Beautiful organizations. But men's and women's experience — and methods — were largely different in that they reflected the era's cultural

One of the favored "gifts" women's clubs offered were drinking fountains. From *American City*, June 1912, p. 788.

A cleaning campaign that resulted in safe bicycle paths and improved train station grounds. From *New England Magazine*, October 1901, p. 206.

assignments based on gender. The methods employed by women in civic improvement continued into the Progressive Era, at which time they were also adopted by men to be used jointly to bring about all manner of civic reform. Women's work remained unaffected by the rise and fall of City Beautiful; indeed, club membership skyrocketed the first decade of the twentieth century. Their methods, as first utilized in villages and then eventually in communities large and small, were based on: a shared belief in personal responsibility of all citizens; a belief in the importance of collective action and cooperation; embrace of small projects that could be easily implemented; a belief in the essential *responsibility* of the governmental body to aid in matters of social welfare; and, a middle-class, elitist attitude of desiring to shape citizen behavior through environmental modification. Only the last could be said to be shared by both men's and women's platforms. Given the essential differences in approaches, a closer examination of women's work is needed.

Women's Improvement Work and the GFWC

It is probable that women's civic improvement efforts have been largely ignored in planning historiography because their activities could not be translated into one of history's big moments, and because they largely represented the accomplishments of women in volunteer organizations and thus were dismissed as inconsequential. Women's volunteerism in the nineteenth century definitely was not inconsequential. The women's club movement is understood to have been significant in the history of the United States. There is a wealth of recent scholarship that addresses not only the club phenomenon but also its impact on the public identity of nineteenth-century American women. Beginning after the Civil War women began to build a non-sectarian public identity. In the 1894 World's Congress of Representative Women, the President of the Woman's Republican Association of the U.S. spoke to its estimated 150,000 attendants about their new public role: "having learned the possibilities of their united ministrations outside home walls, [women] took up the organization

A typical scenario, clubwomen purchased and improved the grounds, the town then took over maintenance. From *American City*, July 1912, p. 870.

of missionary and temperance societies, and began reforms of many kinds; they built fountains for the thirsty and planted shade-trees for the weary.... In these works of charity, philanthropy, and reform, women's leadership is undisputed."[10]

Scholars have debated whether such volunteerism advanced, or defeated, women's status in society. Some have argued that, given the imagery of domesticity that followed the now-public woman, such activities did not advance women's rights. Others, though, see club women as early feminists and credit them to an evolving feminist consciousness. It may be helpful to consider the words of feminist historian, Carroll Smith-Rosenberg: "We see history as an ongoing struggle between women and men actors for control of the script, a struggle that ultimately transforms the play, the players — even the theatre itself. But if we reject the view of women as passive victims, we face the need to identify the sources of power women used to act within a world determined to limit their power, to ignore their talents, to belittle or condemn their actions."[11]

Belonging to a club and doing meaningful work was a way of building authority and self-confidence. It is certain that many club women felt, for the first time, empowered outside of the home. As eloquently stated in the preface to *Clubwoman as Feminist*, "whether dedicated to social reform or to self-improvement, women's clubs had in common their power to afford women a more complete, and therefore a more authentic, self-expression."[12]

According to contemporary accounts one of the first clubs to form did so in 1853 for the purposes of village improvement; improvement work would become a significant call-to-action for middle-class women throughout the century. In its first year of organization the Laurel Hill Association of Springfield, Massachusetts, planted 423 trees, and prizes were given to the best shade tree planted or sidewalk improved.[13] Roughly forty years later, it

was estimated the total number of trees planted was 4,000. As well, the women had successfully lobbied the railroad company to improve its grounds and erect a new "elegant"
station.[14] These small projects — installing water fountains on city streets, paving sidewalks,
cleaning streets, developing small parks, tree planting — provided instant gratification to
women who had previously been anchored to the home. The strength of this can be felt in
just about every printed speech, meeting minutes and correspondence of club women. Consider the words of Julia Ward Howe, representing the New England Woman's Club at a
small gathering of women in New York City:

> When I look upon this assembly it takes away my breath a little to think how much it repre-
> sents.... We shall be witnesses of the truth, of faith to each other and to principle, for the great
> harmonizing power in human nature, which harmonizes the divers and strong power in all these
> things — *a right womanhood* — is placed as the standard. I thank God for the new womanhood, as
> all of you do ... who shall say ... what miracles and opportunities and results and changes it is to
> bring to pass all the world over?[15]

And more poignantly, the words of J.C. Croly, organizer of the meeting: "Today club life
is an accepted thing by men and women. It is admitted to be beneficial, to be doing a work
that is not done in any other direction. It has given what nothing else could, a new life to
middle-aged women."[16]

Once community attention was drawn to the possibilities of improvement, projects
began. In hundreds of communities women raised money or interest or both to have flower
beds installed, unsightly signs and billboards removed, street trees planted and small parks
built. They influenced the look of private residences by holding competitions and awarding
prizes. Endless examples can be given related to this attention to improving the aesthetic,
safety and sanitation status of their communities. Women succeeded in promoting and
building projects which were practical and of direct tangible benefit to the everyday lives
of the people. Women in many communities worked to secure ample supplies of fresh water.
In Lenox, Massachusetts, for example, women improvers raised the funding needed to install
a sanitary sewage system. In Beverly, Massachusetts, Idaho Falls, Idaho, Yankton, South
Dakota, and other communities, refuse was picked up and hauled away, streets were cleaned,
and garbage receptacles were generously dispersed in the landscape. Many organizations
funded and provided the labor for the construction of roads and sidewalks. In the late 1890s
the Women's Town Improvement Association in Westport, Connecticut, provided funds
for the construction of over 2000 feet of sidewalk. In Corte Madera, California, women
improvers during the same period paid for the installation of street lights and maintained
them "until the town realized their value and took over the management and maintenance."[17]
The belief that an improved "public house" benefited the "private house" reverberated
throughout all of these activities. As did the notion that cooperative efforts with public officials and the community at large was essential. Their approach to solving village, town or
city problems was guided by a deep sense of personal responsibility. These were little to no
regional differences.[18] From Petaluma, California, to Huntingdon, Tennessee, to Dayton,
Ohio, the work continued along similar lines. What does stand out is how the success of
one club on a particular project — such as water purification or street paving and cleaning — served as inspiration and guidance nationwide. The vehicle for information dispersal
was the formidable General Federation of Women's Clubs (GFWC), the hugely popular
national organization formed in 1890 — at that small gathering in New York City mentioned
above — to unite women in their diverse club work. News of such successes was presented
at their biennial conferences, sent to State Federation representatives in letter form, and

THE KIRKSVILLE CIVIC LEAGUE'S STREET CLEANERS READY FOR WORK

A Women's League That Keeps the Streets Clean

By Mrs. C. J. Baxter
Chairman Civic League, Kirksville, Mo.

MAYOR'S

PROCLAMATION

Clean-up Week!

From Wednesday, May 1
Till Wednesday, May 8

In compliance with the request of a large number of our citizens, I hereby appoint the first week of May, 1912, as a time for all loyal citizens to co-operate in a general joint effort to put our city ship-shape, by trimming lawns, removing debris, burning brush, painting fences, and by doing all that lies in our power to enhance the beauty and to establish the cleanliness of our homes, as well as the streets and public places, with special effort to the elimination of all unsightly and unsanitary vacant lot accumulations. Our city so beautiful in all its main features, by concerted action of its citizens in attacking the disfiguring details, can become the perfect city for in landscape, as in painting, trifles make perfection, and perfection is no trifle.

G. A. GOBEN, Mayor

IF YOUR STORE FRONT IS DINGY—PAINT IT

IF YOUR AWNING IS RAGGED AND OLD GET A NEW ONE.

IF YOUR WALK IS AN EYESORE TO THOSE TRAVELING OVER IT REPAIR IT OR HAVE A NEW ONE.

IF THERE ARE OLD UNSIGHTLY TRAPS IN FRONT OF YOUR PROPERTY OR IN YOUR ALLEY MOVE THEM

IF THERE HAPPENS TO BE PAPER BLOWING ABOUT YOUR STREET OR BROKEN LIMBS BURN THEM.

IF IN YOUR BACK YARD THERE ARE OLD UNNECESSARY TUMBLE-DOWN SHEDS TEAR THEM DOWN THE GROUND IS VALUABLE AND SUCH THINGS DETRACT FROM THE BEAUTY OF YOUR HOMES—AND THE TOWN

CLEAN OUT ALL BARN YARDS AND STABLES AT ONCE— AND DON'T GIVE THE FLY A CHANCE TO BREED

CLEAN OUT THE ALLEYS BACK OF THE BUSINESS HOUSES AT ONCE

TAKE AWAY ALL ASHES AND RUBBISH FROM YOUR BACK YARD IMMEDIATELY BY ALL MEANS DO YOUR PART TO HELP MAKE KIRKSVILLE A CLEANER AND MORE BEAUTIFUL CITY
                                        G A GOBEN Mayor
                                        KIRKSVILLE, MO.

"A Woman's League that Keeps the Streets Clean." From *American City* 6, July 1912, p. 870.

included in its monthly newsletter to heighten communication among the growing membership. Women learning from women, most of it tactical, the "how to" information needed to get the job done.

Women's improvement clubs thus sought immediate resolution for a host of concerns. They were problem solvers, one project at a time. As a result, projects selected were obvious goals, manageable in scale and able to be implemented immediately. This resulted in the targeting of specific projects such as billboard removal, street cleaning and tree planting at a scale that indicated probable success. Important for the sustainability of their work, this was a method that placed women in the trenches — an aspect which would critically distance their work from that of their male counterparts. They assumed personal responsibility for work to be done, then strove to transfer that ethic onto the larger community to achieve the same essential motivation, feeling that success was to be borne collectively. This cooperative form of organization that involved personal responsibility and shared beliefs remained with these independent improvement organizations as their popularity spread throughout the country.

GFWC was formed so that its members could benefit from others and be mutually helpful.[19] It was an inspired moment for Croly; the GFWC was to become a political forum that would influence national policy on many fronts.[20] But it is the sheer numbers that astound. As early as 1898, and only eight years into its existence, a GFWC report acknowledged there were 595 clubs representing 60,000 individual members and 30 State Federations, composed of 2,110 clubs. Removing the possibility of duplication in membership, the corresponding secretary reported total membership to be 160,000.[21] By 1918, 800,000 individual members were listed nation-wide.[22] Considering that this number does not represent all women engaged in club work (only dues paying GFWC members), the actual number of women involved in voluntary activity nation-wide may have been significantly higher.

It should be noted that GFWC membership was not comprised of radicals. They tended to avoid the controversial issues of suffrage and temperance, drifting instead to more popularly supported topics, staying within the comfort zones of middle class America. Regardless of topic, women's club fever swept the nation. Proudly, in 1892, Croly suggested that women's clubs were so numerous that "you almost tumble over them as you walk the street. Women's clubs have become popular, even fashionable."[23] Echoing that observation, an enthusiastic Mary Caroline Robbins captured the collective spirit of improvement activities in an 1897 *Atlantic Monthly* article: "My lady's quick eye, her relentless spirit, her uncompromising activity, hitherto largely manifested in house-cleaning, here find a broader field to preempt, and the full utilization of that energy which now goes to waste in many futile pursuits may in the end create force enough to sweep this globe from pole to pole, and neatly dust every continent."[24] Women improvers may not have swept the globe, but they did influence the look and function of the American landscape through thousands of individual projects.

Emergence of City Beautiful and Professionalization

> "Civic art is not a fad. It is not merely a bit of aestheticism. There is nothing effeminate and sentimental about it ... it is vigorous, virile, sane" — Charles Mulford Robinson.[25]

Forty-seven years after the first village improvement society was established, and eight years after the GFWC formed, there were some who expressed a need for another national organization — this time inclusive of men — and devoted exclusively to civic improvement. It was in Springfield, Ohio, a small college town located west of Columbus in the heart of a burgeoning mail-order floriculture and publishing center, that interest in a national organization of improvement societies was sparked. In 1898, D. J. Thomas, the local publisher of the monthly magazine *How to Grow Flowers*, printed a series of illustrated articles on improvement societies showing the positive influence of their work. The accounts were written by Jessie M. Good, an energetic, civic-spirited Springfield resident, librarian and avid floriculturist. Neither she nor Thomas anticipated the interest that the articles would generate. Inspired by Good's reports, letters poured into Springfield requesting further information.[26] Heralded as a convening of "Improvement Leagues of America," the magazine organized a convention held on October 10, 1900.[27] Excited about the prospective organization, and perhaps with an eye toward securing a greater customer base, Thomas offered his publication to further broadcast news about improvement work. Corresponding to its added function, in November the magazine name was changed to *Home and Flowers: an Illustrated Monthly Magazine Devoted to The Home Beautiful*. In that revised issue was the expressed ardent belief that "in the home lies the hope of civilization."[28] *Home and Flowers* gave extensive coverage to both improvement activities and floriculture. Its subtitle changed several times, indicating the movement's broadening focus, for example "an illustrated monthly published in the interests of a more beautiful American life," and even, "...devoted to the world beautiful."

Those who attended that first convention in Springfield voted to form a National League of Improvement Associations. It is here that the first signs of change appeared regarding division of labor. The stated objective of the League was "to bring into communication for acquaintance and mutual helpfulness organizations interested in the promotion of outdoor art, public beauty, town, village and neighborhood improvement."[29] While the statement suggests a continuation of the women's previously established emphasis on collaboration, the notion of public beauty and public art is introduced and, if there is significance to the listing order, were considered paramount. As well, the belief in environmental social engineering was now explicitly part of the campaign, as expressed by Thomas: "The power of environment, for good or evil, is coming to be recognized more and more. Those who seek to make the world better are finding that they can do so most effectively through the cultivation of the love of beauty ... the National League of Improvement Associations, therefore, should appeal to all who are interested in the moral welfare of the American people."[30]

Instead of planting trees or improving the grounds of the railroad stations, the language begins to reflect a different set of priorities. It was decided that the League would have a clear hierarchical order with an executive board consisting of president, two vice-presidents, two secretaries, treasurer and national organizer. While women had a strong appearance at the first conference, their future involvement at the executive level, and in membership, would be limited. Women, such as the capable and deserving Jessie Good, would never attain status of President. As the League went through several organizational transitions over the next few years, women were not often seen in positions of authority. Perhaps some of the women involved in the League would not have aspired to such positions. Placed in context, though, I suspect they would have been a minority. This is a time period in which women, more than ever in previous American history, voiced strong opinions against the patriarchal society that limited their own personal aspirations. The existence of an organization such as the GFWC — wholly exclusive of men — with its unwieldy membership,

Women first entered public service under the guise of domesticity, a factor that contributed to their distance from City Beautiful efforts. *American City*, May 1913, p. 599.

suggests, at the very least, a keen restlessness. It is certainly possible that some women looked to the rise of professionalism with deference, even seeking expert aid for their own club. Yet within the pages of GFWC archives there is a strong, unwavering expression of the *ability* of women to bring about change. Indeed one can look exhaustively to find evidence of the League's influence, or any influence by male experts, in vain. Instead individual empowerment was the message, and it ran deep. Yet, to the degree women were involved with the early City Beautiful movement, they were whole-heartedly so. Jessie Good's own words represent that enthusiasm: "No task is too great for these associations to undertake. They will direct the digging of anything from a sewer to a flower bed. They order down your front fences and order up electric lights with equal sangfroid. Water flows at their command."[31]

Through the efforts of Good and others, more local societies joined the National League association. While the organization grew quickly — in 1900 there were just over twenty members; in 1902, 232 members; and in 1903, 340 members — the League represented, in all probability, those clubs in which both men and women were active — a fraction of local groups. The organization's headquarters relocated from Springfield to Chicago in 1902 so as to provide a metropolitan tone which, in turn, would presumably offer greater stature to the male organizers.[32] The League was given further direction from its second President, Charles Zueblin, University of Chicago sociologist. Zueblin was adept at utilizing the power of silence as a dismissive tool. In a retrospective published in 1905 entitled *A Decade of Civic Improvement,* he acknowledged that Stockbridge was the first village improvement society to organize, but does not mention it being a women's club. Ignoring all that took place after that date, he places the country's "great civic awakening" as 1893, the year of the Chicago World's Fair. How to explain the gap? He writes, "The country was not ready for these progressive movements, for the feeling of social obligation was undeveloped."[33] His vision was clearly focused upon the grand scheme of illustrious urban planning and development. In sympathy with a national reform agenda, the name of the association was changed to the American League for Civic Improvement (ALCI) at the second national convention held in Buffalo, New York, and the Chautauqua Institute in August, 1901 (during the Pan-American Exposition). The renamed League now placed its emphasis on "civic" improvement rather than the more limited "village" improvement. With its new national identity came a call for professionalism driven by Zueblin who, prior to being elected president, was on the important committee of Changes in Constitution and By-Laws. That committee played a critical role in the development of a new, divergent identity from that of village improvement. A look at the all-male steering committee membership reads like a who's who in City Beautiful history: Frank Chapin Bray; Albert Kelsey (Philadelphia architect, president of the Architectural League of America); Edwin Shuey, vice-president of the League and member National YMCA; and Charles Zueblin.

Evidence of the new emphasis on large scale master planning is apparent in Zueblin's writing and demonstrates his eagerness for the new agenda. His language served to put nonprofessionals, women and men, in their place. From 1893, he stated that municipal efforts were directed toward something presumably new — goals — determined by "an exchange of experience rather than a blind groping in the dark."[34] He wrote, "unrelated civic improvements, however imperative and worthy, no longer satisfy enlightened citizens. The goal has come to be the comprehensive city plan...."[35] The steady move toward the professionalization of the organization can also be seen in the list of speakers and topics addressed at the second and third conventions and in organizational changes. For example, by 1902 the ALCI had

14 "section councils" or committees in specified interest areas such as "libraries and museums," "municipal art" and "sanitation," with select members — many of whom were professionals — in each interest area to provide expert assistance.[36] During this ideological transition, "village improvement" was demoted to section council status, with Jessie Good as one of only four members.

What eventually emerged from these changes was architect Daniel Burnham's "make no little plans" form of civic improvement, popularly identified as the City Beautiful movement. While grass roots involvement was encouraged, and was thought necessary, it was clearly felt that the village, town or city improvement activities needed to be guided by experts and professionals and that the objectives must be larger, municipal-wide aesthetic planning, the virtual antithesis of the ideas and methods previously developed by the women's improvement organizations. This model for civic change was given greater credibility by journalist Charles Mulford Robinson. While Robinson did not coin the term City Beautiful, he popularized its usage through a number of important publications and directly applied the phrase to the growing male-driven civic improvement movement. At the end of the nineteenth century he published a series of articles for *Atlantic Monthly* and *Harper's Magazine*. The first of those articles gave credit to village improvement associations and the work of women for changing the face of the nation. However, in 1901, while secretary of the ALCI, Robinson published his first book, *Improvement of Towns and Cities*. In it he contributed to the shaping of City Beautiful ideology and, not surprisingly, downplayed the significance of previous improvement efforts: "With a Haussmann or a L'Enfant in our three millions of population, the ideal city, the city beautiful and perfect, would at least be suggested, but what are we doing with it? We are plodding along on village lines, with village methods, marring with patchwork improvements that disfigure, ignoring all teachings of the past, unconscious of all the possibilities of the future."[37]

Only the highly trained professional, Robinson argued, in coordination with enlightened and informed local leaders, was capable of managing the sweeping success that America deserved. Ironically, when Robinson suggested that woman's qualification to be a professional should depend, "not on her experience in wielding a broom, but on the possession of executive ability," women trained to step into such leadership positions were few and far between.[38] As explained by both Robinson and Zueblin, the job of the layperson was to work on small piecemeal projects and to insure the success of large projects by raising money and delivering public support.[39] Zueblin, who argued that the City Beautiful movement was about separate forces unified by the shared goal of improving the urban condition, saw his task (and the task of others in leadership positions) as that of managing the disjointed forces of improvement toward a grander end.

The Merger: Monumental Change and Managed Control

The ALCI was not the only national organization concerned with civic improvement. Landscape architect Warren Manning had founded the American Park and Outdoor Art Association (AP&OAA) in 1897, with the primary task of promoting aesthetic improvement in urban areas. While Manning originally intended the organization to be comprised solely of landscape architects and other professionals with a direct concern for parks in the urban environment, the organization gradually pursued a wider membership.[40] Over time the grassroots improvement was given attention since landscape architects and other planning professionals were few in number. Much of their interest in the improvement movement was spurred by the hundreds of women auxiliary members of the AP&OAA, who focused attention on the topic at national conventions of the organization.[41] Many of the women gave papers highlighting the striking progress village improvement associations had made throughout the nation. Other papers by them scorned the ubiquitous scourge of smoke, dirt, and billboards. By 1902 the AP&OAA, while retaining a large professional membership, had become interested in "considering the question of co-operation and affiliation or union" with the ALCI.[42] While the ALCI had formed from the grass roots and changed to accept leadership and a bureaucracy charged with managing an array of improvement activities, the AP&OAA started as a group of professionals and experts who found it advantageous to broaden its base.

In 1903, Horace McFarland was named president of the ALCI. As president he actively promoted a merger with the AP&OAA since the two organizations had similar interests and many members in common. An agreement was reached at the 1904 Louisiana Purchase Exposition in St. Louis, and the organizations merged to form the American Civic Association (ACA). McFarland was elected president of the new association, a position he held for the next twenty years.

Conclusion

In her exhaustive and far-ranging study of female organizations in the nineteenth century, Ann Firor Scott made the following general observation: "Associations provided careers for many women, careers from which the income was psychic rather than material. In their own groups women learned to be professionals before the traditional professions were open to them, and developed a recognizable female style of professional behavior that relied heavily on cooperation. Reflecting their voluntary-association training, the first women doctors, lawyers, teachers, and ministers often functioned differently from their male counterparts."[43]

In the nineteenth century, the work of women in civic improvement and their membership in organized clubs was profoundly altering. Not only did they alter the physical landscape of their communities, but their self-perception as public individuals. They moved with a collective spirit of female advocacy and advancement; and they moved differently from their nineteenth-century male counterparts regarding civic improvement. History of urban development and of the planning profession has tended to focus on City Beautiful master planning. But there was another critical element to 19th century improvement efforts that was grass roots driven. Had women not come out in force in such large numbers one wonders whether the public ideal of City Beautiful would have ever developed. Certainly women's work manipulating the physical environment in their respective communities would have continued regardless of the guiding hand of a Zueblin or a McFarland. Driven by concerns similar to those of the men — uplifting people morally for greater stability in society — their methods varied significantly. Women worked as equals; they worked together within the community assuming a personal level of responsibility; they effected change from the bottom up. As the national City Beautiful collapsed and the city practical emerged, women's work continued unabated. Male leadership in City Beautiful tended not to concentrate on piecemeal work; in the name of efficiency they utilized the male professional to carve out a master plan. With women's civic work came consistent involvement and personal commitment. They were able to recognize social or physical problems, then took it upon themselves to find a means to intervene in response. The result was not only an improved community, but the feeling of emancipation and growth. The "new woman" of the twentieth century emerged from such unpaid, committed and communal efforts.

Notes

1. An expanded version of this article was originally published in the *Journal of Urban History* 29, no. 2 (January 2003): 107–132.
2. Leonie Sandercock, "Framing Insurgent Historiographies for Planning," in *Making the Invisible Visible: A Multicultural Planning History* , ed. Leonie Sandercock (Berkeley: University of California Press, 1998), reference note 2.
3. *Ibid.*, 6.
4. *The General Federation of Women's Clubs, Ninth Biennial Convention, Official Report,* (Chicago: The General Federation of Women's Clubs, 1908), 128–130.
5. Anne Witz, *Professions and Patriarchy* (London, New York: Routledge, 1992), 11.
6. Penina Migdal Glazer and Miriam Slater, *Unequal Colleagues: The Entrance of Women into the Professions 1890–1940* (New Brunswick: Rutgers University Press, 1987), 3–4.
7. Witz, *Professions and Patriarchy*, 64.
8. *Ibid.*, 64–65.
9. Keith M. Macdonald, *The Sociology of the Professions* (London; Thousand Oaks, CA: Sage, 1995), 125.
10. J. Ellen Foster, "Women as Political Leader," in *The World's Congress of Representative Women*, ed. May Wright Sewall (Chicago: Rand, McNally & Co, 1894), 439–440.
11. Carroll Smith-Rosenberg, *Disorderly Conduct: Vision of Gender in Victorian America* (New York: Alfred A. Knopf, 1985), 17.
12. Annette K. Baxter, preface in *The Clubwomen as Feminist: True Womanhood Redefined, 1868–1914*, by Karen J. Blair (New York: Holmes & Meier, 1980), xii.
13. Referenced in Birdsey Northrup, "The Work of Village Improvement Societies," *Forum* (1895) 95; Mary Caroline Robbins, "Village Improvement Societies," *Atlantic Monthly* 79 (February 1897): 217; Warren H. Manning "The History of Village Improvement in the United States," published in *Craftsman* 5 (February 1904): 426.
14. Northrup, "The Work of Village Improvement Societies," *Forum* (1895), 96.
15. General Federation of Women's Clubs Archives, Founding Documents (Record Group 10). Report of the Twenty-first Anniversary of Sorosis, 1890, 18–19.
16. *Ibid.*, 24–25.
17. Mary Ritter Beard, *Woman's Work in Municipalities* (New York: D. Appleton, 1915), 311.
18. *The American City* 6, no. 6 (New York: The Civic Press, June 1912).
19. J.C. Croly, *The History of the Woman's Club Movement in America* (New York: Henry G. Allen, 1898), 98.
20. Nancy Woloch, *Women and the American Experience*, 2nd ed. (New York: McGraw-Hill, 1994), ch. 12; Priscilla Massman, "A Neglected Partnership: The General Federation of Women's Clubs and the Conservation Movement, 1890–1920, " Ph.D. diss., Department of History, University of Connecticut, 1997.
21. "Fourth Biennial Address," Convention Records (proceedings and reports) 1896–1904, (Record Group 3). Woman's History and Resource Center, General Federation of Women's Clubs headquarters, Washington DC, 1898.
22. Sophonisba Breckinridge, *Women in the Twentieth Century* (New York: Arno Press, 1933), 39.
23. Address written by Jane Cunningham Croly, *Biennial Addresses and Papers*, 102–109, 103.
24. "Village Improvement Societies," *Atlantic Monthly* 79 (1897): 212.
25. Charles Mulford Robinson, *Modern Civic Art*, 1904, 28.
26. Jessie M. Good, "The National League of improvement Associations, a Short History," *Home Florist* 4, no. 1 (1901): 44.
27. "Improvement Associations," *The Press-Republic* (Springfield, Ohio), October 7, 1900, 1.
28. "Name to Our Wider Field," *Home and Flowers*, November, 1900.
29. "Promotion of Civic Beauty," *Home and Flowers*, December, 1900.
30. "A Notable Event," *Home and Flowers*, December, 1900.
31. Jessie M. Good, "The Work of Civic Improvement," *Home Florist* 3, no. 4 (1900): 10.
32. Richard E. Fogelsong, *Planning the Capitalist City: The Colonial Era to the 1920s* (Princeton, NJ: Princeton University Press, 1986), 142.
33. Charles Zueblin, *A Decade of Civic Improvement* (Chicago: University of Chicago Press, 1905), 4.

34. Zueblin, *Ibid.*, 34.
35. *Ibid.*, v–vi.
36. "Work of League," *Home and Flowers*, September, 1902.
37. Charles Mulford Robinson, *Improvement of Towns and Cities* (New York: G.P. Putnam and Sons, 1901), 18–19.
38. *Ibid.*, 47
39. *Ibid.*, 109–110.
40. Wilson, *The City Beautiful Movement*, 36–41.
41. "Park and Art Association," *Home and Flowers*, August, 1901.
42. "Two Civic Events," *Home and Flowers*, October, 1902, 3.
43. Anne Firor Scott, *Natural Allies: Women's Associations in American History*. Chicago: University of Illinois Press, 1993, 3.

Bibliography

"A Notable Event." *Home and Flowers: An Illustrated Monthly Magazine Devoted to the Home Beautiful*. December, 1900.
American City 6, no. 6. (New York: Civic Press, June 1912).
Beard, Mary Ritter. *Woman's Work in Municipalities*. New York: D. Appleton, 1915.
"Biennial Addresses and Papers," "Founding Documents" and "Convention Records (proceedings and reports)." Women's History and Resource Center, General Federation of Women's Clubs Headquarters, Washington, DC.
Blair, Karen J. *The Clubwomen as Feminist: True Womanhood Redefined, 1868–1914*. New York: Holmes & Meier, 1980.
Breckinridge, Sophonisba. *Women in the Twentieth Century*. New York: Arno Press, 1933.
Croly, J.C. *The History of the Woman's Club Movement in America*. New York: Henry G. Allen, 1898.
Fogelsong, Richard E. *Planning the Capitalist City: The Colonial Era to the 1920s*. Princeton, NJ: Princeton University Press, 1986.
"Fourth Biennial Address." Convention Records (proceedings and reports) 1896–1904. (Record Group 3). Woman's History and Resource Center, General Federation of Women's Clubs headquarters, Washington, DC, 1898.
Foster, J. Ellen. "Women as Political Leader." In *The World's Congress of Representative Women*, edited by May Wright Sewall, 439–440. Chicago: Rand, McNally, 1894.
General Federation of Women's Clubs Archives. Founding Documents (Record Group 10). Report of the Twenty-first Anniversary of Sorosis. 1890.
Glazer, Penina Migdal, and Miriam Slater. *Unequal Colleagues: The Entrance of Women into the Professions 1890–1940*. New Brunswick: Rutgers University Press, 1987.
Good, Jessie M. "The Work of Civic Improvement." *Home Florist* 3, no. 4 (1900): 10.
"Improvement Associations." *The Press-Republic*. October 7, 1900, 1.
Macdonald, Keith M. *The Sociology of the Professions*. London; Thousand Oaks, CA: Sage, 1995.
Manning, Warren H. "The History of Village Improvement in the United States." *Craftsman* 5 (February 1904): 426.
Massman, Priscilla. "A Neglected Partnership: The General Federation of Women's Clubs and the Conservation Movement, 1890–1920, " Ph.D. diss., Department of History, University of Connecticut, 1997
Munslow, Alan. *Deconstructing History*. New York: Routledge, 1997.
"Name to Our Wider Field." *Home and Flowers: An Illustrated Monthly Magazine Devoted to the Home Beautiful*. November, 1900.
Northrup, Birdsey. "The Work of Village Improvement Societies." *Forum* (1895): 95.
"Park and Art Association." *Home and Flowers: An Illustrated Monthly Magazine Devoted to the Home Beautiful*. August, 1901.
"Promotion of Civic Beauty." *Home and Flowers: An Illustrated Monthly Magazine Devoted to the Home Beautiful*. December, 1900.
Robinson, Charles Mulford. *Modern Civic Art: Or, The City Made Beautiful*. New York: Arno Press, 1918.
Robbins, Mary Caroline. *Improvement of Towns and Cities*. New York: G.P. Putnam Sons, 1901.
_____. "Village Improvement Societies." *Atlantic Monthly* 79 (February 1897): 212–217.
Sandercock, Leonie. "Framing Insurgent Historiographies for Planning." In *Making the Invisible Visible: A Multicultural Planning History*, edited by L. Sandercock, 1–33. Berkeley: University of California

Press, 1998.

Scott, Anne Firor. *Natural Allies: Women's Associations in American History.* Chicago: University of Illinois Press, 1993.

Smith-Rosenberg, Carroll. *Disorderly Conduct: Vision of Gender in Victorian America.* New York: Alfred A. Knopf, 1985.

The General Federation of Women's Clubs, Ninth Biennial Convention, Official Report. Chicago: General Federation of Women's Clubs, 1908.

"Two Civic Events." *Home and Flowers: An Illustrated Monthly Magazine Devoted to the Home Beautiful.* October, 1902, 3.

Wilson, William H. *The City Beautiful Movement.* Baltimore: Johns Hopkins University Press, 1989.

Witz, Anne. *Professions and Patriarchy.* London, New York: Routledge, 1992.

Woloch, Nancy. *Women and the American Experience.* New York: McGraw-Hill, 1994.

"Work of League." *Home and Flowers: An Illustrated Monthly Magazine Devoted to the Home Beautiful.* September, 1902.

Zueblin, Charles. *A Decade of Civic Improvement.* Chicago: University of Chicago Press, 1905.

Chapter 8

Elsa Rehmann, Ecological Pioneer: "A Patch of Ground"

Dorothy Wurman

Elsa Rehmann was one of America's first women landscape architects. Her visibility was primarily through her writing. She produced three books, one of which, *American Plants for American Gardens*, published in 1929, was unique. This book discussed the use of plant communities (ecological associations) in garden design, a singular approach at a time when garden books espousing the gardenesque style proliferated. The book also translates ecological theory into an art form for the residential gardener. This historic contribution resonates particularly in our new century, in the discourse within the landscape profession concerning ecological aesthetics.

In this venture, Elsa Rehmann's accomplishments include: listing specific plant associations as a basis for design criteria; interpreting these associations, as an art form, into suggested compositions for the home gardener; integrating siting and architectural style as part of the "genius loci"; and writing with scholarly and poetic skill.

This chapter is an attempt to re-establish the lost contribution of a pioneer, as well as present some of her personal background, and the circumstances that produced the book.

Early Life and Education

Ecology apparently did not play any role in the early stages of Elsa Rehmann's life. Elsa Rehmann was born in the Forest Hills "garden city" section of Newark, New Jersey, on 11 April 1886, to Carl F. and Marie Rehmann. Her father had emigrated from Germany to the United States, where he took up the study of architecture. In addition to practicing architecture in Newark, he became principal of a new drawing institution, the Public Drawing School, in 1882, where he presided until his death in 1906. His older daughter, Antoinette, was a graduate of this school, and it is possible that Elsa was as well.

Elsa Rehmann attended Wells College in Aurora, New York from 1904 to 1906, intending to take up writing as a profession. She then transferred to Barnard College in New York City, where she received a BA in 1908. While at Barnard, along with the usual liberal arts subjects, she studied Medieval Architectural History and Geology.

Following her graduation from Barnard, she studied at the Lowthorpe School of Landscape Architecture for Women in Groton, Massachusetts. In reference to this choice of career, Rehmann remembered "that delightful biography [of] *Charles Eliot—Landscape Architect*, to which I owe my first idea of landscape architecture.... This (book) I found by pure chance on a topmost shelf of the Wells College library."[1]

The Lowthorpe School, unique in this country, was founded in 1901 by Mrs. Edward Gilchrist Low. The school trained women to take an active and professional part in gardening, horticulture and landscape architecture, emphasizing, in particular, design and construction. Courses included surveying, engineering, entomology, forestry, and soils. An important focus of the school was to "learn by doing." J.F. Dawson of the Olmsted Brothers taught there during those initial years. The early classes at Lowthorpe were small in number. During the first decade at Lowthorpe, eight students were graduated. Rehmann, having remained at the school until 1911, was probably one of these graduates.[2]

In 1911, Rehmann began an "apprenticeship," working in New York City for tow landscape architects, Charles N. Lowrie of the Hudson County Park System, and Marion Coffin, designer of estate gardens.[3]

During this apprenticeship, Rehmann produced her first book, *The Small Place*, published by Knickerbocker Press in 1918. The book contains fifteen diverse landscape design "problems," each one a chapter. These portrayed residential designs by other landscape architects, among them Marian Coffin, the Olmsted Brothers, Arthur Shurtleff, as well as the firm of Pray, Hubbard and White. Rehmann stated in her introduction that she included "only places that have a well-organized plan." She also said that, "the small places still retains its fascination, for its possibilities, which are generally overlooked, are infinite, and its limitations, which are considered as a drawback, ought to the very means of its making."[4] Numerous reviews praised the book, stating that it was "easily comprehended," "(it) stirs a delightfully personal interest," and was "immensely valuable."[5]

During this same time period, Rehmann also published many magazine articles.[6] These appeared in magazines such as *Garden Magazine*, *Country Life*, *House Beautiful* and *Better Homes and Gardens*. The content of all these articles, in addition to her first two books, comprise the typical "gardenesque" theories of the period.[7, 8]

In 1919, Elsa Rehmann branched out independently. She worked primarily out of her own home at 492 Mt. Prospect Avenue in Newark where her workroom overlooked her own garden.[9] She planned gardens for clients in various parts of Essex County (in Rumson, Elberon, and Tenafly) and other parts of New Jersey, as well as in Pennsylvania, Delaware, New York State and New England. In 1922, Rehmann is listed as teaching a new course, Garden Architectural Design, at the Philadelphia School of Design, noting "Her practical experience as a landscape

Portrait of Elsa Rehmann from Barnard College '08, circa 1907, from the *Mortarboard* 1908, p. 151 (courtesy of the Barnard College Archives).

architect, added to an unusually board training on architectural lines, will make the historical, architectural and practical aspects of the work equally balanced and interesting."

Rehmann produced a second book in 1926, *Garden-Making*, published by the Houghton Mifflin Company. This book included her own garden designs in the gardenesque style. The *New York Times* review states that she "writes with enthusiastic and poetic appreciation."[10]

An example of landscape architecture by Elsa Rehmann taken from the chapter, "The Simplest Kind of Garden" in her book *Garden-Making*, 1926, p. 4.

Similarly, the *New York Herald Tribune* says, "There is a thoroughness and a finish about her work, in writing as well as in her professional activities ... a readable, human and yet scholarly book."[11] Julie Morris, horticulturist at the Blithewold Mansion named *Garden-Making* as a favorite book, and said that Rehmann approached garden making as a fine art, that she was more environmentally aware in many ways than we are today, and that she was skilled in finding the "genius of place." In 1994, Diane Kostial McGuire included a chapter from *Garden-Making* in her book, *American Garden Design*, and said that she believed that Elsa Rehmann wrote with passion and authority.[11]

Ecological Influences

During the 1920s Rehmann became associated with Vassar College, and entered into an association that would alter her landscape philosophy. She is recorded as having lectured in landscape gardening (1923–1924), and in landscape architecture (1925–1927) in the Botany Department. At this time, Edith Roberts, who was considered a pioneer in the new science of plant ecology, was Chair of that department. Roberts had an idea for the development of an out-of-door botanical laboratory for experimental ecology, and in 1920, the College granted the department the use of four acres of land for this project, to become known as the Dutchess County Botanical Garden, financed by Elizabeth Drinker Storer Fund. This botanical laboratory was the first of its kind in the United States.[12] The goal of the project was to establish the plants native to Dutchess County, New York, in their correct associations, with the appropriate environmental factors. It was also hoped that it could demonstrate the use of native plants "blended into an attractive landscape picture."[13]

At this point, a remarkable and significant decision was made — the decision to use the new plant information, not just as a scientific laboratory, but in the context of the fine art of design. Edith Roberts had received her education at the University of Chicago where she undoubtedly was influenced by the "Prairie School" design philosophy of Jens Jensen, and

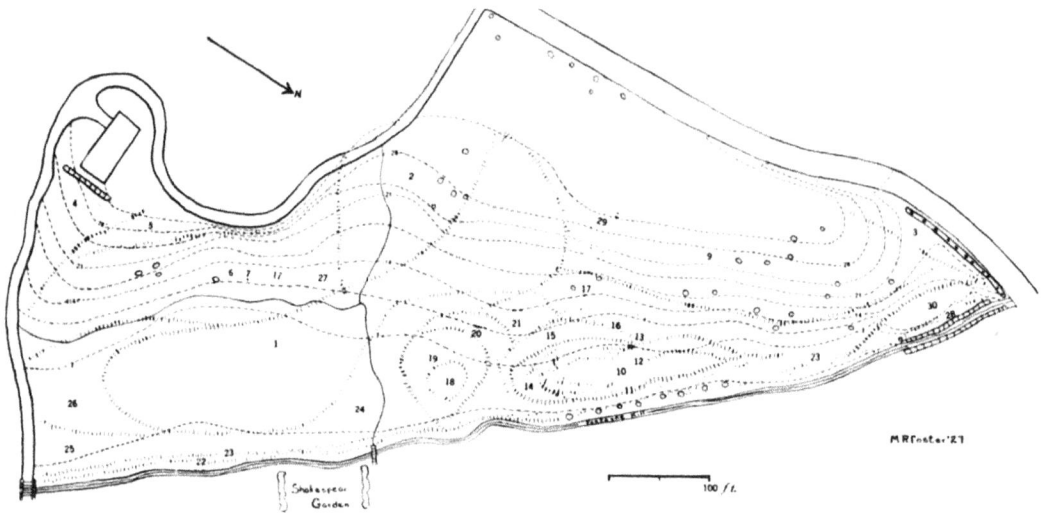

"The Dutchess County Botanical Garden, showing areas assigned to the thirty associations named in Table 1," from *Ecology*, April, 1933, p. 166 (used by permission of the Ecological Society of America).

his friend, Dr. Henry Cowles, professor of botany. Elsa Rehmann became a colleague in the development of this new ecological design idea.

A preliminary study of the plant associations had been made and published by the Conservation Committee of the Garden Club of America, in an earlier pamphlet in 1923, *The Ecology of the Plants Native to Dutchess County*, by Edith A. Roberts and Margaret F. Shaw.[14]

The ecological garden was planted with thirty Dutchess County ecological associations that included ten Upland Associations, and twenty Lowland Associations that were divided into four series — Lake and Pond, Bog, River and Stream, and Ravine. Two years later, some of the results were put into a booklet, advancing the hopes of the Garden Club to be able to present the results to its constituency. In addition, in 1926, the Boyce Thompson Institute of Plant Research, along with the students, produced an exhibit of the project at the New York Flower Show.

Edith Roberts and Elsa Rehmann eventually used the scientific data produced by this laboratory in 1927 in a series of articles entitled "Plant Ecology," published in the *House Beautiful Magazine*. They presented the material with a proper manner for the purpose of interesting the general public in ecological methods. The authors said that they wanted to bring forth the realization that plants are an integral part of their own landscape, to explain this close relationship of plants to the places where they grow, and to outline the *compositions* that they made. They wanted to offer suggestions as to how the plant associations could be interpreted in grounds and gardens, and to show what ecology had to offer to anyone doing naturalistic planting. Finally, in 1929, Roberts and Rehmann published the articles sponsored by the Garden Club of America, as a book, *American Plants for American Gardens*.

Other Contributors

Ecology was a new science. Scientists had studied plant distribution, pollination and seed dispersal, as well as physiological responses in the nineteenth century. Charles Edwin

New students at Vassar College experiment with planting. From *Ecology*, April, 1933, p. 166 (used by permission of the Ecological Society of America).

Bessey, Conway MacMillan, Frederick E. Clements and Henry Chandler Cowles all made major contributions to this new science. The Ecological Society of America was formed in 1914, and by 1928, plant ecology as a study of plant communities had become a recognized science.

Although native plants had become a familiar subject from the mid-nineteenth century on, they were generally considered by gardeners (as they often are, even today!) as isolated plants, as specimens, and occasionally, as groupings for producing naturalistic effects. "Native gardens," or "wild gardens" (an oxymoron?) have been the expression of these interests. These gardens often represented an intensely romantic, spiritual, even a political approach, to landscaping, and were not adverse to the inclusion of exotics. Warren Manning, at the turn of the century, was a passionate advocate of the wild gardens as an expression of the genius of the site, realized through selective editing or through additions.

The ideas about native plants had been generally supported by other gardeners such as Robinson and Jekyll, but their particular ideas represented, basically, a desire for informality, and an approach that also included exotics within their intent of creating an "appearance of the wild in the garden." In the period after World War I, natural gardening design remained mostly romantic is spirit, in spite of the availability of new scientific view. "We need to know more about what to plant, and where to plant in order that the trees, shrubs, and herbs may be placed in their proper environment. Correct environmental planting will insure greater success and lessen the destruction of plants. Also it will insure greater accuracy in the character of naturalistic effects."[15] This view addresses practicality (health and accuracy) rather than morality or nationalism.

Prominent American landscape architects had previously advocated natural landscape: Thomas Jefferson was noted as an early leader in studying and experimenting with native plants at Monticello; Andrew Jackson Downing discussed the natural style; in the design

A planting from the Out-of-door Laboratory. From *Ecology*, April, 1933, p. 173 (used by permission of the Ecological Society of America).

of Hollywood Cemetery in 1848, the architect John Notman produced a notable and successful ecological solution; Frederick Law Olmsted advocated adaptation to the environment and introduced the idea of naturalistic "mass" planting; and Jen Jensen spoke very passionately about regional landscapes and the "families" of plants that lived with each other in perfect harmony. Frank A. Waugh, in his 1917 book, *The Natural Style in Landscape Gardening*, promoted natural landscape composition, "friendly associations," and mentioned a few motifs such as the Squaw Birch Society and the Pitch Pine Society, but without specific compositions of lists of associations. In her park planting at Radburn, Marjorie Cautley used plants from the surrounding land to preserve an "echo of the woods and meadows on which it was built."[16] Harold A. Caparn, in 1929, wrote about "Thoughts on Planting Composition" in *Landscape Architecture*, wherein he discussed the subtle relation of form, proportion, pattern and law in nature on which the plantsman must base his composition, in order for his work to be convincing and stable. He mentioned the "species that get on well together," although he did not specific particular names.

The Presentation

Rehmann's book was very different from any other garden and landscape books produced up to this time. It included extensive listings of native plant associations. A New

York review called the book "a new field of interest for all garden makers."[17] And one advertisement stated that "these *lists* will be especially valuable to the owner of developer of naturalistic plantings, particularly since *they are unavailable elsewhere*."[18]

Rehmann's book developed ecological concepts in greater depth than other garden-book authors, by promoting the use of plant associations for the entire property. This information was placed in the form of specific suggestions for the home-gardener. From the Juniper Hillside, for example, she suggests: "Take the drive. It can be adapted to the contours and made to wind naturally up the hill. Its whole way can be outlined with irregular clumps of cedar and turns marked by groups of black haws. All along the edges masses of blueberries and roses can be planted in broad borders. The plants can surround the turn-around that is sunk inconspicuously into a hollow. They can be brought up to the house itself and arranged against it. The black haw has such an impressive structure that it can be very effective beside the entrance door."[19] And from the Seaside Association, "The spreading flatness characteristic of many of these plants offers an opportunity of trying interesting experiments. Instead of the graded heights that are used in most borders there can be an evenness of height which is better suited to exposed places and makes better foregrounds for views of the sea. Many of the plants are so low, in fact, that they are out of the direct sweep of the wind. Many, too, have billowy undulations like the dunes and the waves. They all are by their nature a part of their environment."[20]

Elsa Rehmann, in her introduction to *American Plants for American Gardens*, stated "Each of these groups (plant associations) is given a chapter in this book. The most important plants are mentioned, the fundamentals that underlie each association are indicated, the natural *compositions* that they make are suggested, and the way they can be used about the house in relation to it are outlined."[21] Not only did this book list native plants by association (as opposed to that of general habitat — woodland, meadow, etc.), but it also provided the patterns (natural order), or design composition in which they grow. *Science was discussed as an art form.* The scientist and the artist were working together. Instead of the method of arranging native plants in a gardenesque style, the book promoted the orchestration of natural patterns. And, this "scientific" approach was being presented for the first time to home gardeners, rather than to horticulturists or professionals.

Consider a sample of the aesthetic Rehmann discusses in "The Seaside Association" chapter. "There is the deep green of the pines, the glossy green of the oaks, all the gray-greens of amelanchiers and bayberries, roses and beach plums, and even the more noticeable grayness of coremas and sand myrtles. This coloring is beautifully harmonious with the rocks and the sand. It is even more effective in the autumn, when the foliage turns to bronze and purple, rose and maroon."[22] And another sample: "And masses of striking wild lupine, beach-peas, lespedezas, and adorable low blue asters with grass foliage can be planted. These alone would make a blue garden as lovely as can be."[23]

Rehmann presented the following plant associations in separate chapters: "The Open Field," "The Juniper Hillside," "The Grey Birches," "The Pines," "The Oak Woods," "The Beech-Maple-Hemlock Woods," "The Hemlock Ravine," "The Stream-side," "The Pond," "The Bog," and "The Seaside." The associations are primarily for New England and the Middle Atlantic states.

She discussed with a professional designer's skill the associations' structural design forms and compositions. For example, structural forms or patterns: for the open field — masses, scattered groups, expanses, clumps, special spots, hedgerows and thickets; for the Juniper Hillside — rocky and irregular barren spaces, and irregular clumps; for the oak, beech, maple,

From the article "Plant Ecology" published in *House Beautiful*, 1927. Reprinted with permission of House Beautiful, 1927.

hemlock woods — layered formations, twiggage, clearings, and filtered light; for the hemlock ravine — luxuriant mats, wet boulders, lavender light, dark and cool green; for the bog — rings, hummocks, springy, spongy, hidden, and unstable; for the seaside — undulating, rocky, outcrops, sandy hollows, great rounded masses, billowy and spreading, gray-green and waxy, and gale-bent. These elements form the basis for constructing the design composition, the art; they were manipulated and enhanced by the designer, Elsa Rehmann.

Rehmann added to these design forms many natural combinations of plant material for different segments of the property — for outlying areas, approaches, house, and edges. Here are some of her suggestions for form and composition for these special areas. From the seaside association: "Sometimes, in very exposed places, they (bayberries) remain low like ground-covers and again in sheltered positions they become great rounded bushes, eight feet high or more, fine enough in form and foliage to be planted as accents beside the main entrance." And another, also from the seaside association: "Such planting leaves no room for a lawn ... sun-scorched and wind-dried. There are however, many natural grasses that stay green during the hot summer and then turn to tan and tawny tones in the fall ... smooth enough to walk upon."[24]

Rehmann not only suggested planting compositions to fit the site, but the siting and the characteristics of the house as well. Her early exposure to architecture contributed to her sensitivities for the building mass and style. In this approach, Elsa Rehmann fulfilled a prime mandate of the landscape architect — the complete study of the land (structure, culture and usage) and its resultant holistic manifestation through siting, building and planting. In a sample from "The Juniper Hillside," she writes, "In this way, the building becomes one with its surroundings. Under the sway of the rugged picturesqueness, the house becomes low and wide-spread so that it nestles into the hillside. Its outlines are irregular so that the winds and walls fit the uneven slope. The roof has gables and overhanging eaves that seem to repeat the contours. The first floor is arranged on several levels to conform to the topography. And the materials of the house are suggested by the environment. Dark brown shingles can blend with the green of the cedars, stucco can take its tone from the color of the ledges, stone can be hewn from the rocks themselves."[25] Again, siting and style from "The Hemlock Ravine," "A great house can be splendidly placed at the top of such a ravine and built so that it will seem to be towering above the hemlock branches into the sunlight. Cliff-like walls, steep-hipped roofs and tall chimneys are appropriate and all the plants of the ravine can be placed immediately about the house."[26]

The caption "Marsh Marigolds can outline the entire stream," describes this image originally published in *American Plants for American Gardens*, by Rehmann and Roberts, 1929.

Elsa Rehmann's early inclination for writing has added a delightful dimension to her logic in the poetic sensitivity with which she describes each scene. Samples of this poetry are: "This scene, filled with varying tones of quiet green, lies in such subdued light and is held in such soft shadows that it seems caught in enchantment."[27]

And, "In their midst, hummocks overgrown with osmunda ferns and black alders rise out of little pools of dark water. It is a dangerous journey. Only the most adventurous descend into the hollow and get a close view of the trees and the bog itself. And only they know what an enchanted place full of rare shrubs and flowers lies hidden there with the thicket-surrounded fastness. It is, to be sure, almost unbelievable that such an undrained place can be a unique and gardenesque spot."[28]

Visibility and Resonance

American Plants for American Gardens was well received by reviewers and experts. R.S. Sturtevant of the Garden Club of America called the book "particularly noteworthy." What is interesting, if disappointing, is that this book did not appear to be overly popular, or adopted as any kind of standard over the years. The prevailing gardenesque type of book seemed to have been the most acceptable to the gardener. In the following years authors such as Taylow in 1931 listed plants by design/soil types. Bush-Brown in 1939 included soil type and habitat in the "Woodland Gardening" section of *America's Garden Book*. Marian Coffin, as late as 1940, discussed native plants by habitat in her book, *Trees and Shrubs for Landscape Effects*. She listed plants by habitats such as woodland, brook garden, river-bank, gave their particular cultural needs as well as some placement information dealing with "edge," "deep woods," and open glades. Although she mentioned "the right plant in the right place" and the observation of nature's groupings, her insight into composition and presentation was primarily in the traditional design forms. Plant ecology was perhaps suggested, but not presented as a focus. And in 1940, Florence Bell discussed soil, moisture, heat, light, and air, and listed some plant associations. Her main reference was Elsa Rehmann.

Darrel Morrison, in his introduction to the reprint of Rehmann's book, writes of some of the reasons for the lack of interest in ecological matters after 1930: the end of the estate era and the onset of mass suburbs, the modernist design movement, and the fast-growing landscape industry, all resulting in a general attitude of expediency and the use of broadly-adapted plant material in contemporary designs.

Elsa Rehmann's first two books were in the gardenesque mode, and so were all of her magazine articles save one. One might suppose, in the case of the magazine articles, that the demand (even after 1929) was for the gardenesque information. In her only magazine article on ecology, in *Landscape Architecture* in 1933, Rehmann wrote again about plant ecology and "unlocking the treasure that, except for the initiated, lay hidden in [the list of associations] and making it available to the general reader."[29] This article continued the support for her earlier ideas, such as this one from the seaside association where she writes, "There is something fundamental in this [seaside] vegetation. It is surprising that it has ever been uprooted and that other plants have been used in its place."[30] In the magazine article, she also mentioned "true reproductions" as well as "sympathetic interpretations" of compositions, and referenced the work of Frank. A. Waugh in these areas.[31]

Even at present, although the idea of native landscape has become most fashionable in landscape design, there are very few, if any, books that address plant associations and their compositions in any complete way. There are, indeed, many books on native plants and natural gardening, but they have "laundry lists" of native plants, or generalized lists of plants by habitat.[32]

Interest in the natural landscape has been revitalized within the profession since the 1960s, fraught with the clashing extremes of emotional ecologists and design elitists. Problems abound concerning the proper era for classifying a plant as native, our new knowledge of the randomness and changeability in evolution, our basic natural resources (air, wind, energy), the value of history and culture, and the global homogenization of the landscape. There is an urgent need for healthy, meaningful balances of natural and cultural landscapes. In the last several years, a laborious quest has been taking its course, hunting for a method for integrating design and ecology. Darrel Morrison has made a plea for Ecological Art, a creative synthesis of ecological understanding with spatial art. The current discourse, with its quandaries and stumbling, is unfortunately lacking an answer, producing a body of enigmatic fragments. John Dixon Hunt said, "It is into that empty space of discourse between culture [*man-made design?*] and nature [*science?*] that Landscape Architecture needs to insert itself again."[33]

I propose that Elsa Rehmann bridged part of that gap in 1929 — her book has helped to disarm the idea of the conflict of art and nature. She has shown a way in which ecological associations can be used as a fine art form in preserving our indigenous, local, natural-as-we-know-it, character: "American," as her book title suggests. Her design theory springs from a desire for practicality (science) and geographic veracity (genius loci), as well as art.

Impasse

Rehmann seemed to have retired from her practice when she moved to Rockport, Massachusetts in 1929 to live with her sister Antoinette. She many have had some connections with the Rockport Summer School (The Cambridge School).[34] She wrote poetry after she moved to Rockport, some which is very depressing, suggesting personal tragedies. Some is of special interest because it is ecological is spirit such as "The Uplands," and "Road Making."[35] A gift of her collection of poetry was made to the Ella Weed Library of Barnard College in 1955.

Elsa Rehmann died on May 30, 1946, in Rockport, Massachusetts. Her book lives on in the native plant history world, but curiously not in the design world. In 1996, *American Plants for American Gardens* was reprinted by the University of Georgia with an introduction by Darrel Morrison, wherein he remarks, "this volume has a message that is as solid today as it was the day it was published."[36] I believe Elsa Rehmann's book is still one of the best I have seen in respect to the use of ecological aesthetics in the residential landscape.

Elsa Rehmann wrote this poem near the end of her life:

ON RECEIPT OF ROYALTY
(believing that a book is dead unless it is read)

One copy sold, one royalty,
Of thousand seeds one found,
In midst of stone,
A patch of ground.

But was it read, that single book?
Seed find fertility?
Or barren's soul's
Sterility?

A slender differentiation,
Dependant on mere chance,
For sustained
Continues.

from *First Poems*, November 6, 1938, revised autumn 1943.

Elsa Rehmann's historic contribution needs its visibility restored. Her ideas deserve a significant place in history, a new life, a larger and more fertile "patch of ground."

The author would like to acknowledge the following for their assistance: Susan Allmendinger, University of Delaware; Charles Birnbaum, National Park Service; Ribert Blackwell, Principal Librarian, Newark Public Library, Newark, NJ; Arlyn Leveel; Jane Lowenthal Lowenthal, Archivist, Wollman Library, Barnard College; Cynthia Peckham, Curator, The Sandy Bay Historical Society and Museums, Inc., Rockport, MA; and Elanien S. Pike, Vassar Special Collections.

Notes

1. Elsa Rehmann, "Notes about Garden-making," *Garden Club of America Bulletin* no. 1, January 29, 1929.

2. Prior to 1919, Lowthorpe records are practically non-existent; in the merging of the school in 1945 with Rhode Island School of Design, many documents appear to have been lost.

3. Dorthea H. Wingert, "Newark Woman is Successful as Landscape Architect," *Newark Sunday Call*, April 3, 1927. In a magazine article, Mary Hartt mentioned that many professionals had stated that it was difficult for a woman to get a start due to existing prejudices in many offices. Hartt also said that if a woman didn't have connections, financial security, or access to a good office, she would have been ill-advised to attempt to pursue the profession as a livelihood. Elsa may have had some entrée through her father, or through one of her contemporaries who had practices in New York. Mary B. Hartt, "Women and the Art of Landscape Gardening," *Outlook* 88 (March 28, 1908): 695–704.

4. Elsa Rehmann, *The Small Place* (New York and London: G.P. Putnam's Sons, 1918).

5. "Review of *The Small Place* by Elsa Rehmann" *Book Review Digest* Vol. 14, ed. Mary Catherine Reely (New York: H.W. Wilson Co., 1919), 371.

6. *Landscape Architecture* magazine carried, in 1918, an article about a competition arranged by Rehmann for the design of a small house lot. Her jury included Marian Coffin, Charles Lowrie, and Rehmann's sister, Antoinette Perrett. Out of twelve submittals from Cornell, Lowthorpe, and the Cambridge School, Rose Greeley received one of the two mentions.

7. At this point, it is important to explain the use of the word "gardenesque." This use is derived from definitions in Jellicoe's *Oxford Companion to Gardens:* it is, a term proposed by Loudon and Kemp for a style of garden design whose object was the development of individual plant character, beauty of line, and general variety — basically an eclectic design that is a mixture of garden features, and typical of many residential gardens of the time. The word used also implies the idea that a garden is a cultivated phenomenon, and a work of fine art, and that it is different from naturalistic planting or Nature (as defined in the *American Heritage Dictionary*: "a primitive state of existence uninfluenced and untouched by civilization or artificiality") itself.

8. One atypical article appeared in 1914 in *Architectural Record* magazine. It discussed the landscape planning merits of the layout of a Krupp Foundation suburb in Germany. Elsa Rehmann, "Margarethenhöhe bei Essen, the Krupp Foundation suburb," *Architectural Record* 36 (1914): 372–78.

9. Dorthea H. Wingert, "Newark Woman Is Successful as Landscape Architect" (a series about business and professional women of New Jersey) *Newark Sunday Call*, April 3, 1927.

10. "All of Us Are Gardeners Under the Skin; Four New Books on Horticulture Which Prove That 'Sumer Is y-Cumen In'" (Review of *Garden-Making* by Elsa Rehmann), *New York Times*, June 20, 1926, BR13.

11. Robert S. Lemmon, "If you Like Flower Gardens" (review of *Garden Making* by Elsa Rehmann) *New York Herald Tribune*, May 14, 1926.

12. Elizabeth Daniels, "Vassar History: 1915–1922," *Main to Mudd: an Informal History of Vassar College Buildings* (Poughkeepsie, NY: Vassar College, 1987).

13. Edith A. Roberts, "The Development of Out-of-door Botanical Laboratory for Experimental Ecology," *Ecology* 14, no. 2 (April 1933): 163.

14. The Garden Club of America, in September 1923, also put forth a notice "Let's Help Research," which asked members to help by sending seeds and information to Edith Roberts for her research in native plant seed germination, which the club felt would benefit members as well as commercial dealers. The appeal was followed by a $750.00 contribution to a fellow for a Vassar student for research work.

15. Edith A. Roberts and M.F. Shaw, "The Ecology of Plants Native to Dutchess County," *Garden Club of America Bulletin Conservation Committee Booklet*, 1924.

16. Marjorie Sewell Cautley, "Planting at Radburn," *Landscape Architecture*, 21 (October 1930): 23–29.

17. "American Plants for American Gardens," *New York Herald Tribune*, April 21, 1929, 28.

18. Advertisement for *American Plants for American Gardens* by Edith Roberts and Elsa Rehmann. Vassar Co-operative Bookshop. Poughkeespie, New York: Vassar College, 1929.

19. Elsa Rehmann and Edith A. Roberts, "Introduction," *American Plants for American Gardens*, (New York: Macmillan, 1929).

20. Rehmann and Roberts, *American Plants for American Gardens*, 111.

21. *Ibid.*, "Introduction."

22. *Ibid.*, 105.

23. *Ibid.*, 110.

24. *Ibid.*, 107.

25. *Ibid.*, 28.

26. *Ibid.*, 70.

27. *Ibid.*, 68.

28. *Ibid.*, 100.

29. Elsa Rehmann, "An Ecological Approach," *Landscape Architecture* 23 (July 1933): 240–41.

30. Rehmann and Roberts, *American Plants for American Gardens*, 105.

31. "Sympathetic reproductions," or orchestrations of natural patterns at the residential scale have been implemented by modern practitioners such as Jens Jensen, A.E. Bye, Patrick Chasse, and Andropogon Associates. In her article, Rehmann also explained the broader uses of her approach, in subdivisions, and in large scale planning.

32. Ken Druse's 1994 book, *The Natural Habitat Garden*, has chapters on grasslands, drylands, wetlands, and woodlands. In his introduction, he mentions plant communities, and advises the reader to learn about them from local sites. His chapters on habitat are very general, and list no associations. His newer version, 2004, attempts to simulate natural habitats, covers many states, but without complete lists or entire property focus. A book by Elizabeth N. DuPont, *Landscaping with Native Plants in the Middle Atlantic Region*, 1978, has more comprehensive information that lists groups of plants for soil regimes; Jeff Cox, *Landscaping with Nature*, 1991, covers the entire country and does not have extensive lists, or address the entire property; *Field and Forest*, by Jane Scott, 1992, discusses four types of forests, open lands, three types of dry-lands, and four types of wetlands. The Brooklyn Botanic Gardens, 1992, published a booklet, *The Environmental Gardeners*, with lists of a few associations and a few general layout suggestions. John Brooks *Natural Landscapes* is global in scale and very general. Jerome Malitz has a book, *Reflecting Nature*, 1998, written by enthusiastic mathematicians, showing beautiful vignettes of wild scenes in Acadia and in their native Colorado; John Diekelman's book, *Natural Landscaping*, 2002, covering plant communities, analysis and planning, design, plans for private and public sites and an appendix of representative species of major plant communities and places to visit, including a broad area, and is like a college textbook with more information than the average gardener wants to digest; two books by Rick Drake, *The American Woodland*, 2002, covering mid–Atlantic forests without site-specific design, and, *The Wild Garden*, 2009, an update of William Robinson and a treatise on informal and natural design, are not as site specific as Rehmann's book; a 2007 book by Beresford-Kruger, *A Garden for Life: the Natural Approach*, presents a very loose and spiritual interpretation of natural gardening.

Some States have been compiling scientific lists; North Carolina Natural Heritage Program has a very comprehensive classification of natural communities; Maine Natural Areas Program has a general classification of natural communities recently published in a book, *Natural Landscape of Maine*, 2010; New York State Natural Heritage Program has produced an Ecological Communities report; Connecticut State Geological and Natural History Survey documents specify nature preserves. These valuable surveys have no design information and are not in an easily usable form for designers or home gardeners. Basically, there are no thorough books on landscape design with plant communities — and none with many specific "local" habitats, or whole property designs. For the most part these books provide inspiration in very general sense. Books that cover a larger region are much too general.

33. John Dixon Hunt, *Gardens and the Picturesque* (Cambridge, MA: MIT Press, 1992), 301.

34. During the 1930's, she is recorded in the Barnard College Alumni Register as an instructor at the Cambridge and the Lowthorpe schools; she also participated in a "short-course" series of lectures with Stephen F. Hamblin sponsored by the Boston alumnae group for The Cambridge School.

35. Elsa Rehmann, *First Poems*, 1933. An example of her environmental poetry:

> (UNTITLED)
> "The uplands lay in dreary drought
> And languish of thirst,
> The lowlands lay where water reached
> And roots were still immersed.
> The upland grass was sun-burnt brown
> The lowland grass was green
> It seemed the water knew the way
> To differentiate the scene."

36. Morrison, Darrel, "Introduction," for *American Plants for American Gardens*, reprint, Athens, GA: University of Georgia Press, 1996. An example of the passing by of Elsa Rehmann's ideas among contemporary landscape architects, see Warren Byrd, "A Century of Planting Design: an opinionated and variegated timeline of planting design," *Landscape architecture* 89 (November 1999): 92–95, 114–119.

Bibliography

Adams, Charles C. "The New Natural History — Ecology." *American Museum Journal* 7 (1917).

Advertisement for *American Plants for American Gardens* by Edith Roberts and Elsa Rehmann. Vassar Cooperative Bookshop. Poughkeepsie: Vassar College, 1929.

"All of Us Are Gardeners Under the Skin; Four New Books on Horticulture Which Prove That 'Sumer Is y-Cumen In.'" (Review of *Garden-making* by Elsa Rehmann) *New York Times*, June 20, 1926, BR13.

"American Plants for American Gardens." (Review of book by Elsa Rehmann). *Hartford Courant.* March 24, 1929.
_____. (Review) *New York Herald Tribune.* April 21, 1929, 28.
_____. (Review). *Rochester Democrat and Chronicle.* March 21, 1929.
Anderson, Dorothy May. *Women, Design, and the Cambridge School.* West Lafayette, IN: PDA Publishers Corp., 1980.
Beresford-Kruger, Diana. *A Garden for Life: the Natural Approach to Designing, Planting, and Maintaining a North Temperate Garden.* Ann Arbor: University of Michigan Press, 2004.
Bramwell, Anna. *Ecology in the Twentieth Century: A History.* New Haven: Yale University Press, 1989.
Brookes, John. *Natural Landscaping.* New York: DK Publishers, 1998.
Brown, Catherine, and Celia Newton Maddox. "Women and the Land: 'A Suitable Profession.'" *Landscape Architecture.* 72 (May 1982): 64.
Brown, Connie. *Colombia University Bulletin of Information,* New York: Columbia University, May 1907.
Byrd, Warren. "A Century of Planting Design: an opinionated and variegated timeline of planting design." *Landscape Architecture* 89 (November 1999): 92–95, 114–119.
Caparn, Harold A. "Thoughts on Planting Composition." *Landscape Architecture* 19 (April 1929): 141–156.
Cautley, Marjorie Sewell. "Planting at Radburn." *Landscape Architecture* 21 (October 1930): 23–29.
"C.F. Rehmann, Head of Drawing School, Dead." *Newark Evening News.* February 19, 1906.
Coffin, Marian Cruger. *Trees and Shrubs for Landscape Effects.* New York: C. Scribner's Sons, 1940.
Cox, Jeff. *Landscaping with Nature: Using Nature's Design to Plan your Yard.* Emmaus, PA: Rodale Press, 1991.
Cronon, William. "The Trouble with Wilderness." *New York Times Magazine.* August 13, 1995, 42–3.
Cunningham, Mary. "New Uses for Native Plants." *Country Life* 47 (February 1925): 34–40.
Daniels, Elizabeth. *Main to Mudd: An informal history of Vassar College Buildings.* Poughkeepsie, NY: Vassar College, 1987.
"Department of Wild Flower Preservation" (Letter from H.N. MacCracken to Mrs. Farwell) *Garden Club of America Bulletin.* November 24, 1923, 53.
Diekelmann, John, and Robert Schuster. *Natural Landscaping: Designing with Native Plant Communities.* Madison: University of Wisconsin Press, 2002.
Drake, Rick. *The American Woodland Garden: Capturing the Spirit of the Deciduous Forest.* Portland, OR: Timber Press, 2002.
_____, and W. Robinson. *The Wild Garden.* Portland, OR: Timber Press, 2009.
Druse, Kenneth, and Margaret Roach. *The Natural Habitat Garden.* Portland, OR: Timber Press, 2004.
DuPont, Elizabeth N., and Wick Williams. *Landscaping with Native Plants in the Middle Atlantic Region.* Chadds Ford, PA: Brandywine Conservancy, 1978.
Edgerton, Frank N. "Ecological Studies and Observations Before 1900." *History of American Ecology.* Ed. Frank Edger, 311–352. New York: Arno Press, 1977.
Egan, Dave, and William H. Tishler. "Jens Jensen, Native Plants, and the Concept of Nordic Superiority." *Landscape Journal* 18, no. 1 (1999): 11–29.
Elger, Frank, and William A. Niering. *Natural Areas of McClean Game Refuge: Vegetation of Connecticut Natural Areas.* Hartford, CT: State Geological and Natural History Survey of Connecticut, 1967.
_____. *The Natural Area of the Audubon Center of Greenwich: Vegetation of Connecticut Natural Areas,* no. 2. Hartford, CT: State Geological and Natural History Survey of Connecticut, 1966.
_____. *Yale Natural Preserve, New Haven: Vegetation of Connecticut Natural Areas,* no. 1. Hartford, CT: State Geological and Natural History Survey of Connecticut, 1965.
Gawler, Susan, and Andrew Cutko. *Natural Landscapes of Maine: A Guide to Natural Communities and Ecosystems.* Augusta: Maine Natural Areas Program, Department of Conservation, 2010.
Gould, Stephen J. "An Evolutionary Perspective on Strengths, Fallacies, and Confusions in the Concept of Native Plants." *Nature and Ideology: Natural Garden Design in the Twentieth Century.* Edited by Joachim Wolschke-Bulmahn, 11–19. Washington, DC: Dumbarton Oaks Research Library and Collection, 1997.
Grainger, John. *Garden Science.* London: University of London Press, 1935.
Greiff, Constance M. *John Notman, Architect: 1810—1865.* Philadelphia: Athenaeum of Philadelphia, 1979.
Groening, Gert, and Joachim Wolschke-Bulmahn. "Changes in the Philosophy of Garden Architecture in the Twentieth Century." *Journal of Garden History.* 9, no. 2 (1989): 53–70.
Hartt, Mary B. "Women and the Art of Landscape Gardening." *Outlook* 88 (March 28, 1908): 695–704.
Heard, E.V.R. "American Plants for American Gardens." *Garden Club of America Bulletin.* July 26, 1929.
Hubbard, Henry Vincent, and Theodora Kimball. *An Introduction to the Study of Landscape Design.* Revised edition, New York: Macmillan, 1929.

Hunt, John Dixon. *Gardens and the Picturesque.* Cambridge, MA: MIT Press, 1992.

Jellicoe, Geoffrey, and Susan Jellicoe. *The Oxford Companion to Gardens.* Oxford: Oxford University Press, 1986.

Karson, Robin. "Warren H. Manning, Pragmatist in the Wild Garden." *Nature and Ideology: Natural Garden Design in the Twentieth Century*, ed. Joachim Wolschke-Bulmahn, 113–130. Washington, DC: Dumbarton Oaks Research Library and Collection 1997.

Kimball, Richard B. "A Little Visit to Lowthorpe." *House Beautiful* 39 (March 1916).

Knight, Jane. "An Examination of the History of the Lowthorpe School of Landscape Architecture for Women, Groton, Massachusetts, 1901–1945." Master's of Landscape Architecture thesis, Cornell University, 1986.

Lemmon, Robert S. "If You Like Flower Gardens." (Review of *Garden-making* by Elsa Rehmann). *New York Herald Tribune.* May 14, 1926.

"Let's Help Research." *Garden Club of America Bulletin.* September 1923, 59.

Libby, Valencia. "Marian Cruger Coffin: Landscape Architecture of Distinction." *Preservation League of New York State Newsletter* 16 (Fall 1990): 4–5.

Maine Natural Heritage Program. *Natural Landscapes of Maine: A Classification of Ecosystems and Natural Communities.* Augusta: Maine Natural Heritage Program, Office of Comprehensive Planning, 1991.

Malitz, Jerome, and Seth Malitz. *Reflecting Nature: Garden Designs from Wild Landscapes.* Portland, OR: Timber Press, 1998.

Marinelli, Janet. *The Environmental Gardener Handbook (Plants & Gardens Brooklyn Botanic Garden Record,* Vol. 48, No. 1 Spring, 1992). Brooklyn: Brooklyn Botanic Garden, 1992.

McDougall, W.B. *Plant Ecology.* Philadelphia: Lea & Febiger, 1949.

McGuire, Diane Kostial. *American Garden Design: An Anthology of Ideas That Shaped Our Landscape.* New York: Prentice Hall, 1994.

McIntosh, Robert P. "Ecology Since 1900." *History of American Ecology.* Edited by Frank Edgerton, 353–371. New York: Arno Press, 1977.

Meyer, Elizabeth K. "The Designer's Dilemma: Giving form to Environmental Values," Speaker at Dumbarton Oaks Center for Landscape Studies Annual Symposium: Environmentalism and Landscape Architecture, May 1998.

Morrison, Darrel. "Beyond Planting Design." *Landscape Architecture* 89 (November 1999): 92–95.

Mozingo, Louise A. "The Aesthetics of Ecological Design: Seeing Science as Culture." *Landscape Journal* 16, no. 1 (1997): 46.

Nevins, Deborah. *The Triumph of Flora; Women in the American Landscape, 1890–1935.* New York: Brant Publications, 1985.

Newark City Directories, 1905–1929. Collection of the New Jersey Historical Society, Newark, New Jersey, Elsa Meyer librarian.

Nicholas, Rose Standish. *English Pleasure Gardens.* New York, London: Macmillan, 1925.

Nichols, G.E. "Plant Ecology." *Ecology* 9, no. 3 (1928): 267–71.

"Noverville Woman Presided at Session." (Dr. Edith Roberts) *Hudson Register.* January 11, 1935.

Parsons, Samuel. *The Art of Landscape Architecture, its Development and Its Application to Modern Landscape Gardening.* New York, London: G.P. Putnam's Sons, 1915.

Pond, W. Bremer, Williams Bradford, and American Society of Landscape Architects. *Transactions of the American Society of Landscape Architects.* Augusta, ME: Press of C.E. Nash & Son, 1927.

Pollan, Michael. "Against Nativism." *New York Times Magazine.* May 15, 1994.

Reed, Howard S. "The Brief History of Ecological Work in Botany." *The Plant World.* 8, no. 5 (July 1905).

"Review of *The Small Place* by Elsa Rehmann." *Book Review Digest Fourteenth Annual Cumulation*, Volume 14. Edited by Mary Catherine Reely, n. 18. New York: H.W. Wilson Co., 1919.

Rehmann, Elsa. "Competition for the Design of Small House Lot." *Landscape Architecture* 8, (July 1918): 186–89.

_____. "An Ecological Approach." *Landscape Architecture* 23, no. 4 (July 1933): 239–245.

_____. *First Poems.* Self published book, Elsa Rehmann gift to Barnard College, Barnard College Archives, 1933.

_____. "Margarethenhöhe bei Essen, the Krupp Foundation suburb." *Architectural Record* 36 (1914): 372–78.

_____. "Notes about Garden Making." *Garden Club of America Bulletin* no. 1, January 29, 1929.

_____. "Planting a Suburban Lot." *Garden Magazine* 17 (April 1913): 167–9.

_____. *The Small Place.* New York, London: G.P. Putnam's Sons, 1918.

Rehmann, Elsa, and Edith A. Roberts. *American Plants for American Gardens*. New York: Macmillan, 1929.

_____. *American Plants for American Gardens*. 1929. With a new introduction by Darrel Morrison. Reprint, Athens, GA: University of Georgia Press, 1996.

_____. "Plant Ecology: Seaside Planting." *House Beautiful* 61 (June 1927): 46, 81–84.

_____. "Plant Ecology: The Contribution to Naturalistic Planting of This Study of Plants in Relation to Their Environment." *House Beautiful* 62 (July 1927): 805, 842, 844–845.

_____. "Plant Ecology: The Juniper Association. " *House Beautiful* 62 (October 1927): 399, 448, 450, 452.

_____. "Plant Ecology: The Pine Association." *House Beautiful* 62 (December 1927): 652.

Rehmann, Elsa, and (Mrs.) Antoinette Rehmann Parett. *Garden-making*. Boston, New York: Houghton Mifflin Co., 1926.

"Rehmann Poetry Gift." *Barnard Alumni Magazine* 45, no. 1.

Riley, Robert B., and Barbara J. Brown. "Editorial Commentary: Analogy and Authority Beyond Chaos and Kudzu." *Landscape Journal* 14, no. 1 (1995): 87–92.

Roberts, Edith A. "The Development of Out-of-door Botanical Laboratory for Experimental Ecology." *Ecology*. 14, no. 2 (April 1933): 163–223.

_____, and Helen Wilkinson Reynolds. *The Role of Plant Life in the History of Dutchess County*. Poughkeepsie, NY: Lansing Bros Print. Co., 1938.

Roberts, Edith A., and M.F. Shaw. "The Ecology of Plants Native to Dutchess County." *Garden Club of America Bulletin, Conservation Committee Booklet*. 1924.

Robinson, Florence Bell. *Planting Design*. New York, London: Whittlesey House, McGraw-Hill, 1940.

Rockport Municipal Office Records. Rockport, Massachusetts, Office of the City Clerk, F.C. Frithsen.

Shafale, Michael, and Alan S. Weakly. *Classification of the Natural Communities of North Carolina, Third Approximation*. North Carolina Natural Heritage Program, Division of Parks and Recreation, North Carolina Department of Environment, Health and Natural Resources, 1990.

Spirin, Ann Whiston. "The Authority of Nature: Conflict and Confusion in Landscape Architecture." *Nature and Ideology: Natural Garden Design in the Twentieth Century*. ed. Joachim Wolschke-Bulmahn, 249–261. Washington, D.C.: Dumbarton Oaks Research Library and Collection, 1997.

Tabor, Grace. *Old-fashioned Gardening: A History and Reconstruction*. New York: McBride, Nast & Co., 1913.

Tankard, Judith B. "Women Pioneers in Landscape Design." *Radcliff Quarterly* 79, nos. 3–4, (March 1993).

Taylor, Albert D., and Gordon D. Cooper. *The Complete Garden*. Garden City, NY: Doubleday, Page & Co., 1921.

Tripp, Amy F. "Lowthorpe School of Landscape Architecture, Gardening and Horticulture for Women." *Landscape Architecture* 3 (October 1912): 14–18.

"Vassar Fund." *Garden Club of America Bulletin*. November 24, 1923, 72.

Waugh, Frank A. *The Natural Style in Landscape Gardening*. Boston: R.G. Badger, 1917.

Wingert, Dorthea H. "Newark Woman is Successful as Landscape Architect." *Newark Sunday Call*. April 3, 1927.

Sargeant, Charles Sprague. "Women as Landscape Architects." *Garden and Forest* 5, no. 242 (1892): 482.

Wright, Richardson. "Women in Landscaping." *House and Garden* 49 (January 1926): 150.

Wyck Papers. Box 296A-File no. 134, series 11, "Philadelphia School of Design for Women." American Philosophical Society, Philadelphia, Pennsylvania.

Chapter 9

An Ecological Approach

ELSA REHMANN

Plant ecology is a comparatively new science. It has its origin at the turn of the century.[1] Scientists seemed no longer satisfied with the taxonomic study of plants nor even with a wider segregation in accordance with geographic and climactic differentiations. They found that vegetation was divided into distinct groupings through the inherent adaption of plants to the environment in which they grew. These groups they called "plant associations." The observations made as to what plants grow together and what they have in common as to soil, light, moisture, and temperature (all of which are the factors which make up what is called the plant's "environment") became the basis of the study of plant ecology.

This study has been kept almost entirely of a scientific turn. It needs, therefore, to be translated into a form that will make it available, in nomenclature and substance, to all those who are doing work in which the landscape and the vegetation which forms so vital a part if it come into consideration. In this list we can include not only landscape architects, owners and gardeners of private estates, and all those interested in national, state, and county parks, parkways, and reservations for the preservation of natural scenery, but those working on watersheds, reservoirs, and other public lands, and as real estate subdividers, city and town foresters, and engineers on roadway construction, including those in charge of roadside planting and maintenance as well as telephone and telegraph linemen. All in these several groups ought to be instructed in elementary ecology at least, if only to stimulate a respect for the native vegetation and the landscape of which the plants are so integral a part.

In *American Plants for American Gardens* an attempt has been made to bring to popular attention the subject of ecology in its relation to landscape architecture. This book had its origin in a pamphlet prepared for the Conservation Committee of the Garden Club of America by Edith A. Roberts, Professor of Botany at Vassar College, with the assistance of Margaret F. Shaw of the same department, who listed the plants native to Dutchess County, New York and arranged them according to ecological associations. With the idea of unlocking the treasure that, except for the initiated, lay hidden in these lists and of making it available to the general reader, a series of magazine articles was written[2]; these were later gathered into book form.[3] The lists were reorganized to fit a wider geographic scope as well as a nonscientific audience, and descriptive and explanatory text was developed in connection with the most

Originally published in *Landscape Architecture* July 1933, p. 239–245. Reprinted with permission from the America Society of Landscape Architects.

significant associations. Important plants were mentioned, the natural compositions that they make were suggested, and the way they can be used about the house and in relation to it were outlined.

For a book of its kind and size, the authors had to content themselves with a rather set plan and with suggestions which were limited to the private estate. But, with a little ingenuity on the part of the reader, the book can be adapted for a wider use. It can, for instance, be used as field book since it is really a primer to a more comprehensive understanding of native plants as well as to a keener appreciation of the relationship inherent between native vegetation and the landscape. It is this inherent relationship that many a landscape architect seems to forget in his eagerness to organize land and landscape for human use and to show his creative ability as an artist.

It must be remembered that, despite its inclusive title, the book deals with but a small section of the United States, primarily the northeastern states, and that it discusses only the plant associations to be found in this section: namely, the open field, the juniper hillside, the grey birches, the pines, the oak woods, the beech-maple-hemlock woods, the hemlock ravine, the stream-side, the pond, the bog, and the seaside. Even a slight knowledge of these plant associations is tremendously worth the while because it increases our enjoyment and understanding of the natural landscape.

There is great need for studies of other sections of the country that would be available to the landscape architect and to the general reader, remembering that a plant is no longer native if it is transferred to a locality in which it is not really indigenous or, in a real ecological sense, to a location not environmentally correct.

The study of ecology stimulates, too, a whole series of earnest questions. It draws attention, for instance, to the artistic waste of uprooting blue berry bushes to replace them with flower beds, and of making lawns on uneven rocky fields that, if not destroyed, are so fascinating in their natural contours and in their native grasses and flowers. It strengthens and ever-increasing dissatisfaction with the general run of hedgings, miscellaneous shrubberies, and so-called naturalistic plantings. It quickens sensitiveness to the loss to native vegetation when extraneous material is added, no matter how sparingly. It emphasizes the shortcomings of the English landscape school when its ideas are imposed upon the wilder and more rugged topography of the American landscape, and lays stress upon the fallacy of using European plant material in the English park manner instead of our native vegetation in its own characterful distribution. It stresses the growing realization that the overactive clearing away of natural growth along the roadside is destroying the foreground which is so important to the beauty of landscape views. It stirs up an ever keener distress at the manner in which the too vigorous leveling and straightening of roads and highways disturb the natural undulations of the whole landscape. And moreover, it starts increasing misgivings as to the necessity of wiping out whole sections of native growth, whole ridges of oak woodlands, for instance, by suburban colonies where owners, who have come for the purpose of living in the country, allow the destruction of indigenous material and natural contours for artificial slopes and exotic vegetation.

But the study of ecology is also of constructive value. It holds an important clue to planting that is based not upon any man-made rules of composition but upon natural groupings. The cataloguing of plants that grow together under given conditions, as they are listed in *American Plants for American Gardens*, id of assistance in the use of these natural groups. But this is not enough. The varying quantities of the plants and the manner in which we find them assembled are also of primary importance. It will be necessary, therefore, to make a quantitative analysis and an accurate charting of actual areas. As far as I know, this has not been done in any comprehensive or systematic manner, if at all from the point of view of the landscape value for his investigation. But the work scientists have done along this line illustrates the method which we shall be able to follow and adapt in plotting larger areas of distinctive landscape beauty. Such scholarly works as John W. Harshberger's *Vegetation of the New Jersey Pine Barrens* and Fred E. Clement's *Plant Physiology and Ecology* have many suggestions for our investigations. And the work done by Frank A. Waugh with his students at Amherst, as shown in recent numbers of *Landscape Architecture*, is significant.

Student investigation in the field can be supplemented by design problems in the drafting room in which native groupings are reconstructed to fit special situations. The problem might be an actual hillside within sight of the drafting room to be transformed into a cedar garden. Here we might concentrate upon the characteristic groupings of *Juniperus virginiana* and the more important members of the juniper association, with a suggestion of a gray birch and an occasional while pine to show that these would be present in the natural evolution when the cedars were reaching maturity. A second problem might be an imaginary spot in a wood with a hemlock as the dominant tree, for the purpose of studying the manner in which the herbaceous plants native to a woods of beech, maple, and hemlock are distributed.

Intensive observation of the landscape, observation ecologically attuned, is of course the best schooling. Scenes of great beauty are to be found everywhere — laurel-filled oak woods; hemlock woods where yews spread their needled branches under the trees; hillsides where cedars stand in monumental arrangements or group themselves in a seemingly more spontaneous manner with ground junipers, wild roses, and sometimes bayberries, sweetferns, and huckleberries; tumbling brooks between fern-encrusted ledges; streams flowing slowly though luxuriant water-loving vegetation. Here are some of the scenes that are ready with many a suggestion fro garden use. To be naturalistic, in the very truest sense, the plants have to be assembled in compositions that are true reproductions or sympathetic interpretations of the landscape scene.

From such beginnings we reach out to larger, more comprehensive problems. Once such a program fixes itself, these scenes are not considered singly but in relation to the entire estate. Such an undertaking has seldom, if ever, been consistently developed throughout. Many a house, even where it might have been, is not adapted to the surroundings. It is, moreover, difficult to overcome usual landscape procedure and to prohibit foreign plant material. But how logical it seems that the style of a country house, the shape, roof lines, plan, and material should be controlled by the "lay" of the land and by the character of the landscape, and that the rocky slopes and woods, meadows, ponds, and streams should comprise a natural setting that is kept intact and re-created in its minutest details. Such an undertaking is not easy, but it becomes more and more significant as the inherent beauty of the natural vegetation becomes manifest to us. And while such a program grows in vision, it is not visionary.

The rural scene is not to be forced upon an urban setting. There is no possibility of retaining the native vegetation intact where houses are placed close together and where streets are laid out in a set manner. The very building of a house and streets, with the enforced changes of contour which such work entails, creates more violent changes of environment than plants will endure. In the leveling of field, the flowers are destroyed; in the filling of streams, the characteristic water-loving vegetation disappears; and when forest trees are left isolated, without their accustomed undergrowth and canopies of interwoven branches, then sicken and die.

But there are still suburbs and rural communities where houses are sufficiently isolated. In such places it would still be possible to build roads that would adapt themselves to the natural contours of the land, to select appropriate house sites, to keep hedgerows and surrounding woodlands intact, and to outline a program for the preservation of vegetation and for the re-creation of such scenes as may have been unavoidably destroyed. The possibilities of such a community are excitingly enticing through they are dependent upon a well-nigh unprecedented cooperation of neighbors based upon a far-sighted policy of subdivider and engineer.

It is not bad to consider such idealistic programs. They are naturally and artistically possible. But there are other programs that may be more easily realized and put into effect. One is the preserving of roadside vegetation and the replanting of a vegetation that is not only native but in keeping with the specific environmental conditions. This is all the more possible as people are awake to the destruction that has taken place and are eager to avoid further lessening of whatever beauty is left. Another problem is the creation of parks and parkways in truly naturalistic spirit. The urban park must become more and more formal to conform to city conditions. Playgrounds can no longer be consistently welded in to the informal park. But once the park approaches country environments, it becomes, to all intents and purposes, a reservation in which the characteristic landscape should be emphasized and retained without a single exotic note.

The work that is being done in the forests of reservations and in the woodlands of private estates is suggestive. It draws attention to the woodlands of private estates is suggestive. It draws attention to the esthetic value of the landscape forest — that is, the forest in its natural state — in distinction from the more obvious commercial value of the stands of trees started in many places as town forests. It has created the profession of landscape forestry in distinction to pure or commercial forestry. The program reduced to its simplest outline consists of clearing our dead wood, thinning overcrowded areas, and rejuvenating and replanting burnt-over tracts. Much work of this kind is being done in entire disregard or ignorance of natural laws. The work demands an understanding not only of ecological groupings but of the manner in which these groups follow one another and interweave in the natural evolution from the open field to the beech-maple-hemlock forest which is termed the climax association.

The most important phase of any work along these lines depends upon the intelligent preservation not only of the vegetation but of the environmental factors that control it. The re-creation of natural scenes is much more difficult. It cannot be done as of yet, except in a fragmentary way or, in exceptional cases, by actual replanting. It must be accomplished by means through which the native vegetation can reestablish itself. This is a slow process, and yet sometimes it is not as slow as it would seem. A ten- or fifteen-year term, in which a not too seriously burnt-over oak woods is helped in reestablishing itself by fostering the young growth, produces unexpected results. And so, while an age-old beech-and-hemlock woods cannot be re-created, even so, if there are nay trees of fair size left at all, the natural habitat which young beeches and hemlocks have of growing up in such a woods produces effects of rare beauty and promise.

Notes

1. In answer to an inquiry as to the origin of Plant Ecology, Professor Henry C. Cowles of the Department of Botany at the University of Chicago writes: "We generally figure that ecology was organized as a definite science in 1895 through the publication of *Oecology of Plants: An Introduction to the Study of Plant Communities*, by Professor Warming of the University of Copenhagen. This book stimulated efforts and research all over the world. However, there were special papers on the subject long before that. The word 'ecology' itself dates back to 1866, when it was coined by Haeckel; and as far back as 1836 an important work was published by Unger on the relation of soil to vegetation." Professor Cowels adds that "plant geography is an older science than ecology, being generally dated back to the time of Humboldt, who wrote a very important treatise on the subject in 1804. Books on the subject were written in the twenties of the last century."

2. "Plant Ecology." By Edith A. Roberts and Elsa Rehmann. In *House Beautiful* (June 1927–May 1928).

3. *American Plants for American Garden*. By Edith A. Roberts and Elsa Rehmann. New York: Macmillan, 1929.

Chapter 10

Garden City Landscapes of Marjorie L. Sewell Cautley, 1922–1937

THAÏSA WAY

If gender has been one of the "most critical lines of differentiation in culture and society," how has it been historically visible in the careers and creative work of landscape architects — of women landscape architects?[1] How does one read issues of gender in the landscape? This in large part defines the core of the book in which this chapter is just one contribution. Nonetheless it is important to note that this particular contribution is intended to not only challenge the canon, but to challenge how historians have defined practice and the profession. It is not enough to merely add women to history — as Van Slyck has noted "add women and stir."[2] This chapter offers to both expand the recognized role of women and frame an alternative focus for the study of twentieth century landscape architectural practice — that of the domestic domain or residential design.

In 1913 an editorial in *House Beautiful* declared:

> From our own grounds the next logical step is to the attention to parkways and streets and from these again to membership on park boards and civic improvement leagues.... The woman who steps from her door step to plant a few handy "yarbs" at its foot, has quite unwittingly taken her first unconscious step towards the suffrage.... Most of us do not realize as we wield trowel and rake that we are doing a deed of national significance.[3]

This was not an unusual claim in the late nineteenth and early twentieth centuries in the United States, as the private and public domains came together in transformative ways under the influence of the Progressive, Country Life, and reform movements. This period of American culture reflected a society in search of a new order, a new rationality. Advocates believed in progress, not merely as evidenced by intangible cultural characteristics but in the visible manifestations of culture.[4] The progressive agenda underscored the importance of environment. Architecture and landscape thus simultaneously shaped and reflected social and cultural values.

The Garden City Movement was one manifestation of this belief in the significance of environment and place. According to planner and landscape architect Henry Wright, the successes of the "new towns" of Radburn, New Jersey, and Sunnyside in Queens, New

An earlier version of this paper was published in "Designing Garden City Landscapes: Works by Marjorie L. Sewell Cautley, 1922–1937," *Studies in the History of Gardens & Designed Landscapes* 25, no. 4 (2005).

York were "definitely and irrevocably related to [their] site and setting."[5] The residential site and setting was designed by Marjorie Sewell Cautley.[6] The work of Cautley for the Stein-Wright design team is particularly interesting as it simultaneously reveals the ideals of the garden city movement as well as a feminist inscription on the land. An analysis of Cautley's landscape designs specifically reflects her experience as a professional landscape architect and a woman and mother. And it is for these reasons that the landscapes may well have been ignored as a scholarly focus — they are about women, mothers, children, family and domestic living.

Women's marginal position in the histories of landscape architecture stems from tenuous assumptions about the breadth of their practice, the numbers of female practitioners, and the importance of residential work among contemporaries. The first assumption has been that women were commissioned exclusively for residential estate design, in particular flower gardens.[7] While residential work was a significant part of their practice, other projects ranged in type from university campuses to city parks to urban housing projects and highway systems.[8] The second assumption describes women in design as a group of elite upper class women leading "bedroom" practices.[9] In fact hundreds of women are documented as practitioners during the first half of the twentieth century.[10] They came from diverse backgrounds, practiced across the nation, were featured in professional exhibits, lectured, and participated in the professional organizations. However, more striking is a third assumption revealed by the general lack of interest by historians and designers in the significant role of residential landscape design, whether by men or women, in the shaping of the profession of landscape architecture. Residential design has since the 1970s been considered of lesser importance in practice as opposed to public and civic design.

The lack of attention to residential design does not accurately reflect the history of landscape architecture as a practice or a profession. Residential landscape design was, in fact, central in efforts to improve society and at the core of landscape architecture's purpose as a practice in the first half of the twentieth century. However, later twentieth century conceptions of the hierarchy of private and public spaces and associated constructions of gender-identity and connection have undermined the role of residential and private practice in the profession.[11] Constructed hierarchies reflected in professional language have suggested that women hold knowledge in the domestic and private domain while men are "naturally" endowed with knowledge of the civic and public domains.[12] In this framework we are lead to believe that as male is to female so architecture is to landscape architecture, public to private, public to domestic, and park to residential, the former assumed to have great significance than the latter. This in turn engenders particular narratives of the designed landscape in which home garden design and gardening are relegated to women's sphere and the design of public parks and city planning to men's domain. This is clearly not a benign construction of knowledge or of practice. And that is at the core of why an investigation of a female landscape architect who designed residential spaces challenges both the male canon but also the hierarchy of public and private space.

Challenging this construction of language, the essay explores the "second" of the aforementioned binary pairs arguing for their essential role in the history of practice of landscape architecture. By exploring residential design we reveal a breadth of practice engaged in by diverse practitioners, male and female. However, as the investigation reveals women playing a lead role in the design of residential landscapes, the exploration is framed by the overlapping domains of women as practitioners and the practice of designing residential landscapes. While this approach provides just one lens with which to discover the richness of landscape history and its practice as a profession in the United States, the analysis begins to build a different history that may inspire a breadth of thinking and creativity yet realized.

The garden city movement was merely one manifestation of the interest in residential and domestic design and planning. Designers and writers since the mid-nineteenth century were concerned with the development of livable cities and towns that supported traditional family life while benefiting from modern technology and transportation. The interest in such improvements and cultural refinements grew in part in reaction to increasing urbanization across the nation. In the 1840s, Andrew Jackson Downing argued for the necessity of establishing communities in which the advantages of the country were within easy access of the cities by railroad. He argued that these towns would be ideal spaces for communities to grow and families to thrive. Parks would be at the heart of these new developments providing a rural framework for the community.[13] Frederick Law Olmsted began his designs for the well-known suburb of Riverside in Illinois in 1868 with a vision similar to Downing's in that it focused on the merging of the best qualities of rural and urban life set within the countryside.[14] Olmsted believed the "manifestations of refined domestic life were unquestionably the ripest and best fruits of civilization." The development of taste was a crucial sign of domesticity and culture for which the home garden was a potentially positive force. He further suggested that American homes should include outdoor areas for domestic activities as well provide plenty of space for children's play. Without such advantages Olmsted was concerned that citizens under the stress and strain of city life would "almost certain, before many years ... be much troubled with languor, dullness of perceptions, nervous debility or distinct nervous diseases."[15]

Designing domestic spaces including a home garden was, as evidenced by these attitudes, a significant undertaking and cultural contribution. Landscape architect Ellen Biddle Shipman wrote "If you are planning to build a home, you are embarked on man's greatest achievement — it is for its protection that wars are fought; and for its beautification that other arts have been developed."[16] By the late 1920s, professional landscape architects, including Stephen Child, Ruth Dean, and Warren Manning had established reputations for small residential projects. In 1923, the Home Owners Service Institute advocated the services of a professional landscape architect to site houses and other buildings, lay out home grounds, and develop planting schemes for middle-class suburban communities.[17] Designs for home gardens were increasingly made available to those of the middle class in the early twentieth century

Women played a significant role in these interests in residential design. Both professional colleagues and clients credited women landscape architects with specific (read "natural") expertise in garden design. A 1928 report on women contended that they "have a natural aptitude for the more intimate type of design that one finds in domestic work, coupled with an instinct for plant design and groupings."[18] Nevertheless, the acceptance of women in the profession was not universal nor ubiquitous. Whether it Olmsted's description of the well-known and respected landscape architect Beatrix Farrand's professional work as a bedroom practice, or fear that women were taking jobs away from men, there remained voices discouraging women from engaging in professional work.[19] These views reflected the perceived need to professionalize landscape architecture along the lines of architecture and engineering, neither of which genuinely accepted women and denied a feminine perspective. Efforts to distinguish landscape architecture from horticulture and gardening, both frequently associated with women, also fed a distrust of female practitioners. Despite these views, there were male professionals who mentored women including Warren Manning, Jens Jensen,

Charles Platt, and the firm of Vitale, Brinckerhoff and Geiffert. By 1915 there were three schools providing programs in landscape architecture for women taught by men as well as at least twenty co-educational programs. Further professional acceptance was evident in the Third National Conference of Instruction on Landscape Architecture's (1922) strong endorsement of the practice of training women in coeducational schools.[20] Thus it was a complex context that framed practice and while historians initially chose to follow a simplified linear narrative (from Olmsted to Hubbard to Eckbo/Kiley to McHarg), this essays suggests a more complicated and nuanced history.

It is within the complex design milieu of the 1920s that the Regional Plan Association of America (RPAA) was organized to explore ideas and visions of the role of planning at every scale — from the house to the neighborhood, to the town, city, and region. Led by the architect Clarence S. Stein and landscape architect and planner Henry Wright, they set out to create such a plan at the level of a new town or a garden city. Their vision for an American garden city or "New Town" was based on the ideas of the English writer, Ebenezer Howard. Howard had described the broad principles of garden city development in *Tomorrow: A Peaceful Path to Real Reform* in 1898.[21] Stein and Wright together with

Portrait of Marjorie Sewell (Cautley), 1917 as she graduated from Cornell University (author's collection).

practitioners and businessmen, including at various times Lewis Mumford, Benton Mackaye, Catherine Bauer, and Alexander Bing, began to formulate plans to implement their vision. The primary problems they sought to solve were a shortage of affordable housing, overcrowding in the metropolitan areas, the impact of the automobile, and the need for more efficient land use policies. Plans and projects were developed over the years in locations as far apart as New Jersey and California.[22] While a number of the towns met with relative success, the lasting legacy of Stein and Wright's work has been the Sunnyside superblock and the Radburn plan both of which included landscapes designed by Marjorie Sewell Cautley.[23] This paper considers four garden city designs within the larger New York metropolitan area: Sunnyside, Radburn, Phipps Garden Apartments, and Hillside Housing each of which is positioned within landscapes designed by Marjorie Sewell Cautley.

Marjorie Louisa Sewell was born into a middle class Navy family in 1891 near San Francisco, California, spending her early years in California, New York, Japan, and Guam.[24] Orphaned at thirteen, she was sent to live with relatives in New York and New Jersey and spent summers with the family at their Lake George campground, discovering nature within the Adirondack wilderness.[25] She enrolled at the Pratt Institute in New York City where she was introduced to Arthur Dow's book, *Compositions*, that shaped the foundation of her work as a landscape designer and writer. She subsequently attended and graduated from the Packer Collegiate Institute in Brooklyn. At the age of 23, Cautley applied to the landscape

design program at Cornell University and graduated in 1917.[26] This was an ideal foundation at a period when professionals believed that "landscape architecture has, like all arts, a certain scientific side, and ... basic and fundamental laws."[27]

Shortly after graduating from Cornell, Sewell went to work first for the Boston-based landscape architect Warren H. Manning and then in Illinois for Julia Morgan, a California architect, on war housing projects under the auspices of the YWCA.[28] In 1920 she opened an office in Paterson, New Jersey and was soon leading an office of three employees specializing in public projects including hospital grounds, housing projects, schools, and parks.[29] She was active as a writer and published articles and photographic essays for professional and popular magazines including *Landscape Architecture, Planners' Journal,* and *Architecture.*[30] In 1925 she was elected to professional membership in the American Society of Landscape Architects (ASLA) under the name of Cautley as she had married in 1922. She was regularly included in the annual exhibits of both the larger association and the New York Chapter through the 1920s and early 30s. Thus she was an active member of and contributed to the profession.

Plan for Roosevelt Memorial Common, Tenafly, New Jersey, 1921–1928. Designed by Marjorie Sewell Cautley. From the Cautley Scrapbook, © Architectural Archives of the University of Pennsylvania.

If the purpose of this scholarship was to merely add women and stir, one might argue that Cautley's contributions to two canonic works in the historic narratives of both city planning and landscape architecture would suffice. Nonetheless, this work argues that there is far more to be learned by reading more closely this work and Cautley's inscription of her own agenda for the profession and, even of more significance, her vision for a new social order. Cautley's designs and writing on landscape architecture and public landscapes propose three significant social objectives: to fully and dynamically integrate natural landscapes into the lives of the lower and middle classes; to design landscapes that would best serve the significant needs of women and children; and to actively and consistently involve the community in the design process. Her designs reveal the high value she placed on community participation, conservation of land and nature, and collaboration with architects and artists.

Cautley's first major public landscape design was the 30 acre Roosevelt Memorial Common in Tenafly, New Jersey (1921–1930).[31] As a memorial to Theodore Roosevelt's conservation efforts, Cautley created an arboretum park featuring native trees and shrubs. She worked alongside the sculptor Trygve Hammer (1878–1947) to weave the monument into the landscape and place. Working with the existing landscape, Cautley designed the park

A GROUP OF HOUSES PLANNED AND PLANTED AS A UNIT

MARJORIE SEWALL CAUTLEY, LANDSCAPE ARCHITECT

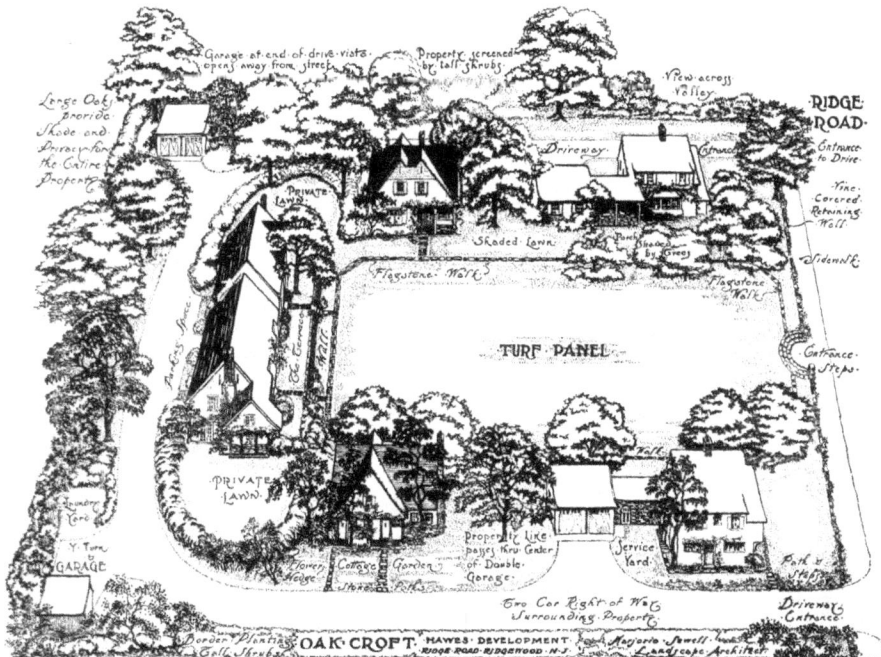

AN UNUSUAL *suburban development, in contrast to the more usual one which consists of houses placed in a row with uniform setbacks, exposed lawns, and a large proportion of land wasted by long drives. Here at Ridgewood, New Jersey, a group of six houses built by Mrs. John Hawes are placed on three sides of a common lawn and served by a single drive which runs behind them*

Plan of Oak Croft Development, Ridgewood, New Jersey, 1921–1929, designed by Marjorie Sewell Cautley and Thomas C. Rogers. As published in *House Beautiful* in 1929, p. 68.

to simultaneously celebrate native landscapes and natural amenities while providing recreational and contemplative spaces for town residents. This was done by a series of small insertions into the existing elements. The park comprised designated areas for observing nature, including a bird and game preserve where vegetation and water networks were carefully stewarded, for active school gardens where students could engage in learning about nature, for athletic activities such as croquet and for more passive activities including a picnic grove where families and active adolescents might interact. An existing creek continued its path through the park and was only damned to create a small pond and skating rink in one corner serving both conservation and recreation concerns.

Reflecting larger social concerns, Cautley encouraged the city to hire "needy men" as well as use local volunteers (particularly children) to plant and construct the park.[32] Not only was the community engaged in planting and constructing the park, but they became embedded stewards and advocates of the park land. Only later was a school built on a part of the park, and yet while the building intrudes on the open spaces, the placement of a school is appropriate to Cautley's vision for public landscapes.

While the Roosevelt Park was an important public space, Cautley was also interested in the design of public housing. In 1923 the *New York Tribune* published the plan of the Tribune Demonstration Houses, Oak Croft, in Ridgewood, New Jersey, with Cautley as landscape architect and Thomas C. Rogers as architect. She worked closely with the patron, Mrs. Hawes who became increasingly interested in new town projects. This project, like

Sunnyside Community, garden court, 1928. Photograph included in essay by Albert G. Hinman and G. Coleman Woodbury, "Landscape Architecture's Role in Modern Housing Projects," *American Landscape Architecture*, October 1929, p. 15.

others of the period, was meant to provide a model for better living within the means of the working middle class family. The designs offered healthy environments for families, particularly those on limited incomes, and to create an alternative model to increasing urbanization and the perceived horrors of contemporary city-dwellings. Important elements of these designs were ample sunlight, air circulation, views of the landscape, and generous recreational space.[33] Cautley's plan accomplished these goals by working with the existing landscape to create an efficiency of use, including shared spaces and densely arranged private spaces. She stipulated that the existing oak trees remain and she used local stone to build the walls, steps, and paths thus serving both an economic efficiency and creating a sense of place grounded in the local. However, historically the most striking part of her plan was to place the houses in a U-shape on the perimeter of a common garden court.[34] This format was very similar to that used to plan the garden city plans with Stein and Wright and may well have caught the eye of those in the RPAA.

In the midst of this practice, Cautley's interest in housing and its relationship to landscape led to travel in Europe, including Sweden, Latvia, Czechoslovakia, Yugoslavia, and Hungary as well as France and England in 1929 and again in 1935. She arranged for meetings and interviews with the European planners from whom she learned many of the current scientific practices applied to the design and analysis of residential spaces and activities.[35] On returning from her first trip, she wrote a book for children, *Building a House in Sweden* with illustrations by her sister, Helen Sewell.[36] The story is of a young family moving to a housing project in the government's garden suburbs of Stockholm where they are able to build their own home and garden in a friendly and collaborative community.[37] Cautley's

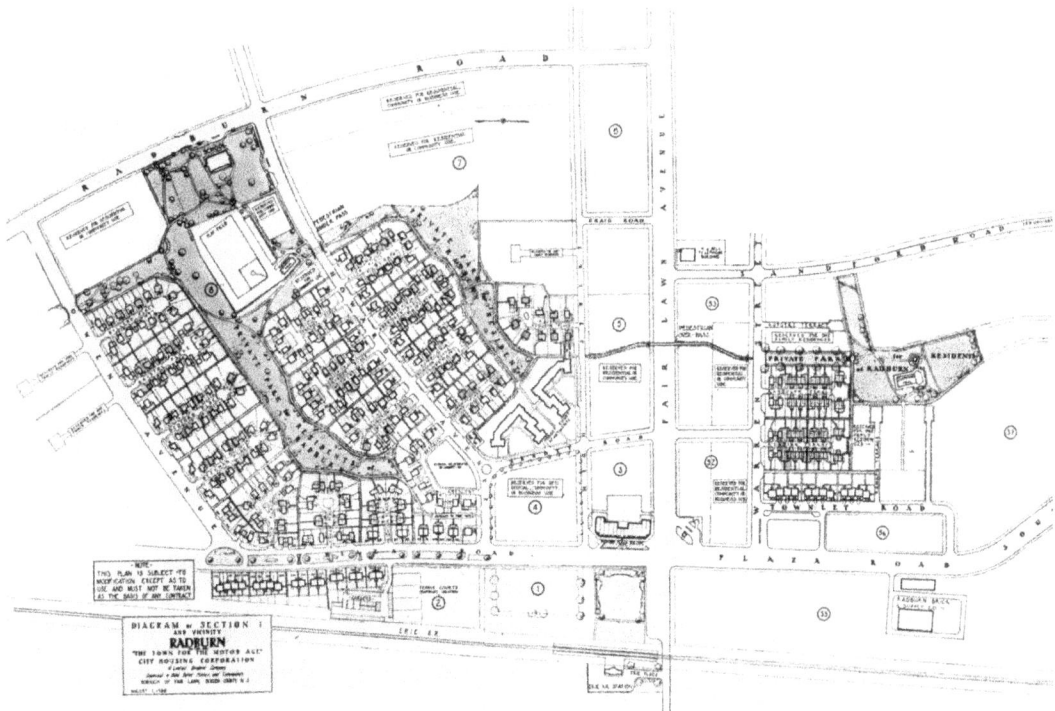

Radburn Plan as used in publicity materials. Clarence Stein and Henry Wright, architects with Marjorie Sewell Cautley as landscape architect (courtesy of the Radburn Association).

story emphasized the value of integrating the home and garden in order to create a healthy environment for children and families, ideals that guided her designs.

While it is unclear exactly when or how Cautley met Stein and Wright, she was selected as a member of the design team for Sunnyside in Queens, New York (1924–1928) the association's first experiment implemented under the auspices of the City Housing Corporation. On an eighty-acre site already marked by an urban grid, a mix of single, two family, and apartment buildings were sited along the perimeter of regular city blocks. The houses and apartments faced the streets while the interior spaces were dedicated to parks and small gardens. The common areas were laid out as horticulturally distinct landscape courts serving as shared space for residents while the gardens were viewed as private spaces to be tended by the respective families.

With the success of Sunnyside, the design team planned a community that might more closely meet the garden city ideal as it would be constructed on farmland rather than within the existing urban grid. Radburn in New Jersey (1928–1930), although due to the depression it was never completed, remains one of the most canonic of the early garden cities.[38] The Radburn plan developed five important themes which became known collectively as the Radburn idea: the superblock provided a development framework; the houses were reversed with a primary entrance facing the interior park, rather than the street; the streets were

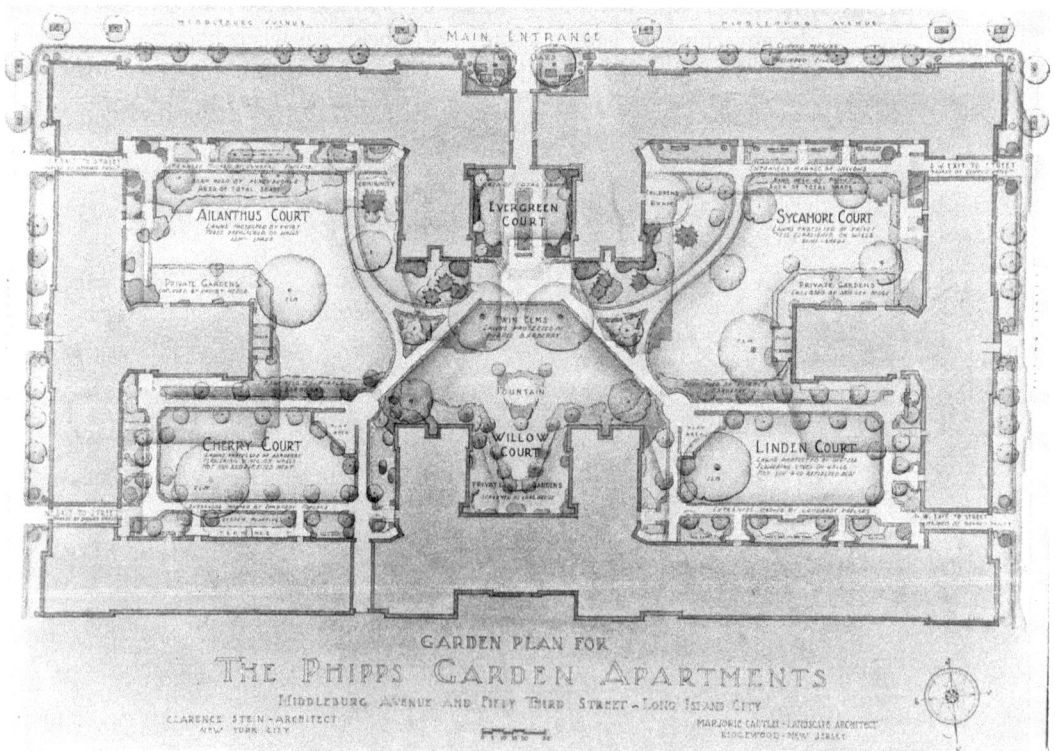

Landscape design for Phipps Garden Apartments, 1931, as designed by Cautley. Note the large circles were the elm trees that were moved into the landscape prior to completion of the building. The courtyards each featured a plant theme and thus became a part of the immediate community of residents, distinguishable from the other courtyards (courtesy Avery Architectural and Fine Arts Library, Columbia University).

minimalized creating a system of dedicated streets and lanes; pedestrian and vehicular traffic were kept separate; and a continuous park ran through the community.[39]

In 1931, the Society of Phipps Houses initiated the addition of an apartment complex as an extension to the Sunnyside community, the Phipps Garden Apartments (1931, 1935).[40] The complex, in keeping with the purpose of the foundation, was to serve low-income individuals and families.[41] This site, which retains its layout and remains committed to serving low-income families, was remarkable for the elaborate garden courts at the core of the complex of four and six-story high apartment buildings providing housing for three-hundred and forty families. The buildings covered only 43 percent of the land leaving a majority of site as shared landscape. Lewis Mumford in announcing the Medal of Honor for large-scale planning awarded by the New York City AIA to the project wrote, "This apartment group shows what can be done in the way of commodious planning when the unit of design is no longer a few buildings lots on the regulation street layout.... The enormous inner court is landscaped with trees and shrubs that have plenty of sunlight for growth; here Mrs. Marjorie S. Cautley has done an excellent job."[42]

Although private space specifically for individual families was minimal, the garden courts provided intimate areas for a variety of activities supplementing related public spaces within the buildings. Each apartment was provided with access to an out-of-door space. The ground floor apartments had private gardens, others had balconies, some had terrace garden rooms, and others access to the roof-scapes. Access to nature and the out-of-doors was considered a requirement for healthy living environments by housing advocates and the Phipps family, which included avid gardeners, and supported efforts to provide such spaces for families living in the garden apartments. To emphasize the permanency and importance of the garden areas Cautley persuaded the Phipps foundation to purchase large trees to be moved into the gardens prior to the completion of the apartment buildings.[43] In addition she persuaded the foundation to dig wells in order to provide a more permanent water system to maintain the gardens. These initial investments emphasized the importance of the landscape in the eyes of the foundation as well as Cautley's persuasive arguments to create a sustainable landscape. The Phipps apartments were a model of low-income housing

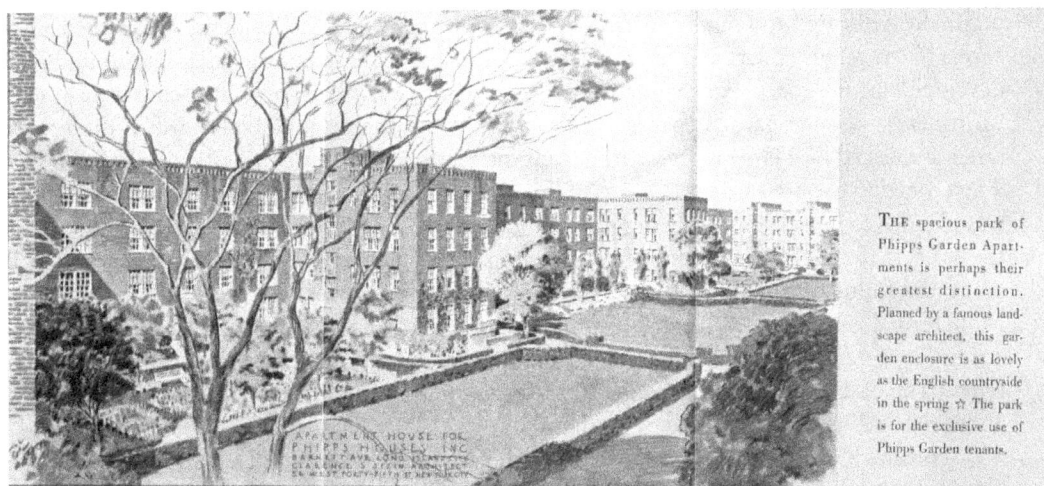

THE spacious park of Phipps Garden Apartments is perhaps their greatest distinction. Planned by a famous landscape architect, this garden enclosure is as lovely as the English countryside in the spring ☆ The park is for the exclusive use of Phipps Garden tenants.

Phipps Garden Apartments, Queens, New York, 1931 as published in publicity brochure (Phipps Houses Group).

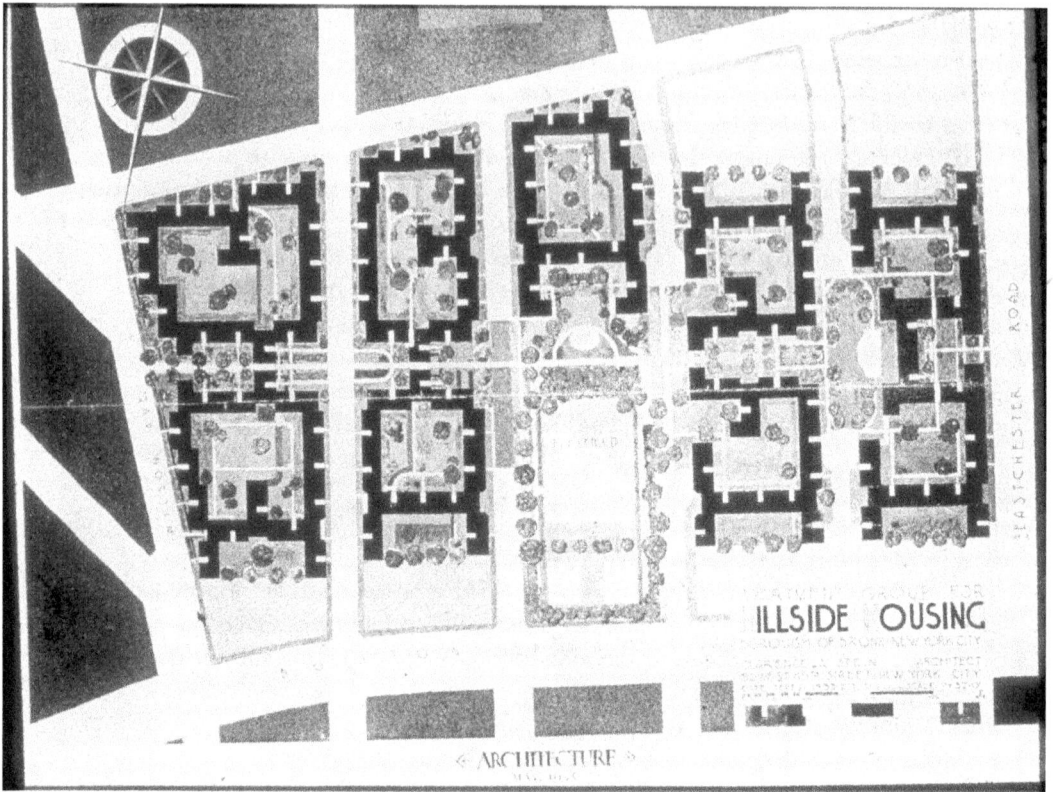

Plan for Hillside Housing as published in an article by Henry H. Saylor, "The Hillside Housing Development," in *Architecture* **May 1935, p. 245.**

for many years and remain fully occupied to this day, with many apartments lived in by second and third generations of the first families.

In 1935 Cautley and Stein were invited to extend the apartment complex over the area originally dedicated to tennis courts. With the agreement that the residents of Phipps had access to the tennis courts and other recreational spaces included in the adjacent Sunnyside development, the complex expanded. Cautley provided the plans for a large courtyard featuring three distinct garden spaces. The entrance from the original courtyard to the new one was marked by a large wisteria arbor framing views of the courtyard and new buildings. There were no private gardens laid out in this courtyard as it was too narrow. The landscape was planned to be efficient while suggesting the experience of a much larger park. To obscure the scale of the buildings, ginkgo trees were espaliered along the walls and hedges planted along the foundations. Open grass areas alternated with flower beds and walking paths. More formal "Dutch" and "English" gardens highlighted the two ends of the courtyard with a simple garden of grass and trees at the center. Like the original courtyard, this landscape remains an oasis of green within a densely urban landscape, including the subway that runs above ground just behind the development.

Hillside Housing, renamed Eastchester Heights, in the Bronx, New York (1932–1937) was the last project that Cautley would work on with Clarence Stein. The land was purchased at a minimal price from Nathan Strauss Jr. and financed through governmental programs. The intent was to create a project similar in quality and detail to the Phipps Garden Apartments but at less of a cost so that it would be within reach of lower-income groups.[44] With only 40 percent of the land as building, the remaining 60 percent of the sloped and marshy site was intended as landscape. This allowed the maximum amount of open space to be dedicated to use by its residents.[45] As with the other designs, the landscape was defined primarily by lawns and hedges with trees as vertical accents.[46] With more space on this site than at the Phipps Apartments, Cautley identified the perimeter of the public park as private gardens opening out from the garden apartments, which were in fact half basement apartments. It is likely that the private garden spaces balanced the disadvantage of being in an apartment that was slightly below ground level made possible by the hillside topography of the site. The ground landscape, like that at Radburn, was large enough to establish distinct spaces for different uses including children's playgrounds and walkways for mothers and young children. The need for recreational grounds for older children and larger open spaces for community activities had been secured through the siting of the project near a school and existing public parks.[47]

Cautley's garden city designs did not merely frame the architecture or the plan as many modern architects imagined. Instead her designed spaces actively engaged the community in experiences of nature and landscape. Writing the editor of *Horticulture Magazine* she

Radburn, Gazebo, 1932 (Radburn Association).

emphasized the horticultural challenges of her projects: "twenty four of the Plant Classifi-
cations in Chapter Vii [of her Garden Design, 1935] are being demonstrated in the development of courts and streets for the Hillside Housing Project in the Bronx, N.Y., a PWA
job covering 20 acres, and quite the most difficult from the horticultural approach that I
have ever undertaken."[48] Although many professional city planners focused on the architecture and engineering aspects of the landscape plans (even when they were trained in
landscape architecture), she considered the horticultural maintenance and stewardship to
be critical elements of the design's ability to meet the needs of the residents and users. It
was this commitment to designing with a strong plant palette that led to women being
labeled as garden designers rather than landscape architects. Yet, as Ellen Shipman is so
famously quoted, "women, instead of working over their boards, used plants as if they were
painting pictures, and as a artist would."[49] Traditionally nineteenth and twentieth-century
women were taught the skills of gardening, the science of horticulture and the art of painting.
The emerging profession of landscape architecture merged these interests and may well have
suggested itself as an appropriate venue for women wishing to pursue a career. This background was shared by many women designers such as Shipman, Beatrix Farrand, Annette
Hoyt Flanders, Rose Greeley, and Marian Cruger Coffin, all of whom drew on their gardening and horticultural knowledge as well as their training as painters and artists to create
works of landscape art.

Cautley's solid knowledge of plant materials and horticultural requirements was an
outgrowth of her childhood experiences in a family of plant collectors, enthusiastic gardeners
and painters, including her mother who was a respected painter of native flowers of California,
as well as a portrait painter.[50] Her parents encouraged her to read and to practice her painting,
music, and gardening, common activities for educated young women, even in the middle
classes. Cautley's education at Cornell University in the "landscape art" program expanded and
refined her knowledge and skills by emphasizing a comprehensive command of plant materials and the ability to apply this knowledge to the design process. Throughout her practice,
she kept abreast of current discussions in the fields of landscape architecture and city planning
and often wrote on the importance of horticultural concerns within these discourses.

Yet neither nature nor horticulture dominated Cautley's designs. She carefully designed
nature in a manner reflecting the idea of three natures, although hers was a compressed and
miniaturized form.[51] This idea comprises the "natural" or the idea of wilderness along the
edges of the development, the cultivated parks of lawn and trees at the center of the community, and the formal garden in close proximity to the home where food was grown and
exotics and other non-native plants might be tended.

Cautley initiated the design process by closely observing the existing topography, soil,
climates, and vegetation, and developed her plan accordingly, creating transitions between
a variety of landscapes both naturalistic and formal.[52] At Radburn she established a buffer
area where the garden city landscape edged a mix of farmland, meadows and waterways.
This edge landscape was designed to appear "natural" with an extensive use of native or
naturalized plants in an informal design. Describing her work she wrote that "[I]t was the
desire of the landscape designer to preserve for Radburn a part of the beautiful natural
growth that is being destroyed so rapidly throughout northern New Jersey."[53] In the southern
park she cultivated a meadow of wild asters and planted a grove of native cedars so that
"when Radburn is a city of twenty-five thousand souls there will still be an echo of the
woods and meadows upon which it was built."[54] These areas could be viewed from the
homes and parks or enjoyed on foot or bicycle.

Hillside Housing plan showing garden courtyard with private and "public" landscapes (courtesy of the Division of Rare Manuscript Collections, Cornell University Library).

Although Cautley was recognized for her use of native plants, she did not limit her palette to botanically-defined native plants; rather she included plants that "naturally" blended into the landscape aesthetically and ecologically. The choice to use native or locally naturalized flora that might survive the local climate as well as the city atmosphere, use little water, and require minimal care was a significant component of Cautley's plan to create low-maintenance, thereby affordable and viable, landscape designs in keeping with the goal of the housing developments and garden cities.[55] Thus it was not an ideological argument for the use of native plants but an economic and practical response to the project and more generally an approach Cautley would consider appropriate as she sought to develop housing plans that were economically sensible, functionally appropriate, and aesthetically valuable.[56] She argued that "the land should not only afford an appropriate setting for the buildings, but also provide a ready means of escape from the noise, dust, and confusion of the city, and offer an opportunity to relax out of doors or to engage in wholesome exercise, which, until recently has been possible only for those city dwellers who are fortunate enough to live near public parks."[57]

In the interior of the communities, Cautley designed park-landscapes. She retained existing landscape forms including the creeks and streams as well as many of the trees.[58] Clumps of birch, viburnum, wild azalea, and highbush blueberries from the neighboring woods were transplanted to the new landscape softening the transition between the existing landscape and the domestic gardens.[59] Although designed and maintained, these areas served as articulations of the regional character — suggesting that they might offer an experience of the "natural" landscape for residents and visitors. Additions of gazebos as noted in the image emphasized the designed nature of the space as well as providing a resting place for residents to view the landscape.

Lawns served a critical role in the park landscapes. The use of lawns was only emerging as a standard for housing projects in the early to mid-twentieth century. As the lawn-care industry encouraged Americans to associate a well-kept lawn with good citizenship, the costs of installation and maintenance remained prohibitive.[60] Cautley designed the lawn spaces to serve as a perceived luxury associated with grander urban parks — think Central Park's Sheep Meadow — while simultaneously limiting the lawns to only those larger spaces where it could be appropriately enjoyed. The community areas of both Radburn and Hillside Housing featured luxurious grass lawns and beautiful trees while the smaller home-gardens featured limited lawn emphasizing terraces, groundcovers, and hedges. The park landscapes at Phipps and Sunnyside were not as expansive but nonetheless featured lawns and trees in the common areas. The lawns visually linked low and medium-income housing project to the wealthy suburbs in a poignant manner.

Yet the lawns were not merely to be viewed or to provide a setting for the homes, as it was often in wealthier suburbs; for the housing projects the grassy areas actively engaged residents by providing spaces for sports, recreation, relaxation, and theatre. It is interesting to compare Cautley's emphasis on activities within the landscape to Stein's focus on the landscape as view, apparent in his speech at the dedication of Hillside Housing in 1935: "We are bringing nature back, grass and flowers and trees ... it will not be long before the vines have grown and the bushes and trees and the lawns have softened the outline of the buildings. It is that that will make Hillside different from the rest of New York. It will be

Opposite: **Audubon Lane Gardens. Note clipped hedges are for edge of lane (courtesy Avery Architectural and Fine Arts Library, Columbia University).**

DETAILS for CLIPPED HEDGING on LANE

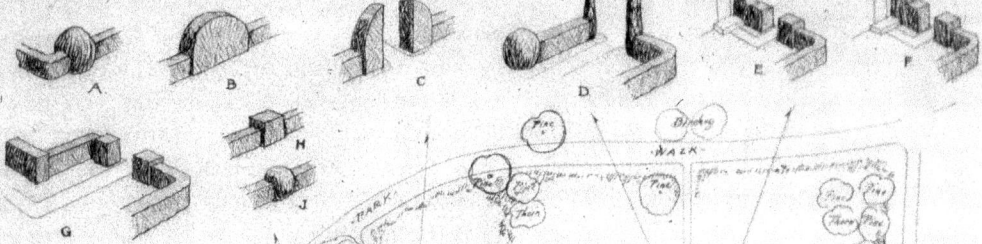

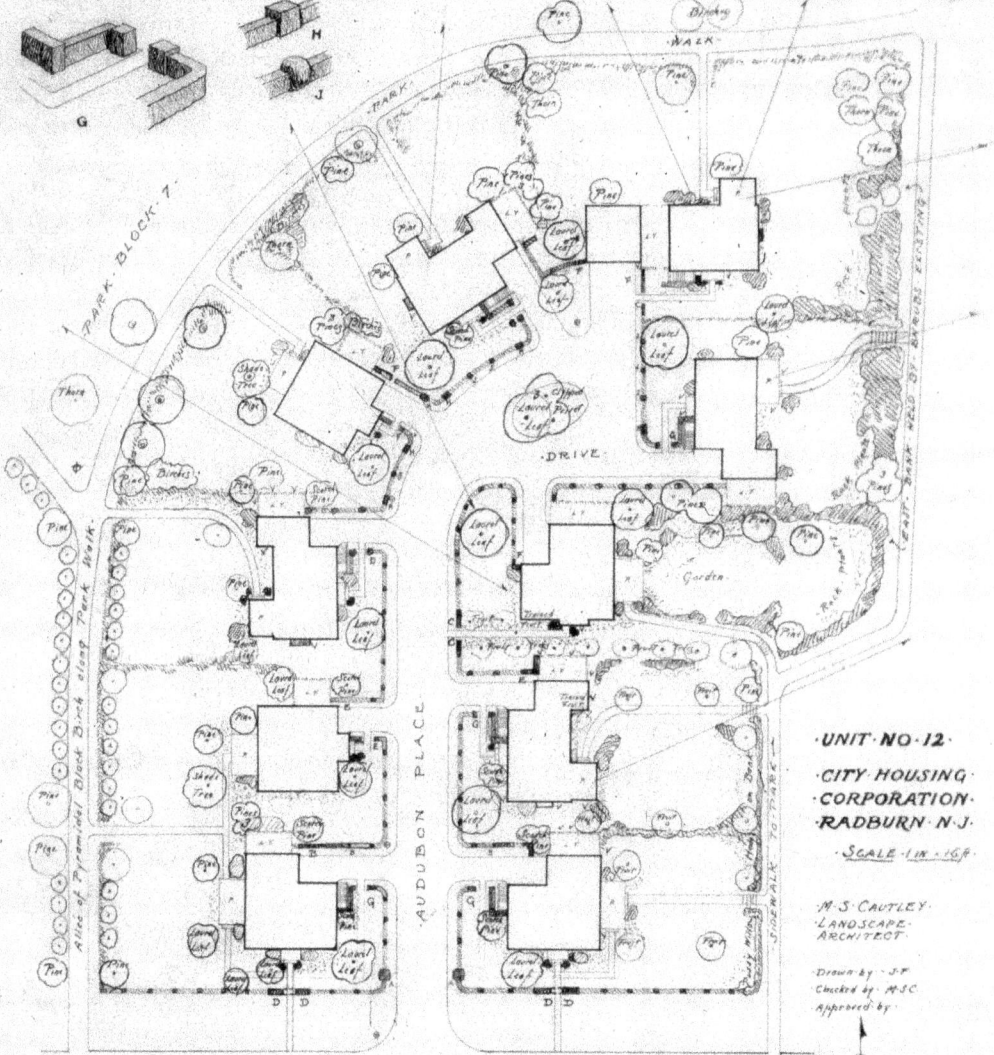

A   B   C   D   E   F

G   H   J

PARK

WALK

PARK · BLOCK 7

Rock · Block 7

DRIVE

Garden

Rock Garden

EAST · PARK · HEAD · OF · BROOKS · EXISTING

AUDUBON PLACE

SIDEWALK · TO · PARK

· UNIT · NO · 12 ·

· CITY · HOUSING ·
· CORPORATION ·
· RADBURN · N · J ·

· SCALE · 1 IN · 16 ft ·

M · S · CAUTLEY ·
LANDSCAPE ·
ARCHITECT ·

Drawn by · J · F ·
Checked by · M · S · C ·
Approved by ·

N · · E ·

· HIGH · STREET ·

AUDUBON · WEST & NORTH
GARDENS

· FOLIAGE · TO · HARMONIZE · WITH · PARK · 7 ·

· TREES · 50 ·
· Oaks · Pines · Birch · Laurel · Leaf · Willow ·
· Pyramidal · Birch · Alice · Existing ·

600' HEDGING & SHRUB · SCREENS ·
150 { Vaccinium · Viburnum · Aronia · along · Park · Walk ·
     Spiraea · prunifolia · between · Properties ·

· VINES · & · PERENNIALS ·
· See · Detailed · Lists ·

· ROCK · PLANTS · EAST · GARDENS ·
· See · Lists ·
Note :- · Flower · Color · is · Indicated
by · Dots ·
· Arrows · Indicate · Views ·

AUDUBON · LANE · & · EAST
GARDENS

· FOLIAGE · GRAY · GREEN ·

· TREES ·
8 · Scotch · Pines ·
21 · Laurel · Leaf · Willows ·

· SPECIMEN SHRUBS · 350 ·
20 · Juniperus · pfitzeriana ·
· Althea · in · variety ·
· Eleagnus ·
· Buddleia ·
· Lonicera ·
· Lycium ·
· Aralia · pentaphylla ·

17 · FRUIT · TREES ·
2 · Trained · Fruits ·

145 · HEDGE · EAST · BANK ·
· Pussy · Willow ·

· STREET · HEDGE · 1000' ·
· Clipped · Privet ·
Hedging 2 ft high ·
Posts 3' ·
Gate Posts 5-6 ft ·
Arches 7 ft high
made of Red Cedars
9 ft tied together ·
For Details
· see · Drawings · Above ·

a quiet peaceful park surrounded by houses. From every room one will look out on broad vistas of gardens and restful lawns or gay play spaces."[61]

Stein and Cautley believed in the vital role of the landscape, yet Cautley's designs encompassed a much more active engagement in the landscape than a mere appreciation of a pretty view. She argued vehemently for the importance of landscape in any vision of better communities and healthier living. In 1933 she suggested "it is time to devote some of our enforced leisure to the study of civic problems and the value of long vistas, open spaces, decent living, and wholesome recreation."[62] It was her mission to design such spaces and places for the working-class communities at Hillside and Phipps.

In a gentle contrast to the "natural landscapes" of the parks and outer edges of the community at Radburn, the domestic spaces in close proximity to the homes were defined by neat hedges and small groupings of medium sized shrubs and trees. The gardens included a mix of native and non-native flora as well as productive (i.e. fruit trees and grape vines) and ornamental plants. The plans emphasized the contrast between the park landscape and the manicured hedges along the streets and lanes. A similar plan was designed for the Hillside Housing Project with private gardens designated for the ground-floor apartments and defined by small flowering hedges. For Phipps Garden Apartments where private gardens were limited to a few ground-floor apartments, Cautley created additional spaces for groups of apartments, each surrounded by a small, neat hedge with formal flowerbeds and benches for the residents. The contrast between a more informal and open approach with the more formal and enclosed character defined the public and private spaces respectively. A similar division of space through plant form is also evident in the Radburn plan for "Audubon Lane." Shrubs are crafted and trained into architectural forms at the edges of the streetscape while an informal massing of trees lines the park walkways.

Drawing on the experience of all three "natures," Cautley offered residents and visitors a range of experiences in the landscape. That these opportunities were created within developments intended for low and middle-income families is of significant consequence. Other

Sitting, surveying and meeting in the park, postcard of Phipps Garden Courtyard, 1936 (Phipps Houses Group).

professionals including Warren Manning, Sarah Orme Jewett, Jens Jensen, Genevieve Gillette, and Elsa Rehmann, advocated for preserving and conserving natural landscapes and making them accessible to a large public. Cautley focused on bringing these landscapes into the daily lives of the working class and in particular women, mothers, and children.

What remains relatively invisible in the design is Cautley's careful attention to visual access in the landscape. Privacy was an increasingly significant issue in modern homes and gardens.[63] It was a modern privilege, one to which many women did not have access. The issues of privacy worked in two directions — it was a privilege of the modern woman and it served to "hide" the domestic realities from the public eye. In suburbia laundry lines, vegetable gardens, and even play areas for the children were often placed behind hedges or fences so that the public need not easily see these activities. For many these precautions were meant to spare the public from the ugly scene of laundry hanging or productive rather than ornamental gardens. Yet for others the design of domestic spaces behind hedges was to provide privacy for mothers as they worked and watched the children.

Cautley addressed issues of privacy in the daily lives of the mothers, through her careful attention to views and the definition of spaces. Privacy was provided for each family immediately adjacent to the house for both functional purposes as well as recreational uses.[64] Laundry yards were provided within easy access of the kitchen door but out of sight of other residents as Cautley recommended in her book *Garden Design.*[65] Productive gardens and orchards were out of sight of the general public as they were set on the park side of the homes. However, such productive landscapes including fruit orchards were sometimes planted across neighboring gardens making them easily accessible to everyone for "to pluck a sprig of parsley or to sample one's grapes ... is to know the richness of simple living."[66] In addition, private areas for family entertaining often overlapped — suggesting a more communal view of community.[67]

Terraces and sitting areas often embraced views of the larger parks and the boundaries of other home gardens. Because the hedges and plant materials defining the edges of the

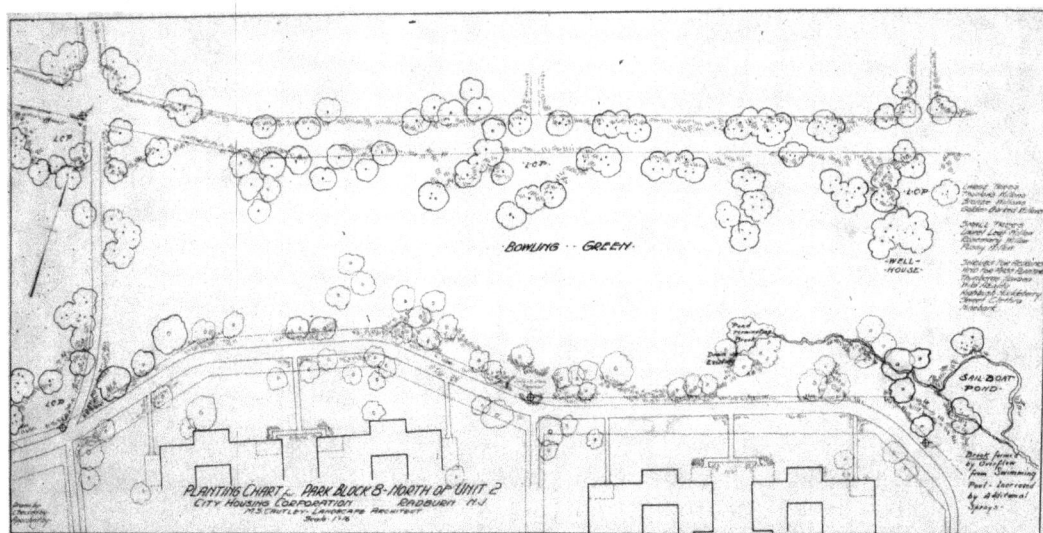

Planting Plan for Park Block 7 (Park A), Radburn, New Jersy, designed by Marjorie Sewell Cautley (courtesy Avery Architectural and Fine Arts Library, Columbia University).

Planting elm tree at Phipps Garden Apartments. From the Cautley Scrapbook, © Architectural Archives of the University of Pennsylvania.

home gardens or other types of small gardens were below eye-level, they formed visual distinctions without blocking the views to and from the private and communal landscapes. The open views blurred the edges of private and public suggesting a more communal lifestyle for residents, particularly mothers and children. These views back and forth might encourage residents to imagine their extended family encompassed the larger neighborhood. Similar to the traditional front porch, the home gardens allowed the experience of standing physically within one's private space while simultaneously being visible to the immediate neighborhood. As these gardens were only visible to other residents, as they were on the park side of the homes, it was not a public view but a neighborhood view that was offered.

Balconies and terraces at the Phipps Garden Apartments provided another type of outdoor space. While each apartment was provided some type of out-of-door space, these varied in specific details. The corner ground floor apartments were provided small garden spaces that were physically and visually adjacent to the common courtyards. Many apartments featured balconies that were part of the fire escape system while others featured wide hanging-balconies. The balconies had individual entrances but remained open to the view of anyone in the common areas and from other windows. Nonetheless through the use of potted plants and screens these could be made more private. The most private were the enclosed terraces. Stone paving and the extensive number of windows made these spaces feel a part of the out-of-doors, yet walls, an extension of the interior architecture, fully surrounded the spaces. Placed on protruding sections of the apartment buildings, these spaces featured excellent views of the common areas and in some cases views of the New York City

Grading the terraces at Hillside. From the Cautley Scrapbook, © Architectural Archives of the University of Pennsylvania.

skyline while protecting inhabitants from views into the spaces. These remained coveted apartments due to the private terrace rooms (some called Florida rooms). In contrast, roof-top landscapes were the most public and it is unclear if any private spaces were marked out. Nonetheless, residents spent much time on the roof hanging laundry, visiting, watching children play, and enjoying the view of the distant city skyline.

The park areas provided another form of community privacy in each of the garden city developments designed by Cautley. While not private for each family or resident, they were private to the community of families. These private/public park landscapes were safe spaces for children and families. Play areas were designed to be within sight of the apartment or home windows, thus mothers knew their children were always under watchful eyes. The "vigilant eye of the mother [who] may supervise the children ... while she sets the table or hangs out the table linen," was significantly aided by the visual access alongside the physical boundaries of the parks.[68]

While these views are often described in aesthetic terms as open and expansive, they are also functional. Shrubs and trees did not entirely block one's view from inside the house to the private yard area or the larger common park spaces. At Radburn the school and its yard were designed to be within sight of neighboring houses. At Phipps and Hillside mothers knew their children were always under watchful eyes of the many apartment dwellers as the playgrounds and open landscapes were all within view of the windows. Cautley valued such a communal view of families and communities and often brought her daughter to work with her to share the experience.[69]

While window views provided one form of surveillance, plentiful seating and active programming offered a more engaged form. All of the parks within the garden city developments offered ample seating allowing mothers, elderly residents, and children to observe each other as well as socialize on a regular basis and in safety. Benches and picnic tables were provided adjacent to the play areas for younger children where mothers might visit with friends while maintaining close attention to their young ones (noted in the plans as LCP). The parks offered a variety of game fields and pageant stages for community events thus suggesting a richness of programming that would encourage older children to remain within the limits of the development and thus within sight of the community.[70] These articulated spaces, visually accessible landscapes, and identifiable circulation systems were on the interior of the community, acting as private community places. As designed, the landscapes were easily defensible by the residents as they had visual access not shared with outsiders. The residents knew who should and should not be present and which activities were appropriate and acceptable.

By being "survey-able" Cautley suggested that the edges of private and community space might be visually read as ambiguous. This can be positioned within the context of utopian community developments, particularly those designed by early urban feminists who, according to Dolores Hayden, endeavored to merge the public and the private in conjunction with the respective male and female spaces in their designs and ideals for model communities.[71] Cautley's spaces suggested a fluidity between those areas designed as private and community, domestic and non-domestic, thereby expanding the "usable" space for women from within the house and its immediate landscape to the entire community.

While Stein and Wright argued for the economy of the architecture, Cautley designed economically feasible landscapes supporting the development of affordable-housing projects.[72] Cautley was adamant that the planning should give careful attention to construction costs and should forecast appropriate maintenance plans and expenses. At least 5 percent of the cost of the buildings she argued should be dedicated to the landscape: "If the development of ... the land is considered as a permanent installation of definite sales' value, why should it receive an allotment which is equal only to such incidentals as radio outlets and awnings?"[73] As for the architecture itself, Cautley argued that the houses "hardly function as a house" specifically in light of the lifestyle modern Americans desired and expected. She advised that the provision of "soundly built dwelling ... at moderate cost is a problem that planner and the architect have not yet solved."[74]

In a similar vein, community participation was highly valued by Cautley. She consistently argued for the power of listening to the ideas and dreams of the public. She invited potential users to comment on the design and subsequently to plant and construct their landscape. In this way, she argued, the space would become a park owned and stewarded by its own particular public. In an essay published in *American City* in 1944, she argued that the park was a "practical asset and laboratory for the development of good citizenship and human character." This was Progressive Era thinking applied directly to parks at all scales.

Cautley took her argument to civic associations, garden clubs, and school districts lecturing on the importance of landscape design and community involvement in the planning and construction phases.[75] She directed the professional never to forget "that you must have your community with you, step by step, even though it means a lot of extra time devoted to publicity and to arousing interest and cooperation. Yes, you are a public servant...."[76] She produced films of the construction process including workers and community members.[77] These films emphasized the active participation by women and children, as well as hired workers, to create the community gardens and parks. At the Phipps Garden Apartments she filmed children planting bulbs while mothers visited and watched. Husbands and fathers were shown helping with the larger planting projects.[78] As opposed to the more traditional photographs of architecture and landscape without people, Cautley's documentary images, many by photographer Clara Sipprell, were filled with individuals engaged in the place. Her focus was on the social functions of the garden cities, and more specifically, how they served to improve the daily lives of the residents.

Cautley pursued other projects in addition to her garden city landscapes. She published *Garden Design: The Principles of Abstract Design as Applied to Landscape Composition* in 1935. She taught as a lecturer at MIT (1934–1937) and Columbia University (1935–1937) on site planning and landscape design.[79] In 1933 she was appointed as Landscape Architect Consultant for the State of New Hampshire, overseeing Civilian Conservations Corps projects in ten State parks. She was actively engaged in the profession and served as a mentor to young professionals including Katherine Cole Church and Alice Recknagel Ireys.

Unfortunately, at the height of her career, in 1937, Cautley suffered a nervous breakdown.[80] She was subsequently committed by her husband to a New Jersey state hospital for the mentally ill, Greystone Park. She was paroled only in 1942 with help from her friends and professional colleagues.[81] She immediately divorced her husband and enrolled in and completed a Master's Degree in the University of Pennsylvania's city planning program. In the ensuing years she collaborated on projects with established practitioners in the Philadelphia region. However, by 1946 she again resided in a sanitarium, and she died in 1954.[82]

Despite the important work by Cautley and that of other women, few have been credited with work in the public sector during the early part of the twentieth century. Stein collaborated with women, yet often neglected to credit them for any significant contributions, even when their social agendas were as closely intertwined, as his were with those of Cautley.

Instead Cautley has been credited for "handling of plant materials" in the plans and creating a nurturing community rather than creating the landscape composition as a whole.[83] These are the skills and talents historians and designers traditionally felt comfortable attributing to women: the domains of horticulture and the domestic arena.

As the practice of landscape architecture matured in the twentieth century, the professional mainstream moved away from domestic and residential design toward public work. This move reflected increasing concerns within the professional community regarding the legitimacy of the practice as a profession and its relationship to architecture and engineering. Housing as a national interest was changing. The emerging profession of city planning distanced themselves from issues of housing as they identified planning as a public effort while housing was increasingly labeled a private issue. Instead, the focus was on transportation, traffic, streets, and civic and public buildings.[84] A similar trend can be traced in landscape architecture although it came later, in the 1930s. Private and residential work was too easily associated with gardens and gardening and thus the profession needed to break with such practice. Jens Jensen, after resigning from the ASLA wrote that there was a "strong tendency by the American Landscaper to get away from gardening, as if that word smelled of cabbage. He has a fear of being classed with the craftsman instead of the professional, and today the art is practically killed, because of his efforts to make a profession of it."[85]

But housing had in fact been and remained an important domain of design practice. Leading practitioners from Frederick Law Olmsted to Garrett Eckbo argued for the value of good design in residential landscapes. Design was significant at every scale, from the home garden to the planning of a region. Nevertheless, in time efforts to disassociate residential work from the profession of landscape architecture dominated the perception of practice and its historic narrative. While practitioners including the Olmsted Brothers designed small residential gardens and landscapes, by the 1940s they did not allow the practice to define their oeuvre.

A focus on women's designs for residential landscapes is one alternative lens through which to consider a history of designed landscapes. It does not make the argument of women's natural affinity to domestic space, nor does it claim an essential feminine expertise. However, it does claim that contemporary culture ascribed to women an expertise in domestic issues and thus authority in the design of such spaces and their use. This lens reveals how women accessed this authority and, in turn, promoted and advocated a shared vision of a better nation. Women including Martha Brookes Hutcheson, Annette Hoyt Flanders, Ellen Biddle Shipman, as well as Cautlley believed well-designed modern landscapes would improve the American culture and the lives of its citizens. They brought to their designs a (not the, but one of) woman's perspective and therefore, in contemporary culture, an authority in the creation of homes and their respective gardens. They exerted this authority to pursue a social agenda to improve the living standards of the average American citizen and cultivate American society.

It is the residential designs by women that reflect the combined authority of women as housekeepers and as professional designers. One can identify the inscriptions of women in the attention paid to the improvement of the daily life of the mother, wife, child, and family. While men might acknowledge such matters, their designs rarely exhibited specific knowledge or awareness of the realities of family life. Men did not write of the vigilant mother or of the need for her to have an outdoor room of one's own. By exploring residential work and the practice of women, as well as others marginalized over time, we begin to understand a breadth of historical practice in landscape architecture not often acknowledged by designers or historians. We can begin to trace threads of practice that might not otherwise be visible to the historian's inquiry and yet might offer rich lessons and narratives for future practices.

Acknowledgments

This paper was published in an earlier version as "Designing Garden City Landscapes: Works by Marjorie L. Sewell Cautley, 1922–1937" in *Studies in the History of Gardens and Designed Landscapes*. I want to thank John Dixon Hunt as the editor and subsequent reviewers for the excellent comments that were a part of revising the paper. The paper has also been presented and discussed in a variety of scholarly venues each of which has been an important part of developing the arguments. It is the community of scholars that I want to thank for the ongoing pursuit of a more rigorous discipline of landscape architectural history.

Notes

1. Lynn Avery Hunt, *The New Cultural History* (Berkeley: University of California Press, 1989), 18.
2. Abigail Ayres Van Slyck, "Women in Architecture and the Problems of Biography," *Design Book Review* 25 (1992): 19.
3. Anne Higginson Spicer, "The Gardening Women in Our Town," *The House Beautiful* 33, no. 3 (1913): 103–4.
4. Daniel T. Rodgers, *Atlantic Crossings: Social Politics in a Progressive Age* (Cambridge, MA: Belknap Press of Harvard University Press, 1998), 190.
5. Alan Mather, "Henry Wright," *Pencil Points* 21, no. 1 (1940): 14.
6. This omission on the part of landscape historians has been noted as well by Elizabeth Meyer, "The Expanded Field of Landscape Architecture," *Ecological Design and Planning*, ed. George F. Thompson (New York: John Wiley, 1997) 60–62. Martin has more recently discussed the landscape of Radburn, although it is more of a discussion of use and experience than an historical analysis. Michael David Martin, "Returning to Radburn," *Landscape Journal* 20, no. 2 (2001).
7. Historians such as Norman Newton endorsed such a view by including just three examples of women in his history of landscape architecture and discussing only their residential garden work.
8. For a lengthier discussion on the breadth of women's practice see Thaïsa Way, *Unbounded Practice: Women and Landscape Architecture in the Early Twentieth Century* (Charlottesville: University of Virginia Press, 2009); Thaïsa Way, "Women as Force in Landscape Architecture, 1893–1942," PhD diss, Cornell University, 2005.
9. Frederick Law Olmsted is credited with having so described the practice of Beatrix Jones Farrand who in fact ran an office with commissions across the nation over a fifty year period.
10. Way, *Unbounded Practice: Women and Landscape Architecture in the Early Twentieth Century*.
11. Meyer, "Expanded Field of Landscape Architecture"; Ann E. Komara, "The Glass Wall: Gendering the American Society of Landscape Architects," *Studies in the Decorative Arts* 8, no. 1 (2000): 22–30.
12. Important arguments for this discussion include the following: Judith Butler, *Gender Trouble: Feminism and the Subversion of Identity* (New York: Routledge, 1999); Joan Wallach Scott, "Excerpts from 'Gender: A Useful Category of Historical Analysis,'" *Gender Space Architecture: An Interdisciplinary Introduction*, ed. Jane Rendell (London; New York: E & FN Spon, 2000), 74–87.
13. A. J. Downing, George William Curtis and Fredrika Bremer, *Rural Essays: Horticulture—Landscape Gardening—Rural Architecture—Trees—Agriculture—Fruit, Etc., Etc.* (New York: R. Worthington, 1869), 236–43.
14. Cynthia L. Girling and Kenneth I. Helphand, *Yard, Street, Park: The Design of Suburban Open Space* (New York: J. Wiley, 1994), 47–54.
15. Charles E. Beveridge, Paul Rocheleau and David Larkin, *Frederick Law Olmsted: Designing the American Landscape* (New York: Universe Publishing, 1998), 115.
16. Ellen Biddle Shipman, *Garden—Notebook*, Ellen McGowan Biddle Shipman Collection, #1259, Division of Rare and Manuscript Collections, Cornell University Library.
17. David L. Ames and Linda Flint McClelland, "House and Yard: The Design of the Suburban Yard,"

National Register Bulletin, Historical Residential Suburbs, U.S. Department of the Interior, National Park Service, 2002, http://www.cr.nps.gov/nr/publications/bulletins/suburbs/part3.htm (accessed 10 January 2006).

18. Henry Atherton Frost and William R. Sears, *Women in Architecture and Landscape Architecture: a Study for the Institute for the Co-ordination of Women's Interests* (Northhampton, MA: Smith College, 1928), 24.

19. Dorothy May Anderson, *Women, Design, and the Cambridge School* (West Lafayette, IN: PDA Publishers Corp., 1980), 19.

20. Donna Palmer, "An Overview of the Trends, Eras, and Values of Landscape Architecture in America: From 1910 to the Present with an Emphasis on the Contributions of Women to the Profession," Master's thesis, North Carolina State University, 1976, 25.

21. For a discussion of the idea of the garden in this vision, see M. Elen Deming, "The Place of the Garden in Garden Cities: A Utopian Romance," *Proceedings of Council of Educators in Landscape Architecture. Selected Papers, Vol. VIII: Our Community and Our Neighborhood* (1996): 38–45.

22. Clarence S. Stein, *Toward New Towns for America* (Cambridge, MA: MIT Press, 1969).

23. It is not clear at exactly what point Marjorie Sewell Cautley came to the attention of the garden city movement leaders, Clarence Stein, Henry Wright, and others. It may have been notice of her work at Oakcroft, her Cornell connections through Frederick Ackerman, or her personal friendship with Robert D. Kohn (architect, planner, and leader in the field).

24. Her first published article is on the landscape of Guam: Marjorie Sewell, "The Magic of Guam," *Atlantic Monthly* 111, no. 5 (1913): 649–52.

25. Marjorie spent the summer of 1914 running a small camp for children at Lake George with her sisters. They daily recorded their activities in a journal accompanied by sketches and photographs of the landscape. Cautley-Sewell-Moore Family Papers, 1840–2002, Private Collection of Patricia Cautley Hill, Brunswick, Maine: 1840–2002.

26. Cornell's Professor Ralph Curtis successfully recommended Marjorie to Warren Manning writing that she was "unusually single-minded in her determination to succeed in the profession ... that keen kind of outdoor student that you [Manning] enjoy" (31 March 1917). Marjorie Sewell Cautley, Correspondence, Marjorie Sewell Cautley papers, #4908. Division of Rare and Manuscript Collections, Cornell University Library.

27. Ruth Dean, *The Livable House, Its Garden* (New York: Moffat Yard and Co., 1917), vii.

28. Her work for Morgan is documented in her professional resume although it has not been verified by any Morgan scholar. See resume in Marjorie Sewell Cautley papers, #4908, Box 1, Division of Rare and Manuscript Collections, Cornell University Library.

29. Projects included the Bamburger Ideal Home, a hospital in Newark, New Jersey, the Town Park for Bolton, New York on Lake George, Pierce Arrow Service Station off Bloomfield Avenue, the Ellis Motor Car Company, Newark, a Studio for the Ethical Culture School, New York City.

30. In 1922 *Architecture* featured her photographic essay, "A City Garden," in which she described how an empty city lot might be designed as a garden to be enjoyed from the apartment across the street. In the same year she collaborated with her sister, Helen, as illustrator, and Charles Cutler, an architect, to produce a seven part series for the popular magazine, *Country Life* entitled "New Houses of Old Flavor."

31. The monument and part of the park are under consideration for listing on the National Historic Register and is listed as a part of the New Jersey Women's Heritage Trail. My thanks to Kevin Tremble, former chair of the Tenafly Historic Preservation Committee, for guiding me through the current status of the park.

32. Marjorie Sewell Cautley, "Landscape Gardening for the Unemployed," *New Jersey Gardens* (1928).

33. Marjorie Sewell, "A City Garden," *Architecture* 45, no. 4 (1922): 125–126. Marjorie Cautley, Helen Sewell and Charles Cutler, "New Houses of Old Flavor," *Country Life* 91, no. 1–6 (1922).

34. See Marjorie Sewell Cautley, "A Group of Houses Planned and Planted as a Unit," *House Beautiful* 65, no. 1 (1929): 68–69, "Community Development Advantages Demonstrated by Tribune: Houses in Jersey Group Open to Public Next Sunday," *New York Tribune*, September 9, 1923.

35. In 1935 she visited the town planner, Raymond Unwin, in England, while touring English town developments. The Unwins visited her in New Jersey in 1936 while he was lecturing at Columbia University where Cautley was teaching. Raymond Unwin lectured at Columbia on residential site planning and the dialogue of public and private landscape according to Michael David Martin, University of Iowa.

36. Marjorie Sewell Cautley, *Building a House in Sweden* (New York: Macmillan, 1931). She also produced a photographic essay on the view of Sweden from the air, Marjorie Cautley, "New Horizons from Aloft," *The American Landscape Architect* 3, no. 6 (1931): 17–19.

37. Cautley, *Building a House in Sweden*.

38. Drawings for these projects are currently in the papers Marjorie Sewell Cautley, Drawings, Collections of the Drawings and Archives Department, Avery Architectural & Fine Arts Library.

39. For a good description see Marjorie Sewell Cautley, "The Garden Walks of Radburn," *New Jersey Gardens* (1930): 21–22. Girling and Helphand, *Yard, Street, Park*, 54–64.

40. Now the Phipps Houses Group.

41. Radburn, N.J. and Phipps Garden Apartment, N.Y., 1928–1935 vol. 1 folder, 3 rolls, Marjorie Sewell

Cautley Papers and Drawings, Drawings and Archives, Avery Library, Columbia University; Marjorie Sewell Cautley, Phipps Garden Apartment, NY, Phipps Houses Group, 1931, 35, vol. multiple rolls and correspondence, Phipps Houses Foundation Archives, New York.

42. Lewis Mumford, "The Sky Line," *The New Yorker*, April 16, 1932.

43. Stein, *Toward New Towns for America*, 87–88.

44. Henry H. Saylor, "The Hillside Housing Development," *Architecture* 71, no. 5 (1935): 245–47.

45. Marjorie Sewell Cautley, "Landscaping the Housing Project," *Architecture* 72, no. 4 (1935): 186.

46. Royal Cortissoz, "Impressions of Art," *New York Herald Tribune*, March 25, 1933. Landscape architects of the NY chapter of the American Society of Landscape Architects reviewed Cautley's Phipps Garden Apartments as "an inspiring example of urban gardening."

47. Saylor, "The Hillside Housing Development."

48. Cautley, Correspondence.

49. Anne Peterson, "Women Take Lead in Landscape Art," *New York Times*, March 13, 1938, 83.

50. Paintings and watercolors by Minnie Sewell are included in the private collection of Cautley's daughter, Patricia Cautley Hill. Cautley-Sewell-Moore Family Papers.

51. John Dixon Hunt, *Greater Perfections: The Practice of Garden Theory*, Penn Studies in Landscape Architecture (Philadelphia: University of Pennsylvania Press, 2000).

52. Cautley, "Landscaping the Housing Project."

53. Marjorie Sewell Cautley, "Planting at Radburn," *Landscape Architecture* 21 (October 1930): 24.

54. Cautley, "Planting at Radburn."

55. This approach extended to her park designs for the State of New Hampshire for which she noted that the "Property has been developed to utilize existing features, & to conserve natural character & beauty. Building located at strategic points to control use & simplify maintenance." See plans for Kingston Park and Dorrs Pond Park, 1934, in Cautley, Correspondence, Cornell University.

56. Marjorie Sewell Cautley, "Potted Plants? Or Adequate Landscaping for Community Projects?," *American City* 50 (August 1935), Cautley, "Landscaping the Housing Project."

57. Cautley, "Landscaping the Housing Project."

58. See the landscape plans for Ashburn and Berkeley Parks and the Apartment buildings in the Cautley, Drawings, Cornell University.

59. Cautley, "Planting at Radburn."

60. Virginia Scott Jenkins, *The Lawn: A History of an American Obsession* (Washington, DC: Smithsonian Institution Press, 1994).

61. Dedication for Hillside, 29 June 1935, CUA, CSP, #3600 box 2, folder 5. Clarence Stein Papers, #3600, Division of Rare and Manuscript Collections, Cornell University Library.

62. Society, "Mrs. Marjorie Cautley Talks on Landscape Architecture," *Ridgewood Herald*, March 10, 1933.

63. Dianne Harris, "Making Your Private World: Modern Landscape Architecture and House Beautiful, 1945–1965," *The Architecture of Landscape, 1940–1960*, ed. Marc Treib (Philadelphia: University of Pennsylvania Press, 2002), 180–205.

64. At Port Sunlight, by Lever Soap manufacturers, developers were frustrated to see housewives hanging laundry on the fences as the design had not accounted for an appropriate area. *Clara Greed, Women and Planning: Creating Gendered Realities* (New York: Routledge, 1994), 95.

65. Marjorie Cautley, *Garden Design; the Principles of Abstract Design as Applied to Landscape Composition* (New York: Dodd Mead, 1935), 58–62.

66. Cautley, Sewell, and Cutler, "New Houses of Old Flavor."

67. These values reflect both contemporary utopian developments as well as the arts and crafts movement, in particular, efforts to design cooperative housing communities. Dolores Hayden, *Seven American Utopias: The Architecture of Communitarian Socialism, 1790–1975* (Cambridge, MA: MIT Press, 1976); Greed, *Women and Planning: Creating Gendered Realities*, 88–106; C. B. Purdom, *The Garden City; a Study in the Development of a Modern Town* (London: J. M. Dent & Sons, 1913), 98–103.

68. Cautley, Sewell and Cutler, "New Houses of Old Flavor."

69. Patricia recalls her mother telling her to pay close attention to the Radburn project as it was the most important project that she was involved in. Patricia Cautley Hill, interview with author, Brunswick, Maine, February 8–11, 2003.

70. As Michael David Martin has noted, "Radburn's landscape protected children, not just from cars but from the uncertain dangers inherent in the very publicness of the community street." Martin, "Returning to Radburn," 158.

71. Dolores Hayden, *The Grand Domestic Revolution: A History of Feminist Designs for American Homes, Neighborhoods, and Cities* (Cambridge, MA: MIT Press, 1981), 7.

72. "Landscape Artists Helps to Reduce Property Costs," *New York Herald Tribune*, Sunday, June 29, 1930, was one of the number of her articles and interviews addressing her concerns.

73. Cautley, "Potted Plants?."

74. Marjorie Cautley, "Effects of the American Standard of Living on Planning," *The Planners' Journal* (1937).

75. Topics included: "The planting of streets and highways"; "Developing Community Recreation Parks"; "The landscape problems of housing projects"; and "Garden Cities of Finland, Sweden, and Czechoslovakia."

76. Marjorie Sewell, "Small City Parks for Community Use: How Neighborhood Parks Meet Public Needs," *American City* 59 (May 1944): 66.

77. Cornell University holds 7 films that are currently being archived. Also see Cautley, "Landscape Gardening for the Unemployed."

78. Cautley's films are now on DVD held in the Marjorie Sewell Cautley papers, Marjorie Sewell Cautley #4908, Cornell University.

79. According to the MIT *President's Report 1935–1936* Cautley co-taught an undergraduate course in Landscape Construction (later renamed Site Planning and Construction Details) with Ralph Eberlin, a consulting engineer. The course was a preparation of engineering and architectural site plans and construction details for a group of sixty houses, as well as detailed cost estimates made of the completed work.

80. Correspondence, Marjorie Sewell Cautley papers, Marjorie Sewell Cautley #4908, Cornell University.

81. Supporters included Francis White and Dean William Emerson, MIT, who set up a trust fund for her use, Russell and Mary Van Nest Black, and Robert D. Kohn.

82. Upon release, she divorced, reclaimed the name Marjorie L. Sewell, and enrolled in the master's in fine arts degree program at the University of Pennsylvania and received her degree with honors in the city planning program in 1943. Her thesis on transforming blighted areas of Philadelphia suggested familiar reconstruction themes with superblocks, community space, and parks. Her only major project was with Russell Van Nest Black on the development of Meuser Park in Wilson Burough, Pennsylvania. During this time, she also completed a course in Industrial Camouflage for O.D.D. certificate. Marjorie Sewell, "How Blighted Areas in Philadelphia and Boston Might Be Transformed," *American City* 58 (October 1943): 47–48; Sewell, "Small City Parks."

83. Norman T. Newton, *Design on the Land; the Development of Landscape Architecture* (Cambridge, MA: Belknap Press of Harvard University Press, 1971), 489; Stein, *Toward New Towns for America.*

84. Rodgers, *Atlantic Crossings*, 195–96.

85. As quoted in a letter from Jensen to Mrs. and Mrs. Boardman, n.d., in the Morton Arboretum archives. Robert E. Grese, *Jens Jensen: Maker of Natural Parks and Gardens* (Baltimore: Johns Hopkins University Press, 1992), 61.

Bibliography

Ames, David L., and Linda Flint McClelland. "House and Yard: The Design of the Suburban Yard: History and Education, Cultural Resource Program." National Register Bulletin, Historical Residential Suburbs, U.S. Department of the Interior, National Park Service, 2002. http://www.cr.nps.gov/nr/publications/bulletins/suburbs/part3.htm (acessed 10 January 2006).

Beveridge, Charles E., Paul Rocheleau, and David Larkin. *Frederick Law Olmsted: Designing the American Landscape.* Revised edition, New York: Universe Publishing, 1998.

Butler, Judith. *Gender Trouble: Feminism and the Subversion of Identity.* New York: Routledge, 1999.

Cautley, Marjorie. "Effects of the American Standard of Living on Planning." *The Planners' Journal* (1937): 88.

_____.*Garden Design; the Principles of Abstract Design as Applied to Landscape Composition.* New York: Dodd Mead, 1935.

_____. "New Horizons from Aloft." *American Landscape Architect* 3, no. 6 (1930): 17–19.

Cautley, Marjorie Sewell. "A Group of Houses Planned and Planted as a Unit." *House Beautiful* 65, no. 1 (1929): 68–69.

_____. *Building a House in Sweden.* New York: Macmillan, 1931.

_____. Radburn, N.J. and Phipps Garden Apartment, NY, 1928–1935. Vol. 1 folder, 3 rolls. Marjorie Sewell Cautley Papers and Drawings. Drawings and Archives, Avery Architectural and Fine Arts Library, Columbia University,

_____. Correspondence, papers, drawings, sketches, photographs. Marjorie Sewell Cautley Papers, 1847–1995, #4908. Division of Rare and Manuscript Collections, Cornell University Library.

_____. "Landscape Gardening for the Unemployed." *New Jersey Gardens* (1928).

_____. "Landscaping the Housing Project." *Architecture* 72, no. 4 (1935): 182–86.

_____. Phipps Garden Apartment, NY. Phipps Houses Group, 1931, 35, vol. multiple rolls and correspondence. Phipps Houses Foundation Archives, New York.

_____. "Planting at Radburn." *Landscape Architecture* 71 (October 1930): 23–29.

_____. "Potted Plants? Or Adequate Landscaping for Community Projects?" *American City* 50 (August 1935): 51–52.

_____. "The Garden Walks of Radburn." *New Jersey Gardens* (1930): 21–22.

Cautley, Marjorie, Helen Sewell, and Charles Cutler. "New Houses of Old Flavor." *Country Life* 91, no. 1–6 (1922).

Cautley-Sewell-Moore Family Papers, 1840–2000. Private Collection of Patricia Cautley Hill. Brunswick, Maine. 2 boxes.

"Community Development Advantages Demonstrated by Tribune: Houses in Jersey Group Open to Public Next Sunday." *New York Tribune.* September 9, 1923.

Cortissoz, Royal. "Impressions of Art." *New York Herald Tribune.* March 25, 1933.

Dean, Ruth. *The Livable House, Its Garden.* New York: Moffat Yard and Co., 1917.

Deming, M. Elen. "The Place of the Garden in Garden Cities: A Utopian Romance." *Proceedings of Council of Educators in Landscape Architecture. Selected Papers, Vol. VIII: Our Community & Our Neighborhood* (1996): 38–45.

Downing, A. J., George William Curtis, and Fredrika Bremer. *Rural Essays. Horticulture — Landscape Gardening — Rural Architecture — Trees — Agriculture — Fruit, Etc., Etc.* New York: R. Worthington, 1869.

Frost, Henry Atherton, and William R. Sears. *Women in Architecture and Landscape Architecture: a Study for the Institute for the Co-ordination of Women's Interests.* Northampton, MA: Smith College, 1928.

Girling, Cynthia L., and Kenneth I. Helphand. *Yard, Street, Park : The Design of Suburban Open Space.* New York: J. Wiley, 1994.

Greed, Clara. *Women and Planning: Creating Gendered Realities.* London; New York: Routledge, 1994.

Grese, Robert E. *Jens Jensen: Maker of Natural Parks and Gardens.* Baltimore: Johns Hopkins University Press, 1992.

Harris, Dianne. "Making Your Private World: Modern Landscape Architecture and House Beautiful, 1945–1965." *The Architecture of Landscape, 1940–1960*, edited by Marc Treib, 180–205. Philadelphia: University of Pennsylvania Press, 2002..

Hayden, Dolores. *Seven American Utopias : The Architecture of Communitarian Socialism, 1790–1975.* Cambridge, MA: MIT Press, 1976.

_____. *The Grand Domestic Revolution : A History of Feminist Designs for American Homes, Neighborhoods, and Cities.* Cambridge, MA: MIT Press, 1981.

Hunt, John Dixon. *Greater Perfections : The Practice of Garden Theory.* Philadelphia: University of Pennsylvania Press, 2000.

Hunt, Lynn Avery. *The New Cultural History: Essays.* Berkeley: University of California Press, 1989.

Jenkins, Virginia Scott. *The Lawn: A History of an American Obsession.* Washington, D.C.: Smithsonian Institution Press, 1994.

Komara, Ann E. "The Glass Wall: Gendering the American Society of Landscape Architects." *Studies in the Decorative Arts* 8, no. 1 (2000): 22–30.

Martin, Michael David. "Returning to Radburn." *Landscape Journal* 20, no. 2 (2001): 156–73.

Mather, Alan. "Henry Wright." *Pencil Points* 21, no. 1 (1940): 3–14.

Meyer, Elizabeth. "The Expanded Field of Landscape Architecture." *Ecological Design and Planning.* Edited by George F. Thompson, 45–79. New York: John Wiley, 1997.

"Mrs. Marjorie Cautley Talks on Landscape Architecture." *The Ridgewood Herald.* March 10, 1933, S 5, 7.

Mumford, Lewis. "The Sky Line." *The New Yorker.* April 16, 1932.

Newton, Norman T. *Design on the Land; the Development of Landscape Architecture.* Cambridge, Mass.: Belknap Press of Harvard University Press, 1971.

Palmer, Donna. "An Overview of the Trends, Eras, and Values of Landscape Architecture in America: From 1910 to the Present with an Emphasis on the Contributions of Women to the Profession." Master's thesis. North Carolina State University, 1976.

Petersen, Anne. "Women Take Lead in Landscape Art." *New York Times.* March 13, 1935, 83.

Purdom, C. B. *The Garden City: A Study in the Development of a Modern Town.* London: J. M. Dent & Sons Ltd., 1913.

Rodgers, Daniel T. *Atlantic Crossings : Social Politics in a Progressive Age.* Cambridge, MA: Belknap Press of Harvard University Press, 1998.

Saylor, Henry H. "The Hillside Housing Development." *Architecture* 71, no. 5 (1935): 245–52.

Scott, Joan Wallach. "Excerpts from 'Gender: A Useful Category of Historical Analysis.'" *Gender Space Architecture: An Interdisciplinary Introduction.* Edited by Jane Rendell, 74–87. London; New York: E & FN Spon, 2000.

Sewell, Marjorie. "A City Garden." *Architecture* 45, no. 4 (1922): 125–26.

_____. "How Blighted Areas in Philadelphia and Boston Might Be Transformed: Rehousing for a fuller social." *American City* 58 (October 1943): 47–48.

_____. "Small City Parks for Community Use: How Neighborhood Parks Meet Public Needs." *American City* 59 (May 1944): 63–66.

_____. "The Magic of Guam." *Atlantic Monthly* 111, no. 5 (1913): 649–52.

Shipman, Ellen Biddle. *Garden — Notebook.* Ellen McGowan Biddle Shipman Collection, #1259. Division of Rare and Manuscript Collections, Cornell University Library.

Spicer, Anne Higginson. "The Gardening Women in Our Town." *The House Beautiful* 33, no. 3 (1913): 103–04.

Stein, Clarence S. *Clarence Stein Papers, #3600.* Division of Rare and Manuscript Collections, Cornell University Library.

_____. *Toward New Towns for America.* 3d ed. Cambridge, MA: M.I.T Press, 1969.

Van Slyck, Abigail Ayres. "Women in Architecture and the Problems of Biography." (Book Review.) *Design Book Review* 25 (1992): 19–22.

Way, Thaïsa. "Designing Garden City Landscapes: Works by Marjorie L. Sewell Cautley, 1922–1937." *Studies in the History of Gardens & Designed Landscapes* 25, no. 4 (2005): 297–316.

_____. *Unbounded Practice: Women and Landscape Architecture in the Early Twentieth Century.* Charlottesville: University of Virginia Press, 2009.

_____. "Women as Force in Landscape Architecture, 1893–1942." Ph.D. diss., Cornell University, 2005.

Chapter 11

Strolling Down Main Street with Dolores Hayden: A Perspective on Celebration, Florida

ILARIA SALVADORI

The inspiration for writer and director Todd Haynes's 1995 movie *Safe* was a story he saw on television about a group of housewives who were developing extreme reactions to everyday chemicals. In the movie, actress Julianne Moore plays Carol White, the perfect housewife with a wealthy husband and a beautiful house. At the beginning of the film she seems safer in life than just about anyone you could imagine. However, as the eerie plot of the movie unfolds and Carol starts becoming ill, starting with headaches, Carol's illness worsens until she finds out that she's become sensitive to the common toxins in today's world such as exhaust, smog and fumes. Diagnosed "environmentally ill," she leaves her family to find respite in an insulated new-age retreat.

Feminist Critique of the Urban Environment

The powerful image of Carol White becoming ill and rejecting her environment inverts the unfair but too common conception of woman's role in her social environment. Men have been usually associated with the public domain, while women have been associated with the domestic realm of family and leisure. Concepts such a "woman's sphere" and a "man's world" reflect such a separation of roles in the urban environments.[1] The entire history of the industrial city represents, according to the current feminist discourse, "an increasing spatial, functional, and temporal separation between home and work, on a continuum from the early industrial home workshop to the suburban home."[2]

After World War II, suburban home design brought this polarization to the extreme with the commodification of the domestic environment. The suburban dwelling became a bare box "to be filled up with mass-produced commodities."[3] This new environment presumed model inhabitants: a mononuclear family sustained by a man-earned wage. Men would receive "family wages" and become, therefore, homeowners, while women, as managers of the home, would take care of the members of the family. The great explosion of the suburban environment as a "perfect haven" for its mononuclear families has been, from the beginning, a man's solution: the polluted city with its stressful, congested spaces was the space of competition and production, while the home was a restful, non-threatening environment where men could recuperate after an intense day of work. The figure of the woman was necessary in this schema to maintain the peaceful quality of the home. It was also necessary for her to consume a great amount of goods in order to fulfill her role. From the Victorian interior of the parlor, to the early twentieth century engineered space of the kitchen, to the postwar suburban kitchen and its electric, functional parts, the evolution of the domestic environment has been a steady evolution of woman, first as a domestic and sexual care-taker, and, second as a major consumer of mass-produced items.[4]

Working hand in hand with this definition of the private home as woman's sphere was the exclusion of women from public space. "As long as the domestic world remains a romantic haven outside of public life and the political economy, politically active women can always be sent back to it, and men can justify the exclusion of women and children from their public debates and analyses."[5]

Thus, unless they were willing to be objects of harassment or aggressive attention, women were denied each aspect of public life. In contemporary society, such public spaces have themselves become increasingly privatized, in an effort to provide security to supposedly "vulnerable" women.

"A woman's place is in the home"

Women's place in the public, social environment of the contemporary metropolis has been tenuous at best, and sometimes entirely absent. In her discussion about the city, feminist scholar Dolores Hayden brings to our attention such conception through the analysis of two common feminist arguments and their relationship to public and private space. The first common feminist argument has assumed that public and private spheres have been, through out history, gendered and unequally valued. As stated above, men have been usually associated with the public domain, while women have been associated with the domestic realm of family and leisure. According to feminist discourse, the specialized land use patterns of the industrial city extended and solidified the separation of home and work spheres in time, place, and purpose. The corresponding expectation and identification of the private realm as female and the public realm as male resonates across decades of city-making. The new privatized spaces of the contemporary city and the contemporary suburbs have come, like the home similarly controlled, to be used by women for the practice of beauty and other rituals of consumption. Shopping malls, fitness centers, juice bars and hair parlors all belong to the "woman's sphere" and often replicate and reinforce spatial separation of gender roles. For their constructed and artificial nature, they also constitute a fragmentary environment and a discontinuous series of experiences.

The ways in which the design of both public and private spaces serve to thwart, entrap, and harm woman have become a focus of the analysis and critique of the planner Hayden, one of the most prominent contributors to the feminist discussion of the city and its relationship to gender and ethnicity. In her 1986 book *Redesigning the American Dream*, Hayden describes the transformation of the role of women from the late 1920s to the suburban sprawl of the 1950s, and explains how the increased energy consumption and the lack of community relationships were extended by this societal gender imbalance. "While the woman was expected to stay home and raise the child, the media invaded the private space of the home and pushed the necessity for bigger and better material possessions. These include the washing machine, the refrigerator, and even the weekend convertible."[6] Along with an increased efficiency such mechanization of the domestic realm also increasingly confined the woman's role to the home. As a consequence the domestic woman became more and more withdrawn from the public and the potential opportunities of solidarity with other women in the surrounding environment.

Domestic labor's function as the "most basic cause of women's inequality" was already identified by the first "material feminists" at the turn of the twentieth century. These feminists made the initial attempt to rethink urban design to address the condition of women. Dolores Hayden explains: "I call them material feminists because they dared to define a 'grand domestic revolution' in women's material condition. They proposed a complete transformation of the spatial design and material culture of American homes, neighborhoods and cities."[7]

Since that time, other changes have occurred, including progressive change of the family structure, increased number of women heading families, and higher participation of women in the labor force. Hayden, along with historian of planning and architecture Gwendolyn Wright and others, has argued that such factors require consideration in any urban design that would address the condition of women and other underrepresented groups in man-made environments. Current feminist discourse develops around several main issues particularly useful and relevant to the study of the urban environment. They include transportation, housing, safety, and human health as particularly relevant to the analysis of women's environments.

Transportation is probably one of the most important issues originating from the geographical isolation of suburban development and its consequent segregating effects on women's lives. MacGregor writes, "Women with children have different requirements of public transit and more complex pattern than men have. Because of various domestic responsibilities, women tend to make more short trips at different times during the day to a number of spatially dispersed facilities such as childcare centers, grocery stores, and children's recreational activities."[8] The destinations of these short trips not only are dispersed geographically but also located far from the home. The absence of public transportation can become — especially for women — a barrier to their participation in public urban life. Women isolated in residential suburban environments can be excluded by other activities that they could easily access in an urban environment.

Transportation is also interconnected with the central issue of land-use controls. From the feminist perspective, municipal zoning regulations have only exacerbated problems in mobility especially after the most recent changes in family and household structure. Single-use residential zoning for example has been, according to Hayden, "particularly detrimental for women's emancipation from the domestic zone, precluding the communalization of domestic tasks such as childcare, laundry and food preparation, and thus perpetuating the double burden of women in families."[9] Moreover, a majority of daily life activities usually managed by the female side of the family are still perceived as private matters. In addition, as mentioned above, essential services are often placed far from residential areas and are rarely accessible by public transit. Lack of time, money, or private means of transportation become a private problem of the family and, ultimately, of the woman. This problem is a structural one: since every detail has been carefully thought out and centered around the concept of mononuclear family, little space for flexibility and alternatives is left for women residents.

A higher degree of flexibility, claim feminist theorists, is needed for the spaces of the new city, where different functions can be accommodated accordingly to the different needs.[10] Urban theorist Kevin Lynch, in a related critical discussion, talks about flexibility as one of the variables determining a good city form. Under his definition of "fit" he lists the concept of manipulability as a particular necessity for the city to the changing needs of its inhabitants. He defines manipulability as "the extent to which a behavior setting can be changed in its use or form, in an easy and incremental fashion, and whether that ability to respond is likely to be maintained in the predictable near future."[11]

Similarly, Hayden discusses integration and flexibility as main aspects of a new, feminist model of the city. Reconsidering the human environment from the household to the city, Hayden proposes "an alternative set of design guidelines."[12]

Hayden's alternative model, called HOMES, is conceived to be applied, first, to existing suburban and urban environments and, then, as a guideline for new developments. The model would be implemented, according to Hayden, by Homemakers, small participatory organizations working cooperatively. Her model includes as a main characteristic the integration of home, employment and services through mix-used development. Flexible building codes and zoning would accommodate different typologies of households, while simple retrofitting of existing suburban homes and other urban dwellings is the most appropriate strategy of change. Single-family homes would be therefore subdivided and converted into multi-unit apartments, and front lawns would be turned into private gardens, enhancing the focus on a central green space at the center of the suburban block. This agglomeration of the formerly privately owned yards in a larger shared space combined with the subdivision of the houses in a higher number of units would, in Hayden's own words, "turn the block inside out."[13]

As a direct consequence of such actions, the wasteful replication of uses typical of the repetitive and monotonous aspect of the suburban landscape would be completely dissolved. Hayden's new environment transforms suburban icons into functional, commonly shared spaces. An efficient transportation system would guarantee mobility at different times of the day, while vans with employed drivers would be located in each lot in order to give families the necessary mobility to accomplish daily duties. Hayden's model introduces shared house duties to housing developments with services such as common industrial kitchens, laundry spaces, and day care. The consequent substantial increase of common spaces would also facilitate the employment of new workers and generate new local jobs. Such a model necessitates a review of the notion of private property — a cornerstone of the suburban environment. Cooperative ownership appears to be the most appropriate form of management of HOMES.

Often, women's concerns are associated by the planning process only with the private sphere. Safety and childcare, as mentioned above, are considered private matters rather than concerns of the extended community. The feminist urban environment is instead a place where community is built, an idea too often disregarded by the traditional planning approach, as well as by some new planning approaches in developments like Celebration, as we will discuss later.

The New Urbanism

Hayden's perspective on environmental design helps expose the limitations of the supposedly innovative planning of the New Urbanism movement, especially as it is embodied in the community of Celebration. The "New Urbanism" movement started in 1994 and has become enthusiastically accepted in much current urban planning and design theory in the United States. The Congress of the New Urbanism became a milestone of the history of American planning. The Charter, illustrating the principles of the Congress, states: "We stand for the restoration of existing urban centers and towns within coherent metropolitan regions, the reconfiguration of sprawling suburbs into communities of real neighborhoods and diverse districts, the conservation of the natural environments, and the preservation of our built legacy."[14]

The document has become probably the most cited set of ideas in the last fifteen years of urban theory. New Urbanism has met also a considerable number of opponents such as planner Alex Krieger, who, in 1998 in an article in *Architecture* magazine, criticized principles hardly contested by the planning community before then.

> Your broad aims are dead on. History, however, rarely evaluates a movement on the basis of its stated aims. The success of New Urbanism will eventually be measured by comparing is achievements against its claims.... To date you have helped to produce: more subdivisions than towns; an increased reliance on private management communities, not innovative forms of elected local governance; densities too low to support much mixed use, much less to support public transportation; relatively homogeneous demographic enclaves, not rainbow coalitions.[15]

Responding to Krieger's criticism in the December 1998 issue of the same journal, planner Andres Duany, a paladin of the movement, responded: "Krieger is correct that the typical New Urbanist projects have a lower density. The reason is not the abdication of principle, but the more complex criteria of diversity — a variety of human needs and desires, some fulfilled by an urban apartment and others by a house with a yard. New Urbanism requires inclusive housing, the full range of choices provided in close proximity within each neighborhood."[16]

What people were debating about was the essential suburban character recurrent in the New Urbanist projects and its contrasting term "Urbanism." The presence of a large number of low-density housing in the New Urbanist projects was seen by its designers as a feature to be offered on the market along with other typologies, but it was interpreted by its opponents as an essentially suburban aspect of this supposedly innovative development. More pointedly, the suburban woman had been re-framed in a conservative way.

Celebration, Florida

The Disney Corporation's Celebration is an example of this essential conservativism, as far as women are concerned, of New Urbanism. In the 1960s, Walt Disney conceived of EPCOT (Experimental Prototype Community of Tomorrow) as a vertical city covered by a large-scale structure interconnected by an internal monorail system. His utopian community was never realized, as he died in 1966. However, thirty years later a study by Michael Eisner, at the time chairman of the Disney Company, assessed the potential of 10,000 acres of land left over from Disneyworld development. Eisner realized that this land, which would never be used by Disneyworld, could be turned into a profitable enterprise. Soon, Disney's dream of the ideal community was pulled off the shelf, dusted, polished and delivered to the real estate market. The technological vision of EPCOT was transformed into the New Urbanist vision of Celebration, whose name was chosen through marketing strategies and numerous focus groups.

Developed by The Celebration Company, a subsidiary of the Walt Disney Company, Celebration is located on 4,900 acres of flat swampy land southwest of Orlando, 15 miles from Cinderella's Castle. The first residents — the so-called "Pioneers" — moved to Celebration in June 1996. The town officially opened in November 1996. Its population in November was 2,500, with a projection of 20,000 in ten to fifteen years, with a maximum potential buildout of 8,000 residences. The Disney Corporation takes care of all the management aspects of daily life. In spite of the concerns for the disappearance of true public spaces denounced by the New Urbanism, Celebration is entirely privately owned. Nevertheless, faced with the challenge of creating a real community in an authentic urban space, Celebration's founders are quite optimistic. Bob Shinn, senior vice president of Walt Disney Imagineering, has declared: "With Celebration we are giving something back trying to blaze a trail to improve American family life, education, and health. This project allows us to fulfill Walt's idea for a town of tomorrow."[15]

Accordingly, in authentic New Urbanist tradition, the development is surrounded by 4,700 acres of protected greenbelt. Robert Stern's fine-grained plan of Celebration is organized around a loose grid of streets, putting into practice the New Urbanist concern with traffic reduction, helping to create both safe spaces for children and walkable streets with accessible facilities — concerns often raised by feminist critiques of the suburb. Both slower car traffic and an enhanced pedestrian experience are reinforced by the "anti-suburban siting" created by the location of the houses close to the curb and including small set-backs and a variety of arrangements and styles. The resulting fine grain of the small sized lots creates an engaging rhythm at a human scale. Street trees planted already in mature stage create a

View of typical street in Celebration. Copyright © 1994–2009 Scott Gilchrist. Image from stock.archivision.com.

View of downtown Celebration. Copyright © 1994–2009 Scott Gilchrist. Image from stock.archivision.com.

"historic" feeling, the scaling of the architecture pays attention to proportions and cars are removed from the main streets and hosted in alleys. The disappearance of the classic suburban icon of the garage is a strong New Urbanist statement, as is the reappearance of the porch, an icon of neo-traditionalist towns. The porch is the trademark of any "true" New Urbanist development and it is considered an effective catalyst of community. The homes of Celebration are the strong point of the development's selling packet. Subjected to strigent aesthetic restrictions, they are available in a catalogue and include a wide range of possibilities: Classical, Victorian, Colonial, Revival, Coastal, Mediterranean, French. In a tradition with roots in Victorian homes, the *Pattern Book* of New Urbanist Architecture illustrates all the design features offered by each design. One entry reads: "Celebration's Mediterranean style comes out of a Florida tradition established by early-20th-century architects, who created well-composed and eclectic homes by combining a number of different styles. This is evident in the asymmetrically placed windows, doors, and arcades all within a simple stucco frame. Porticos and loggias face the streets, while tile roofs provide color and character. Available in Bungalow and Estate home sites."[16] The catalogue presents a restricted set of alternatives: the homes in Celebration must be glamorous, stylized, in fashion and substantially obeying to a precise middle-upper class decor. This fact is also confirmed by the average price of the homes in Celebration, which range from 25 to 40 percent more than average real estate prices in the area.

The public spaces of town are organized around 18-acre downtown, the core of the development. The site includes a bank, a post office, cinema, retail shops, restaurants and apartments. Disney's special place in American culture, its powerful skills of place-making, and its ability to shape people's behavior through physical space are here combined with the New Urbanist design vision: the vernacular architecture of Main Street, preserved in Disneyland "Main Street U.S.A," is refreshed and updated in Celebration's main street. The walkable character of the streets and succession of pleasing public spaces are what both Disney downtowns have in common.

In Celebration Disney employed the most prominent American and European architects to create its collection of public buildings. The list of names is astoundingly prestigious: the Celebration Preview Center — the promotional center for the town — by Charles Moore, a bank by Robert Venturi, a post office by Michael Graves, two movie theaters by Cesar Pelli, office buildings by Aldo Rossi, the town hall by Philip Johnson. Such a collection, created in the best Disney tradition, only helps to realize a typical postmodern environment, appropriately, since not only architectural dissonance but also civic irresponsibility has been seen to characterize postmodernism.[17] In Celebration, escape from suburban alienation is translated into a small-town nostalgia through the implementation of a quite conservative vocabulary, which alludes to a simpler, easier, friendlier past — the same past in which a "woman's place is in the home."

The political realm of the town is only apparently so: behind the abundance of columns of the Philip Johnson's postmodern town hall there is no public arena but Disney Corporation instead. Moreover, as mentioned above, the town of Celebration is not incorporated: the county takes care of the main infrastructure, while Disney manages the town indirectly through the Homeowners Association, the fastest-growing form of political association in the country.[18] Disney is, in fact, involved in the town politics to such a degree that the town manager, Disney Corporation's Brent Herrington, is defined as "sort of the Mayor of Cel-

Designed by Philip Johnson, Celebration City Hall is one of the civic buildings designed in postmodern style. Copyright © 1994–2009 Scott Gilchrist. Image from stock.archivision.com.

ebration."[19] This confusion between private and public, between real and fake, is the essence of Celebration, as a kind of artificially created "natural community."

Community has emerged as one of the features most prized by new home buyers, according to the trade journal *Builder*. As the Preview Center's brochure explains, Celebration's cornerstones are, in fact, "Community, Education, Health, Technology and Place." This community is a technological one: a fiber-optic network of information systems links the town's homes, school, healthcare facilities and offices. The virtual "Front Porch" provides information online about community events and newsgroups. Among the events listed for the months of October and November, is the "Home Decoration tour," promoted by the Women's Club and the "Snow Show on Main Street" four times every night between November and January, provided by the Disney Corporation.

In Disney's town, the home is only one part of a larger effort to recreate a small town ideal long time gone. The effort is to do so reinterpreting the existing language of the suburbs, enriching it and articulating it with an "urban" lexicon. This is the project of Celebration and more generally of the New Urbanism at large. Nevertheless, as Andrew Ross has concluded, "there is a relationship in the mind of the New Urbanist planners between the houses' typologies and the urban form of town. Capitalizing on popular sentiment for the lost community of the small American town, New Urbanism adopted neo-traditional style as a vehicle for its goal of restoring prewar planning. Mindful of the charges of pandering to the conservative taste of the Victorian values, the New Urbanism insists that the traditional housing styles are simply a tool to promote the town-planning principles and have no particular significance in and of themselves."[20] By doing so, though, the movement is promoting a very specific vocabulary, dialoguing only with a white middle-class audience, and subtly excluding any other possible resident's identity.

"Community" in Celebration is the ultimate commodity: it can be purchased on the market as a feature that raises the residences' property value. The artifice of community is linked to the larger phenomena of privatization of public spaces and the attempt to purify urban environments considered as chaotic, dangerous, unhealthy and ultimately "toxic." Community in Celebration is strictly monitored, not lived; it is defined a priori, not achieved; its rules are learned, not negotiated.

The Authenticity of Community

The problem of authenticity is not only a problem in the specific case of Celebration; in reality it is a dilemma for the New Urbanist movement at large. Through the mere creation of streets, public places and buildings, to what degree can physical design ever regain a lost sense of community? Spaces such as shopping malls, coffee houses, festival market places, fitness centers, themed historical destinations, while publicly accessible and supportive of public life,

A street sign in Celebration, featuring the city logo with a white picket fence (photograph by the author).

are private or public-private in ownership. Several critics lament these spaces as exemplary of capitalism's conquest of the public environment.[21] Disney's Celebration seems to capture this critique. It is completely owned by one corporation and based on the key premises of private ownership for a targeted audience, emphasis on consumption and leisure, security, and controlled behavior and design.

These environments, privatized in nature, not only reflect social inequality but often serve to reinforce that inequality. Feminist theorists, as we discussed at the beginning, have explicitly criticized the "lack of fit" between the activities women are trying to carry out and the environments in which they live. As new guidelines for development, New Urbanism must, in the future, consider more needs of women, as well as those of a wider range of people coming from diverse social classes and ethnic backgrounds. The "tradition" New Urbanism refers to is a reinvented one, and it includes only a specific segment of the American population.

Celebration, like many planned communities before it, relies on the belief that the pre-planned arrangement of features in space — from public spaces, trees, and houses, to front porches and curtains' color — will help to realize a utopian vision of society. This overly planned community instead, through the use of covenants, codes and restrictions, controls space while bringing a substantial lack of freedom in the life of its residents.[22] The Homeowners Association is subordinated to the town's owner, the Disney Corporation. In the short and in the long term, if any change is proposed, the association is required to ask the Disney Corporation for permission. Like Carol White's, these homes are perfectly manicured objects in the landscape of town. The homes, and the women with their families in it, are safe because they are precisely designed and controlled.

The heightened security associated with Celebration's privatized space is a major feature offered to attract their residents. The disproportionate fear that women experience in public space has, therefore, been cultivated and reproduced in the historic development of the city. Nowadays, other new contemporary privatized public space, similarly oriented toward the enhancement of security, tame that fear only apparently. High security in "fortressed" spaces reaffirms a fear of less controlled, more flexible public spaces, tying women even more than before to conventional roles. Safety as a major feature that the controlled environment of Celebration offers is only a marketing tool for the perpetuation of gender-based division of roles and for the exclusion groups with a different ethnic and social background.

"Safe," while showing us the critical fault of overly planned environments like Celebration in the vain search for security and well-being through predictability and behavioral norms, also points in a different direction. It points toward a notion of community that is not found on the market but is a product of struggle and conflict, and idea of community that suggests the constant critical questioning of our social and physical environment as a possible solution.

Notes

1. Dolores Hayden, "What a non-sexist city would be like? Speculations on Housing, Urban Design and Human Work," *Women and the American City*, ed. Catherine Stimpson, Elsa Dixler, Martha Nelson, Kathryn Yatrakis (Chicago: University of Chicago Press, 1984), 170–187.

2. Sherilyn MacGregor, "Deconstructing the Man-Made City: Feminist Critiques of Planning Thought and Action," *Change of plans. Towards a Non-Sexist Sustainable City*, ed. Margaret Eichler (Toronto: Garamond Press, 1995), 25–49.

3. Dolores Hayden, *The Grand Domestic Revolution: A History of Feminist Designs for American Homes, Neighborhoods, and Cities* (Cambridge, MA: MIT Press, 1981), 23.

4. Hayden, "What a non-sexist city would be like?"
5. *Ibid.*, 212.
6. Dolores Hayden, *Redesigning the American Dream: The Future of Housing, Work and Family Life* (New York, London: W.W. Norton, 1986), 23.
7. *Ibid.*
8. MacGregor, "Deconstructing the Man-Made City," 31.
9. *Ibid.*, 32.
10. *Ibid.*
11. Kevin Lynch, *Good City Form* (Cambridge, MA: MIT Press, 1981),171.
12. Hayden, "What a non-sexist city would be like?"
13. *Ibid.*, 183.
14. Congress for the New Urbanism, *Charter for the Congress of New Urbanism* (San Francisco: Congress for the New Urbanism, 1994).
15. Alex Krieger, "Whose Urbanism?" *Architecture* 87 (November 1998): 73.
16. Andres Duany, "Our Urbanism," *Architecture* 87 (December 1998): 69.
17. Bob Shinn, senior vice president of Walt Disney's Imagineering, quoted in Michael Pollan, "Town-Building Is No Mickey Mouse Operation," *New York Times Magazine*, December 14, 1997, 59.
18. From "Pattern Book," Celebration's website, www.celebrationfl.com (accessed November 1999).
19. Kristen Day, "Introducing gender to the critique of privatized public space," *Journal of Urban Design* 2 (June 1999): 155–178.
20. See Pollan, "Town-Building Is No Mickey Mouse Operation," cf. also Celebration web site.
21. Pollan, "Town-Building Is No Mickey Mouse Operation."
22. Andrew Ross, *The Celebration Chronicles: Life, Liberty and the Pursuit of Property Value in Disney's New Town* (New York: Ballantine Books, 1999), 77.
23. See Kirsten Day, "Introducing Gender."
24. Michael Pollan, "Town-Building Is No Mickey Mouse Operation," 77.

Bibliography

"Celebration-Pattern Book." www.celebrationfl.com (accessed November 1999).
Congress for the New Urbanism. *Charter for the Congress of New Urbanism*. San Francisco: Congress of New Urbanism, 1994.
Duany, Andres. "Our Urbanism." *Architecture* 87 (December 1998): 69.
Hayden, Dolores. *The Grand Domestic Revolution: A History of Feminist Designs for American Homes, Neighborhoods, and Cities*. Cambridge, MA: MIT Press, 1981.
_____. "What a non-sexist city would be like? Speculations on Housing, Urban Design and Human Work," in *Women and the American City*, edited by Catherine Stimpson, Elsa Dixler, Martha Nelson, Kathryn Yatrakis, 170–187. Chicago: University of Chicago Press, 1984.
_____. *Redesigning the American Dream: The Future of Housing, Work and Family Life*. New York, London: W.W. Norton, 1986.
Day, Kristen. "Introducing Gender to the Critique of Privatized Public Space." *Journal of Urban Design* 2 (June 1999): 155–178.
Krieger, Alex. "Whose Urbanism?" *Architecture* 87 (November 1998): 73.
Lynch, Kevin. *Good City Form*. Cambridge, MA: MIT Press, 1981.
MacGregor, Sherilyn. "Deconstructing the Man-Made City: Feminist Critiques of Planning Thought and Action." *Change of plans. Towards a Non-Sexist Sustainable City*. Edited by Margaret Eichler, 25–49. Toronto: Garamond Press, 1995.
Pollan, Michael. "Town-Building Is No Mickey Mouse Operation." *New York Times Magazine* December 14, 1997, 58–63, 76–81, 88.
Ross, Andrew. *The Celebration Chronicles: Life, Liberty and the Pursuit of Property Value in Disney's New Town*. New York: Ballantine, 1999.

Chapter 12

Engendered Spaces

Dagmar Grimm-Pretner

Public parks and squares in dense urban quarters of Vienna are rare. As previous research shows, five times more boys than girls are making use of these sites. Especially when girls are ten years and above they withdraw from public parks. The reasons can be located in a complex of social, spatial and gender-specific aspects. Herein we discuss the design and use of public parks in Vienna and the efforts which have been undertaken to get a fairer distribution of space among female and male users. This chapter explores the role of landscape architecture and female landscape architects who raised the discussion on "gender specific park design" in Vienna and investigates the characteristics of public parks and squares within the social context of urban quarters. The investigation draws on previous research findings on the use of public space in urban renewal areas of Vienna and on recent design research findings in newly built or redesigned sites in different parts of the city. It examines the premises required for reclaiming space and focuses on the question of how these sites can become meaningful territory that will serve girls. The aim was to learn about girls' requests and special interests and to better integrate these into future park design. It explains a number of ingredients that are responsible for making open spaces appropriate for girls, and that are also useful for an evaluation of existing designed open spaces.

Although some argue that public parks and squares in urban areas have lost relevance because of mobility, virtuality, privatization and individualization, public open spaces can still be seen as a frame for urban communication and an indispensable part of a democratic society. As the Danish architect Jan Gehl points out, "the information society is providing new meaning and significance to the city as meeting place."[1] Public open spaces are an important part of urban life: they provide sites in which different generations, social groups, and cultures can meet and intermingle. Social planners and sociologists have stressed the importance of public open space in daily life.[2] They view public open space in terms of its symbolic and cultural aspects and emphasize the difference between life-cycles (age, family structure, employment) and social groups (income, education, profession). Especially for young people, public open spaces open up a much wider range of social and communication experiences than are possible in private and institutionalized places.[3] Gehl also notes an intensified appropriation of public space in many European cities during the past two or three decades.[4]

But this general development should be viewed through a more diverse lens. Empirical studies conducted from a gender perspective show that an equal share between women and men in the use of public parks and squares has not been achieved.[5]

Herein, I will discuss the design and use of renewed public parks and squares in Vienna along with the efforts which have been undertaken to get a fairer distribution of space among female and male users. I am basing my discussion on several years of researching public space in Vienna. My studies focused on the relationship between design concepts and social use of these public open spaces. They took into account the social and cultural differences of the users and were conducted from a gender perspective.

I define "public space" as open space in urban areas, and use the term "public" in its three dimensions: the legal dimension — public property in contrast to private property; the sociological dimension — public use in contrast to private use; and the political dimension — public use as one that makes possible free forming of opinion and joint action.[6]

I pose the following questions: what can the role of landscape architecture be in enabling girls to have the same possibilities as boys in using public space? What can be done to provide a fair distribution of space within public parks and squares? How can these encourage social interaction and communication? And what is the role of landscape architecture in expanding the range of girls' activities and, thus, their presence in public spaces? Girls should not have to leave the park when they outgrow the sand-box, nor should their access to park resources be measured by male standards.

Public Parks and Squares — Sites for Everyday Life

The quality of urban space depends — amongst other values — on urban structure, spatial and social criteria and, last but not least, on the design of the space. Public parks and squares in densely built-up quarters of urban Vienna are small and rare and intensively used. Surveys within these sites have shown that five times more boys than girls make use of public parks and squares, and that most girls ten years and above withdraw from these public spaces altogether.[7] One of the reasons for these behaviors is that many older small parks are based on functionalized design concepts. Such concepts provide exclusive — often fenced in — areas for such sports as soccer and basketball, a separate playground, and a sitting area for the elderly, and hardly provide any space for multifunctional use. The above-named sports activities are favored by boys and young male adults.

Nevertheless these public open spaces in densely built-up urban quarters have an important function within each such quarter — they are not only meeting-sites for many age-groups and for outdoor-activities and recreation but also a means of orientation within the quarter — and therefore should not be reserved by design for a few user-groups or a few predefined functions.

A city as safe as Vienna can offer public space for adolescents to experience their growing independence. Young people need experiences within their peer groups without adult interference, and this social life among children and adolescents needs space — public space. Before discussing further design concepts it would be helpful to understand the development of Austria's landscape architectural gender discussions.

Landscape Architectural Gender Discussion in Austria

In Austria, academic education in landscape architecture is very young. In German-speaking countries, the first studies on gender in architecture were undertaken in the mid-seventies and were published by female architects. Inspired by the architecture discussion, in 1987 an international symposium organized by female landscape architecture students questioned the professional paradigm and the educational framework at the University.

In 1991 an exhibition was presented by two female planners with the title "To whom does public space belong? Women's everyday life in the city." The exhibition dealt with issues of mobility, accessibility, open spaces and places generating fear, amongst other topics. This exhibition specifically noted children's playgrounds as one type of women's workplaces. The exhibition stimulated a public discussion about women and planning not only in Vienna but throughout Austria. Public opinion was very much divided. Men in particular, who had never thought about gender issues before, agitated against what they felt was a personal attack.

Later, the discussion focused on safety in public space, and in 1999 a design competition on gender-sensitive park design was initiated by the Coordination Office for Planning and Construction Geared to the Requirements of Daily Life and the Specific Needs of Women, a subdivision of the City Planner's Office of the Vienna Municipal Directorate. Two existing parks in a very densely built-up area were selected to be redesigned. The responsible person within this Coordination Office was one of the women who created the exhibit previously described. The Office's goal was to develop design ideas that would support a more balanced distribution of open space amongst girls and boys and would also strengthen the value of these sites as neighborhood parks.

Since that initial effort, all park design projects initiated by the Vienna Gardening Department are assessed as to their focus on empowering women and girls. The Coordination Office performs the assessment tasks. The challenge is a list of criteria which is more than just a list of favored playground-equipment. For this reason, in 2001 a research project was undertaken by the Institute of Landscape Architecture (IFL/ILA) for the Coordination Office with the aim of pointing out design solutions in 14 existing parks, which could encourage girls to use these parks (Grimm-Pretner et al. 2002).

Design Aspects

A complex of social and spatial factors influence the use of public space. In the following analysis, the focus lies upon spatial factors which might contribute to enhancing girls' access to park resources. These spatial factors are the ones which are primarily influenced by the design of a site.

Spatial and Functional Structure

The hypothesis for the following is that the spatial concept of a design by itself influences the mixture of users and their range of activities. The spatial structure of a site design is the most durable design decision and forms the basic structure into which further elements and equipment are fitted.

Learning from the ineffective aspects of functionalized design concepts — and responding to changing requirements of park visitors — a spatial concept should ideally offer open, versatile and functionalized spaces in reasonable proportions. Where a public park offers spaces for a wide range of activities, it is more difficult for any single group to dominate most of the park, or to dominate one space most of the time. A flexible group structure

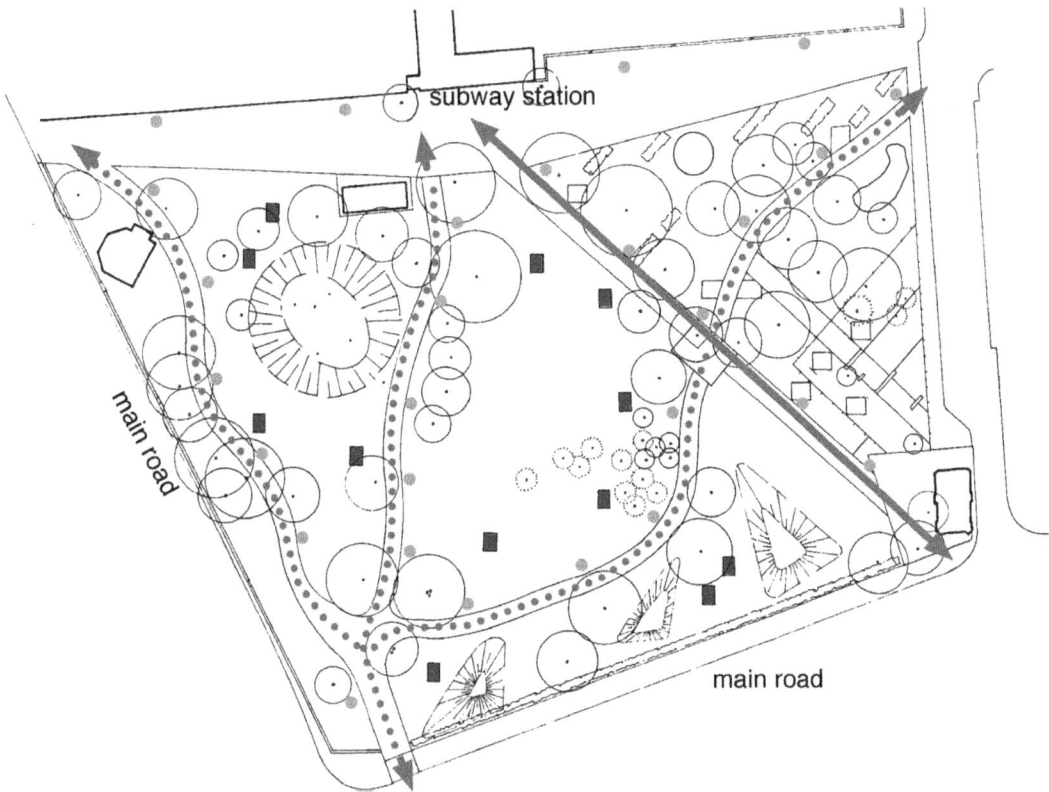

St. Johann-Park, plan overview (author illustration).

enables weaker users to appropriate space at least temporarily. Flexibility of space also allows the users to interpret spatial structures differently, according to both gender-specific and age-specific patterns of perception and appropriation.

This open design concept was used for St. Johann-Park, which is only 10,000 square meters in size (about ¾ of an acre). It offers open, grassy areas partly shaded by groups of trees, as well as functionalized areas such as a toddlers' playground and an area for playing ball.

The Possibility of Appropriating Space

As I mentioned before, the fenced-in courts for ball games are almost exclusively used by male users. We have to base our assumptions for now on girls' position in today's society. Great care has to be taken not to force girls into particular role patterns, and to understand girls' space appropriation behavior. Girls tend to observe the scene of action from outside before moving in to claim the space for themselves. Establishing inviting observation points near or along areas of action would encourage girls to utilize action areas without having to step into a predefined role. Erecting a second fenced-in soccer court would hardly turn girls into ardent players overnight even though they might be interested in the game itself. What does seem realistic is to induce gradual changes in their sports behavior by expanding the range of sports that they already favor or may have an interest in.

It was important for the planners of St. Johann-Park (Kose Licka Landscape Architects)

Red wooden platforms in St. Johann-Park (photograph by the author).

to offer easier access to the former soccer-court area. They eliminated the fencing and lowered the grade. The resulting "bowl" can be accessed from the grassy area around it and still keeps the ball inside it. The climbing poles in the bottom of the bowl can also be used for attaching ropes and playing volleyball.

Points of Activity Crystallization

In larger sites, points of activity crystallization within the open and versatile structure are necessary — they are starting points for girls to use adjacent space. In St. Johann-Park, red wooden platforms offer small, single islands which can be appropriated by single persons as well as small groups for motion, role-playing or board-games, as meeting places, or as places to relax.

The Need to Feel Comfortable and Safe

Safety in public space is a basic requirement for unlimited use. Design concepts can contribute to objective and subjective safety. The integration of the foot-paths into the district's trail system creates streams of motion. For example, in St. Johann-Park a main path was built with an unobstructed view from the exit of the subway to the adjacent main street that leads into the residential area. People passing through offer a certain amount of social control within the park, as well as a visual connection from the side-walk into the park. Generally, the designers intended to create clearly arranged spatial structures, so as to provide good overview and orientation to support personal control. Efficient lighting for the main paths is a matter of course.

Another key contributor to feeling comfortable and safe is the regular maintenance of the parks. While this is primarily a question of financial resources, it must also be considered during the development of a design.

Park Equipment

Equipment in parks in general, and playground equipment in particular, changes due to trends in material and design as well as leisure-time activities. But equipment design is most positive when the equipment can be used flexibly: for example, equipment can promote communication as well as action and exercise of, and can also facilitate development in risk-taking and strength.

Communicating Gender Sensitive Park Design

During the redesign of the neighborhood parks, based on the design competition on gender sensitive park design, it was very difficult to communicate to the public the complex issues of fair distribution of space between male and female users and the possibilities of landscape architecture. In the media, the issue was shortened to, and labeled with, "girls' parks," with no mention that the major goal was to strengthen the value of neighborhood parks by offering space for more activities and users, and thereby to create a vital environment. As a result, the public's expectations were completely different. Some girls expected animals for cuddling, like cats, rabbits or even small horses, a play-house, Barbie dolls, a pool and a park supervisor to keep out the boys. Disappointment was high, as can be easily imagined. It certainly would have been helpful to integrate a community-participatory project into the planning process.

Conclusions

The design of a site can offer possibilities for appropriation of space for girls, but cannot ensure adoption by girls for their cultural uses. Further steps on a socio-pedagogic level have to be undertaken to change socially formed role patterns. One example is the so-called "Child and Youth Care in Parks," a project which was launched in 1993 to minimize the potential of conflicts and to break up existing structures of power and hierarchies in parks. It is an important district-oriented measure, aiming to enable a democratic use of public parks. This is one additional possibility — but, as I said before, there is also a need for non-supervised space.

The discussion about gender-sensitive park design brought forward further developments. The gender discussion sensitized decision makers and planners in the city planning and gardening department — even if they did not want to get involved, or thought it unnecessary. They now have to deal with the gender discussion because of the assessment tasks. As part of feasibility and site design, the review team includes staff representing both girls' interests and barrier-free issues. In such planning and design efforts, it is critical to consider spatial aspects and not just develop a list of favored playground equipment that fits into a predetermined space.

The gender-sensitivity initiative started a discussion about design and use of space that was desperately needed. Improvements that have developed include:

- design improvements in accessibility and flexibility of spaces in general
- improvements in safety by increasing social control
- a better integration of the toddlers' play-grounds into overall park design, which improves safety for all users as well as offering more comfort for accompanying adults
- sports activities, now more broadly defined (playing, spectatorship, or just meeting friends at a sports-court)
- an increase in the range of user-activities on several sites.

The renewed interest in public life and public open spaces as meeting places is a chance to strengthen the role of the city as a democratic forum. It offers the opportunity for participation and representation in the public realm to all users. Furthermore it is a chance for landscape architects to contribute to socially relevant developments in society.

Notes

1. Gehl, Jan, and L. Gemzoe, *New City Spaces* (Copenhagen: Danish Architectural Press. 2001), 20.
2. Gehl, Jan, *Life between buildings*, (New York: Van Nostrand Reinhold, 1987); Spitthoever, M. *Frauen in staedtischen Freiraeumen* (Cologne: Pahl-Rugenstein, 1989).
3. Deutsches Jugendinstitut, ed. *Was tun Kinder am Nachmittag? Ergebnisse einer empirischen Studie zur mittleren Kindheit* (Munich: Deutsches Jugendinstitut, 1992); Emmenegger, M., *Zuerst ich denke: Schweiz ist Schwein, aber jetzt ist besser. Neuzugezogene fremdsprachliche Jugendliche, Situationen — Orte — Aktionen: eine sozialgeographische Studie in Basel* (Bern: Peter Lang, 1995).
4. Gehl and Gemzoe, *New City Spaces*, 20.
5. Grimm-Pretner, D., *Oeffentliche Freiraeume in Wiener Gruenderzeitgebieten — Ein Potential zur Verbesserung der Lebenssituation von Kindern und Jugendlichen ODER Verschaerfung sozialer Gegensaetze?* (Vienna: Kammer fuer Arbeiter und Angestellte fuer Wien, 1999); Paravicini, U., S. Claus, A. Muenkel, and S. von Oertzen, *Neukonzeption städtischer öffentlicher Räume im europäischen Vergleich: Forschungsbericht.* (Hannover: NFFG, 2002).
6. Paravicini, Claus, Muenkel, and von Oertzen, *Neukonzeption städtischer öffentlicher Räume im europäischen*, 12.
7. Grimm-Pretner, D., U. Krippner and L. Jeschke, *Differenzierungen — Gestaltanalyse oeffentlicher Parks und Plaetze in Wien unter besonderer Beruecksichtigung geschlechtssensibler Gestaltungsansaetze* (Vienna: Institute for Landscape Architecture and Landscape Management [IFL], 2002).

Bibliography

Deutsches Jugendinstitut , ed. *Was tun Kinder am Nachmittag? Ergebnisse einer empirischen Studie zur mittleren Kindheit.* Munich: Deutsches Jugendinstitut, 1992.
Emmenegger, M. *Zürst ich denke: Schweiz ist Schwein, aber jetzt ist besser.* Neuzugezogene fremdsprachliche Jugendliche, Situationen — Orte — Aktionen: eine sozialgeographische Studie in Basel. Bern: Peter Lang, 1995.
Gehl, Jan. *Life Between Buildings.* New York: Van Nostrand Reinhold, 1987.
_____. and L. Gemzoe. *New City Spaces.* Copenhagen: Danish Architectural Press, 2001.
Grimm-Pretner, D. *Oeffentliche Freiräume in Wiener Gruenderzeitgebieten — Ein Potential zur Verbesserung der Lebenssituation von Kindern und Jugendlichen ODER Verschaerfung sozialer Gegensaetze?* Vienna: Kammer für Arbeiter und Angestellte für Wien, 1999.
_____., U. Krippner, and L. Jeschke. *Differenzierungen — Gestaltanalyse öffentlicher Parks und Plaetze in Wien unter besonderer Berücksichtigung geschlechtssensibler Gestaltungsansaetze.* Vienna: Institute for Landscape Architecture and Landscape Management (IFL), 2002.
Paravicini, U., S. Claus, A. Münkel, and S. von Oertzen. *Neukonzeption städtischer öffentlicher Räume im europäischen Vergleich: Forschungsbericht.* Hannover: NFFG, 2002.
Spitthoever, M. *Frauen in staedtischen Freiraeumen.* Cologne: Pahl-Rugenstein, 1989.

Chapter 13

Homes Across the Waters: The Construction of Gender and Landscape within a Trans-Pacific Life

SHENGLIN ELIJAH CHANG

In depth interviews with three housewives (whose husbands work within the computer industry on both sides of the Pacific Rim) about their trans–Pacific lifestyles and how their homes reflected a sense of their individual identities form the basis of this chapter. An analysis of their dual-home lifestyles points to several new ways of conceiving the relationship between home/landscape and personal identity. Melissa's, Winnie's, and Julie's home-across-the-water stories lead to a reexamination of the modern notion of idealized and coherent relationships among identities (self), experiences (lifestyle), and forms (home/landscape). Traditional idealized and coherent relationships were dissolved by the three women's "global sense of place." The new relationship among themselves, their life, and their homes/landscapes were randomly mixed entities. The three housewives' individual sense of self points to the need to reformulate the traditional static and linear construction of the connection between self and place. A newly formulated construction of self-home-landscape challenges a modern set of assumptions about the rootedness of place, the singularity of identity, the separation between multiple cultures, and the definition of migration as a one-way phenomenon.

Most research regarding the phenomenal growth of Silicon Valley focuses either on economic and industrial networks, or on technological innovation. And not surprisingly, when researchers ask questions about any of a number of things they are curious about related to Silicon Valley, they ask men. Men make up the majority of the engineers and executives within the Silicon Valley high-tech sector. Within my research, it is women rather than men, housewives rather than their husbands, who have informed my investigation of what I call "the trans–Pacific home phenomenon."

"Trans-Pacific home phenomenon" is a phrase that refers to a trend that emerged in the late 1990s. The economic boom of the 1990s that led to the rapid rise of computer hardware and software companies (located on both sides of the Pacific Rim) also led to the emergence of a new trend in global commuting, in which thousands of Taiwanese-born high-tech engineers realized that they could greatly increase their career opportunities by establishing a lifestyle that allowed them, and their families, to regularly commute between two homes, one in Silicon Valley and the other in Taiwan.[1] They not only commuted in their cars to get from their homes to their workplaces, but also commuted across the Pacific Ocean, in jet planes, to get from their Silicon Valley homes to their Taiwanese homes.

Since 1997, I frequently flew back and forth between Silicon Valley and Hsinchu Science Park because I wanted to understand how high-tech engineers and executives, who commuted regularly between their homes on both sides of the Pacific, constructed the new relationship between their identities and their homes. As it turned out, it was not the overworked male engineers or the executives, but the "high-tech housewives" in their 40s — the stay-home spouses of high-tech professionals — that brought me the new insights not only on the "trans–Pacific lifestyle" but on our assumptions about the relationship of landscape and identity.

Home Beyond the Walls of the House

Each of us has a sense of ourselves that we have developed from our personal history.[2] Our sense of self, of "who we believe we are (our identity)," is something that we express, knowingly or unknowingly, at all times.[3] The styles of clothes we wear, the music we like or dislike, and our hairstyles are all channels to express who we are. The home that we live in is also one of the many things that enables us to expresses our individual identity.[4] When I talk about "home identity" I am referring to the psychological-physical system of inter-relationships in which the home and its surroundings represents someone's personal entity. While a home can be thought of as an object that exists at a particular place, on a particular street, in some particular city, I think of home as more than a mere object. A home and its surroundings provide the residents with a sense of belonging, a sense of community, and a sense of self.[5]

Home, in other words, is not an object that is separate from us, its inhabitants. Home is connected to us in a very significant way: allowing us to express who we are. In exploring the connection between home and self (home and identity), it is important to understand the connection between home and its surroundings. In the conversations that I had with high-tech housewives, all of them, at one point, talked about their home as part of the larger context of its surroundings. For some, a home was a place that included an adjoining garden. For others the boundaries of the house extended to their neighborhood, their community, their district, or even their region. So when I use the phrase "home place" or "home environment," I do so to relay the personal map that people have in mind when they talk about their relationship with their home — a map that extends, in small and large degrees, beyond the actual walls of their house.

The Emerging Bi-gration Pattern Creates Transcultural Lifestyles Interconnecting the Pacific Rim

Within the last ten years the issue of "home identity" (how homes reflect people's personal identities) has been an emerging topic within contemporary intellectual discourse in fields as diverse as Asian-American studies, anthropology, cultural geography, cultural studies, literary criticism, and landscape architecture. But few studies have focused on the immigrants' experience of struggling between their old identities and their newly forming American identities, as well as the role that their old and new homes and landscapes play within that struggle.[6]

In the past, when immigrants arrived in the United States, they were severed from their old homeland and *either* assimilated into the mainstream of American culture *or* lived isolated from the mainstream culture.[7] Chinatown's population is a good example of immigrants who lived apart from the mainstream American culture by reproducing their home culture in a new land.[8] And for the most part those Chinese immigrants who, in the past, chose not to live in Chinatown, adopted an American lifestyle and identity. But since the emergence of the bi-gration phenomenon, the either/or of having to choose between staying Chinese or becoming American is a thing of the past. Since the 1990s, the ease of air transportation, accessible telecommunication, and instant global connection through the internet has given immigrants more than an either-or choice of assimilating into or separating from mainstream America.

The high-tech housewives I spoke with, who consistently traveled back and forth between their original and their new culture, experienced a "two-way migration," or what I call a "bi-gration." For them, the fact that they were born into a Taiwanese culture at one point in their lives, and found themselves in an American culture at another point in their lives, did not lead them to think that they had to choose between America or Taiwan as the cultural basis of their identity. Because they did not think of Taiwan and America as discrete and separate cultures, they were able to give up the old idea that their migration was a one-way journey that led from a homeland to a foreign land.[9] Their new transcultural lifestyles, in which the Taiwanese and American ingredients of their homes, their landscapes, and their identities, mixed and melded, enabled them to give up the traditional thought that their migration to a new culture would mean that they had no choice but to leave their rich set of cultural and personal experiences behind.

Transcultural Home Identity

I was fascinated to speak with the trans–Pacific housewives about how their sense of self related to their sense of home. This is what has been called "home identity." The housewives I spoke with are global commuters and have homes in two very different countries. As they talked to me about their global lifestyles, they helped me understand how one person could have a sense of her home identity even though she commuted back-and-forth between two homes and two cultures. These women possess what I call a "transcultural home identity" because their sense of self includes the connection across two cultures, and between their old and new homes. Homes, landscapes and communities appear within the transcultural lifestyle of global commuters in the form of physical as well as virtual realities. In the case of the high-tech housewives whose lives I observed, their "transcultural lifestyles" were constructed through various combinations of Taiwanese urban environments and American suburban homes and landscapes.

In describing the trans–Pacific commuters relationship between home and self, I have intentionally avoided the use of the term "multicultural" to describe their lifestyles. Instead, I used the term "transcultural lifestyle."

In his essay "Transculturality: The Puzzling Form of Cultures Today," Wolfgang Welsch points out that traditional concepts of cultures — including classic single culture, interculturalism and multiculturalism — assume that "every culture can be distinguished and remain separated from other folks' cultures."[10] However, transculturalism "sketches a different picture of the relation between cultures, not one of isolation and conflict, but one of entanglement, intermixing, and commonness."[11] Welsch argues that we already live in a transcultural context. "Lifestyles no longer end at the borders of national cultures, but go beyond these.... There is no longer anything absolutely foreign.... Today, in a culture's internal relations — among its different ways of life — there exists as much as foreignness as in its external relations."[12] Welsch's conception of transculturalism as an entangled, intermixed relation between cultures is a useful starting point for analyzing the relationship between identity and home.

Welsch's observation that the experience of living a transcultural lifestyle has led to the intermingling of one's domestic culture with many other foreign cultures coincides with the melding and mixing of cultural elements that I observed trans–Pacific high-tech housewives use to construct their lifestyles and identities. The trans–Pacific lifestyles carried by Taiwanese high-tech housewives point to several new ways of conceiving the relationship between home/landscape and personal identity, ways that take into account the collapse of the deep rooted home, the dissolving of the static identity, the separation between multiple cultures, and the one-way migration. Yi-Fu Tuan's 1996 book entitled *Cosmos and the Hearth* helps frame the new relationship between home and self that members of the trans–Pacific commuter culture have adopted. Tuan writes, "[a]t a basic (reflex) level, the shift is surprising if only because the life-path of a human being moves naturally from 'home' to 'world,' from 'hearth' to 'cosmos.'"[13] Tuan argues that the dramatic change in today's transcultural background and context is foreignness intertwining with folk. Home is seen as the world; hearth extends to the cosmos.[14]

Unconventional Identity, Unconventional Women

I now turn to three housewives' personal stories: Melissa, Winnie, and Julie. Each of these women constructed a relationship between identity and landscape that is very different from the way that immigrants of the past have constructed that relationship. Their different way of constructing a sense of how the self and the landscape interrelate helps us redefine the importance of home identity for women as well as suggesting a new way of constructing gender.

Melissa: Home Here and Home There

My husband and I live in Taiwan, but my parents and daughters live in Fremont, a city in the so-called Silicon Valley. I fly between our Taiwan home to our Fremont home five times a year, and exchange emails with my daughter daily. Anyhow I don't quite feel the distance between Taiwan and Silicon Valley. The reason is simple. I can enjoy my perfect Taiwanese life in Silicon Valley these days, driving my mom to visit our friends in her Fremont neighborhood, shopping at Ranch 99.[15] You know, those things you usually can only do in Taiwan. I also can buy all the Taiwanese groceries plus enjoy very good Taiwanese food, trimming and styling my hair in the hair salon at the Ranch 99 Mall [1998 interview].

Melissa represents a new prototype for the construction of one's sense of self: the shifting home identity. This is a construction of the self that I feel is more responsive to the context of the twenty-first-century lives that many of us presently lead: a life in which we communicate across the globe with ease, in which we travel on super-fast jets that render our world a global village. Melissa strongly identified with two houses and two landscapes in two societies, Taiwan and the United States. She didn't feel that one home was primary to her sense of self, while the other was secondary — or foreign — to her sense of self. Rather, she felt that both of them were her homes, because she could engage or accomplish the same tasks and activities at both locales; she could socialize and hang out with a circle of family and friends in either house on either side of the Pacific.

Melissa leads a transcultural life. In her view neither her Taiwanese nor American culture was the primary source of her sense of self. By giving up the old tradition of needing one home that is confined to one distinct culture and one distinct place (made of brick, mortar, paving, and perhaps foundation shrubs) Melissa moved physically from one to another of her homes, but remained psychically attached to both homes through her personal use of twenty-first century technologies. She had replaced a traditional sense of self as singular, with a self that was multiple. The construction of a multiple self has enabled her to attach to both of her Pacific Rim homes at once, through new media that

Within Melissa's experience of buying groceries at "Tawa 99" in Fremont, California, she was able to find the fruits, vegetables and household products that filled the shelves of stores she shopped at during the Taiwan portion of her commute between her two Pacific Rim homes (photograph by author, 2000).

enabled her to feel she was virtually at one home when she was actually at the other. A shifting, multiple self, a self that does not need a rootedness at an actual place, enabled Melissa to "shift" from one to another of her homes, from one to another of her landscapes and social networks with ease. A "shifting home identity" enabled her to "virtually return" to the home that she left just hours earlier.

The conversations that I had with Melissa challenged me to rethink some of my assumptions about the construction of an Asian-American home identity, assumptions bounded by a conception of immigration as a one-way event.[16] After my conversations with Melissa and others I stopped thinking of members of trans–Pacific commuters as one-way immigrants, and started thinking of them in terms of their experiential process of bi-gration. I started understanding how one person could have a sense of her home identity even though she commuted back-and-forth between two homes and two cultures; even though she called two very different countries home.

The conventional wisdom of the past suggested that it was natural for immigrants to arrive in the new land and to gradually erase the memory markings of their homeland and over time render a new picture of themselves — a picture that reflected their new social and physical surroundings. Because Melissa did not regard Taiwan or America as so discrete, distant and therefore separate cultures, she was able to transcend the old notion that her migration was a one-way journey that led from a homeland to a foreign land. For her, the home's surrounding landscapes, as well as her identities, mixed and melded.

For Melissa giving up the notion that migration by definition must be a one-way journey, was not an idea or choice that came by way of theorizing or longing. Rather it emerged from within her very own experiences of bi-grating, of journeying back and forth between cultures. Many members of the trans–Pacific commuters subculture that I spoke with embodied the same kind of transcultural home identity that Melissa experienced. They did not think that they had to choose between one home or the other in order to gain a healthy, normal sense of themselves. Instead they developed ways of intertwining their old home landscapes in Taiwan with their new ones in Silicon Valley. They did not feel that they left either their California or Taiwanese landscapes behind because they constantly commuted between the two. In a physical way, they constantly traveled back and forth between two places, just as psychologically, they constantly switched back and forth between their fluid, and multiple selves.

Winnie: Transplanting Culture

Winnie's Taiwanese-accented Mission Revival style residence house greeted me when I visited her. Situated in the Hsinchu Science Park community in Taiwan, Winnie's house, like many others, was of that familiar California suburbia: red-tile roof and white, faux adobe walls. Winnie and her family had lived in a residential area within Hsinchu Science Park known as the Bamboo Village for ten years, and in Palo Alto, California, for one year. She was in her early fifties, having raised three children. All of her children attended the local bilingual school. Her husband's extended family had already moved to the U.S. by the time that he and Winnie instead moved in the other direction, from Silicon Valley to Taiwan. However, having relatives in the U.S. enabled Winnie and her husband to relive their earlier bi-gration pattern through regular visits to the United States — visits that occurred at least twice a year, with one always planned for the Christmas holiday season. In addition to their frequent family trips to America, their children attended youth camp in Silicon Valley every summer. As I spoke with her it became clear that the frequent trips back to California served to keep the embers of Winnie's Silicon Valley memories warm and alive.

At one point of our conversation she excitedly told me, perhaps "I feel it is great to have a community like this. The life that I and the other wives had was very happy and joyful there in Silicon Valley. We hung out together and chatted, and did nothing. However, our husbands had to work very very hard. Nevertheless, I often ask my husband if we can go back to Silicon Valley, or if we can migrate there." Winnie went on to tell me that although she and her family only stayed at their Palo Alto house for one year, it was one of the most memorable years she could remember. That year started off when her neighbor greeted her with a homemade house-warming cake the first day that she had moved into her new Palo Alto home. After sharing how that first experience "deeply touched" her, she went on to describe the more mundane, everyday portions of her life, but with no less excitement in her voice. She took pleasure in telling me all about the Silicon Valley public services she appreciated; how, for example, she enjoyed recycling her garbage.

Winnie believed that the garden that fronted her Hsinchu, Taiwan, home presented a face to the public. Her own identity was enmeshed with the garden; she perceived it as if it were her own face (photograph by author, 2002).

Winnie's Palo Alto home was a single-detached house with a swimming pool in the backyard. As she recalled how much she "loved" the house, the image of the garden, adjacent to the house, became clearer to her. She said, "I loved that garden very much. I liked living in a house with a garden. The garden is so important to me. I never took care of my garden before I lived in America." She observed that Americans were more likely to spend their time maintaining their gardens than their houses — that it was quite acceptable for an American home to be in the average-looking range, if the garden was beautiful. She then confessed that she never maintained any of her gardens before her Palo Alto residency.

"I never took care of my garden before I lived in America," Winnie explained, "now, I think a garden is even more important than a house. It is just like the face of our house. I should spend my time to decorate my garden. It's for the public. I think beautiful public landscape enhances the quality of life. This is what I learned from my American life experiences." The garden was a face that Winnie's home presented to the public. Her own identity was enmeshed with the garden that she described as her "home's face;" she perceived it as if it were her own face. It was important for her to present a beautiful face that rivaled the beautiful American faces that her neighbors' homes presented. The year she lived in Palo Alto was the first year that she followed her mostly Caucasian neighbors in the annual tradition of Christmas light decorations for the gardens and house exterior. "The whole house becomes very charming and beautiful over the Christmas season," she told me.

Winnie's recollections of the American use of the front yard as a public face became the prelude for a story of victory and defeat. That story began in Taiwan, shortly after she and her family had returned to Bamboo Village after their one-year American residency. With images of her late father's ritualistic adorning of the front entry with the national flag hanging on national holidays, she tried convincing her neighbors to join her in decorating their lawns and homes with flags in celebration of the October 10th National Day, birth of the Republic. But despite her enthusiasm, no one bought into the idea.

Nonetheless, Winnie was undeterred by this local defeat, and went on to tell me about how her "Christmas lights campaign" resulted in brilliant victory. Less than eight weeks after a complete lack of support for a block-wide national flag installation, her neighbors rallied with excitement in joining her by setting up Christmas lights that lit up their Bamboo Village neighborhood. Winnie had succeeded in what she called "transplanting" those pieces of her life in America that she valued and felt passionate about.

Winnie's stories about American objects, like lights and gardens that she had "transplanted" into the cultural soil that comprised her neighborhood, enabled me to better understand how she constructed her transcultural home identity. The "transplanting" of Taiwanese flags and Christmas lights pointed to Winnie's shifting, entangled and culturally overlapping sense of her self. By "transplanting" objects that recalled and indicated both her childhood and American experiences, she was able to sustain the two sides of her Taiwanese and Asian-American dual identity.

The bi-gration experience that she had undergone enabled Winnie to let go of the "im"-migration, the one-way migration, set of rules that prescribed either a tenacious retention of one's previous identity and culture or a practical adoption of the local identity and cultural framework that one arrives in. Her identity was not prescribed or predetermined, but rather it was self-determined. Winnie was just as interested in importing the Taiwanese flag decoration scenario that was embedded within her memory of childhood, as she was in importing American Christmas lights into her Taiwanese life. Her cultural references were mixed and matched rather than pure: the Taiwanese flag referred to one culture, while the American Christmas lights referred to another, and yet both became equally strong and valid rationales for her home decorating projects. This mixing and matching enabled her to mix and match the two sides of her self, and ultimately gave her control of her personal process of self-creation.

In addition to "transplanting" Christmas lights, Winnie told me that her children, having experienced an American Halloween and Easter, looked forward to trick-or-treating and Easter egg hunting despite the fact that these two rituals had never been a part of life in Taiwan. It may sound like Winnie and her family had been very Americanized. However, one phenomenon revealed an alternative perspective that was rather stunning — her house in Bamboo Village had an American outside but mostly a Taiwanese interior. It consisted of an American garden, a modernist living room, and a very Taiwanese kitchen.

Clearly, an American house form with a landscaped garden was very important to Winnie, but the interior arrangement of her house was rather mixed. Her garden was well-manicured and very colorful in floral diversity. Her modern living room was a little bit dark but cozy. However, her kitchen and dining room were wonderfully chaotic. Without any pleasant decorations, piles of Chinese paintings and books occupied the dining table and chairs. She had to rearrange those piles to make room for me to sit. Her daily life blended a beautiful outdoor garden (a reflection of her American suburban community life), a neat and cozy living room that she transplanted from her Palo Alto home, and a cluttered kitchen that revealed her Taiwanese culinary tendencies.

Inhabiting a home that contained three very different types of spatial experiences did not bring up any conflicts or contradictions for Winnie. She made no pretense at integrating the spaces; each of the spaces embodied a unique essence that did not need to be explained in relation to the others. Winnie's transcultural construction of self enabled her to dissolve the problem of cultural uniqueness rather than to spend time solving the problem. Instead of thinking that she needed to strive for a coherent or beautiful explanation of how such unique cultures could exist together under one roof, she playfully used her knowledge of those cultures to create an ever-changing story about her house, her garden and her self.

Julie: A Collage of Cultural Experiences

Julie was in her late forties. Her family was one of the first families to move back from America to live in the Hsinchu Science Park. She frequently traveled back and forth across the Pacific with her husband. They visited the U.S. a couple of times a year for business and family trips, as well as for their children's summer camps. Before we talked about her current home, Julie fondly recalled the house that she had grown up in — a house that no longer existed physically, but nonetheless seemed as if it would always occupy a space for her in memory. Her childhood home had been located in the wealthy Tienmoo district, just north of central Taipei. Her beloved house had been a timber-frame Japanese-Colonial house with a very large garden that resembled a small orchard, with rows of azalea and camellia, and other ornamental plants that sprang up to her eye-level. She said she often cheerfully visited the colors, shapes and leaves of various plants. As we chatted through the interview, she remembered how she and her father often sat in the garden, sipping tea, and telling stories until midnight.

Julie also recalled leaving her childhood home for the first time. That was in 1971, when she graduated from National Taiwan University and journeyed overseas to continue her studies in the United States. Although she found herself half a globe away from her homeland, that house would often re-surface in her consciousness. Then, one summer day, her mother called her at her New Jersey home to tell her that they were going to sell their old house in Tienmoo District. "I flew back just for the last chance to stay in it for three months. After my departure, my parents sold it." Our conservation brought up some difficult memories for her. "I have been attached to this house deeply for my entire life," Julie told me. "I had many special memories with this house. I enjoyed sitting in the yard alone, immersed within the poetic atmosphere. I learned to play Chinese zither there during my college years. My father got two stone benches with a stone table for me, though I didn't know where and how he got them. The most memorable feeling for me was when I played my Chinese zither. The sounds of the string vibration harmonized as they bounced off the stone table and echoed throughout the garden. It was so peaceful but lonely. I haven't had the same feeling anywhere later in my life."

As the tide of memory began to ebb, Julie began describing her current home in the Bamboo Village within Hsinchu, Taiwan. She and her family were among the first "foreigner" groups to move back from the United States. They had lived in the Bamboo Village for nearly sixteen years. Although they rented the house, Julie felt it was hers, saying, "When you live here long enough, you don't quite feel the difference regarding the legal ownership." So even though, technically, renters were not permitted to modify homes, Julie's felt ownership motivated her to make the changes that she wanted and felt were necessary.

Julie and her husband converted a front porch into an entrance foyer. Although local legal restrictions deterred most Bamboo Village renters from modifying their homes, Julie's "felt" ownership led her to make the changes that she wanted and felt were necessary (photograph by author, 2002).

Julie described how she and her husband:

> extended the house and took over half of its front porch and back yard. We tore down the exist-
> ing outside walls on both sides. At the front entry, we added the acrylic-glass panels to create a
> foyer out of the leftover porch space, since it's windy and often rainy here. In the back, we
> added a tatami tearoom, which created a peaceful corner space at the edge of our central public
> area. The central public area is our living and dinning room. We took out the interior wall and
> connected the two places. It looked more spacious. I like to live in a bigger suburban house in a
> quiet area. I am not willing to move into an apartment. Luckily enough, I have never lived in
> an apartment my whole life.

I was intrigued by Julie's story of having overcome local legalities to create the home
that she wanted, and by the process by which she had collaged various types of spaces recalled
from her different residential experiences in different cultural settings. In the beginning of
our conversation, she mentioned that she could not return to her childhood neighborhood,
because everything that she had been so familiar with as a child had been much altered.
She told me she would rather return to her memories of the place than return to the real
place, because in her memory nothing had changed, whereas in reality lots of things had.

Julie would never return to Tienmoo for fear of finding that things had changed, and that would lead to an unwanted disruption of the time and space that she had preserved in her memory. But despite her fear of facing the changes that she would certainly encounter if she returned to Tienmoo, she was preoccupied with changing her Hsinchu home. She controlled the past by keeping her childhood home just the way it was within her memory, and at the same time she controlled the present by changing her adulthood home to suit her needs and tastes.

Because the form of her childhood home would be forever frozen in her memory, the form of her present home was not important for Julie. What really mattered for her was participating in the home building process. Her status as a renter did not deter her from modifying her recent American-style duplex home to fit her needs. The physical elements of the home reflected the four residential cultures she had experienced in her life: American, Taiwanese, Chinese, and Japanese. First, she added a fabric-covered porch. This was a very popular form of wind and rain protection in Hsinchu, Taiwan. Second, the tatami room echoed the tranquil Japanese garden experience of her childhood. Third, her dining room was Chinese, with a large Chinese round table at its center. The table could fit about twenty people and served as the house's social gathering hub, when a group of good friends visited her. Finally, her living room was not only spacious, but housed a modern leather sofa set and a fitness machine. A strong sense of openness was the most important quality for her. Julie emphasized that the American detached house and the Japanese house provided her with the spacious quality she liked — a quality that she constructed for herself by modifying her home despite the legal restrictions.

The mosaic home that Julie created was a collage of sorts. Its overlapping cultural materials were sheltered within an American house form that provided the main body, a Taiwanese porch that softened its front facade, a Japanese tatami tea room that embellished the back, a Chinese dining room that defined its center, and a modern living room that greeted all visiting guests. As she refused to return to her childhood neighborhood, she had created a mosaic home that integrated her past experiences; she re-constructed certain portions of her life experiences and installed them into a home that did not belong to her from the legal stand point (she is a tenant), but did very much belong to her from the standpoint of her own memories of multiple cultures and multiple times in her own life. Unlike many others within the trans–Pacific commuter culture, whose homes existed simultaneously within multiple places, Julie's various memories, multiple places, and assortment of cultural experiences existed simultaneously within that one home.

Bi-gration and Individuation

Melissa's, Winnie's, and Julie's home-across-water stories challenge us to re-examine the modern notion of idealized and coherent relationships among identities (self), experiences (lifestyle), and environments (home/landscape). The idealized and coherent relationships are dissolved by the three women's "global sense of place."[17] The new relationship among themselves, their lifestyles and their homes/landscapes are randomly mixed entities. The relationships are shifting, ambiguous, virtual, and unsystematic.

Melissa, Winnie and Julie were three among many trans–Pacific commuters I spoke with, who consistently traveled back and forth between their original and new cultures. For the trans–Pacific commuters, the fact that they were born into a Taiwanese culture at one point in their lives, and found themselves in an American culture at another, did not lead them to think that they are obligated to choose between America or Taiwan as the cultural basis of their identity. Because they do not think of Taiwan and America as discrete and separate cultures, they have been able to give up the old idea that their migration was a one-way journey that led from a homeland to a foreign land. Their new transcultural lifestyles, in which the Taiwanese and American ingredients of their homes, landscapes, and identities mixed and melded, enabled them to pass up the traditional thought that their migration to a new culture meant an abandonment of one culture for the sake of another.

Within their construction of self and place the idea that one possesses an everlasting home culture that is set against all other "foreign" cultures was replaced by the experience of embodying a cultural mix where the foreign and familiar co-exist simultaneously.

Elements in traditional lifestyles that had previously existed in isolation from one another existed simultaneously in the transcultural lives of trans–Pacific commuters. Homes, landscapes and communities appeared within the transcultural lifestyle in the form of phys-ical as well as virtual realities. Melissa, Winnie and Julie exemplify the trans–Pacific com-muter's transcultural lifestyle: a lifestyle constructed through various combinations of Taiwanese urban environments and American suburban homes and landscapes. Within their individual constructions of a lifestyle, there are several shared aspects that mark a very uncommon approach to constructing landscape and identity. All of them are part of a grow-ing number of global commuters whose twenty-first century lifestyles have enabled them to cross the width of an ocean with speed and comfort that their parents could never have imagined. They share the kind of life in which jets, computers, cell phones, and satellites have made the Pacific commutable rather than impassible. As a result of the disappearance of insurmountable physical boundaries that had characterized the past, the vast psychological boundaries between homeland and new-land that previous generations of immigrants have had to construct have become more of a footnote to history than a currently lived reality within trans–Pacific commuter culture.

It is possible that members of the trans–Pacific commuter culture are the first generation of immigrants whose journey across the width of an ocean has not demanded that they choose between a homeland or new-land identity. Instead of migrating, instead of having to choose one or another identity, this newly emerging population of immigrants is bi-grating. Bi-gration has become a new type of experience that has enabled global commuters to construct a sense of self and a sense of home that is not ultimately a choice between cultures. Within the two-way migration experience, the old notion of either/or choice of culture, identity, home and landscape is dissolved, and replaced by a process in which the immigrant's sense of self is constructed by mixing and matching cultures, identities, homes, and landscapes.

As the housewives who I have introduced you to above shared their daily life stories with me, as I interviewed each of them and analyzing their described connections between home and landscape, I came to understand how their trans–Pacific life had led them to invent new sets of nontraditional relationships between their identities and their homes. The women I spoke with did not think about their homes in traditional terms. For them, home was not a single object rooted in a single geographic piece of land. For them, home existed simultaneously at multiple places. They had constructed new nontraditional identities in which both the home and the self were embraced as multiple, non-static, shifting and changing within their daily set of life experiences. As a group of women Melissa, Winnie and Julie have been presented here because they embody certain characteristics that reflect the newly emerging trans–Pacific commuter culture. At the same time, each of the women in this chapter has constructed a home and an identity that is unlike the others, and this is important because it points to their having freed themselves from an old conception of self and home as essential, an old conception of self and home as a static and predetermined entities. This attempt to de-essentialize the definitions of human identity, home and land-scape reflects the emergence of a recent feminist and postmodern critique of the traditional notion of "an essential home that mirrors an essential self."[18] The newly emerging discourse, guided by this critique, seeks to replace the notion that the purpose of life is to strive for purity and perfection, with the understanding that life can be enjoyed by playing with the chaotic, diverse, complicated and imperfect set of persons and events that are constantly crossing one another's path.

Seen through the lens of this new discourse, the mixing and matching of cultures in the construction of each of these women's homes can thus be seen as a process of appre-hending and making creative use of the chaos-driven diversity and cultural contingencies that one comes in contact with toward one's own ends — toward one's own individual sense of agency.

Notes

1. Jinn-Yuhm Hsu, "A Late-industrial District? Learning Network in the Hsinchu Science-based Indus-trial Park, Taiwan," Ph.D. diss., Department of Geography, University of California, Berkeley, 1997, 73; Anna-Lee Saxenian, *Silicon Valley's New Immigrant Entrepreneurs* (Berkeley: Public Policy Institute of California, 1999), 34.

2. David Lowenthal, *The Past Is a Foreign Country* (Cambridge, New York: Cambridge University Press, 1985), 197.

3. Manuel Castells, *The Power of Identity*, Vol. 2 of *The Information Age: Economy, Society and Culture* (Oxford: Blackwell, 1997), 6.

4. Marcus, Clare Cooper. "The House as a Symbol of Self," in *Designing for Human Behavior: architecture and the behavioral sciences*, ed. Jon T. Lang (Stroudsburg, PA: Dowden, Hutchingon, 1974), 435–448; Marcus, *Environmental Autobiography* (Berkeley: Institute of Urban and Regional Development, 1979); Marcus, *House as a Mirror of Self* (Berkeley: Conari Press, 1995).

5. Donald Appleyard, *Home* (Berkeley: Institute of Urban and Regional Development, 1978); David E. Sopher, "The Landscape of Home," in *The Interpretation of Ordinary Landscapes: Geographical Essays*, ed. D. W. Meinig (New York and Oxford: Oxford University Press, 1979), 129–152; Marcus, *Home-as-Haven, Home-as-Trap: Explorations in Experience of Dwelling* (Berkeley: Center for Environmental Design Research, 1986).

6. In contrast to the scholarly focus on urban ethnic enclaves, urban sociologist, Gottdiener, discussed the ethnic suburban phenomenon in his book *The New Urban Sociology*. He specifically points out that the Asian newcomers have modified the traditional American suburban landscape. See Mark Gottdiener, *The New Sociology* (New York: McGraw-Hill, 1994), 172–174.

7. Alejandro Portes and Ruben G. Rumbaut, *Immigrant America: A Portrait* (Berkeley: University of Cal-ifornia Press, 1990).

8. Kay J. Anderson, "The Idea of Chinatown: The Power of Place and Institutional Practice in the Making of a Racial Category," *Annals of Association of American Geographers* 77, no. 4 (1987): 580–598; Gwen Kinkead, *Chinatown: A Portrait of a Closed Society* (New York: Harper Pereninal, 1992); Mark Lai Him, *From Chinese Immigrants to Chinese American: A Social History of Chinese American in The Twenty Century (in Chinese)* (Hong Kong: Joint Publishing [H.K.] Co., Ltd., 1992).

9. Liisa H. Malkki, *Purity And Exile: Violence, Memory, and National Cosmology Among Hutu Refugees in Tanzania* (Chicago: University of Chicago Press, 1995).

10. Wolfgang Welsch, "Transculturality: The Puzzling Form of Culture Today," in *Spaces of Culture*, eds. M. Featherstone and S. Lash (London: Sage, 1999), 195.

11. *Ibid.*, 205.

12. *Ibid.*, 197–8.

13. Yi-Fu Tuan, *Cosmos & Hearth: a Cosmopolite's Viewpoint* (Minneapolis: University of Minnesota Press, 1996), 2.

14. *Ibid.*, 8–9.

15. Ranch 99 is the name of a supermarket chain specializing in Chinese food and home supplies. It is often the anchor for dozens of other Chinese restaurants, bookstores, and groceries.

16. David Seamon, "Reconciling Old and New Worlds: The Dwelling-journey Relationship as Portrayed in Vilhelm Moberg's 'Emigrant' Novels," in *Dwelling, Place, and Environment: Toward a Phenomenology of Person and World*, eds. Seamon and Mugerauer (New York: Columbia University Press, 1985), 227–246.

17. Doreen Massey, *Space, Place, and Gender* (Minneapolis: University of Minnesota Press, 1994), 146–173.

18. In *House as a Mirror of Self*, Clare Cooper Marcus follows a modernist tradition that I am calling the construction of the essential self. See Clare Cooper Marcus, *House as a Mirror of Self* (Berkeley: Conari Press, 1995). There are numerous feminist and postmodern critiques of the essential self-view. Two of the most influential are: Alison M. Jaggar; Susan R. Bordo, eds, *Gender/Body/Knowledge: Feminist Reconstructions of Being and Knowing* (New Brunswick, N.J.: Rutgers University Press, 1989), and Richard Rorty, "The Contingency of Selfhood," in *Contingency, Irony, and Solidarity* (New York: Cambridge University Press, 1989), 23–43.

Bibliography

Anderson, Kay J. "The Idea of Chinatown: The Power of Place and Institutional Practice in the Making of a Racial Category." *Annals of Association of American Geographers* 77, no. 4 (1987): 580–598.

Appleyard, Donald. *Home*. Berkeley: Institute of Urban and Regional Development, 1978.

Castells, Manuel. *The Power of Identity*, Vol. 2 of *The Information Age: Economy, Society and Culture*. Oxford: Blackwell Publishers Ltd., 1997.

Gottdiener, Mark. *The New Sociology*. New York: McGraw-Hill, 1994.

Him, Mark Lai. *From Chinese Immigrants to Chinese American: A Social History of Chinese American in the Twenty Century (in Chinese)*. Hong Kong: Joint Publishing (H.K.) Co., 1992.

Hsu, Jinn-Yuh. "A Late-industrial District? Learning Network in the Hsinchu Science-based Industrial Park, Taiwan." Ph.D. diss., Department of Geography, University of California, Berkeley, 1997.

Jaggar, Alison M., and Susan R. Bordo, eds. *Gender/Body/Knowledge: Feminist Reconstructions of Being and Knowing*. New Brunswick, NJ: Rutgers University Press, 1989.

Kinkead, Gwen. *Chinatown: A Portrait of a Closed Society*. New York: Harper Pereninal, 1992.

Lowenthal, David. *The Past Is a Foreign Country*. Cambridge; New York: Cambridge University Press, 1985.

Malkki, Liisa H. *Purity and Exile: Violence, Memory, and National Cosmology Among Hutu Refugees in Tanzania*. Chicago: University of Chicago, 1995.

Marcus, Clare Cooper. "The House as a Symbol of Self." In *Designing for Human Behavior: Architecture and the Behavioral Sciences*, edited by Jon T. Lang, 435–448. Stroudsburg, PA: Dowden, Hutchingon, 1974.

_____. *Remembrance of Landscape Past*. Berkeley: Institute of Urban and Regional Development, 1978.

_____. *Environmental Autobiography*. Berkeley: Institute of Urban and Regional Development, 1979.

_____. *Home-as-Haven, Home-as-Trap: Explorations in Experience of Dwelling*. Berkeley: Center for Environmental Design Research, 1986.

_____. *House as a Mirror of Self*. Berkeley: Conari Press, 1995.

Massey, Doreen. "Double Articulation: A Place in the World." In *Displacements: Cultural Identities in Question*, edited by A. Bammer, 110–124. Bloomington and Indianapolis: Indiana University Press, 1994.

_____. *Space, Place, and Gender*. Minneapolis: University of Minnesota Press, 1994.

Portes, Alejandro, and Ruben G. Rumbaut. *Immigrant America: A Portrait*. Berkeley: University of California Press, 1990.

Rorty, Richard. *Contingency, Irony, and Solidarity*. New York: Cambridge University Press, 1989.

Saxenian, AnnaLee. *Silicon Valley's New Immigrant Entrepreneurs*. Berkeley: Public Policy Institute of California, 1999.

Seamon, David. "Reconciling Old and New Worlds: The Dwelling-journey Relationship as Portrayed in Vilhelm Moberg's 'Emigrant' Novels." In *Dwelling, Place, and Environment: Toward a Phenomenology of Person and World*, edited by D. M. Seamon and Robert Mugerauer, 227–245. New York: Columbia University Press, 1985.

Sopher, David E. "The Landscape of Home." In *The Interpretation of Ordinary Landscapes: Geographical Essays*, edited by D. W. Meinig, 129–152. New York and Oxford: Oxford University Press, 1979.

Tuan, Yi-Fu. *Cosmos & Hearth: a Cosmopolite's Viewpoint*. Minneapolis: University of Minnesota Press, 1996.

Welsch, Wolfgang. "Transculturality: The Puzzling Form of Culture Today." In *Spaces of Culture*, edited by M. Featherstone and S. Lash, 194–214. London: Sage, 1999.

Chapter 14

Constructing Gender[ed]
Outdoor Public Space

SOPHIE NICHOL SAUVÉ

> Openness permits exchange, ensures movement, prevents saturation in possession or consumption. But openness dwells in oblivion ... because it cannot be represented, nor made into an object, nor reproduced in some position or proposition. Who knows that the possibility of exchange is born from two lips remaining half open?[1]

As a "voyageuse," I consciously remove myself from settings to explore them from an observer's perspective and to mull. As a designer, I often physically move myself from a city, country or continent, seeking something other than accepting a static condition, which I still believe it is possible to change. This intentional distancing has enabled me to "dwell in oblivion," as Luce Irigaray states. It has allowed me the luxury to become an observer and observed, participant and critic of outdoor public space as a woman.

The premise of my work is based on the feeling that despite woman's improving status in society "woman's access to outdoor public space remains problematic and constrained." This manifestation reveals itself as a desire to address an ever changing socio-cultural demographic which is not yet reflected in outdoor public space.

In doing so, I wish to identify the gap or build the links necessary to allow us to reach true equal status in the urban landscape. This collection of reflections on gender[ed] outdoor public space document my research, first as a student of landscape architecture in the pursuit of a Masters degree. Where the practicum compared three distinct cities' form and content launched primarily from Gordon Cullen's *Townscape*, it was highly dependent on my experiencing these places "on the ground." The ensuing "product" that materialized from the research was a quilt, resembling patterns of the ground from the air. This "product" was first presented at "A Century of Women in Landscape Architecture" a conference at the University of California, Berkeley, a few short months prior to completing my degree and transitioning into the world of professional practice. Since the completion of my degree, I have continued to explore the answers to the questions I asked then. Nearly a decade of conscious wanderings as both an observer and a participant have been collecting in both mind and spirit, impacting upon both my journeys and my designs.

The introspection that arises out of weaving in and out of the "practice" of landscape architecture is one that sends me in and out of literature and the shelter of buildings, to visit and revisit places from a woman's perspective. As the nature of the concern of women in outdoor public space suggests, that is, as contested and questioned, my research has lead me to other disciplines' theories to find a way to communicate by way of exchange. By visiting feminist philosophers' writings and reinforcing my medium of investigation, I have also identified and accepted the variables of life that have without any doubt, altered my point of view. Nevertheless, most outdoor public spaces remain unmistakably gendered and without identifying an open space in which an exchange within the discipline can occur, the status quo will prevail.

Motivation

My needs, wants, and desires are not being met. I desire to be a *flâneuse* and wander the streets of my city at any time of the day, in any place. I want to be able to be perpetually lost in thought, rather than needing to consciously organize a safe path, or a comfortable journey where I do not feel like an *object* in outdoor public space. I want to be able to continue to take public transportation, to feel equal to others, to step outside of built walls, comfortable boxes, and into the "playgrounds" of this world. Yet, the world outside of buildings has not been planned with me in mind, nor has it been upgraded to meet the needs, wants, and desires of many who remain marginalized in the exterior built environment.

"Landscape" is bound to the society and to the soil upon which it is shaped. The perception of place and the comfort within spaces that people sense, are attached to previous experiences, as well as to similarities found in spatial configurations. Indeed, neither people nor landscapes are separable; each molded by personal stories, collective memories, and traditions; all come together to form a continuous weaving of motions and emotions. Yet, as a discipline, Landscape Architecture struggles with the malady of binary opposition. While in the field of design, it is often perceived as "other" to building architecture outside it is a place-making art and science that remains highly undervalued and unacknowledged by the general public. Thus, the fact that the practice of landscape architecture is increasingly becoming permeated by women has not meant that the outdoor public spaces through which we journey have been automatically upgraded to reflect either the changes within our profession, or the changes of makeup in the primary users of "landscape." Indeed, in a world engrossed in capital, a patriarchy still remains in control of who and what priorities are to be addressed and upgraded in (outdoor) public space. The places of transition through which we must inevitably move too often do not meet the needs, wants, and desires of those deemed "other."

The exploration of gender in outdoor public space was the focus of my practicum (the practical application of knowledge to conclude a degree) in Landscape Architecture. The subject and subsequent objects that emerged from this study came from the desire to inscribe my own story onto the urban palimpsest, while exploring everyday spaces and my feeling of "otherness," which emerges in different environments.[2] In North America in particular, I have experienced not only varying senses of detachment from the cities in which I have lived and traveled, but also experienced an overwhelming feeling that there is a lack of gender positive space.

I also recognize that as designers, women subscribe to a perpetuation of a dichotomy from within, by overlooking that which makes us different from our colleagues. In a quest to gain equality and to "fit in"-to the realm of design, we, both collectively and individually, have maintained the system without having access to its secrets.[3] Simply being part of the field does not mean that (1) the rules of inclusion have changed and (2) the characteristics

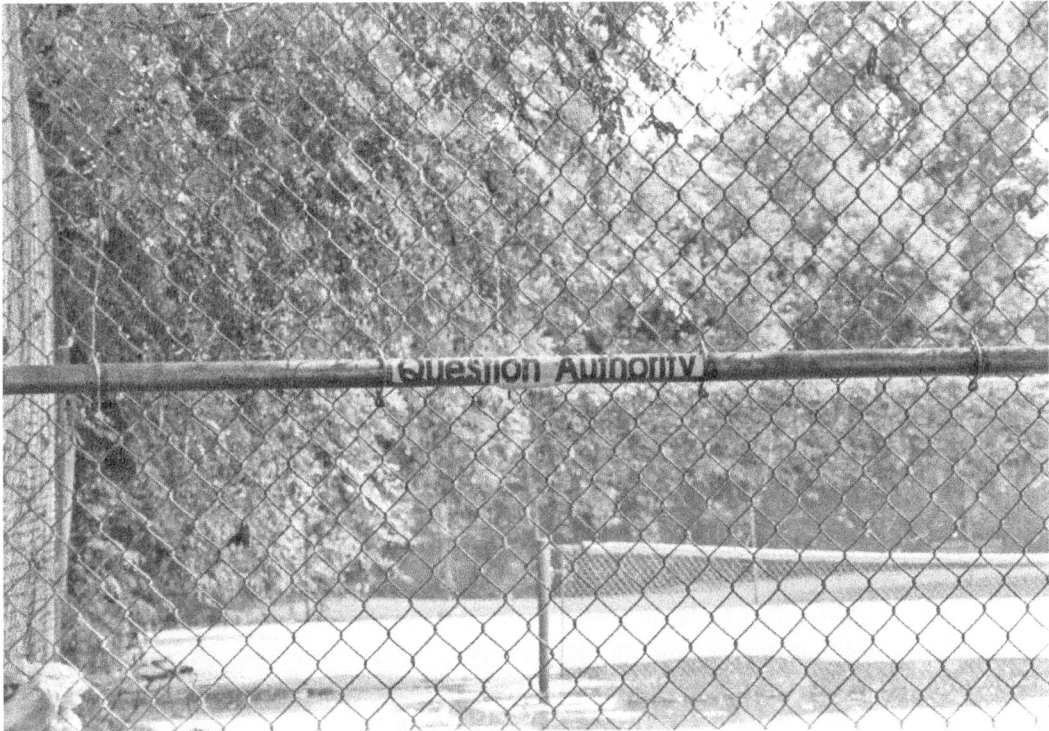

Question authority: Black and white photograph taken in a residential neighborhood in downtown Winnipeg, Manitoba, Canada, during preliminary research, summer 2001 (photograph by the author).

that identify us as women have been encompassed in our methods of approaching design, of observing design, or even of being part of the field of design. Notwithstanding that some may not accept that there are psychological differences between the sexes, biological and physical diversity make it inevitable that we all experience space and undergo designing in dissimilar ways.

Power

There is always power in space. Whether the varying degrees of power come from or through designers, from clients who request (and will only pay for) a definite type of space, or a certain hierarchy which existing places segregate amongst users, space can evoke a feeling of exploitation in those deemed "other," reinforcing a dichotomy of space, and hence, of people. Often lacking clear delineations, or simply put, walls, urban public spaces are difficult to pinpoint in terms of control. Yet, recognizing that the "landscape carries multiple layers of meaning" and is a complex cultural product, a reflection on a society, is imperative in the discipline of design.[4] It is crucial to acknowledge that though we construct landscape, it also constructs us; namely, via movement through and/or the alterations of spaces, our own personal boundaries are continuously altered.

In the hope of bridging a continued gap, even if women and men experience all things in different ways, I recognize and agree that some men do increasingly feel excluded from the world in which we live. But I also attest that women forget their sex far less often than men do.[5] The following is a study emerging from the experience of one woman.

Storytelling

Women, in both their social and biological differences from men, have a tendency to exchange stories in order to further their understanding of an issue, and each other, rather than to seek an elevation (by way of competition) of their ego.[6] Hence, the idea of telling my story, the only one over which I do have an authority (without seeking it) has become, at this time, the best way to express my interpretations of gendered outdoor public space. It is not a collective account, but I hope that it can help others recognize or consciously identify their own versions.

Background

Before all learned social and cultural attributes, I am a woman. I am from an incredibly privileged society called Canada. Gratefully, I have had the means (or credit) to travel to and live in cities and communities spanning the globe, from west to east and north to south. Despite being from a middle-class family, I have been a student for so long that my debt-load has certainly contributed to my need to walk throughout cities, which in more and more instances have been engineered for cars. These factors contribute to how I view and experience the city and outdoor public space, specifically, on a daily basis. For sociological purposes, I also add that I am a francophone (French-speaking) Canadian, white, single, able-bodied and heterosexual. These frames of reference are offered as this, my work, is decidedly personal.

I was born and raised in Cornwall, a city of approximately 47,000 people in south-eastern Ontario, on the northwestern border of New York State and close to the southwestern border of Québec. I spent many of my first seventeen years lamenting the claustrophobia I felt in the city. Luckily, in 1992, I was given the amazing opportunity to study abroad for a year, in the city of Aalborg, Denmark, while still in high school. For the ten years after I first lived in Denmark, the city and the country represented to me what the real feeling of *place* entails. With the desire to unravel this mystery of my complete comfort in a city to which, despite my relentless desire not to be, I *am* a foreigner, I returned in January of 2002 to participate in an urban design studio for six months, ready to face the possibility that this utopia might have nothing to do with space, but with the simple fact that I had been away from home for the first time.

Journey

In order to discern what makes Aalborg unique in my heart and mind, I decided to record my journey traveling and living in different places over a span of 150 days. Envisioning an end product deemed gendered by tradition, I proposed and developed a series of images, motivated by W.J.T. Mitchell's five families of images — graphical, optical, perceptual, mental and verbal — in order to expose that which, to me, contributes to making space gendered.[7]

Aside from Aalborg and Cornwall, Bangkok, the capital of Thailand, also became a part of the study when our design studio traveled and lived in this city of smiles for a month while conducting site analysis and consequently proposing a studio-based design for the city. Gordon Cullen's *The Concise Townscape* (1971), a seminal text in design education, became the tool forming the basis of analysis of the three cities. Cullen's desire for and depiction of quality spaces, especially the connections he represents as vital to linking spaces and their contexts, are based on his context of the United Kingdom. Outside of this context, the interpretation has been left to desire, but at a second glance, enables the reader to see beyond the objects and solid forms he portrays to the social connections and to space he seeks. As such, he states: "there is an art of relationship just as there is an art of architecture. Its purpose is to take all the elements that go to create the environment: buildings, trees, nature, water, traffic, advertisements and so on, and to weave them together in such a way that drama is released."[8] Although beautiful as a notion, it is imperative to note that many of the terms and illustrations he used are gendered. However dated his work may be, it is not an excuse to overlook vocabulary such as *penetrating, colonizing, commanding, arousing*, and *exploiting*, as autocratic and imperialistic. Moreover, these terms are still used to describe projects and sites in contemporary design studios and circles.

From Utopia to Myopia

In 1992–1993, I lived in Aalborg, Denmark as an exchange student. During my year abroad, I lived with three host families, in three distinct neighborhoods. Although none of these homes were located in the downtown, the relationship to the city as a whole was evident. The frontages of houses are not far from the sidewalks. There are speed bumps on residential roads, and a creative use of vegetation on private land. While the sidewalks distinguish between cyclists and pedestrians, cobblestones are common in older areas, slowing traffic, and buses and trains have schedules that connect and readily accommodate bicycles and strollers. The second time I lived in Denmark (2002), the area where I lived was a bridge away from the city center of Aalborg, in Nørresundby, which was its own city until amalgamation with Aalborg. To emphasize the made-for-people feeling which I experienced and which Cullen clearly articulates in his work, it is worthy to mention that a five minute walking radius around my apartment brought me in contact with: a butcher, a fisherman, two bakeries, two grocers, two banks, a florist, a photographer, a post office, a pharmacist, a farmers' market on Fridays, a corner store, a bus stop for local buses, a bus stop for out of town buses, and a fine view of the fjord (and I am sure I am missing something). Overall, there is a fascination which comes with seeing small details in the outdoor public spaces in Aalborg, similar to Alain de Botton's delight in an airport sign at Schiphol, Amsterdam where: "[a] plug socket, a bathroom tap, a jam jar ... may tell us more than the designers intended, it may speak of the nation that made it."[9]

Since my first visit, change has arrived in Aalborg, where in the span of ten years, the "mall" (Bilka) has developed from a single, but large store, to a true North American style *container*. Complete with Pizza Hut and KFC, it endangers a place which had been trying so hard to remain *purely* Danish.[10] Additionally, the overall sense of security in this comfortable Scandinavian community is slowly diminishing. While my memory serves to portray Aalborg as a gender-positive and accessible city with safe and comfortable outdoor public spaces, many Danes were quick to suggest that my comfort was no longer accurate; I was often warned not to hold onto the confidence to which I had become accustomed to a decade ago and had retained in my mind.

Bangkok, "Krung Thep" (the city of angels), on the other side of the world, is at the other extreme of a Cullen spectrum. As the capital of Thailand, Bangkok is not dull and boring, rather, it is an overt attack on auditory, olfactory, palpatory, and gustatory senses. After a day in the streets of Bangkok, conducting site analysis and wandering around local environs, my body ached from the absolute chaos of the city. The buildings, the transportation systems, the advertisements, coupled with (the unofficial statistics of) 10 million people, are ingredients for nothing short of anarchy. Though I embrace the irregularity of roads, of twists and turns in Europe, Bangkok is overkill. There is a lack of balance between chaos and order.

Meanwhile, the transportation system maintains an exclusive system of class, in turn affecting gender. The new skytrain and the elevated highways are too expensive for regular Thais to use and, as a result, traffic continues to move at an average speed of nine kilometers an hour on the streets below, while tourists and business*men* barely fill the skytrain at most times of the day. Alternatively, walking is strenuous (darting street vendors and stray dogs) and cycling is impossible (even taking the tuk tuk is risky); and still an elevated bicycle path is found deserted in the middle of this hectic city.

However, private and public space is blurred: walking on the sidewalks can sometimes be equated with walking in somebody's bedroom due to the large number of homeless people, shantytowns and squatters. We observed large parking areas under one of the elevated highways used as a sleeping area at night, while in another neighborhood, a group set up a movie screen and projector under their part of the elevated highway (which is debated private/public space). Shantytowns and squatter settlements are established directly beside rail lines, and houses are literally on the river (supported by stilts), adding to the blurring of boundaries within the megapolis.

While the speed of change can be seen in both Bangkok and Aalborg, a crisis of identity is experienced in Cornwall.[11] The "Friendly Seaway City's" approach to destroying historical buildings leaves even its most loyal and diligent citizens calling it a dreary city, yet quickly excusing it as geographically ideal, located one hour by car from either Montréal, Québec or Ottawa, Ontario.

Cornwall is typically Canadian: dispersed and with numerous "big box" stores forming "new" downtowns. With its three separate "cores," Cornwall isolates parts of the city from others and it can take up to an hour to travel from one end of the city to a destination by public transportation. In addition to little protection from the elements for pedestrians, there are not any bicycle lanes in the city, though it features a recreational bicycle *path* along the river, which is commonly deserted during the week. Meanwhile, the new developments are massive, windowless boxes that are divorced from their outdoor environment, not to mention their frontages, which are seas of parking.[12] The buildings which had historical character have been replaced by two things: (1) murals recalling a glorified past and (2) modern yet generic buildings housing functions; that is, buildings that lack any regard for context. Containers consistently *à la Learning from Las Vegas* "style" are strewn throughout the city.[13] Meanwhile neighborhoods are increasingly impersonal and retracted, the downtowns are largely devoid of people during the day, and frighteningly empty at night. Surprisingly, in terms of neighborhood character, it is those areas which have no large lawn frontages, but "nooks and crannies" of dynamism, such as porches and stairways, and windows close to the sidewalk, which based on class, are judged unsafe to walk through. Meanwhile, the lethargic, lifeless middle/upper-class neighborhoods are devoid of any connection with the sidewalk, where, as Oscar Newman describes, four levels of territory separate impersonal main thoroughfares: public space, semi-public space, semi-private space and private space.[14] Indeed, "The porosity of home and street may be something that is lost in the most developed societies as families, architects and planners clarify distinctions between public and private."[15]

The cycles and patterns I observed between Cornwall and Aalborg may have been very different, if not illegible, had my journey been restricted to two known and western environments. Although these three cities, countries, and continents were the focus of the research, two other cities also had an impact upon my perceptions, reactions, and reflections, as they were visited during the 150 days of study. The cities of New York City and Al-Qahira (Cairo, Egypt) enabled me to distance myself from my research and return with new appreciation and understanding to the cities in the study. It is imperative to note that family and/or friends surrounded me in all circumstances, adding to the understanding, and in some cases, struggles, that I faced in the various places. The exploration of the three different cities and countries not only enabled me to compare how different city structures and cultures affect the feeling of gendered outdoor public space, but also allowed me to be removed from my comfortable surroundings, and to become an observer (and observed in many cases), in addition to being a part of the landscape.

While experiencing these cities within the context of Cullen's *Townscape*, that is, by finding examples of his "visions" outside of the United Kingdom where his examples stemmed from, it became obvious how clearly space and culture are inseparable. Three different cultures, three different views and ways of viewing and depicting, of including and excluding women, equaled three different experiences in space. As human beings, we are constantly aware of our position in the environment: our distance from buildings, the climate that surrounds us, and the way things "look." But what the general public and many in the design realm may fail to see are the surpluses that come with simply walking through spaces as "vision is not only useful but it evokes our memories and experiences, those responsive emotions inside us which have the power to disturb the mind when aroused."[16] This power, at once liberating and dangerous, depends on the possibility of being unseen. As Cullen suggests, as humans we possess the capacity to meld all the "opposing" parts such as Here/There together, eliminating or at least subduing the hierarchies existing in space.

In attempting to express the path on which my work has taken me, I came across a difficulty in articulating my thoughts and ideas to the general public. Moreover, I also found obstacles in engaging those in the field of design, as well as non-feminist audiences, without simply provoking reactions of disdain in regards to my research. It is difficult to engage a docile world in the discussion of gender, an issue or "focus group" which is seen by many to have been exhausted simply because women have the right to vote or to an education in many parts of the world. Ironically, even if people admitted that they had never thought of gender and landscape architecture or gender and outdoor public space, some automatically became defensive rather than reflective and were quick to point out that "there is no problem." Despite this reactionary affront, I wanted to engage those around me. Moreover, I was concerned that my work would be unread and unexplored by those unfamiliar with the field of landscape architecture. Personally, I saw my inability to express myself with the traditional plans, sections, and elevations, which usually constitute a "practicum," regarding such a multi-faceted and multi-disciplinary issue as gender and space.

Construction

While assembling a bookwork that formed my personal understanding of the issue of gender and outdoor public space during the summer of 2001, I came to see that not only were all the pages difficult to assemble in a certain "order" which is necessary to form a book, but these pages were all interconnected, as are all the issues I felt need exploration in landscape architecture. Visually, the "piecing" of these pages together (they measured 5½" × 5½") formed an interesting patchwork. From this observation, the idea of translating the images into material resulted in a final process and product into the "construction" of a quilt.

Patchwork, or the making of quilts, has long been a medium through which messages amongst people have been conveyed and translated. As a strong symbolic medium of communication, as well as work typically associated with women and about women's relationships, creating a tactile entity representing gender and space was ideal. Generally regarded as a historical craft, though there is now much debate on the artistic merits of quilts, these objects have managed to play important roles in North American history, from keeping families warm during frugal times, to enabling women to voice their political opinions when they did not have the right to vote. Quilts were also part of the strong division of labor that

Land quilt: Inspired by the landscape of the prairies from above, this photograph is of the quilt that was constructed as a final piecing of thoughts and observations of my practicum research. The quilt was created and completed in Cornwall, Ontario, Canada, between July and October 2002 (photograph by the author).

occurred during the Victorian era, emphasizing beauty and femininity in both process and product. Historically, the quilt as a medium is both symbolic, and, characteristically, a voice for words and opinions that cannot necessarily be vocalized. Having chosen a topic which is not always warmly received in contemporary circles, the quilt became a haven for my work, as well as an essential symbol which set the tone for dialogue about the issue of gender and outdoor public space.

In terms of process, the construction of the quilt was, in many ways, parallel to building site models in studio. All too frequently regarded as the final product to be completed in order to demonstrate the three-dimensions of space, the model requires hours of handwork and is labor-intensive (whether computer-based or not). The quilt, equally tangible, was similarly time-consuming and helpful, both in the development or continuation of thought, of re-adjustments, of re-thinking, and of mind-wanderings with regards to the deconstruction of outdoor public space. Due to the nature of the issue being explored, as atypical and personal, in addition to the constant bewilderment and harsh reactions to the concept of space as gendered, the quilt became, and continues to be, a soothing process and product.

While stitching one of the first squares to the quilt, my selection of this medium became obvious. In order to be admitted into the Masters' program of Landscape Architecture at the University of Manitoba, I had to complete three semesters of pre–Masters, two of which were with the architecture pre–Masters students. During the first semester of that year, I had the task of putting together my first "working model." After a bit of a jump-start into landscape architecture with only one other female student and being surrounded by a majority of "architecture boys," the model was a bit of a shock to my system. The review that followed was not very encouraging, where my *craftsmanship* [*sic*] was deemed nothing short of horrible. Despite the feeling of discouragement, I sought out the professor to ask for help and additional feedback. I do not remember his reply in its entirety, but part of it was: "but didn't you build model airplanes and cars when you were a kid?" I thought he was joking. I was not a stereotypical "girl" when I was young, but building model airplanes, sir, was not part of my childhood. I had a wood burning kit once ... does that count?

This recollection only served to remind me that I had entered a male-dominated discipline. This happened at a point where inserting myself into the "containers" of men's experience and priorities had the potential to leave me numb in exploring my own methods of designing space through an entrenched bias, which otherwise has the potential to help create a more "balanced" approach to spatial design, or of provoking me to leave the field altogether. In the end, how can space reflect the "other" gender if the systems from which skills are learned does not change to include other approaches to design?

Throughout the research, an assortment of comments and discussions spurred both negative and positive reactions to the issue of gender and outdoor public space. Although the work is based primarily on my own findings, these reflections surfaced through my interactions with other people, the existing literature related to gender, space and urban design, as well as the feedback I continue to receive. Sometimes frustration, but often strength, is the final outcome of such encounters. With this in mind I decided to open a "dialogue" with fifty women I have known throughout my life by asking them to participate in the generation of their own "image" of space, which also came to form a part of the quilt. Questions were asked, and the respondents were to answer with either form or color in a "patch" for the quilt.

The questions:

1. Do you think public outdoor space is gendered?
2. Do you think the way public outdoor spaces are designed have an effect on how people feel in space?
3. Do you think that public outdoor spaces can alter people's actions or non-actions?
4. Have you ever had an experience in a public outdoor space which somehow changed or shaped how you now view that type of space?
5. How many other women, whom you know personally, have had an experience in public outdoor space which changed, or shaped, how they viewed space thereafter?

The following shapes and colors provide the answers to the questions:

1. yes: include red in the image
2. yes: include green in the image
3. yes: include a triangle in the image
4.–5. include and repeat a figure in the image*

*The amount or size of the "answers" should reflect how strongly you feel about the answer.

Although I asked for a quilt piece, I also suggested that other materials could be used; hence, there are some quilt pieces made from paper or cardboard, as well as wood, stained glass, and plastic. I also suggested that the piece could be as small as 5½" × 5½", but that decision was left up to each individual. The reactions to the "homework" varied, but what emerged was surprising and exciting. Only a few of the pieces depict spatial scenes, one of which I later learned is a "safe" space for one woman (a school, where she teaches); the other is an area which the woman criticizes for its recent transformation and lack of use (a plaza). Most of the pieces are abstract, while others are symbolic in either the material used or the patterns formed with the medium.

One of the deliberate choices of mediums was the stained glass piece — the response reads: "The medium I chose was glass. The transparency of the colors

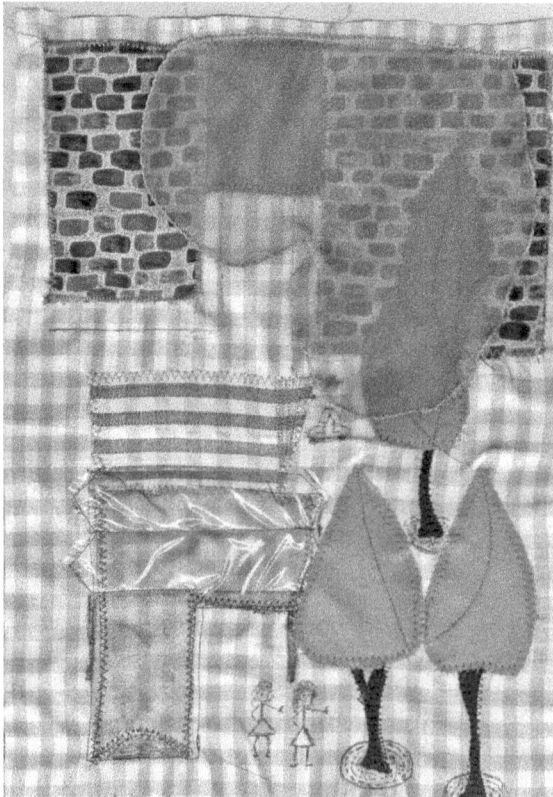

Nete's quilt piece: This quilt piece was submitted by my second Danish host mother, Nete Hvitfeldt. It was the first piece I received from the women I invited to participate in the dialogue about whether space is gendered. To add to this beautiful piece, Nete brought me to the plaza she had in mind when reflecting upon my questions and in creating her piece (photograph by the author).

varies so as to reflect the intense beauty of the unity of colors when the piece is held up to the light ... symbolic of the intensity and diversity of spaces around us that certainly shapes (or taints) our experiences. Out of the light, the piece is dark, unknown, and less accessible, evoking a very different emotion.... I separate this space into the space I see myself in during the lightness of the day as opposed to the darkness of the night."[17]

The diversity in responses can be seen in the pieces themselves. These all line the sides of the quilt. Out of fifty women invited to participate, thirty-two did. Out of the thirty-two participants, only four did not include the color red in their pieces, which was meant to symbolize space as gendered. With some responses came details of their thinking, or stories of experiences. For example: "[I]t represents an environment which marked me during my trip to Mexico in 1975 (when I was pregnant for my first child) — a young mother sitting on a bench in a park under the shade of a tree, breastfeeding her baby ... an oasis of tranquility and of respect in such a 'macho' world...."[18]

The quilt is my story, of my thoughts, reactions, reflections, perceptions, and finally actions that emerged out of *consciously* experiencing outdoor public space. For 150 days, I explored different places, and in turn, created different images, for what I had experienced that day. The images were created based on my wanderings and journeys in both foreign and homeland, both unknown and known places. Three continents, three different languages, and three different experiences came to shape my understanding of how I experience space and how I believe space shapes my experiences. Of 150 images, 46 emerged to form part of the quilt.

The explanations for each piece are included in a bookwork that accompanies the quilt. The overall assembly of the pieces, however, does have an overarching meaning, or a story, starting in the left corner and meandering maze-like through to the "end" at the bottom right corner. To me, the left side is about space being gendered in terms of exclusivity or having a negative impact upon women, while the right side highlights more positive experiences, or the experience of change as one moves towards the end piece.

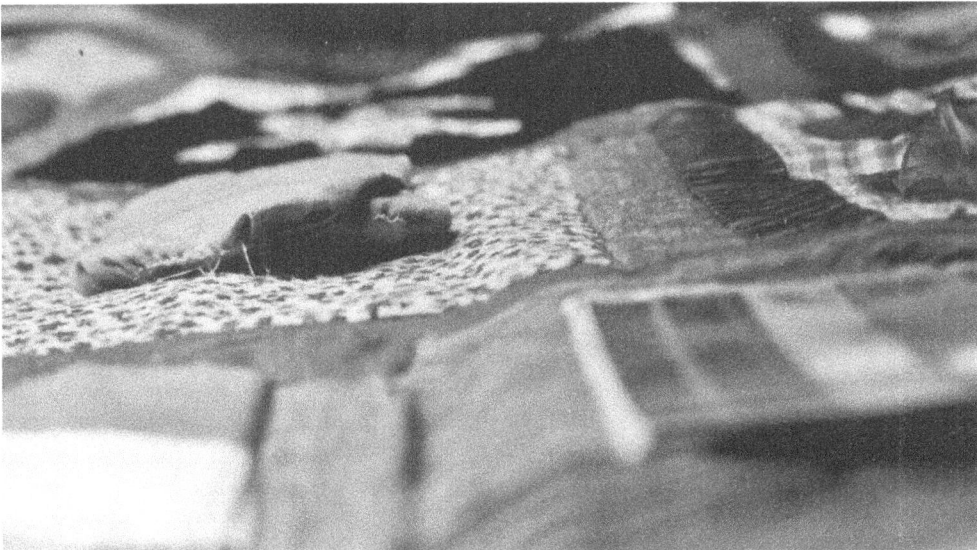

Quilt closeup: While the quilt may appear as a flat medium of expression, this photograph illustrates that it was three dimensional (photograph by the author).

Some examples include the corners, where, from top left corner, the journey begins with "sphere of confusion," where the experience of Bangkok, a city deemed generic by urban designers, leaves one in awe of the "progress" of commercialization, and hence, the commodification of people in outdoor public space. Moreover, the changes that have occurred in Aalborg in the ten years since I was first there are mind-boggling. The city now has a mall and its surrounding suburbia is growing.

"Access" (top left: black lines on white background) was created in the haze of not knowing how to approach a subject that has so many paths, while attempting to confront the initial feeling of averting the initiative of revealing that which has shaped my experience on a daily basis.

"Exit" (bottom right: resembles a star on a black background) on the other hand, becomes a question of "what next?" or where does one physically go from here? It is also the feeling of having to change one's perception of space as one changes locality and, in my case, continents. Returning to North America means changing one's attitudes towards freedom of movement in space.

One of the middle pieces, which is a half-way point between "access" and "exit," is a set of doors, which was created on one of my first days back in Denmark. The doors, both opening and closing, symbolize the unknown of positivity or negativity, dark or light. Other pieces on the diagonal with the doors include the "gaze" represented by an eye — which in my previous work was especially focused on the "male gaze" and the feeling of space which is inhibited by different methods of creating a hierarchy in space — a common example being vertical elements allowing someone to "overlook" others, while those on lower levels are either unaware of the other presence, or by their awareness create a sort of unease in space. The gaze in this instance, however, has become more of an internal gaze, where the reality of being an outsider in another place, and especially a foreign country, can become a difficult balance of judgment, of personal

Access? Mannequins before their work day begins or the way I feel about wandering through outdoor public space as a woman. Aalborg, Denmark, 2002 (photograph by the author).

values versus cultural norm. Examining the direction of the gaze can inform the basis of one's reaction. The gaze can be further elaborated in terms of the internal gaze at ourselves in outdoor public space, which is maintained and sometimes created by the various media outlets to which we are subject on a daily basis. That is, sometimes our psychological discomforts with ourselves add to our feeling of unease in outdoor public spaces.

Reflections

Throughout the work, the main obstacles came from attempting to identify that which makes space gendered, without defaulting to a pre-determined methodology. Consequently, opponents to the notion of gender and outdoor public space have kept pressing for both "concrete" examples and a formula or a quick-list of "solutions" to remedy space that is gendered. Others have defended the contribution of symbols of "femininity" within outdoor public space as an adequate form of emancipation to counter the male and power-centered symbolism which exists and has been debated within the city, the most argued example being the modern skyscraper. Meanwhile, my own battle was in identifying the images and memories in space that contribute to the gendering of space, while trying to keep my own "gaze" from becoming judgmental rather than informed. In these cases, I deferred my thoughts to recording my impressions with words.

Wariness of the danger of re-inventing or re-labeling parameters of design in a pseudo-feminist voice has led me to focus on reviewing how design is undertaken and executed, rather than offering a new set of parameters for design. In doing so, I assert that there *is* an alternative to the current approaches of design which can be essentially patriarchal when left unquestioned in theory and methodology. However, rather than espouse the system as it exists and create illusionary neutrality in the process of design, I chose to pull away from the order, even if it has often meant creating an internal struggle through chaos within myself. Yes, I have identified some details in outdoor public space which make places gendered, but I also acknowledged early on the complexity of space, of landscape architecture, and of culture, and their interdependence, which make it impossible to provide a clear set of guidelines for designers. In truth, I continue to believe that a conscious, rather than passive, alertness to accessing and to assessing space will begin to lead to a construction of gender in outdoor public space.[19] It is neither by ignoring gender as an issue, nor continuing to pursue an incessant authoritative position *on* space, that we can design something *about* people and for *all*:

> As David Harvey observed, the "proper way to see" is wholly dependent on who is looking, what they are looking for, and why. Now, I would like to posit that in traditional design practices, the "proper way to see" has historically been guided by principles that seek to master site, and that this desire for mastery contributes to, and reinforces the habitual practices of "overlooking" ... the relationship between maker and site (embodied by operations of overlooking) has historically been one of domination, analogous to the "enclosure of women in men's conceptual universe."[20]

I believe that this method and its product suggest that we do not necessarily need to "move earth" to be landscape architects, or to apply acquired knowledge. Similarly, rather than feel a constant need to move the land, maybe it is worth reflecting on how to move and to challenge thoughts. I have designed and "built" a quilt, one which is emotive and responsive to the deconstruction of outdoor public space as gendered, one which has led to constructive discourse between women and (some) men, one which is an informed reading of existing everyday spaces. After all, outdoor public space, like the land and its people, is not powerless. It is how that power is engaged (or disengaged) that makes it gendered.

I have revisited and will continue to revisit sites that I *think* I understand. The quilt *constructs* space, while trying to appreciate the value of space to represent multiple factors, to demonstrate that site is dynamic rather than passive, and to see outdoor public space as "mobile ground" rather than stale and fixed in identity.[21] It is a starting point for dialogue, for which there is no clear-cut conclusion.

Ruminating About Professional Discourse

When I presented my research at "A Century of Women: Evaluating Gender in Landscape Architecture," I was decidedly "green." No experience in the practice of landscape architecture outside of my university studies could be attached to my name, but I was optimistic. I sought to push the boundaries of a discipline entrenched in "thinking outside the box" from a woman's perspective and the conference provided me with an exposure to like-minded professionals and an "other" history lesson in landscape architecture which I felt incredibly privileged to hear. The ensuing deliberations were inspiring and what followed reaffirming. Unfortunately, those who professed that "gender" is not an issue today in the profession were remarkably absent from all presentations aside from their own.[22] What do such actions indicate about discourse?

In the years that have passed since completing my Masters research, I have continued to explore spaces with an analytical lens and admittedly contributed to some very and some much less, inspiring design.[23] Though one must not always "investigate," the contemplations begun during my degree and evidently still "open," leave me wondering and questioning the places I traverse and the design work I am vested in. I am often deliberately conscious of my surroundings and (still) always acutely aware of my sex as I explore and design outdoor public space. I admit that I have been unable to leave my theories and academic ruminations at the "practice" door: a recipe for a challenging professional experience thus far.

If I were focused on the end-piece, I might have found the words to clearly qualify my need to address sexual difference in the realm of design. I would express sexual difference in the context of landscape architecture specifically, and in the design of the built environment generally. But in an attempt to find the "right" dialectic to articulate the space which exists between woman and man, men and women, as both users and creators, and the social constructs which envelop these interpretable words, this reflection forms part of the struggle I have in finding a language where words are to be perceived as sharing — a space in between — rather than criticizing.[24]

Practice

While constructive criticism on projects can be taken in stride by most in the design profession, especially having lived through the rigors and (sometimes) upsetting pin-ups during the pursuit of our degrees, not everyone is open to reflecting upon their approaches to design. As a subjective discipline, questioning methodology can shake the very core of not only what one has been taught, but also executed for perhaps years, or decades. While initially I set out into the practice world with a desire for change, trying to make a place for myself within a firm has admittedly taken priority. As a consequence, I have delved into research while weaving in and out of professional practice for different firms.

Roots

To be able to seek out an applicable language, to develop the foundation upon which the issue of women and urban design can confidently be rooted, I have found myself becoming absorbed in the philosophy of feminist scholars such as Luce Irigaray and Hélène Cixous to be essential. These works of wisdom by women, who have challenged the rules of patriarchy without creating new hierarchies, heighten my wonder and ground my passion. Although provoking much mental *jouissance,* the abstracted and contested views nevertheless do not point directly to an "application" of sexual difference to design.

Meanwhile, I continue to turn to the other design disciplines for existing research on the issue of gender. Where in her contribution to the compilation *The Architect: Reconstructing her Practice,* Margrét Harðardóttir writes: "Explaining the search for what one intuitively knows to exist but has not yet captured is a delicate task. However, as it is a vital attribute of an architect not to avoid the uncomfortable, I feel compelled to write this

Violence of contrast: As one of the terms used by Cullen in *Townscape,* this violence of contrast shows what most North American cities clearly overlook during planning and designing exercises. Black and white photograph taken during preliminary research, summer 2001 (photograph by the author).

text."[25] My research is motivated by Margrét Harðardóttir's words. It is sometimes difficult to describe something internal, that which we are unable to ignore, to others.

As a result, I grapple inwardly with the desire to find the correct speech to translate the thoughts back out from their internalization, first into discussion, and then, into the realm of design. It is still a challenge to broach this subject with colleagues without sounding or being perceived as judgmental; it seems that most of us have a socialized predisposition to feel that an approach to questioning the way we "do things" as personal and negative. I am no exception. As I am constantly aware (and reminded) of the requirement to grind concepts into reality, I grapple with the standard modus operandi of the discipline. (Are men predisposed to technical issues such as landscape architectural details, just like building models based on their airplane model skills?)

The wish to focus research on the "needs" of women in the landscape is often assumed to imply addressing concerns of safety or of women's assumed roles as caregivers, whether of aging adults or of young children. But there is something intrinsic about outdoor public space that does not meet my needs, wants and desires as a woman: whether as a designer or a user of space. Dolores Hayden (1995) and Daphne Spain (1992) are just two individuals who have approached research on gender and space using empirical analysis as the foundation for their arguments. I wish to build on the relations such theorists have made in urban space, but by mingling with and around their assertions. Recently I began to look at the origins of women's exclusion from space in terms of social hierarchy. It is hoped that linking women's position in society in relation to the history of the city can document (if there are any) changes reflected in urban design.

My Modus Operandi

Walking continues to be my medium. Historically, walking has had many functions ranging from a mode of transportation, to a political mode of expression. As a collective, philosophers place a great deal of importance on the act of walking throughout urban spaces,

where "[w]alking is an art from whose loins spring the menhir, sculpture, architecture, landscape. This simple action has given rise to the most important relationships man [sic] has

Meter maids: Often these shadows are unrecognizable to those who see this photograph. Taken in black and white in downtown Winnipeg, Manitoba, Canada, during the summer of 2001, I find it ironic that the shape of these tools is so feminine. Meanwhile, if you do not have the correct change or it expires before you can "feed" it again, it can create feelings of anger and grief (photograph by the author).

established with the land, the territory."[26] But I wonder if women are hindered in their wanderings, what great thoughts and creations have we missed?

Søren Kierkegaard might have stressed the issue of this type of existence in today's world where "power" seems to remain unquestioned in patterns and traditions. In a time where there is a world-wide trend grasping at history, in addition to one widely embracing the North American development model, one may ask whether the longings for a past are well-intended and whether one can overlook the desires to import spatial design as possibly unsuitable. Indeed, the move to restore and to preserve existing cultural and physical infrastructures (whether building, park, plaza or other) can be said to be founded on an increased nostalgia for the past, while globalization continues to imply that "cutting and pasting" specific environments all over the world is forward-thinking. These longings and patterns are causes for concern, when historically many people have remained on the margins of society thanks in part to these physical forms, patterns and content. "Spatial segregation is one of the mechanisms by which a group with greater power can maintain its advantage over a group with less power. By controlling access to knowledge and resources through the control of space, the dominant group's ability to retain and reinforce its position is enhanced."[27]

Foreground

While my research continues along a winding path, the social lens through which I peer at the world and experience space has greatly changed. My wanderings are almost never alone now: I often wear my son on my back, and sometimes we are fortunate enough to have my community planner and urban designer husband along for the debate. As discussed in Annmarie Adams and Peta Tancred's *"Designing Women": Gender and the Architectural Profession*, I must now imagine how to "knit" my private responsibilities with the public nature of landscape architecture; a challenge that I both look forward to and dread, as I know the nature of the profession to be insanely entrenched in itself and perhaps too much so to allow a tipping of priorities into the private lives of its authors.[28] This fact, of course, is one which affects both men and women, but as is still evident is women's assumed relationship to the domestic sphere, it has not been socially reinvented — yet.

Notes

1. Luce Irigaray, *Elemental Passions*, trans. Joanne Collie & Judith Still (London: Athlone Press, 1992), 63.
2. Susana Torre, "Claiming The Public Space: The Mothers of Plaza de Mayo," in *The Sex of Architecture*, ed. Diana Agrest, Patricia Conway, and Leslie Kanes Weisman (New York: Harry N. Abrams, 1996), 241.
3. Mark Wigley, "Untitled: The House of Gender," in *Sexuality and Space*, ed. Beatriz Colomina (New Jersey: Princeton Architectural Press, 1992), 348.
4. Denis E. Cosgrove, *Social Formation and Symbolic Landscape* (London: Croom Helm, 1984), 13.
5. George Simmel, *Philosophische Kultur (Philosophical Culture)*, 1911, quoted in Stevi Jackson and Sue Scott, "Introduction," in *Gender: A Sociological Reader*, ed. Stevi Jackson and Sue Scott (London: Routledge, 2002), 6.
6. Luce Irigaray, *Speculum of the* Other, trans. G. Gill (Ithaca, NY: Cornell University Press, 1985), quoted in Mimi Arnstein, "Consciousness Razing: Self-Defining Feminism and the Problem of Post-Modern Politics," in *Feminist (Re)visions of the Subject: Landscapes, Ethnoscapes, and Theoryscapes*, ed. Gail Currie and Celia Rothenberg (Oxford: Lexington Books, 2001), 174.
7. James Corner, "Eidetic Operations and New Landscapes," in *Recovering Landscape*, ed. James Corner (New York: Princeton Architectural Press, 1999), 153.
8. Cullen, Gordon, *The Concise Townscape* (Oxford: Architectural Press, 1994 (1971)), 8.

9. Alain de Botton, *The Art of Travel* (London: Hamish Hamilton, 2002), 69.

10. David Sibley, "comfort, anxiety, space," in *Architecture: The Subject Is Matter*, ed. Jonathan Hill (New York: Routledge, 2001), 110.

11. Cullen, 13.

12. Larry R. Ford, *The Spaces Between Buildings* (London: Johns Hopkins University Press, 2000), 40.

13. Robert Venturi, Denise Scott-Brown and Steve Izenour, *Learning from Las Vegas* (Cambridge, MA: MIT Press, 1977), 11.

14. Ford, 50.

15. Sibley, 108.

16. *Ibid.*

17. Anne Young, personal letter to author, September 2002.

18. Nichole White, personal letter to author, September 2002.

19. Andrea Kahn, "Overlooking: A Look at How We Look at Site ... or ... site as 'discrete object' of desire," in *Desiring Practices: Architecture, Gender and the Interdisciplinary*, ed. Katerina Rüedi, Sarah Wigglesworth, and Duncan McCornquodale (London: Black Dog Publishing, 1996), 176.

20. Kahn, 181.

21. Kahn, 186.

22. And yes, these were women.

23. Unfortunately, those projects coined "bread and butter," that is, the less meaningful, but hugely socially influential work, is the "raison d'être" of many landscape architectural firms. That is, the participation of firms in much more "important" but not as financially logical nor guaranteed work is only possible because of regular, often standardized, contracts.

24. I am also cognizant that feminists are divided on the continued reference to humans as split into "women" and "men" and the patriarchal constructs this may uphold. However, that discussion is beyond the scope of this addendum, given its briefness.

25. Margrét HarÔardóttir, "A Cold View," in *The Architect: Reconstructing Her Practice*, ed. Francesca Hughes (London: MIT Press, 1998), 222–223.

26. Francesco Careri, *Walkscapes: Walking as an Aesthetic Practice* (Barcelona: Editorial Gustavo Gili, 2002), 20.

27. Daphne Spain, *Gendered Spaces* (Chapel Hill: University of North Carolina Press, 1992), 15.

28. Annemarie Adams and Peta Tancred, *"Designing Women": Gender and the Architectural Profession* (Toronto: University of Toronto Press, 2000), 109.

Bibliography

Adams, Annemarie and Peta Tancred. *"Designing Women": Gender and the Architectural Profession.* Toronto: University of Toronto Press, 2000.

Agrest, Diana, Patricia Conway, and Leslie Kanes Weisman, eds. *The Sex of Architecture.* New York: Harry N. Abrams, 1996.

Amidon, Jane. *Radical Landscapes: Reinventing Outdoor Space.* New York: Thames and Hudson, 2001.

Andreotti, Libero and Xavier Costa, eds. *Theory of the Dérive and Other Situationist Writings on the City.* Barcelona: Museu d'art Contemporani de Barcelona ACTAR, 1996.

Augé, Marc. *In the Metro.* Translated by Tom Conley. London: University of Minnesota Press., 2002. Originally published as *Un Ethnologue dans le métro* (Paris: Hachette, 1986).

Baumgardner, Jennifer and Amy Richards. *Manifesta: Young Women, Feminism and the Future.* New York: Farrar, Straus and Giroux, 2000.

Bech-Danielsen, Claus, Ole Michael Jensen, Hans Kiib, Gitte Marling, eds. *Urban Lifescape.* Aalborg: Aalborg University Press, 2004.

Belsey, Catherine. *Poststructuralism: A Very Short Introduction.* Oxford: Oxford University Press, 2002.

Blackburn, Simon. *Think.* Oxford: Oxford University Press, 1999.

_____. *Being Good: A Short Introduction to Ethics.* Oxford: Oxford University Press, 2001.

Blyth, Ian, and Susan Sellers. *Hélène Cixous Live Theory.* London: Continuum, 2004.

Bourdieu, Pierre. *Outline of a Theory of Practice.* Cambridge: Cambridge University Press, 1977.

Broadbent, Geoffrey, and Thomas Lorens. *Meaning and Behavior in the Built Environment.* New York: John Wiley, 1980.

Brooks, Ann. *Postfeminisms: Feminism, Cultural Theory and Cultural Forms.* New York: John Wiley, 1997.

Bulos, Marjorie, ed. *Making a Place for Women: A Resource Handbook on Women and the Built Environment.* London: Women's Design Service, 1989.

Bruno, Giuliana. *Atlas of Emotion.* London: Verso, 2002.

Bunschoten, Raoul, Takuro Hoshino, and Hélène Binet, eds. *Urban Flotsam: Stirring the City.* Rotterdam: 010 Publishers, 2001.

Butlers, Christopher. *Postmodernism: A Very Short Introduction.* Oxford: Oxford University Press, 2002.

Calvino, Italo. *Invisible Cities.* London: Vintage, 1997. Translated by William Weaver as *Le città invisibili, 1st ed.* (Torino: Einaudi, 1974).

_____. *If on a Winter's Night A Traveller.* Toronto: Lester, and Orpen Dennys Ltd., 1979.

Cameron, Julia. *The Right to Write: An Invitation and Initiation into the Writing Life.* New York: Jeremy T. Tarcher/Putnam, 1998.

Careri, Francesco. *Walkscapes: Walking as an Aesthetic Practice.* Barcelona: Editorial Gustavo Gili, 2002.

Carr, Stephen. *Public Space.* New York: Cambridge University Press, 1992.

Carson, David and Philip B. Meggs. *Fotografiks: An Equilibrium Between Photography and Design Through Graphic Expression that Evolves from Content.* London: Laurence King Publishing, 2002.

Cavallaro, Dani. *French Feminist Theory.* London: Continuum, 2003.

Chapman, Rowena and Jonathan Rutherford, eds. *Male Order: Unwrapping Masculinity.* Oxford: Oxford University Press, 1988.

Chicago, Judy. *The Dinner Party.* New York: Penguin Books, 1996.

Chomsky, Noam. *Manufacturing Consent: Noam Chomsky and the Media.* Montreal: NFB Canada, 1994.

Cixous, Hélène, Deborah Jenson, et al. *Coming to Writing and Other Essays.* Cambridge, MA: Harvard University Press, 1991.

Clark, Thomas A. *Distance and Proximity.* Edinburgh: Pocketbooks, 2000.

Cline, Ann. *A Hut of One's Own: Life Outside the Circle of Architecture.* Cambridge, MA: MIT Press, 1988.

Code, Lorraine. *Encyclopedia of Feminist Theories.* London: Routledge, 2000.

Coleman, Debra, Elizabeth Danze, and Carol Henderson, eds. *Architecture and Feminism.* New York: Princeton Architectural Press, 1996.

Colomina, Beatriz, ed. *Sexuality and Space.* Princeton, NJ: Princeton Paper on Architecture, 1992.

Cooper Marcus, Clare and Carolyn Francis. *People Places: Design Guidelines for Urban Open Space,* New York: Van Nostrand Reinhold, 1988.

Corner, James, ed. *Recovering Landscape: Essays in Contemporary Landscape Architecture.* New York: Princeton Architectural Press, 1999.

Cosgrove, Denis E. *Social Formation and Symbolic Landscape.* London: Croom Helm, 1984.

Cullen, Gordon. *The Concise Townscape.* London: Architectural Press, 1971.

Currie, Gai, and Celia Rothenberg, eds. *Feminist (Re)visions of the Subject: Landscapes, Ethnoscapes and Theoryscapes.* Oxford: Lexington Books, 2001.

de Beauvoir, Simone. *The Second Sex.* Translated by H.M. Parshley. New York: Alfred A. Knopf, 1993. Originally published as *Le Deuxième Sexe* (Paris: Gallimard, 1949).

de Botton, Alain. *The Architecture of Happiness.* London: Penguin, 2006.

_____. *The Art of Travel.* London: Penguin, 2002.

de Certeau, Michel. *The Practice of Everyday Life.* Translated by Steven Rendall. Berkeley: University of California Press, 1984. Originally published as *Arts de faire* (Paris: Union Générale d'Éditions, 1980).

de Pisan, Christine. *The City of Ladies.* Translated by Rosalind Brown-Grant. London: Penguin, 2005. Original work published as *Livre de la cité des dames* (1405).

Dear, Michael. *The Postmodern Urban Condition.* Oxford: Blackwell Publishers Ltd., 2000.

Debord, Guy. *Society of the Spectacle.* New York: Zone Books, 1994.

Delamont, Sara. *Changing Women, Unchanged Men? Sociological Perspectives on Gender in a Post-Industrial Society.* Buckingham: Open University Press, 2001.

Deutsche, Rosalyn. *Evictions: Art and Spatial Politics.* Cambridge, MA: MIT Press, 1996.

Dimitrakaki, Angela, Pam Sketlton, and Mare Tralla. *Private Views: Spaces and Gender in Contemporary Art from Britain to Estonia.* New York: Women's Art Library, 2000.

Dorrian, Mark, and Gillian Rose. *Deteritorialisations ... Revisioning: Landscape and Politics.* London: Black Dog Publishing, 2003.

Dotterer, Ronald, and Susan Bowers, eds. *Sexuality, the Female Gaze and the Arts.* London: Associated University Press, 1992.

Dovey, Kim. *Framing Places: Mediating Power in Built Form.* New York: Routledge, 1999.

Dowler, Lorraine, Josephine Carubia, and Bonj Szczygiel. *Gender and Landscape: Renegotiating Morality and Space.* London: Routledge, 2005.

Durning, Louise, and Richard Wrigley. *Gender, and Architecture.* Chichester: John Wiley & Sons, 2000.

Eichler, Margrit. *Change of Plans: Towards a Non-Sexist Sustainable City.* Toronto: Garamond Press, 1995.

El Guindi, Fadwa. *Veil: Modesty, Privacy and Resistance.* Oxford: Berg, 1999.

Elam, Kimberly. *Geometry of Design.* New York: Princeton Architectural Press, 2001.

_____. *Grid Systems.* New York: Princeton Architectural Press, 2004.

Ellin, Nan, ed. *Architecture of Fear.* New York: Princeton Architectural Press, 1997.

Fitch, Stanley K. *Insights into Human Behavior.* Boston: Holbrook Press, 1974.

Footitt, Hilary. *Women, Europe and the New Languages of Politics.* London: Continuum, 2002.

Ford, Larry R. *The Spaces Between Buildings.* London: Johns Hopkins University Press, 2000.

Ford, Simon. *The Situationist International: A User's Guide.* London: Black Dog Publishing, 2005.

Foucault, Michel. *The History of Sexuality: An Introduction.* Translated by Robert Hurley. New York: Vintage, 1990. Originally published as *Histoire de la sexualité* (Paris: Gallimard, 1976).

Freud, Sigmund. *On Sexuality: Three Essays on the Theory of Sexuality.* Translated by James Strachey. London: Penguin, 1953.

Friedan, Betty. *The Feminine Mystique.* New York: W.W. Norton, 1963.

Fuller, Margaret. *Woman in the Nineteenth Century and Other Writings.* Oxford: Oxford University Press, 1994. Originally published 1843.

Gallagher, Ann-Marie, Cathy Lubelska, and Louise Ryan, eds. *Re-Presenting the Past: Women and History.* Harlow: Pearson Education, 2001.

Gandelsonas, Mario. *X-Urbanism: Architecture and the American City.* New York: Princeton Architectural Press, 1999.

Gehl, Jan. *Life Between Buildings: Using Public Space.* Translated by Jo Koch. Copenhagen: Danish Architectural Press, 2006. Originally published as *Livet mellem husene* (Copenhagen: Arkitekzens Forlag, 1971).

_____, and Lars Gemzøe. *New City Spaces.* Copenhagen: Danish Architectural Press, 2000.

Goldsworthy, Andy. *Wood.* New York: Harry N. Abrams, 1996.

Ghent Urban Studies Team, eds. *Post.Ex.Sub.Dis. Urban Fragmentations and Constructions.* Rotterdam: 010 Publishers, 2002.

_____, eds. *The Urban Condition: Space, Community, and Self in the Contemporary Metropolis.* Rotterdam: 010 Publishers, 1999.

Harman, Graham. "Heidegger on Objects and Things." In *Making Things Public: Atmospheres of Democracy,* edited by Bruno Latour, and Peter Weibel. London: MIT Press, 2005.

Hayden, Dolores. *The Power of Place.* London: MIT Press, 1995.

Healey, Pasty, Stuart Cameron, Simin Davoudin, Stephen Graham, and Ali Madani-Pour, eds. *Managing Cities: The New Urban Context.* Chichester: John Wiley & Sons, 1995.

Hill, Jonathan. *Occupying Architecture: Between the Architect and the User.* London: Routledge, 1998.

_____, ed. *Architecture: The Subject Is Matter.* London: Routledge, 2001.

Hiller, Bill, and Julienne Hanson. *The Social Logic of Space.* Cambridge: Cambridge University Press, 1984.

Hodgson, Barbara. *No Place for a Lady: Tales of Adventurous Women Travelers.* Vancouver: Greystone Books, 2002.

Holston, James. *The Modernist City.* Chicago: University of Chicago Press, 1999.

Hopkins, David. *Dada and Surrealism: A Very Short Introduction.* Oxford University Press, 2004.

Hughes, Francesca, ed. *The Architect: Reconstructing Her Practice.* Cambridge, MA: MIT Press, 1998.

Irigaray, Luce. *Elemental Passions.* Translated by Joanne Collie and Judith Still. London: Athlone Press, 1992. Originally published as *Passions élémentaires* (Paris: Minuit 1982).

_____. *An Ethics of Sexual Difference.* Translated by Carolyn Burke and Gillian C. Gill. London: Continuum, 1993. Originally published as *Ethique de la différence sexuelle* (Paris: Editions de Minuit, 1984).

_____. *Democracy Begins Between Two.* Translated by Kirsteen Anderson. London: Athlone Press, 2000. Originally published as *La democrazia comincia a due* (Turin: Bollati Boringhieri, 1994).

_____. *To Be Two.* Translated by Monique M. Rhodes and Marco F. Cocito-Monoc. London: Continuum, 2000. Originally published as *Essere due* (Turin: Bollati Boringhieri, 1993).

_____. *The Way of Love.* Translated by Heidi Bostic and Stephen Pluháček. London: Continuum, 2002.

Jacobs, Jane. *The Death and Life of Great American Cities.* Toronto: Random House, 1961.

Jewson, Nick and Susanne MacGregor. *Transforming Cities: Contested Governance and New Spatial Divisions.* London: Routledge, 1997.

Joyce, T. Athol, and N.W. Thomas, eds. *Women of All Nations: A Record of Their Characteristics, Habits, Manners, Customs and Influence.* London: Cassell, 1911.

Juel-Christiansen, Carsten, and Gilbert Hansen, eds. *Transitions: space in the dispersed city.* Copenhagen: Architectural Magazine, 2001.

Jung, Carl Gustav. *Aspects of the Feminine.* Trans. R.F.C. Hull. London: Routledge, 1982.

Kierkegaard, Søren. *Johannes Climacus.* London: Serpent's Tail, 2001.

Latour, Bruno, and Peter Weibel, eds. *Making Things Public: Atmospheres of Democracy.* London: MIT Press, 2005.

Leach, Neil. *Rethinking Architecture: A Reader in Cultural Theory.* London: Routledge, 1997.

_____. *Camouflage.* London: MIT Press, 2006.

Loidl, Hans, and Stefan Bernard. *Opening Spaces: Design as Landscape Architecture.* Berlin: Birkhauser, 2003.

Low, Setha. *On the Plaza: The Politics of Public Space and Culture.* Austin: University of Texas Press, 2000.

_____, and Neil Smith, eds. 2006. *The Politics of Public Space.* London: Routledge, 2006.

Lupton, Ellen. *Mixing Messages: Graphic Design in Contemporary Culture.* New York: Princeton Architectural Press, 1996.

_____, Donald Albrecht, Susan Yelavich, and Mitchell Owens. *Inside Design Now.* New York: Princeton Architectural Press, 2002.

Macey, David. *Dictionary of Critical Theory.* London: Penguin Group, 2000.

Marling, Gitte. *Urban Songlines/Hverdagslivets Drømmespor.* Aalborg: Aalborg Universitetsforlag, 2003.

Marshall, Barbara L. *Configuring Gender: Explorations in Theory and Politics.* Peterborough: Broadview Press, 2000.

Marx, Karl. *Le Capital: Critique de l'economie politique.* Paris: Editions Sociales, 1948.

McCorquodale, Duncan, Katerina Rüedi, and Sarah Wigglesworth, eds. *Desiring Practices: Architecture, Gender and the Interdisciplinary.* London: Black Dog Publishing, 1996.

Massey, Doreen. *Space, Place & Gender.* Cambridge: Polity Press, 1994.

McDowell, Linda. *Gender, Identity and Place.* Minneapolis: University of Minnesota Press, 1999.

_____, and Joanne P. Sharp, eds. *Space, Gender, Knowledge.* London: Arnold, 1997.

Metz, Tracy. *FUN! Leisure and Landscape.* Netherlands: NAi Publishers, 2002.

Mill, John Stuart. *The Subjection of Women.* Edited by Susan M. Okin. 1869. Reprint, Indianapolis: Hackett Publishing, 1988.

Miller, David. *Political Philosophy: A Very Short Introduction.* Oxford: Oxford University Press, 2003.

Mouffe, Chantal. *Democratic Paradox.* London: Verso, 2000.

_____. *The Return of the Political.* London: Verso, 1993.

Nedo, Michael, Guy Moreton and Alec Finlay. *Ludwig Wittgenstein: There Where You Are Not.* London: Black Dog Publishing, 2005.

Oliver, Kelly, ed. *French Feminism Reader.* Lanham, MD: Rowman and Littlefield, 2000.

Osborne, Catherine. *Presocratic Philosophy: A Very Short Introduction.* Oxford: Oxford University Press, 2004.

Poullaouec-Gonidec, Philippe, Michel Gariépy, and Bernard Lassus, eds. *Le paysage: territoire d'intentions.* Montréal: Harmattan Inc, 1999.

Rendell, Jane, Barbara Penner, and Iain Borden, eds. *Gender Space Architecture.* New York: Routledge, 2000.

Rüedi, Katerina, Sarah Wigglesworth, and Duncan McCornquodale, eds. *Desiring Practices: Architecture, Gender and the Interdisciplinary.* London: Black Dog Publishing, 1996.

Sadler, Simon. *The Situationist City.* London: MIT Press, 1999.

St. Norbert Arts and Cultural Centre. *The Arch in Patriarch: a residency exploring recent feminist critiques of the built environment.* St. Norbert, Manitoba: St. Norbert Arts and Cultural Centre, 1996.

Saunders, Joel, ed. *Stud.* New York: Princeton Architectural Press, 1996.

Scary, Elaine. *On Beauty and Being Just.* New York: Princeton University Press, 1999.

Sellers, Susan, ed. *The Hélène Cixous Reader.* London: Routledge, 1994.

Shurmer-Smith, Pamela, and Kevin Hannam. *Worlds of Desire, Realms of Power: A Cultural Geography.* London: Arnold, 1994.

Sibley, David. *Geographies of Exclusion.* New York: Routledge, 1995.

Smith, Theresa Ann. *The Emerging Female Citizen: Gender and Enlightenment in Spain.* London: University of California Press, 2006.

Smithson, Robert. *The Writings of Robert Smithson.* New York: New York University Press, 1979.

Solnit, Rebecca. *Wanderlust: A History of Walking.* Toronto: Penguin Books, 2000.

_____. *A Field Guide to Getting Lost.* Edinburgh: Canongate, 2006.

Songe-Møller, Vigdis. *Philosophy Without Women: The Birth of Sexism in Western Thought.* Translated by Peter Cripps. London: Continuum, 2002. Originally published in Norwegien (Oslo: Cappelen Akademisk Forlag AS, 1999).

Spain, Daphne. *Gendered Spaces.* Chapel Hill: University of North Carolina Press, 1992.

Squires, Judith. *Gender in Political Theory.* London: Polity Press, 1999.

Stahel, Urs, ed. *If Only On A Winter's Night ... Roni Horn.* Göttingen: Steidl Verlag, 2003.

Tooley, James. *The Miseducation of Women.* London: Continuum, 2002.

Ventury, Robert, Denise Scott-Brown, and Steven Izenour. *Learning from Las Vegas.* Cambridge, MA: MIT Press, 1977.

Weber, Max. *Economy and Society: An Outline of Interpretive Sociology.* Berkeley: University of California Press, 1978.

Weil, Simone. *Simone Weil: An Anthology,* new edition. Edited and introduction by Sîan Miles. London: Penguin, 2005.

Weisman, Leslie Kaynes. *Discrimination by Design: A Feminist Critique of the Man-Made Environment.* Urbana: University of Illinois Press, 1992.

Wekerle, Gerda R., Rebecca Peterson, and David Morley. *New Space for Women.* Boulder: Westview Press, 1980.

Winch, Peter. *The Idea of a Social Science.* Bristol: The Burleigh Press, 1958.

Wollstonecraft, Mary. *A Vindication of the Rights of Woman,* revised edition. London: Penguin Books, 2004.

Chapter 15

Landscape Architecture: A Gendered Past, a Potential Feminist Future

SALLY SCHAUMAN

Thirty-five years ago another woman landscape architect and I met after work for a drink with a staff person from the Landscape Architecture Foundation (LAF) in Washington, D.C. Our intent was to lobby him for money to support women in the profession. The meeting was cordial. LAF gave us funds to organize the first just-for-women landscape architects conference in 1976, at Airlie House, Virginia. But after several drinks, this man said, "We have always had women in the profession, but I sure hope women never enter it in great numbers. Landscape architecture is already misunderstood and not respected worth a damn. If we have lots of women, the profession will be seen just like interior design — full of fags and females." His homophobic, misogynic crudeness still shock me. Later, I understood that the alcohol allowed him, a straight male, simply to blurt out his perceptions of the world. It is a view feminists and gays still struggle with — the insidious cultural constraints against women and homosexuals arising from the perceptions, power and penchants of a patriarchal society. Understanding how these constraints have impacted women in our profession and still impacted the entire profession reveals compelling truths. The public lacked respect for our profession thirty-five years ago and still does in too many noticeable ways.

Using his statement as a paradigm, I will explore four themes: the changing roles for women in landscape architecture through as seen through the lens of feminist history; an explanation offered by feminist theory as to why landscape architecture still lacks widespread public admiration; two feminist concepts of gender, both implicit in his remark, that together could provide a basis for advocacy, and finally, a proactive strategy for women landscape architects based on these concepts.

The Roles and Limitations of Women in Landscape Architecture

Early in the twentieth century, women in all professions functioned in what feminist historians refer to as "separate spheres." Women had moved into professions through doors left slightly ajar by men, who perceived these endeavors to be either domestic, thus more appropriate for women, or financially insignificant since the wages were minuscule. Women were physicians, but few were surgeons. Women became university professors but mainly in "female" disciplines such as domestic science, elementary education and social work.

In these early years, a few women studied landscape architecture primarily with male professors; others were self-taught. Wealthy patrons, such as Abby Aldrich Rockefeller and Mildred and Robert Bliss, commissioned Beatrix Farrand to create estate gardens at grander scales and with budgets larger than ordinary "domestic" projects. But these clients were the exceptions. Most women landscape architects did not design beyond the residential garden gate, although historians are now discovering the amazing work of a few that did, such as Florence Yoch.

The misogynist's statement is true. Women landscape architects have been accepted from the beginning, but for more than half of the twentieth century, these women designed mainly in limited "separate spheres" or as assistants to men, who designed the major projects.

During the first three decades of the twentieth century, new technologies of steel and structure gave designers the ability to create exciting new bridges and skyscrapers, the beginnings of the modern city. No women have been credited with the design of these structures. A few women engineers did practice but the conventional wisdom of the design professions identified none involved in these exciting projects. Indeed, the number of women in civil engineering was still less than 10 percent in 2003.[1] Fortunately, women have the intelligence to understand that beautiful buildings did not then, or now, make a city livable, healthy or safe. Needs for more than aesthetically pleasing structures were especially felt by new immigrants from Europe, blacks from the American South and small town women who came to the city to earn a living. While well-paid architects and landscape architects, like Olmsted, created the beginnings of the modern American city for well-financed clients or governments, unpaid women volunteers, who cared about sanitation, garbage and dead horses in the streets, made cities livable. Documentation of their work has emerged slowly as in the book by Daphne Spain, *How Women Saved the City*.[2] From the turn of the century until World War I, in the deceptively named Progressive Era of American history, vast numbers of volunteers created urban redemptive places for those who needed baths, shelter to sleep or a place to learn to read.[3]

Many other examples of women's contributions to the livability of the city likely exist but remain hidden. Design history books describe the skyscrapers and urban parks in great detail but say almost nothing about the work of the "other" sphere, domestic landscape architecture and what some women of that era referred to as "municipal housekeeping."[4] During this same era, Dr. Alice Hamilton campaigned against workplace pollution. Today, few people realize that, in doing so, she founded the field of occupational medicine. Conventional design history has not valued domestic landscape design and municipal housekeeping, but there is no doubt that women contributed to the quality of life for families and disadvantaged groups in urban places. Ultimately their work gave rise to the social considerations in landscape architecture and urban design.

During the same era, but in stark contrast, the environment, as both an organizing concept and an advocacy, became entrenched entirely as a male domain. Historians credit a woman, Rachel Carson, with the birth of American environmental consciousness, but the number of women prominent in the environmental movement has been scant until the past two decades. We can now point to the ground breaking ecological designs of landscape architects Carol Franklin and Peggy Gaynor or the ecological planning scholarship of Kristina Hill. But the most often heard and quoted voices of environmental design in our profession remain male. Environmental history is clear as to how this began.

After President Theodore Roosevelt raised trophy animal hunting to a must-do manly activity, he and his U.S. Chief Forester, Gifford Pinchot, turned to bringing the vast land-scapes of the Western states into the federal domain to conserve them for public use. President Roosevelt signed legislation creating the National Wildlife Refuge program and many National Parks, including the Grand Canyon. He preached a robust gospel of conservation. Hearing his sermons and perceiving him as a roughrider and a man's man, the dominant culture coded these conservation messages to be for males only. His goals were similar to those of John Muir and a band of Stanford University and UC Berkeley professors, who founded the Sierra Club. Their shared goals were to define and conserve America's land resources and heritage — goals appreciated then almost solely by educated, upper class, white males who could use the conserved land for their own recreation. While they laid the ground-work for later environmental action in the 1970's, these men meant to conserve landscapes, not to protect the environment.

Women seldom ventured into these landscape preserves or conservation activities. Wives were occasionally included, but 60 years passed before women became leaders in groups like the Sierra Club. The few exceptions were the women mountain climbers who early on were leaders in the Mountaineers. In contrast, the Sierra Club had only one woman as president from the turn of the century until the 1980's. Women have been American Society of Landscape Architecture (ASLA) members from the beginning, but almost 80 years passed before a woman became President of ASLA. Mark Dowie, an environmental writer, argues that both the Anglo Saxon male leadership model and the dichotomy between conservation and environmental goals have thwarted modern environmental action at every decision point.[5]

The elitist control of environmental groups denied diversity. One group left out devised their own agenda. People of color pursued issues of environmental equity, but remain some-what disconnected to broader ecological goals such as preserving species diversity. Women were also left out, but women failed to organize around special environmental issues. Women remained focused on trying to have parity with men to speak and work for the environment. Until the 1990's, only a scant few women achieved this parity.

Clearly environmental organizations did not consider women and people of color; they also designed their outreach for the wealthy. The appeal to upper class populations using beautiful photos of remote landscapes has "had the unfortunate result of defining environ-ment as an ex-urban phenomena, separate from most people's daily lives."[6] This male author recognized that men extolling the majesty of wilderness throughout the last century likely shared the same mindset and values as men designing majestic skyscrapers at the turn of the century. Neither group was, and perhaps still is now, concerned with the lives and values of ordinary people. In recent years much of this has surely changed, but the cultural mindsets and images of more than eighty years linger as residual baggage thwarting the popularity and politics of the environmental movement for far too long.

When World War II began, landscape architecture programs for women like the Cam-bridge School closed their doors forever, and women landscape architects like Dorothy May Anderson went to the work to win the War. "All the 4-F guys and all the women either went into cartography or camouflage," Anderson told me in 1975. After World War II, opportunities and education for women in landscape architecture began to change slowly. Even the limitations that thwarted, but did not impede, my generation have completely disappeared. Yet the 1998 ASLA Survey shows only 24 percent of the members are women, (20 percent teaching, 23 percent private practice and 30 percent public). Unfortunately, ASLA fails to compare salaries between genders.

In landscape architecture, women have achieved some modicum of parity by 2010. Women now have the right to equal professional education, to teach and to be the majority gender in an academic program such as the University of Washington, to enter all practice forums, to lead the profession, to select whatever project type suits them, to charge exorbitant fees or do pro bono projects. Most important, women now own the right to have their design opinion and product count. While all is not equal everywhere in all situations, our gender has gained much in the profession in the thirty-five years since an LAF staff member declared his bigotry.

If most of our professional rights have been achieved, why did hundreds attend the University of California, Berkeley conference, "A Century of Women: Evaluating Gender in Landscape Architecture" in November 2002? Why do many of us feel the need to talk in a community of women about our profession? I believe we gather to discuss because we are asking the Peggy Lee question, "Is that all there is?"

Parity is important, but as we struggled for equal professional rights, what have we neglected? Prof. Elizabeth Kiss, former Director of the Kenan Institute for Ethics at Duke, has helped me answer the question of neglect: "rights cannot, by themselves, answer the question of what equality means and requires. Rights don't provide us with the capacity to critically scrutinize our assumptions, or the ability to imagine and pursue better things."[7]

For my professional life I now wonder: Do I want to be as one among equals, or a woman with a gendered point of view pushing professional envelopes for as Kiss suggests, "better things?" Dr. Kiss tells me that professional parity is only a small first step. I have come to a clearer understanding about myself as a landscape architect, about the public's lack of respect for our profession and about the possibility of pursuing better things.

Regardless of gender, most landscape architects choose our profession because at some time, often in our childhood, we fell in love with the landscape, climbing trees, wading in streams, hearing birds and smelling flowers. We feel good when we hear love messages about gardens from the public, read landscape design articles in the media and see our profession's best works. The public now to some degree understands what our profession can do. Gardening is a major industry. The media covering gardens and landscape design has burgeoned.

But can we use these indices as measures of Americans' loving actions toward the landscape? Are American landscapes healthier because more people write about landscape architecture and everyone loves gardens? Do Americans read more garden beautiful articles and then think of landscape architects as premier artists? My answer is NO to all these questions.

By many measures, landscape architecture is not the profession leading the way in environmental design. McHarg wrote *Design with Nature* almost forty years ago, but some landscape design projects are still not ecologically healthy. Ecological design and planning do exist, as ASLA Awards attest. But they are not the common way America creates new places. Until the recent real estate downturn slowed development, many new residential areas displayed little water conservation features. Even so called "smart growth" is not necessarily good environmental design; neither is New Urbanism. The non-design media rarely mentions landscape architects as green designers. American builders think green only if the ecomantra comes from the lips of an architect. Campus ecology, a movement to green American campuses, started in small liberal arts colleges and not in universities with landscape architecture programs. With the exception of a few, like Mississippi State, landscape architecture programs are still not housed in green buildings. Few housing developments function as sustainable design to the degree that Village Homes, built more than thirty years ago, does. These situations do not exist because the profession has been silent. Landscape architectural authors have delivered compelling ecological message for years. Consider the powerful examples given by Anne Whitson Spirn more than twenty years ago.[8]

Is America not listening? Are people just slow mentally? Attitude shifts do take time, but in a flash we have learned to order double mocha skinny lattes and chosen to drive hybrid SUV's. Is it public ignorance, landscape architecture ineptness, or something more powerful and insidious preventing American decision makers at all levels, the popular media, and consumers from recognizing that landscape architecture is THE lead environmental design profession? The answer is complex, but for me most of it emerges by examining the subtle, unacknowledged, but detrimental coding given to landscape architecture by those who control policy and money. As a result, these people often gloss over or ignore our advice. I believe feminist theory explaining the coding of gender also explains the instinctive, but negative, coding of landscape architecture.

One Explanation for the Conflicted Respect Landscape Architecture Garners

For my entire professional life, whenever three or more landscape architects are gathered together, the uniform whine has been "Nobody understands us." The LAF staff member echoed this "LA's get no respect" statement. The whine prevails in spite of wondrous designs, engaging literature and sophisticated professional education. For a long while I thought it was a function of an immature profession. But we are over 100 years old! Now I have a different interpretation of our inferiority complex.

Landscape Architecture scholar Prof. Elizabeth Meyers gave me a clue when she used Leo Marx's conclusion that "The backlash against architectural modernism ... replays a deeply rooted American conflict of ideas ... traced to the nineteenth-century opposition between the dominant culture (with its patriarchal view that natural beauty is a lesser, soft, 'feminine' concern and its uncritical commitment to technological progress) and the adversary culture (with its belief in the need for a greater harmony between the man-made and the natural as exemplified by the Jeffersonian ideal of a society of the middle landscape)."[9]

Meyers goes on to critically consider Marx's conclusion: "While this conflation may be a necessary component of the constituent facts of modern art and architecture, the ideological biases of these dominant discourses tend to suffocate the emergence of an alternative, minor voice of modernism — that of landscape architecture."[10] She was quite correct but in my judgment, Meyers was too gentle toward Marx in her article.

Only with arrogance or ignorance can Marx place Jefferson and himself outside the dominant culture. He and Jefferson were eloquent spokesmen for the patriarchal culture, however egalitarian both may have considered themselves to be. Marx's argument does further his case for his "middle landscape" concept and his devotion to the pastoral landscape, but it does not explain the "suffocation" of landscape architecture. Basically, Marx ignored landscape architecture as a modern design force. I believe feminist theorists give us answers to why Marx ignored our profession and why American power and politics, with a few exceptions, has not credited either our profession's environmental design ideas as mainstream or our art as sophisticated.

The underlying reason is that landscape architecture is invisible. Visibility does not depend on acuity. Visibility does not depend on media coverage; it depends on the color and coding of the lens through which one sees. How do American capitalism and representative democracy, composed mainly of men, see the landscape we love and therefore our profession? Marx got this answer correct but attributed it to only part of the American culture and completely missed the fact that the word "pastoral" itself is a code. American power worlds clearly, consistently and irrevocably code the landscape, especially pastoral landscapes, as female, as insignificant.

The earth as female is not a new notion, but the pervasiveness and depth of the coding in this country are unique. A highly respected American studies scholar, Annette Kolodny, analyzed the language of early American writers and concluded that these writers, all white men, systematically and persistently described the American landscape or their experiences in the land using the metaphor of land-as-woman. She explained this as a love/hate relationship in her book, *The Lay of the Land*.[11] Kolodny argued convincingly that the coding has taken on increased importance in this country as an unconscious, imbedded filter for seeing and making decisions about the landscape. She labeled the "pastoral impulse," as an ingrained reaction, a uniquely American "yearning to respond to the landscape as feminine."[12] She continued: "My decision to label the pastoral vocabulary, with all its related images, as metaphorical was based on my observation that the American landscape has not been experienced as something similar to, or merely comparable to, but as the female principle of gratification itself, comprising all the qualities that Mother, Mistress, and Virgin traditionally represent to men."[13]

According to Kolodny, these male responses may have been preconscious, but in labeling the landscape pastoral and female, they made it vulnerable to destruction. She recognized that this metaphor humanized American land, thus making it attractive for immigration and pioneers. But it also masked the actions of these same white men in the landscape. Speaking of the landscape in loving terms has done nothing to diminish its destruction and degradation. In other words, referring to landscape as female, thinking of it as Marx's "middle landscape," seeing its pastoral qualities as the home of Jeffersonian agrarian husbandmen of the land, made it easier to rape the landscape in the nineteenth and the twentieth centuries and to continue to rape it today.

What Kolodny proposed is a well-argued theory that landscape as female is ingrained deeply in American culture, and has "pyscho historical import"[14] for understanding all our reactions to the term "landscape." Voters, businesspeople and legislators, still act on their "pastoral impulses." They profess their fondness for the landscape, even while deciding to degrade it and ignore natural process constraints.

To be landscape is to be female is to be ignored, or worse, abused. To care for the landscape is to care for something insignificant. In spite of all our attempts as landscape architects to be eco-relevant, scientifically accurate or artistically significant, the dominant American culture, capitalism, a commodity marketplace and power politics unconsciously code landscape and the design of it as a "female." In other words, the man in the bar meeting thirty-five years ago was correct; landscape architecture garners little respect because it deals with the landscape, a female domain. Women in landscape architecture have spent most of the last century striving for parity with men in a profession that other men, those in power and money, will value and treat as they have historically dealt with women. Is this a comforting conclusion?

Two Feminist Concepts of Gender

The ingrained cultural mindset marginalizing women and landscape has existed for three centuries and may exist in some form for a long time. The dominant culture has always described female attributes in terms of women's closeness to the earth's cycles, concluding that both women and nature were created as utility for man. Feminists have dealt with this insidious coding in one of two ways. Ecofeminists embrace the notion that woman means earth. Other feminists vehemently disagree, arguing that the coding is cultural and therefore susceptible to modification. One feminist describes this gender conundrum: "Throughout the history of Western feminisms ... a consistent divide has informed feminist thought and action. On one side are feminists whose thoughts and actions work to tear down the category of woman, to promote the equality of women.... On the other side, feminists have worked to reclaim and revalue the category of woman, to promote change based on solidarity among women, and to celebrate gender differences."[15]

Considering these two sides takes us back to the LAF staff member's "fags and female" comment. Do these destructive stereotypes still exist within landscape architecture? Perhaps. I do not presume to know the answer to the stereotyping question, but I have educated guesses. My hunch is that all firms are politically correct and none believe they marginalize women. But as soon as the practice becomes large, institutional and corporate or becomes a subsidiary of a male dominated engineering firm, destructive stereotyping seeps in.

The strategy of contemporary feminists, who value the similarities between the genders, is to strongly deny any special attributes of women and/or attribute these characteristics to centuries of cultural conditioning. Women nurture because culture expects mothers to nurture. Culture has also conditioned wealthy clients to believe women cannot make high dollar decisions, especially blonde women. When I was in my first design position and was still a natural blonde, I remember the principal of the firm telling clients, "Yes I know she is a woman, but she thinks like a man." I imagine that opinion still exists in the minds of some male clients and design firm principals albeit more subtly voiced.

What this landscape architect did not say was, "Lucky for you she is a woman, you'll get a different approach to design." Neither he nor the LAF staff person could conceive that women would bring any unique desirable abilities to bear in creating a design. My hunch is that many women landscape architects also do not want to think of themselves as different when it comes to design. They want to be successful in the office game they are in without realizing how much of those personal interactions are stereotypical. Like some feminists, many women designers will ignore the disquieting reactions they receive occasionally from colleagues and clients or attribute them to be a culture of male rudeness.

Feminists who attribute all difference to culture responded as a backlash to the ecofeminists' exuberance. In the 1970's, ecofeminists celebrated the differences between the genders in wild and wonderful ways. They formed Goddess groups, demonstrated in anti-war protests and boasted the female connection to the earth. These women believed their major goal was to turn around the huge battleship of American politics and our war-making machine. They advocated loving not bombing Mother Earth. Many ecofeminists, especially those in the academy, socially and intellectually embarrassed the cultural construction feminists. The cultural proponents, believe that celebrating differences only validates the dominant culture's opinion and thus perpetuates inequities. "For gawd's sake don't act emotional about the earth." A similar embarrassment has not taken place in our professions because not enough women landscape architects are yet bold enough to proclaim the differences and to celebrate these in their designs.

Fortunately, contemporary ecofeminism has become more nuanced and intellectually complex. Philosophy professor Karen Warren identified twelve directions of contemporary ecofeminism, each with a variety of literature and expressions.[16] More importantly, ecofeminists have become much clearer in connecting the problems of the environment with the problems of women, ethnic groups and the underclass. Noel Sturgeon, Professor of Women's Studies at Washington State University defines ecofeminism as a "movement that makes connections between environmentalisms and feminisms; the theory that the ideologies that authorize injustices based on gender, race and class are related to the ideologies that sanction the exploitation and degradation of the environment."[17] Regardless of multiple directions and applications of ecofeminism, the basic idea still prevails that gender differences exist and provide the mindset for thoughts and actions.

Although ecofeminism has become intellectually more acceptable, the preponderance of feminist literature discusses the cultural construction of gender. Understanding the cultural coding of the landscape as female, may help individual women landscape architects as they negotiate the minefield of practice, but understanding does not help a woman to form a stronger design self-identity. When we accept the cultural construct and only ask for parity, we have, as Elizabeth Kiss pointed out, "less ability to imagine and pursue better things."

Nor does understanding the coding actually remove landscape architecture from Kolodny's label of pastoral as "Mother, Mistress and Virgin." My hope is that women landscape architects would follow ecofeminism and decide that we speak and act for nature with authority. Simply stated, we should not follow its patriarchal conventions or the dominant culture's stereotyping of our profession or us. Rather we should intellectually lead this profession by using our special earth insights. But how? We appear damned if we do and damned if we don't.

Double Visions: A Strategy for Landscape Architectural Design

The two feminist concepts, thinking about the similarities or thinking about the differences between genders, represent both a conundrum and a strategy for women in landscape architecture. Either can be effective. We need not chose one over the other. To select either ecofeminism (differences) or cultural construction (similarities) as the situation demands seems to me to be an excellent strategy for the women in landscape architecture. In my mind, both concepts have applicability in varying degrees depending on the context. To claim authority in environmental design as the gender most closely related to the earth in one context and then to turn around and point out how the cultural construction of the landscape has impeded the implementation of ecological design or the recognition of our art in another context is also an excellent strategy. It is flexible and could be extremely powerful.

Unlike feminist theorists, women landscape architects are not usually ideologues. Just because many feminist theorists try to present ecofeminism and cultural construction as a mutually exclusive binary does not mean these theorists are correct, much less have a strategy for life. Using both notions whenever appropriate is not original with me. Meredith Kimball, a feminist psychology professor, advocates this strategy and terms it; "double visions" which she claims are "theoretically and politically richer and more flexible than visions based on a single tradition."[18] Using double visions in landscape architecture provides an exciting opportunity for women in our profession. Professor Elizabeth Meyer's list of suggestions for landscape architectural theory in her chapter in *Ecological Design and Planning*, could be included in a double visions strategy.[19] My suggestions build on hers.

First, remember that nothing exists in a vacuum, everything is related, and nothing is static. Even Spirn's genres of landscape in *The Language of the Landscape* are flexible.[20] A play landscape for one may be a spiritual landscape for another.

Secondly, resist deconstructing nature and design and people into understandable but immutable categories. Spirn reminds readers of Dame Sylvia Crowe's 1957 definition of our profession as a "bridge between art and science."[21] Fifty years later that bridge is less visible and quite flimsy. My great hope is that landscape architects could practice as if the gap does not exist or design the best bridge possible in each project. Demand the best science and produce the best science — demand the best art and produce the best art. Remember sustainable landscape architecture should not be a subset of the profession and neither should landscape art.

Thirdly, understand the answer to the most important question. At the beginning of each term, Prof Anne Whitson Spirn asks her students — what is nature? Our answer to ourselves, to our clients and to our students should always be: I am nature. Nature is spiritual me, is physical me, is biological me.

No matter how we model it, measure it, or shape it, we must consider our actions in terms of ourselves — what we do to nature we do to ourselves. Nature is not other. When we design as though nature is other, we are accepting the dominant culture's coding of nature as other, of the landscape as other and of women as other. We should adopt what feminist theory calls a "subject-subject" relationship with nature. This means rethinking design not as the centuries old practice of manipulating "other," but a survival tactic for humankind.

My last and most ardent suggestion is not a new one. Almost sixty years ago Dame Sylvia Crow said our profession's "greatest task is to heal the breach between science and humanism, and between aesthetics and technology."[22] The profession has not truly walked this familiar talk. The way I think of Crow's suggestion is to think of every design as not only a hypothesis awaiting proof but more importantly, as a sensual, dynamic story. No matter how we practice or what we call ourselves or how we recognize the implications of gender, we as women in this profession should find our voices to tell these landscape stories. Our voices should resonate among us to gain volume, to find the truth and to speak with clarity. We should passionately tell the story of the land in order to heal those who listen, to heal the storyteller and to heal the land.

Notes

1. American Association of University Women (AAUW), "A Place for Women," *Outlook* (fall/winter, 2003): 5.

2. Daphne Spain, *How Women Saved the City* (Minneapolis: University of Minnesota Press, 2001).

3. Spain, xii.

4. Spain, 72–78.

5. Mark Dowie, *Losing Ground: American Environmentalism at the Close of the Twentieth Century* (Cambridge, MA: MIT Press, 1995).

6. Dowie, 20.

7. Elizabeth Kiss, "Alchemy or Fool's Gold? Assessing Feminist Doubts about Rights," *Dissent* 42 (1995): 3, 347.

8. Anne Whitson Spirn, *The Granite Garden: Urban Nature and Human Design* (New York: Basic Books, 1984).

9. Leo Marx, "The American Ideology of Space," in *Denatured Visions, Landscape and Culture in the Twentieth Century*, ed. S. Wrede and W. H. Adams (New York: Museum of Modern Art, 1991), 74.

10. Elizabeth Meyers, "The Expanded Field of Landscape Architecture," in *Ecological Design and Planning*, eds. G.F. Thompson and F.R. Steiner (New York: Wiley, 1997), 49.

11. Annette Kolodny, *The Lay of the Land, Metaphor as Experience and History in American Life and Letters* (Chapel Hill: University of North Carolina Press, 1975).

12. Kolodny, 8.

13. Kolodny, 150.

14. Kolodny, viii.

15. Meredith M. Kimball, *Feminist Visions of Gender Similarities and Differences* (New York: Harrington Park Press, 1995), 1.

16. Karen Warren, "New Directions in Ecofeminism, 12 Key Areas," Session handout from "Women Sustaining Environment Sustaining Women" conference, University of St. Thomas, St. Paul, MI, October 19–21, 2001.

17. Noel Sturgeon, *Ecofeminist Natures: Race, Gender, Feminist Theory and Political Action* (New York: Routledge, 1997), 23.

18. Kimball, 2.

19. Meyers, 70–76.

20. Anne Whitson Spirn, *The Language of the Landscape* (New Haven: Yale University Press, 1998).

21. Spirin, 246.

22. Spirin, 246.

Bibliography

American Association of University Women. "A Place for Women." *Outlook* (fall/winter, 2003): 5.

Dowie, Mark. *Losing Ground: American Environmentalism at the Close of the Twentieth Century.* Cambridge, MA: MIT Press, 1995.

Kimball, Meredith M. *Feminist Visions of Gender Similarities and Differences.* New York: Harrington Park Press, 1995.

Kiss, Elizabeth. "Alchemy or Fool's Gold? Assessing Feminist Doubts About Rights." *Dissent* 42 (1995): 342–347.

Kolodny, Annette. *The Lay of the Land, Metaphor as Experience and History in American Life and Letters.* Chapel Hill: University of North Carolina Press, 1975.

Marx, Leo. "The American ideology of space." In *Denatured Visions, Landscape and Culture in the Twentieth Century.* Edited by S. Wrede and W. H. Adams, 62–78. New York: Museum of Modern Art, 1991.

Meyers, Elizabeth. "The Expanded Field of Landscape Architecture." In *Ecological Design And Planning.* Edited by G.F. Thompson and F.R. Steiner, 45–79. New York: Wiley, 1997.

Spain, Daphne. *How Women Saved the City.* Minneapolis: University of Minnesota Press, 2001.

Spirn, Anne Whitson. *The Granite Garden: Urban Nature and Human Design.* New York: Basic Books, 1984.

_____. *The Language of the Landscape.* New Haven: Yale University Press, 1999.

Sturgeon, Noel. *Ecofeminist Natures: Race, Gender, Feminist Theory and Political Action.* New York: Routledge, 1997.

Warren, Karen. "New Directions in Ecofeminism, 12 Key Areas." Session handout from "Women Sustaining Environment Sustaining Women" conference. University of St. Thomas, St. Paul, October 19–21, 2001.

About the Contributors

Shenglin Elijah **Chang** is an associate professor in the Graduate Institute of Building and Planning at National Taiwan University. Her book, *The Global Silicon Valley Home: Lives and Landscapes Within Taiwanese American Trans-Pacific Culture*, was published by Stanford University Press in 2006.

Terry L. **Clements**, an associate professor of landscape architecture at Virginia Polytechnic University, has researched the recent professional history of landscape architecture for over a decade. A licensed practitioner and teacher, she is active in professional and academic organizations that promote landscape architecture education and practice and an understanding of the impact landscape architects have.

Dagmar **Grimm-Pretner** is an assistant professor at the Institute of Landscape Architecture, BOKU Vienna, Austria. Her research and writings focus on contemporary landscape architecture and urbanism. Important issues are public open spaces in densely populated urban areas and the interrelationship of usage and design of open spaces.

Linda **Jewell** is a professor of landscape architecture in the Department of Landscape Architecture and Environmental Planning at the University of California Berkeley. Her publications and design work have won numerous ASLA awards, including the prestigious Presidential Award in Communications and the Bradford Williams Medal. She was the first woman to chair the Landscape Architecture departments at Berkeley and Harvard.

Daniel W. **Krall** is an associate professor in the Department of Landscape Architecture at Cornell University where he has taught design studios and historic preservation classes for over 25 years. His research interests embrace the early years of the profession with a particular focus on education and women practitioners. In 2005 he was named a fellow of the American Society of Landscape Architects.

Laura J. **Lawson** is the chair of the Department of Landscape Architecture of Rutgers University. A scholar and advocate, her teaching and research concerns community gardens, underutilized parks revived by residents, and other types of neighborhood activism to improve the local landscapes. Among her many publications is *City Bountiful: A Century of Community Gardening in America* (2005).

Valencia **Libby** is a landscape historian living in Blue Hill, Maine. She holds degrees from Cornell University and the University of Delaware. She was an associate professor of landscape architecture and horticulture at Temple University in Philadelphia. Her accomplishments were recognized in 2004 with a Fulbright Distinguished Chair in Landscape History.

Louise A. **Mozingo** is a professor in the Department of Landscape Architecture and Environmental Planning at the University of California Berkeley. Her articles, chapters, and reviews have appeared in numerous publications including *Places, Landscape Journal, Journal of the History of Gardens and Designed Landscapes*, and *Landscape Architecture*. She is the author of *Pastoral Capitalism: A History of Suburban Corporate Landscapes* (2011).

Elsa **Rehmann** was a landscape architect who practiced in New England in the early twentieth century. A prolific writer and lecturer she advocated for the regionally appropriate and ecologically sound planting design of residential landscapes. Ahead of her time, her writings have continued to educate landscape architects to the present day.

Ilaria **Salvadori** has degrees in architecture, landscape architecture, and city planning and is currently an urban designer and planner for the City Design Group of the City of San Francisco. Her research and professional practice focuses on community planning, neighborhood revitalization, and place-making in both the United States and Europe.

Sophie Nichol **Sauvé** studied landscape architecture at the University of Manitoba and has practiced traditional design with private firms in Toronto, Phoenix and Santa Fe. She continues to research urban landscapes with accessibility to great spaces and is attempting to live a simple life in the South while building upon her skills as a critic of urban spaces.

Sally **Schauman**, FASLA, began her career in private practice, was chief landscape architect for the Natural Resources Conservation Service of the USDA, and chaired the Landscape Architecture Department at the University of Washington. Since retirement, she has been a visiting scholar at Duke University in Women's Studies and now is an adjunct professor in Duke's Nicholas School of the Environment.

David C. **Streatfield**, an emeritus professor of landscape architecture at the University of Washington, is a landscape and garden historian. His research concentrates on modern landscapes in the western states. His interest in gender issues was initiated by research for the restoration of the garden at Rancho Los Alamitos, Long Beach, California.

Bonj **Szczygiel** is an associate professor of landscape architecture at the Pennsylvania State University. Her research has been on women's voluntary organizations as they impacted nineteenth-century built environments. She has also written about the role of medicine in the same period of urban development, and on the gendered configuration of the profession.

Judith B. **Tankard** is a landscape historian, author, editor, and preservation consultant based in Massachusetts. She received a master's degree in art history from the Institute of Fine Arts, New York University, and taught at the Landscape Institute, Harvard University, for 20 years. She is the author of eight books, including *Beatrix Farrand: Private Gardens, Public Landscapes*, and in 2000 was awarded a Gold Medal by the Massachusetts Horticultural Society.

Thaïsa **Way** is an associate professor of landscape architecture and adjunct faculty in architecture at the University of Washington. Her book *Unbounded Practice: Women and Landscape Architecture in the Early Twentieth Century* (2009) received the J.B. Jackson Book Award of the Landscape Studies Foundation. She is currently researching the role of women in the emergence of modern landscape architecture.

Dorothy **Wurman** is an architect and landscape architect, earning degrees with honors in both fields from the University of Pennsylvania, where she trained with Louis Kahn and Ian McHarg. In her practice and teaching, she continues to integrate the two disciplines. Her research interests include investigations into systems of visual logic, and the integration of art and ecology.

Index

Numbers in **_bold italics_** indicate pages with illustrations.

www.ingramcontent.com/pod-product-compliance
Lightning Source LLC
Chambersburg PA
CBHW080552270326
41929CB00019B/3279